D1794757

ISBN 978-0-265-67423-9
PIBN 10877736

THE LIFE

OF

THE RIGHT HONOURABLE

WILLIELMA,

VISCOUNTESS GLENORCHY,

CONTAINING

EXTRACTS FROM HER DIARY AND CORRESPONDENCE.

By T. S. JONES, D. D.

MINISTER OF HER CHAPEL, EDINBURGH.

EDINBURGH:

PRINTED FOR WILLIAM WHYTE AND CO.

ST ANDREW'S STREET;

AND LONGMAN, HURST, REES, ORME, AND BROWN,

LONDON.

PREFACE.

The Author of these Annals is fully aware that they contain topics which may not prove interesting to the ordinary readers of biography. Should any who move in the higher circles of life, and seek their happiness in scenes of dissipation and folly, be induced to look into this volume, they will soon find themselves disappointed, because such persons can neither understand nor appreciate the nature of the life exhibited, which was a life of constant and unwearied devotedness to the service and glory of God. After a few pages have been read, the whole will most probably be thrown aside as destitute of entertaining incident, and the conduct delineated be branded with the common-place epithets of enthusiasm, fanaticism, and madness. But the Author confidently hopes, that by all who know the gospel in its spiritual character, these Annals will be read with heart-felt interest; not because they contain any thing strange and novel, or unfold any experience which is not more or less common to other Christians, but because they bring them to a more distinct and particular acquaintance with one whose memory is highly and justly honoured in the religious world, and evince how powerfully she felt the obligation of Christian principle, and how solicitous she was to walk, like Enoch, with her God.

The Author claims no merit in bringing these Annals before the eye of the religious public. He has done little more than arrange and connect the facts and circumstances to which he had access. If, however, by his doing so, any new light shall be thrown upon the influence of Christian principles on the heart and conduct—if the friends of Christ shall be thereby stimulated to more active exertions in the cause of truth, and be encouraged and comforted in the course of their diversified experience, and thus the interests of religion and the honour of the Redeemer be in any measure advanced, his object is completely gained, and, so far as this Work is concerned, he has received his full reward.

Edinburgh, May 8. 1822.

CHAPTER XII.

CHAPTER XIII.

CHAPTER XIV.

CHAPTER XV.

CHAPTER XVI.

CHAPTER XVII.

CHAPTER XVIII.

CHAPTER XIX.

LIFE

OF

THE RIGHT HONOURABLE

WILLIELMA,

VISCOUNTESS GLENORCHY.

CHAPTER I.

Willielma Maxwell's birth and parentage—Her mother enters into a second marriage—Her sister married to the Earl of Sutherland—Willielma marries Lord Glenorchy—Makes the Tour of Europe—Returns to Britain—Enters into the dissipations of the world—Forms resolutions of leading a devout and religious life—Becomes acquainted with the Hawkstone family—Particularly with Miss Hill—Goes to Taymouth—Is there visited by sickness; under which, lasting impressions of religion are made on her heart—Letter of Miss Hill to Lady Glenorchy—Happy effects of it on Lady Glenorchy's mind.

William Maxwell, Esq. of Preston, in the stewartry of Kirkcudbright, a branch of the Nithsdale family, was a medical gentleman, and possessed a large fortune.

In the year 1739 he married Elizabeth Hairstanes of Craig, in the same county. Their family consisted of two daughters. The eldest was Mary, afterwards

Countess of Sutherland. The youngest was Willielma, the subject of these Annals, born after her father's death, on the 2d of September 1741.

Mrs Maxwell having lived a widow twelve years, was on the 27th of August 1753 married to the Right Honourable Charles Erskine of Tinewold and Alva, a Senator of the College of Justice, with the title of Lord Alva; in consequence of which, by the courtesy of the times, she enjoyed the title of Lady Alva till her death. She survived her daughter Willielma twenty years. Lord Alva was, soon after his marriage, raised to the high office of Lord Justice Clerk, equivalent in Scotland to that of Lord Chief Justice in England. Under the parental roof of this much respected Judge, the Misses Maxwell spent the last seven years of their unmarried state; and of his Lordship's kindness during that period, Lady Glenorchy always spoke with much reverence and affection.

The Misses Maxwell were in their day celebrated for their beauty, accomplishments, and amiable manners, as well as for their fortune. Their mother, lofty and ambitious, had, from their infancy, destined them, in her own mind, to the attainment, by marriage, of high rank.

She obtained her object; but, alas! as is often the case in schemes of worldly ambition, it was followed with many bitter consequences.

[1761.] Mary, the eldest, was married, with every flattering prospect, on the 14th of April 1761, to William the seventeenth Earl of Sutherland, and premier Earl of Scotland. To the finest person, he united all the dignity and amenity of manners and character which give lustre to greatness, while she was every thing which could be desired by such a husband. But their earthly career was of short duration. "As for man, his days are as grass; as a flower of the field so he withereth."

About the time of Lord and Lady Sutherland's union, a proposal of marriage was made to Willielma by John Lord Viscount Glenorchy, the only son and heir of John the third Earl of Breadalbane; a young man, in every respect, except in rank and fortune, the very opposite of Lord Sutherland. Lord Breadalbane had been bred at Court, and possessed very extensive property and influence. He was proprietor of one of the most magnificent seats in Scotland, where he lived in princely splendour. A suitor placed in the circumstances, and possessing the prospects of Lord Glenorchy, was a temptation, if not too great for Miss Maxwell, yet beyond a doubt too great for her mother to resist. His character must have been at this time in a great degree unknown to them both, as it had not yet been fully developed. Pushed on by mistaken friends, and deceived by the fascinations of grandeur, which had no doubt been increased by the marriage of her sister a few months before, she was, in the twentieth year of her age, on the 26th of September 1761, married to Lord Glenorchy, who on that day was twenty-three years old.

Lady Glenorchy had fine talents, and she had profited much by a very liberal and expensive education. She was esteemed one of the first amateur musicians, and had a charming voice, which, after she became a decided Christian, she seldom used but in the worship of God. She was naturally vivacious, gay, peculiarly formed for hilarity, and commanded a very considerable portion of pleasantry, which she was capable of using with great effect. In short, she seems to have been endowed with every talent calculated to communicate delight to a virtuous and well regulated mind.

[1762.] Lord Glenorchy, the year after his marriage, succeeded to the estate and mansion of Great Sugnal in Staffordshire, which he derived from his mother, the heiress of John Pershall, Esq. There Lady Glenorchy and he sometimes resided. Lord Breadalbane had a house in London, and magnificent apartments in the Abbey of Holyroodhouse in Edinburgh, besides the celebrated Castle of Taymouth in Perthshire. His Lordship generally resided during the winter in London, and Lady Glenorchy with him. After Lady Breadalbane's death, he resigned to Lord and Lady Glenorchy the establishments of Edinburgh and Taymouth. Although, therefore, Lord Breadalbane was generally with them wherever they were, Lady Glenorchy had the direction and command of the whole establishments.

[Aged 21.] Soon after Lady Breadalbane's death, which took place at Bath, September 1. 1762, Lord and Lady Glenorchy, accompanied by Lord Breadalbane, went abroad, intending to make the usual tour of Europe. They had spent some time in France, and had proceeded to Nice, when Lord Breadalbane left them, being called home by the death of his sister, who was maid of honour to the Princess Amelia. Lord and Lady Glenorchy pursued their journey to Italy and Rome; and after spending about two years on the continent, they returned home.

[1764. Aged 23.] Lady Glenorchy was now about twenty-three years of age, and during all that time "had walked according to the course of this world, without God, and without hope." This is the account which she herself gave about two years afterwards in her Journal, which shall presently be brought before the reader.

Whilst Lady Glenorchy was sinking in the deep waters of conviction of sin, and her strength and hope were about to perish, she received the following letter from her friend Miss Hill.

"*July*, 1765.

"It gives me great pleasure to hear that your illness has been so sanctified to you, as to shew you in any measure *that* in yourself, to which before you confess you were a stranger; that is, that you had too great an attachment to this vain unsatisfying world, the most pleasing appearances of which are nothing more than transparent baubles, which present gay colours that will soon fade. Allow me to congratulate you on this discovery; and may He, in whose hand our breath is, shew you more and more of the uncertainty of all earthly happiness, and convince you more of the substantial joys that are to be found in him alone. It is a common and no less dangerous prejudice which many entertain against the ways of true evangelical holiness, that they are dull, forbidding, and melancholy, and that to live godly in Christ Jesus is to exchange every enjoyment for austerities and mortifications; whereas, on the contrary, none enjoy so much inward peace and security, none have so much cause for cheerfulness and joy, as those who seek *first* the kingdom of God and his righteousness. It is indeed the interest of the grand enemy of our salvation to pervert the good ways of the Lord, to frighten us from pursuing them by lying suggestions, and, like the spies who went to view the promised land, to

clean copy, written by Lady Glenorchy's own hand, which has been found among her papers, and from which we shall be able to gather some idea of the state of her Ladyship's mind during this period.

bring against it an evil report; and to insinuate, that instead of flowing with milk and honey, it devoured the inhabitants thereof. But surely God never intended that religion should lessen our enjoyments, or make over to a world living in rebellion against himself, a happiness greater than his own children should possess. No; the ways of religion are ways of pleasantness, and all her paths are peace. You say you wish to overcome the fear of death. In order to this, I would advise you to examine whether you are really building upon the only sure foundation of hope; and what that hope is, the apostle expressly declares in the following words: 'Other foundation can no man lay than that is laid, which is Jesus Christ.' Try then, whether, as lost and undone in yourself—deeply sensible of the natural apostasy of your heart from God—weary and heavy laden with the burden of sin—and renouncing all hope and help in your own righteousness, repentance, resolutions, &c.—try if you really rest upon Christ as your only Saviour, relying solely upon his blood applied by the Spirit to pardon you, his righteousness imputed to justify you, and his grace to be given to sanctify you. It was He who came to seek and to save that which was lost, and we must see and feel ourselves thus lost without him, before we can in earnest seek an interest in that salvation which he hath purchased, for 'they that are whole need not a physician, but they that are sick.' So long as, either in whole or in part, we cleave to our own doings, and are not brought off from all dependance on the covenant of works, one or other of these two things must happen; either we shall have so high a conceit of ourselves as to think lightly of, and greatly undervalue the redemption that is in Jesus, or else we shall walk in continual darkness and want of comfort, under a slavish dread of wrath, whereby all our endeavours to avoid sin will proceed from a wrong principle, a principle of fear, instead of love and gratitude, and all our obedience will be the forced drudgery of a slave, and not the effect of the filial disposition of a child. This, I am convinced, is the case with many sincere people, and it is wholly owing to a lurking spirit of self-righteousness and unbelief, which prevents them from submitting to the righteousness of God, and closing with that full, free, all-sufficient salvation which the Gospel holds forth to guilty, helpless sinners, shewing them, that by the obedience of Christ unto death, the law is fulfilled, and Infinite Justice satisfied to the uttermost—that by his resurrection from the dead, God accepted the payment which he had made for his people, and discharged him from the prison of the grave in token of their full acquittal, and that he is now at the right hand of God, having entered the holy place as their head and forerunner, dispensing his gifts according to their various necessities, and making intercession for them, that where he is they may be also. Well, then, may we say with the apostle, 'Who shall lay any thing to the charge of God's elect? It is God that justifieth, who is he that condemneth? It is Christ that died, yea rather, that is risen again, who is even at the right hand of God, who also maketh intercession for us. Who shall separate us from the love of Christ? Shall tribulation, or distress, or persecution, or famine, or nakedness, or peril, or sword—in all these things we are more than conquerors, through him that loved us. For I am persuaded, that neither death, nor life, nor angels, nor principalities, nor powers, nor things present, nor things to come, nor height, nor depth, nor any other creature, shall be able to separate us from the love of

God, which is in Christ Jesus our Lord.' Many, I know, object against thus living wholly upon the blessed Redeemer, making him our all in all, our Alpha and Omega, as a doctrine that tends to licentiousness, and to the prejudice of morality and good works; and this is sometimes done even by those who pretend to mighty zeal for the interests of holiness, whilst they themselves are living after the course of this world. Whoever makes this objection, hereby plainly shews himself to have never received the grace of God in truth, and to be a stranger to the nature of justifying faith, and to the constraining power of Christ's love; for how is it possible that we should be one with Christ, and not endeavour to be like him? If we partake of his Spirit, will not the fruits of that Spirit appear in our lives and conversation? Can he that is brought into the marvellous light of God's dear Son, have any longer fellowship with the unfruitful works of darkness? Can the head be holy, and the members unholy? Can he who is united to Christ be employed in the service of Satan? Can the new creature delight in the works of the old man? Certainly not. It is true, (as the Church of England observes in her 11th article), 'we are accounted righteous before God, only for the merit of our Lord and Saviour Jesus Christ, by faith, and not for our own works or deservings. Wherefore, that we are justified by faith only, is a most wholesome doctrine, and very full of comfort;' but then it is as true, that there can be no real faith which does not produce good works, for the tree is known by its fruits, and as faith is the *root* of works, so works are the *fruit* of faith. We do not then make void the law through faith. God forbid: but we establish the law; for although through our weakness we cannot be justified by it, yet it still remains as a rule of life to every justified believer. Besides, the real Christian does not only look upon holiness as his *duty*, but also as his *privilege*; for being vitally united to Christ by faith, he receives from him a new nature, being, as saith the apostle Peter, 'made partaker of a divine nature;' which nature as much inclines him to holiness, as the old corrupt nature does to sin. Thus, being regenerated and born again, he is transformed in the spirit of his mind, he has put on Christ, and is renewed in every faculty of his soul. But still let us remember, that we are but renewed in part; so long as we are in the body, we shall find a law in our members warring against the law in our mind; the old man will be still striving for the mastery, and if he must die, will die *hard*. May this consideration make us ever watchful against the first risings of sin, and may we be continually looking to Jesus for strength to check it in the bud. It is this Jesus, my dear friend, who has conquered the only enemies we had to fear; he has disarmed death of his sting—looking to him we may overcome all fear of its approach, for when he is our friend, death is no other than an advantage; if he is our life, we shall surely find death our gain. The following questions I have found useful to myself: if we are able to give a comfortable answer to them, death cannot be to us a king of terrors, but a messenger of peace. Have earthly or heavenly things the chief place in our thoughts and affections? Do we prize that great salvation which the gospel offers to sinners, beyond every thing else in the world? Are we crucified to the world, and the world to us? Are we dead to its pleasures, riches, honours, and esteem? Does the humble temper of the meek and lowly Jesus reign in us? Is his service our delight, is sin our burden? Are we hungering and thirsting after righteousness? Are we taking up our cross daily, denying ourselves, and following Christ? Are we working out our own salvation with fear and trembling? Are we giving diligence to make our calling and election sure? Blessed indeed is the person who can say, *I find this to be my case.*"

This letter, by the blessing of God, produced what was intended by Miss Hill, and what was desired by Lady Glenorchy. It was the means employed by the grace of God, to bring her out of the horrible pit and the miry clay of despondency, to set her feet on the Rock of Ages, to establish her goings, and to put a new song into her mouth, even praises unto God. It may now be said of Lady Glenorchy, Behold she prayeth.—She arose from her knees at Taymouth, as Saul of Tarsus did from the ground near Damascus, a wonderful monument of the power and grace of God. From that interesting moment, without hesitation or conferring with flesh and blood, she resolutely turned her back on the dissipated world, and without reserve devoted herself, and all that she could command and influence, to the service of Christ and the glory of God; and in this she invariably persisted to her latest breath. Her future path of life lay through evil report and through good report; in the midst of deep adversity and of high prosperity; of severe trials and strong temptations, both temporal and spiritual. But none of these things moved her from the steadfastness of her Christian profession. Although her road was often rough in the extreme, and her enemies cruel, strong, and numerous, yet on she went in her Christian course, never deviating to the right hand nor to the left, but ever pressing toward the mark for the prize of the high calling of God in Christ Jesus.

CHAPTER II.

Lady Glenorchy becomes sensible of her spiritual weakness—Miss Hill writes to her on this subject—Goes to London—Is afraid of being thereby diverted from serious subjects—Letter from Miss Hill endeavouring to strengthen her in her resolutions to resist the temptations there.

LADY GLENORCHY, like every other well informed Christian, very soon began to discover her spiritual weakness and infirmities. Of these, it seems, she complained to her friend Miss Hill, who accordingly wrote to her the following letter:—

" *August* 30. 1765.

" IT gives me great concern to hear of your bad state of health. May that God, in whose hands you are, command a blessing on the means used for your recovery! or, if it should be his will that this sickness be a sickness unto death, may you, as you see the outward man decaying, see the inward man renewed day by day! The Lord has merciful intentions even in his most bitter dispensations. Whom he loveth he chasteneth; and he scourgeth every son whom he receiveth. May you, my dear friend, be enabled to see *love* in his rod, as well as *justice* in his dealings; and may the bitter cup which he has given you to drink be so mixed with sweet ingredients, that you may look forward with comfortable assurance that all shall work together for good! It is the Lord, he cannot mistake your interest; his will be done: if it is his will, most earnestly do I wish and pray for your recovery. I am persuaded that you belong to Christ; and therefore desire patiently to wait his will in the event. What poor helpless creatures should we be, full of inward fears and outward pains, unwilling to die, and yet dissatisfied with a wretched life, could we not discover some tokens of the Lord's merciful intentions towards us, and of our interest in him! Press on, my dear friend, and be not discouraged: he that is for you is greater than he that is against you. Although trials await you from without as well as from within, he who I trust has brought you out of darkness into his marvellous light, and has refreshed your soul with the light of his countenance, will now be with you when you pass through the fire and water of affliction. These are the strokes of a loving Father's hand, whose wisdom knows how to temper them to your case and strength, and to make you not only bear them with submission, but to kiss the rod that smites, and to sing of judgment as well as mercy. The trials and temptations which you have to encounter are indeed great and many; but having taken to you the whole armour of God, you may bid defiance to them all. You fight against conquered enemies. The Lord of Hosts is engaged in your behalf; look to him then by faith and prayer for strength; he will assuredly shew himself to be a strong-hold in the day of trouble, in which the weary may take shelter and be safe. He is faithful that promised, 'I will never leave thee nor forsake thee.' 'Fear not, for I am with thee; be not dismayed, for I am thy God.' 'Cast thy burden on the Lord and he shall sustain thee;' and above all let us remember, and we shall never want comfort, the gracious declaration, 'In that he himself hath suffered, being tempted, he is able to succour them that are tempted!'—O may your eyes and mine, my dear friend, be ever upon the Lord Jesus. Fixed upon him, we must be happy. He it is that has overcome Satan, death, and hell: they cannot hurt the soul that rests on Christ; he cannot fail the weakest believer that builds upon him. Strong in the Lord, and in the power of his might, we are enabled amidst every distress, and every trial, and every temptation, to endure: as some massy rock supported by pillars of basaltes, though surrounded by tempestuous waves, and beat upon by storms and winds, yet remains unmoved, so we, built upon the rock Christ, are enabled to look down on the foaming billows of affliction, and défy their impotent rage. If we are in Christ, we shall have strength, and none shall be able to pluck us out of his hand. The more we are encompassed with trials and temptations, the more earnestly let us fly to him, and then shall we find by sweet experience, that he is able to keep us from falling, and that when we are weak, then shall we be strong—strong in the Lord, and in the power of his might. I have found that I am no where safe, but at the foot of the Cross; *there* would I always be in the lowest prostration and subjection; in that posture I would always be looking to Jesus, viewing the fulness of the all-sufficiency which dwells in him: and when in that posture of soul, deeply sensible of my own nothingness, and firmly believing his faithfulness, as well as fulness, I dare defy all the powers of darkness. Again, although I desire always to approach the throne of grace with lively actings of faith, and pleading the divine promises, yet I would appear, not in the character of a saint, but of a sinner; and (as a friend of mine observes) there are two things in which I need not fear excess, in thinking humbly of myself, and highly of the Lord Jesus. I would approach him as my dread sovereign, and yet as my dearest friend, who hath loved me with everlasting love, and drawn me with everlasting kindness. Within this fortnight I have met with a severe trial in the death of a most dear and intimate friend, who has been as a sister to me from my infancy; but my comfort is, that I firmly believe she is gone to glory, and my loss is her gain. There can be little doubt that she was washed, sanctified, and justified in the name of the Lord Jesus, and by the Spirit of our God, as it evidently appeared both in her health and sickness. Although she was in the bloom of life, and God had given her such a portion of the good things of this world as might have attached her heart to it, yet did she wisely consider that this was not her rest, and looked beyond this transitory life to the world of spirits, where she was persuaded she must ere long appear before the judgment seat of Christ, to receive the things done in the body, according to that she had done, whether it was good or bad. This awful consideration led her to inquire into the nature, ground, and object of her hope, and through mercy she found it not only to be such as would administer comfort to her in a dying hour, but such as would give her confidence towards God in the great day of Christ's appearing. When she was in health, she was often under doubts and fears with respect to her interest in Christ, the reality of her grace, and the truth of her conversion. But in the time of her sickness, the Lord was pleased to remove this burden, and to give her (as she told me) a settled and composed confidence in his pardoning love through Christ. Hence she was enabled to look upon death as a disarmed enemy, who had no power to hurt her, Christ Jesus the Captain of her salvation having given her the victory over him, through faith in his most precious blood, through which she had redemption, even the forgiveness of her sins according to the riches of his grace. Happy souls, who, from a well grounded hope and confidence in the God of their salvation, can, when on the borders of eternity, look the king of terrors in the face, and say in the triumphant language of Scripture, "I am persuaded that neither death nor life can separate us from the love of God which is in Christ Jesus our Lord." I was not present when my dear friend resigned her spirit into the hands of Jesus, but was with her not long before; the last words she spoke to me were,—"Pray for me that my faith fail not;" and taking me affectionately by the hand, rested her head on the pillow, which lay on the table by her, (for she took not to her bed till just before she expired). After this, I withdrew almost immediately, being greatly affected. Her last words were, "Lord, let thy will be done in me," and presently after she fell asleep in Christ, with a sweet smile in her countenance. May our latter end be like hers! With regard to myself, I cannot say that I have been quite well lately; but when I consider my own deserts, I am amazed that the Lord deals so gently with me, and that the heavy rod of his displeasure has not long since fallen on so unprofitable a branch, with this dreadful sentence, "Cut it down, why cumbereth it the ground?" But grace is free, or it would not be grace. *Here* then will I set my foot—Grace is free, and comes by Jesus Christ; and he saith, look unto me and be ye saved. O for a steadfast faith on his infinite merits and glorious work. The believing heart through the power of the Holy Ghost applies them to itself, and fails not to reap every real advantage, both in time and through eternity. I cannot express how greatly I think myself indebted to you for the kind regard which you shew me; I trust we have established a friendship upon such solid foundations as can never be overthrown. Our meeting again in this world is very uncertain; God only knows if it will ever be: but, through grace, the time will come, when we shall meet to part no more; when a period shall be put to all our worldly troubles, and we shall join the heavenly host, who are day and night singing praises to the Lamb who redeemed them by his blood. Before I conclude, I must beg leave to offer you, my dear friend, a word or two of advice, which you may find useful in your Christian course, of which experience has taught me the necessity. Be earnest and diligent in prayer, and however backward you may at times find yourself to be to this exercise, yet never give way to sloth or listlessness; but if you find your heart cold and dead, pray, (as was Luther's custom), till it be warmed and enlivened. Never rest satisfied with the mere performance of this duty, but always seek to maintain that communion with God in it, without which it will be dry and unprofitable, and perhaps nothing better than lip labour. Be diligent also in reading the word of God, and supplicate that Spirit which inspired it to be your teacher, to lead you into all truth, and to enlighten your understanding, that you may see the wondrous things of his law. Avoid, as much as your situation will allow, whatever may be destructive of a holy, lively, and spiritual frame of mind, such as vain company and unprofitable discourse, which greatly tend to injure and impair the life of God in the soul. I would also beg leave to caution you against the unprofitable walk of professors. Let us always remember, that there is a great and a wide difference between knowledge in the head and grace in the heart. Beware, my dear Madam, that you are not encouraged to go beyond your Christian liberty in any matter, because you see others do so; but whilst you copy their graces, be very careful not to stumble by their falls, or be led aside by their infirmities. I am in a particular manner bound to repeat this caution to you, from a consciousness, that my example before you has not been such as becometh the gospel; but be assured, that the reflection of my undutifulness affords me constant matter of humiliation, and that it is the earnest desire of my heart to be daily more and more conformed to the image of Christ, and more and more meet to be a partaker of the inheritance of the saints in light. As the directions here suggested are diametrically opposite to the principles and practices of a world lying in wickedness, it will be no wonder if your adherence to them should bring upon you reproach and opposition from those who are yet in a state of blindness and alienation from God, whether they be totally careless or outwardly decent. There cannot be conceived any two things so contrary, as the Spirit of Christ which dwells in all true believers, and the spirit of Satan which dwells in all the children of disobedience. " If ye were of the world," says our Lord, " the world would love his own; but because ye are not of the world, but I have chosen you out of the world, therefore the world hateth you;" but be of good cheer, he who spoke these words tells you likewise, that he has " overcome the world." If we would have Christ, we must have his cross also; and if we suffer with him, we shall likewise reign with him."

[Aged 24.] The only place of public religious instruction to which Lady Glenorchy had at this time access, was the parish church of Kenmore. But then the service was chiefly conducted in the Gaelic language, which she did not understand, there being only one short sermon delivered in English. Neither had she any friend but Miss Hill who could aid her; she of course was obliged to apply to her, to solve her inquiries and her difficulties. In answer to a letter conveying intimation of these, Miss Hill thus wrote.

"*October* 1*st*, 1765.

"I began to entertain many anxious and uneasy thoughts respecting you, and am most truly concerned to find that my apprehensions were but too well grounded, and that you have been so much worse. But thanks, all thanks be to the Great Physician, who has again been merciful to my dear friend! His name is Wonderful. None is like him. His skill and power are beyond comparison. There is no disease which he cannot cure. There are none so poor whom he is not willing to heal. No one ever applied to him, even in the most desperate case, and perished. Indeed, how can they? For his name is Jesus, his nature is love! Love all mighty to save his people, and that from the first moment of their conversion to the last moment of their lives, even to the endless ages of eternity. He is and ever will be our Saviour, to keep us from all evil, and to bless us at all times with every good. Your letter seems to be written on purpose to humble me. *I* be your monitor! O, my dear friend, what an unworthy object have you employed! Conscious of my own demerit, my pen is ready to shrink back, lest it should do injustice to the cause which it wishes to promote. Yet encouraged by the hope that God often makes use of the weakest instruments for the greatest ends, I presume to offer you all the assistance in my power towards your progress in the road to Zion. And for more serious than the world around me? Have I given proof of this when in the company of those who are otherwise disposed? Have I had courage to think, to speak, and to act, in opposition to their opinions and practices; and have I done so when necessary, upon the very spot?—There is nothing in this age which can so much evidence the determination of our wills for God, as such a conduct in the world; and much need have we, especially in times like the present, of the assistance of the Holy Spirit, to enlighten our minds, to keep open our eyes, and to confirm our hearts in such a resolution; but we shall not fail if we pray as we ought, and seek for greater humiliation under a sense of past miscarriages. I received, the other day, an account of the experience of a young person on her death-bed, which, as it is both comfortable and encouraging, I shall insert without apology.—'My mind,' said she, 'has been kept in perfect peace and composure, intermixed sometimes with lively views of the glory that is to be revealed. I have no doubts, nor any fears of death; I am happy. I beg you to press on, and not to faint by any means. I can assure you that you shall be well recompensed; the reward is *present* as well as *future*. I would not part with the knowledge which I have of God in Jesus Christ, for ten thousand worlds; I only lament that I have done no more for the glory of God, and lived no more to promote it. Beg all to pray for me that I may wait the Lord's time, and glorify him by a patient submission, as becomes a humbled penitent sinner under the chastening of an Almighty God, and most merciful Father in Christ. I have been taken out of bed but once this fortnight. My disease is worse, attended with most violent pain, and such excessive thirst as is almost insupportable. I am passing a time of the greatest trial; but Satan is kept under. I have peace, hope, and joy beyond expression; but I still find myself a corrupted creature, and have the greatest reason to cry with my latest breath, God be merciful to me a sinner! I have no wish to return to life again, but I desire to wait God's time with patience.'

"In this young person's happy death, we receive a testimony of the power and grace of the Redeemer. It is a peculiar blessing, my dear friend, that you are resigned to his will, and that you can see that the sting of death is removed. O may all who suffer by your illness be equally submissive, and not the worse but the better for the cross. I am and shall be earnest at the throne of grace in your behalf, that the Lord may pour out upon you the influences of his Holy Spirit, that what he calls you to, he may fit you for; but you have a better intercessor than I am, whom the Father heareth always. Now our Lord Jesus Christ himself, and God, even our Father, be your support under, and do you good by this dispensation. Believe me to be, more than I can express, your sincere and affectionate friend."

The family usually left Taymouth at the close of the autumn. This year, it would seem, they had taken their departure sooner, for Lady Glenorchy was in London early in October. This probably was intended by her friends to divert her mind from those serious subjects which occupied it. Aware of the danger attending this return to the seat and centre of dissipation, she had made up her mind to resist it, and had informed Miss Hill of her determination. In this resolution her friend endeavoured to confirm her, by addressing to her the following letter.

attention turned to them, and, as might naturally have been expected, was anxious to have the opinion of her friend Miss Hill upon them. This Miss Hill gave, in her usual frank and kind manner, as follows:—

"*November* 16. 1765.

"My heart and thoughts, my very dear friend, have been much with you during your journey; and were it not for the reflection that you have a merciful God, whose watchful eye is ever over you, to keep you from all evil, my uneasiness on your account would have been abundantly heightened, as in your last letter you mention being afflicted with great doubts and terrors. This is far from being an uncommon complaint; and I believe there are few truly brought out of the captivity of sin and Satan, who have not at times experienced the same or similar distress. When this great adversary sees his kingdom likely to be overthrown in the heart of any one, he never fails, either by force or fraud, to attempt to regain it. But the Lord Jesus Christ, the great Captain of their salvation, ever has, and ever shall most undoubtedly enable them to come off more than conquerors. With respect to the doctrine of the new birth, on which you ask my opinion, it is plainly taught by our Lord in his discourse to Nicodemus, when he says, 'Except a man be born again, he cannot see the kingdom of God.' The sinner, in his natural state, has unquestionably in God, life, motion, and animal being; but he is not conscious of his presence, and is an entire stranger to those influences of the Holy Spirit which nourish the divine life in the new creature. The things of God which are so continually present to the souls of the children of God, make no impression on his mind. God speaketh to him by his word and his providences; he calleth him, but he heareth not his voice. Christ offers himself to him as the bread from heaven, but he tastes not how good the Lord is. God would manifest himself to him, but the eyes of his understanding are so darkened, that he cannot discover him. He is, in fact, as the apostle Paul expresses it, 'alienated from the life of God through the ignorance which is in him.' He may, however, at times have some serious thoughts and affections; he may occasionally feel some good desires, and make some faint efforts to turn to God; but his heart being yet attached to this world, his spiritual senses not being yet exercised, he is not able to behold the Sun of Righteousness, for he is not yet born of God. Whatever peculiar circumstances may attend such a change as is implied in being born again, there is every reason to believe that none can have truly experienced it, and yet remain entirely ignorant that such a change has been effected. The sinner, in fact, is no sooner born of God, than he feels the presence of God, and becomes capable of discerning spiritual objects. God no longer calls to him in vain; he hears, he knows the voice of God, he draws near to God, he tastes the good word of God, and the joys of the world to come. In short, his spiritual senses are all in action; the veil is taken off from his eyes; the things of the Spirit of God are no longer foolishness to him; he receives them, he comprehends them; he feels the peace which passeth all understanding; the love of God is shed abroad in his heart; and living in love, and knowing that God is love, he knows also that he is born of God, and that he dwelleth in God, and God in him. Having suggested these few hints respecting the doctrine of regeneration, I shall now proceed to say a word or two, which may, by the blessing of God, be of use to you towards repelling those fiery darts with which Satan frequently attacks believers, bringing them under doubts and fears respecting their interest in Christ, and the reality of their regeneration. The great deceiver (who, like a roaring lion, goeth about seeking whom he may devour) may possibly take advantage of the weakness of your body, and thereby bring you under many distressing fears. But, my dear friend, the God of truth has declared, that he cannot hurt you; 'for in that Christ himself hath suffered, being tempted, he is able to succour them that are tempted.' Keep this text constantly in your view; I know of none more strengthening or comforting; it has often been blessed to me in like circumstances. Our dear Redeemer, in his sufferings, seemed to be cast off by his Father, when, in bitter agony, he cried out, 'My God, my God, why hast thou forsaken me?' And yet, even then, he obtained a glorious victory over the powers of darkness. The Israel of God, his spiritual children, through him, likewise, are more than conquerors, although they may sometimes be tempted to think that God has cast them off, and suffer most severely by particular conflicts. God, however, is in these circumstances often most near to them, and thus exercises the strength of their love towards him, and tries their faith and patience. A lively faith in the divine promises will convince us, not only that the God of Peace shall bruise Satan under our feet shortly, but that it is also the Father's good pleasure to give us the kingdom. When, therefore, my dear friend, you feel the force of temptation, and you are assaulted with doubts, fears, and terrors, (than which nothing can be more burdensome to a real Christian), do not fail to exercise faith on the Son of God; consider his triumphs on the cross; and remember, that all he did, and all he suffered, were for *you*. Lay hold on him as your only and all-sufficient Saviour, then shall he be to you, as Isaiah expresses it, chap. xxxii. v. 2. 'As an hiding-place from the wind, and a covert from the tempest; as rivers of water in a dry place; as the shadow of a great rock in a weary land.' When Christians are distressed with convictions of sin, as David was, or fatigued with the troubles of this world, as Elijah, they find *that* in Christ, in his undertaking, his promises, and his consolations, which revives them, and keeps them from fainting; they who are weary and heavy laden, do indeed find rest in Christ. All the precious privileges of the new covenant are purchased by his blood, and communicated by his Spirit. How sweet are the promises to a believing soul! How delightful the knowledge of pardon, the assurance of God's love, the joys of the Holy Ghost, the hopes of eternal life, and the present earnests and foretastes of it, to those who have their spiritual senses exercised. If the pleasures of sin are hateful to us, divine consolations shall be sweet to our taste, sweeter than honey and the honey-comb. Now if Satan attempt to destroy your comfort, by suggesting that you must *do so and so, and be this* and *be that*, repel his temptation, by calling to your remembrance, that Christ has paid the whole debt, even to the uttermost farthing; and that in him you have a fulness of pardon, peace, wisdom, strength, righteousness, and salvation, all treasured up for you. O blessed free grace of God! O blessed be his name, for Jesus Christ! What a gift! and for *whom?* for *sinners!* for me and for you, my dear dear friend, to whom I am now writing. What says the everlasting God? Believe on the Lord Jesus Christ, and thou shalt be saved. Can God lie? Can we have a better foundation to build upon than his promise and oath? O then, may we ever cast all our burden upon the Lord, seeing we are thus encouraged, and invited to do so, and lean on the beloved of our souls, and upon the promises of God in him. This will bear us up under all troubles, and fortify us against all temptations, for the Lord Jesus is our *strength and our Redeemer*. You complain of weakness, see then in whom you have strength, strength sufficient for you in every time of need; for, saith the Scripture, 'As thy day is, so shall thy strength be. God is faithful, who will not suffer you to be tempted above that ye are able; but will with the temptation also make a way to escape, that ye may be able to bear it.' My dear friend, lay up these gracious words of promise in your heart as your richest treasure, and confide in them as your surest support, counting nothing so certain as what God has said. While his children can live upon this fixed dependance on the Saviour's grace, all things shall work together for their good. The abiding sense of our own weakness will keep us dependant upon Jesus, and anxious to receive out of his fulness, so that the more we feel of our utter helplessness, the stronger we shall grow, because we shall live more upon him; which illustrates that seeming paradox of the apostle's, "When I am weak, then I am strong;" when I am most sensible of my own weakness, then am I strong in the Lord, his strength is then perfected in me. According to the express testimony of the Scriptures, it is faith that brings peace and resignation to the soul; 'Being justified by faith, we have peace with God through our Lord Jesus Christ.' And again, 'Thou shalt keep him in perfect peace whose mind is stayed on thee, because he trusteth in thee.' The conscience being first awakened to see its own defilement, and afterwards pacified by an application of the blood of sprinkling, attains a sweet composure; and resting on the faithfulness of the Redeemer, and the all-sufficiency of his undertaking, is confident that all things shall work together for good to those who love God, and are the called according to his purpose. This consideration makes it the desire of the Christian's heart, that the will of God may be done in him, and by him; and therefore, under the most distressing circumstances and sharpest sufferings of body or mind, he can say, 'not my will, but thine be done.' Moreover, the soul thus brought out of its natural darkness into the marvellous light of the Gospel, sees an amiableness and an excellency in Christ Jesus, of which before it knew nothing. Once the man could look upon the blessed Redeemer as having no form nor comeliness that he should desire him; but now he sees him to be altogether lovely, the chief among ten thousands, full of grace and truth. Having now obtained the precious faith of God's elect, *Jesus* is become precious to his soul; for saith the Apostle Peter, 'Unto you which believe he is precious.' Time was when this poor perishing world, and its riches, honours, or pleasures, engrossed his affections; but the bent of his heart being now changed, he seeks only the unsearchable riches of Christ, the honour which cometh from God, and those pleasures which are at his right hand for evermore. Time was when his own will was his rule, and the commandments, ordinances, and people of God, were irksome to him and unwelcome; but now, being born from above, and passed from death to life, it is the desire of his heart to be guided by the word and Spirit of God; he counts his commandments no longer grievous, but a light and easy yoke; he says of the ordinances, 'It is good for me to be here;' and his delight is in the saints, who in his estimate are the excellent ones of the earth. These things, my dear friend, I am convinced you now know by happy experience; and most certain it is, that if you do know them in truth, flesh and blood hath not revealed them unto you, 'For the natural man receiveth not the things of the Spirit of God, neither can he know them, because they are spiritually discerned;' and human nature can rise no higher than its source; but the anointing which you have received of God abideth in you, and shall teach you all things. Although, however, it has pleased the Lord to reveal himself in you, you must be earnest in prayer for fresh supplies of knowledge, faith, grace, and strength; and you have all possible encouragement to be so, since (as I observed before) in Christ all fulness dwells, and out of that fulness we receive grace for grace. Learn then to guard against self-dependance, and to live more upon Christ. Resign yourself to him in all his offices, as a Prophet to teach you, a Priest to make atonement and intercession for you, and a King to rule over you and in you. View him also in his pastoral office, in the character of a shepherd, 'the good Shepherd who gave his life for the sheep.' Consider his watchfulness and care of his little chosen flock, that 'little flock to whom it is the Father's good pleasure to give the kingdom,' and of whom he himself says, that 'none shall pluck them out of his hand.' O my dear fellow-traveller in the road to Zion, how are we bound to magnify and adore the good Shepherd, when we remember how that, when we like sheep had gone astray, he sought us and brought us back by the cords of love, and when we were wandering farther and farther from his fold, made us 'hear his voice and follow him.' O this indeed is love which passeth knowledge! May it fill our hearts with gratitude, and our lips with praise! May it constrain us to live more to him who died for us, and to grow more and more in conformity to his blessed image! that so we may adorn the doctrine of God our Saviour in all things, and by well doing put to silence the ignorance of foolish men, who would falsely accuse our good conversation in Christ. But I tire you, and engross too much of your time by the length of my letters. You will, I know however, pardon the freedom with which I write, for with shame and sorrow I confess, that I am a miserable proficient in the school of Christ, and have great need myself to be taught. I love indeed to think, talk, and write of the blessed Jesus; my sinful soul seems refreshed when I meditate on the glories which compose his name. But O, how dark, how ignorant am I! how little, how exceedingly little do I know of him! O thou light of the world, enlighten my soul, teach me to know more of thy infinite and unsearchable riches, that I may love thee with increasing ardour, and serve thee with growing zeal, till thou bringest me to glory. Since I wrote the above, I have been very ill, but I thank God that I am now better. In the midst of my pain, I felt a sweet composure, and experienced a hope that God was my reconciled Father in Christ. When I looked at myself, the sight frightened me, for I saw nothing but a black catalogue of actual sins arising from the impure fountain of my corrupt nature; but in looking at Jesus, how was the view changed! I was enabled to see every sin blotted out by his precious blood, and that the law, as a covenant in its utmost rigour, could have no demands against me. In general, I find it the hardest thing in the world to believe this; a certain legal self-righteous spirit cleaves to me, and I am looking for that in myself which I can never find but in my blessed Surety.

It is this that obstructs the actings of faith, and prevents us from submitting to the righteousness which is of God. I thought much of you, my beloved friend, and even almost wished that I could bear your sickness for you; but this was not a proper submission to the will of him 'who orders all things well,' and *thus* visits you for the good of your immortal soul. I dedicate part of every day to pray to God for your recovery, and for your increase in grace, strength, faith, and holiness, so that you may come out of the furnace of affliction, refined as gold purified in the fire, and be made more and more meet for an inheritance amongst the saints in light. May the Lord vouchsafe an answer to my petitions! Sometimes the consideration of my great unworthiness would draw me back from the throne of grace; but I am encouraged by the reflection, that it is God's command that we should make our requests known to him, and that I shall be heard, not because I am worthy, but in virtue of the merits of my Redeemer. O what a privilege is it, that the God of heaven allows poor sinful worms to pour out their complaints before him! What an ease to an oppressed heart to breathe its wishes, and confess its fears, and tell its griefs to a loving Father, whose ears are open to the humblest prayer! O that the time spent in this heavenly exercise may be more and more delightful to me, and not to me only, but to all who love the Lord Jesus in sincerity! I fear our prospect of meeting again is very distant; perhaps it may not be permitted us in this life; but we may, I trust, hope for a far happier meeting, where sickness, pain, disappointments, and sin, (the woeful cause of them and of every other evil), shall be no more!—Blessed existence! May God vouchsafe to bring us, together with the whole Israel of God, to the haven of everlasting peace and rest, even to the eternal state of holiness and bliss, through the merits and intercession of our dear Redeemer! Help me with your prayers, my dear friend, to the end that I may be enabled to experience in my own soul, what I most sincerely recommend to you, and most earnestly pray for you."

Lady Glenorchy passed this winter in London and Bath, where every means had been employed to induce her to return to the dissipated world. Her judgment and her conscience however were decidedly against it; and neither severity nor art, both of which were put in practice, could divert her from her purpose. In this steadfastness Miss Hill rejoiced, and thus expressed the pleasure which she felt.

"*January* 17. 1766.

"I was last night made happy by the receipt of your kind letter, which I perused with uncommon interest and feeling. Greatly did I rejoice to find that there is any amendment in your bodily health, and above all, that you have once more through grace conquered the snares which Satan had industriously laid to seduce you again into the world—a world, friendship with which, the Scriptures declare, is enmity with God. It is truly amazing that so many people, professing to believe the Bible, should count it an act of prudence and good sense to cultivate, in the manner they do, the esteem and friendship of this vain and foolish world. Such persons certainly forget, that there is no precept in Scripture laid down with more express authority than this, 'Be not conformed to this world, but be ye transformed by the renewing of your mind;' nor than this, 'Love not the world, neither the things that are in the world. If any man love the world, the love of the Father is not in him.' How does it happen then that so many love the world, and yet remain perfectly at ease with respect to the state of their souls? I can attribute this to nothing but to the fatal blindness and desperate deceitfulness of the heart, and to the temptations of Satan, the father of lies. This arch deceiver is ever persuading us to think, and to live, and to act in direct opposition to the sacred oracles of truth in some point or other; well aware that as long as we are the willing servants of any known sin, so long are we his; as the Apostle emphatically expresses it, 'Know ye not that to whom ye yield yourselves servants to obey, his servants ye are to whom ye obey?' It is because the god of this world hath blinded their eyes that worldly people are so contented and satisfied with themselves; and hence it is that the religion of the heart is so much despised amongst us, and that engaging in the round of ceremonies and formal services passes for the whole of religion. The Gospel, however, is the power of God unto salvation; and when its influence is truly felt, it purifies the heart, sets it upon God, and is as inconsistent with the love of this vain world, as light is with darkness. This accounts at once for all the opposition which has been raised against it. The Lord says, 'Son, give me thine heart;' and when the heart, deeply affected with the love of the Redeemer, yields itself up to God, Satan has no more place *there:* this he well knows, and therefore stirs up the enmity of the world to use its utmost efforts to shake the pillars of the kingdom of God within the soul. This is evidently the cause why inward vital religion is so much rejected and despised, and why that dull, stupid, inefficacious *lip-labour*, in which worldly people are so fond of trusting, passes current amongst us. O that God may open the eyes of all who are thus deluded, and shew them that nothing but the love of God in the heart can avail before him, and that every thing else is false and counterfeit! O may God then, my very dear friend, by his Spirit shed abroad his love in our hearts, and cause us to live more and more under its holy and heavenly influence! Happy they who like Mary have chosen that good part, which shall not be taken away from them! They have abundant cause to rejoice before God on account of what he hath done for their souls, in as much as he has enabled them to know the things which belong unto their everlasting peace, and to prefer the service of Jesus to all that the world can present. Doubtless the world condemns their choice, and has been telling them that they are sadly lost to their friends and acquaintances, and, with an affected sort of pity, would fain again entangle them in its snares. But they are happy, let the world form what opinion of them it may, for the Spirit of God and of glory resteth on them; and whatever they may meet with from the contempt of an unbelieving world, they shall rejoice and be exceeding glad, for great is their reward in Heaven. 'Remember,' saith our blessed Lord, 'the word that I said unto you, the servant is not greater than his Lord; if they have persecuted me, they will also persecute you; if they have kept my saying, they will keep yours also. These things have I spoken unto you, that ye should not be offended.' These words of our Lord are sufficient consolation to every believer. Under their influence let us, my dear friend, learn daily that glorious lesson, to 'count all things but loss for the excellency of the knowledge of Christ Jesus our Lord;' and think it our highest honour, that as we can *do* so little for Christ, we should be called in some way or other to *suffer* for him, till he gives us our discharge, and takes us to share in the triumphs of that victorious faith which overcometh the world. May this be our happy lot! I rejoice you had resolution and fortitude to resist all places of public amusement at Bath, and that you were enabled to see the vast danger you were in of being again entangled by the world, whose delights you now happily find to be so truly empty, and so greatly disproportionate to the moral capacities of the soul, that they are no more capable of yielding any solid contentment to an immortal mind, than the glow-worm glistening in the hedge is capable of giving light to the universe. Let us remember, that whatever we make our chief delight, to the neglect of Christ and his salvation, as it is vanity in the fruition, so it shall surely be very bitterness in the end. But if the blessed Jesus say to us, ‘Be of good cheer, your sins are forgiven you’—if he add that precious promise, ‘I will never leave you nor forsake you’—if he in the hour of death receive our departing souls into his tender and compassionate bosom—if in the day of judgment he bid us enter into the joy of our Lord—if this be our portion, we cannot but be truly happy. Let me warn you not to give way to unbelieving doubts and fears, which are highly dishonourable to God, and most destructive to your own peace and comfort. God's Spirit has been striving much of late with you, and will, I am persuaded, not suffer you to rest short of a true conversion. *Do trust him*, he will certainly perfect the work he has begun. I do from the very bottom of my heart bless the Lord, who is dealing so kindly with you. Every one of your spiritual complaints is, in my mind, matter of rejoicing on your behalf, and your case is the common one of all God's children. What if your duties are imperfect, your graces at times weak, and your comforts fail; is not

Christ still the same? Is he not able and willing to pardon the imperfections of your duties, and to strengthen your graces, and to cause your consolations to abound? He is shewing you that you must live wholly upon him. This is one of the most important lessons he has to teach you; and whatever brings it to your experience is a great and valuable blessing. What can make Christ so precious as seeing our continual need of him? What can endear him so much to our hearts as a full persuasion that we cannot do any one thing without him? My dear friend, you seem not to have perfectly learned this lesson. Let not your faith be discouraged by a sense of fresh wants, but live closer and nearer to the Lord Jesus. Look upon him as a *full* Saviour, and rest satisfied that he can save to the uttermost. Here you may build upon a foundation which cannot possibly fail you. Strive to make use of this blessed Immanuel upon all occasions; by faith and prayer carry your wants, your sins, your infirmities to him, that he may deliver you from them all. May the Lord teach and enable you to do this by his word and Spirit! The *justified* person shall live by faith; and, says the Apostle, the life which I now live in the flesh, I live by the faith of the Son of God. May you, my dearest friend, know this truth in your mind, love it in your heart, and enjoy it in your experience every moment of your life, and then all the present evils of which you complain shall work together for your good."

CHAPTER IV.

Lady Glenorchy continues to suffer much from various causes—Miss Hill, in two letters, endeavours to comfort her—Death of Lord and Lady Sutherland—Miss Hill writes Lady Glenorchy on the occasion—Lady Glenorchy, from bad health, leaves home—Miss Hill, in one letter, laments her indisposition—And in another, discovers much fidelity and affection to Lady Glenorchy—Details her own experience—Lady Glenorchy is exposed to reproach—Miss Hill gives her advice and opinion on the subject.

Lord Breadalbane, although he did not enter into the ideas of Lady Glenorchy in matters of religion, highly respected her integrity and talents; and entertained for her the greatest esteem and affection to his latest hour, which extended to no great distance from her own. Lady Glenorchy, however, suffered much from other causes, and wrote to her friend Miss Hill on the subject, who immediately directed her, in the two following letters, to the best of all consolations—those which are drawn from religion.

" *January* 1766.

" You say you have troubles of various kinds. Of whatever nature they may be, I most sincerely sympathize with you; but you may be persuaded that you have not one which you could do well without. Even in the midst of the greatest tribulations, while they are besetting us, and falling heavy upon us on every side, true Christians can triumph, having peace with God, and rejoicing in hope of his glory. They who are acquainted with that greatest of all blessings, the sense of enjoying the favour of the almighty and all-sufficient Jehovah, and who behold endless glory awaiting them, and, as it were, just before them, cannot fail to experience thereby incomparable consolation and support. It is God, our God in Christ Jesus, who can only be our stay in trouble. A covenant God! transporting thought! a God graciously condescending to be a God to us in time and for eternity, through Jesus the Mediator. Have we then taken hold of the covenant? Have we come to God by Jesus Christ? Do we cleave to him as our portion, our greatly and only desired portion? And do we know of a truth that he is a reconciled God to us, and that he will be our God for ever and ever? Thus minded, we shall rejoice even in tribulations; neither shall it be in the power of affliction, or of sin, or of Satan, of oppression or persecution, or even of death itself, to take this our joy from us. O how singular and peculiar are the blessings which belong to real Christians, who are related to God as dear children! and how should this engage us to give all diligence to make our calling and election sure! A Christian is a most honourable character—one who has fellowship with the Father and with his Son Jesus Christ. May we then make it evident to our own souls that we are partakers of that fellowship, by living a life of faith on the Son of God, and adorning the doctrine of God our Saviour in all things! Without this, all is nothing. In every trouble we must strive to exercise the graces of humility, faith, and hope; and when these are in full operation, patience will be the infallible result. Humility shall effectually stop the mouth of complaint; faith shall give the well-grounded persuasion that the affliction is good; and hope shall bring in the enlivening prospects of growth in grace and approaching glory. How then can we do otherwise than rejoice in tribulations, knowing that 'tribulation worketh patience; and patience, experience; and experience, hope? Afflictions are sent to prove us, whether grace be in us or not. Now, if they work in us the sorrow of the world, and make us fly to worldly succours, what do they but unquestionably prove the depravity of our hearts? But if they have a contrary effect, and work patience, they produce in us an experimental acquaintance with various circumstances relative to God and to ourselves, to this world and to the next, which are of the most interesting and comfortable importance. When afflictions bring us to a more resigned and mortified spirit, to a more sure trust in God, and a more entire casting of our care upon him; and when the Lord supports us under them, and blesses our souls by them, then they bring along with them a comfortable experimental proof of his love. 'If you endure chastening, God dealeth with you as with sons.' It is afflictions which distinguish the chaff from the wheat; and by our deportment under them, we shall be able to discover whether or not we are sincere and upright in heart. If we cleave to God and duty patiently in a cloudy and dark day, this shall clear up our evidences, and help us to an experience of our integrity in which we may rejoice. If at such a season we do not confer with flesh and blood, and do not yield any thing to ease, interest, or worldly esteem, but maintain a good conscience, patiently suffering since the will of God is so, hereby we evince that we regard God's will more than our own. Thus it is, my dear friend, that sufferings may be considered as special seasons and means of giving to the children of God experience of their integrity towards him. I rejoice to think that my last letter afforded you any consolation; but I beg you on no account whatever to look on the unworthy writer in a higher light than she deserves. If God make use of me to be in the least degree instrumental towards strengthening you in the blessed paths of righteousness and peace, I shall indeed be happy; but to him give all the glory. My heart is much with you, and I cannot be employed more to my satisfaction than in this intercourse, which I must beg may never again be interrupted. Perhaps the Lord may in his good time permit us to meet again here below; if not, the transporting hour is drawing nigh, when we hope to meet above, and leave all our sins and sorrows behind us. In the mean time, may faith supply the defects of sense, and feed upon the privileges of spiritual communion! Do we not meet at the same throne of grace? Do we not drink of the same water of life? Are we not fed with the same heavenly bread, and supported by the same divine promises? Are we not animated by the same glorious hopes, and pressing towards the same heavenly mark? Does not he who comforts *you*, vouchsafe to comfort *me* also? When we pray in retirement, do we pray *alone?* O no, my dear friend, how would it raise our spirits to consider the countless multitudes that are joining with us every hour! All our eyes and hearts are fixed upon the same Jesus, and he, like the sun in the firmament, shines forth at one and the same moment, filling every eye with his light, and warming every heart with his love. Nor is this all; nay, this is the smallest part of the view of the communion of saints. We join not only with the church below, but with the church above, that glorious assembly, which is enlarging every moment, by the accession of new voices out of every kindred, and tongue, and nation, and constantly singing, 'Worthy is the Lamb that was slain,' and ascribing all the praise to 'him who loved us, and washed us from our sins in his own blood.' It is true, as one observes, that the saints in light do not feel our imperfections, and consequently cannot mourn over them; for in heaven that which is in part is done away, and that which is perfect is fully come. They do not *now*, but they did *once*. There was a time when they *were* as we *are*. They in their day passed through this vast howling wilderness; they were beset with our enemies; they were tempted, wounded, and sore thrust at that they might fall; but the Lord was their stay. Many of them have been hard put to it, and in an hour of unbelief have almost despaired of seeing the goodness of the Lord in the land of the living; but now their conflicts are over. After all their struggles, they are made more than conquerors, by the blood of the Lamb and the word of his testimony. And we, who experience the same trials, expect the same deliverance; for the arm that protected them is stretched out still; the fountain whereof they drank is full and flowing for us also; the word on which they hoped is in our hands; the rock on which they were built is the Rock of Ages, a foundation sure in every age; therefore we need not fear. Every one who has gone to heaven before us, is a witness to the power, faithfulness, and love of our Saviour. And O, with what a cloud of these witnesses should we see ourselves encompassed, could we but penetrate beyond the veil of flesh, and open our eyes upon the glorious realities of the unseen world! May God bless you, my very dear and honoured friend, and pour out upon you the choicest of his mercies! Strive to have Christ always in your heart, heaven in your eye, and the world under your feet, and then you can never be unhappy."

"*February* 5. 1766.

"Many things in your last letter I will answer now more particularly. The more I consider the matter, the more I see proofs of the Lord's gracious dealings towards you. He seems to be, by the enlightening influences of his Holy Spirit, both working in you a more perfect knowledge of himself, and of your own state and character. These two things are indispensably necessary towards our progress in the Christian race. For until we see something of the infinitely condescending love of God to sinners, in sending his own Son to suffer for them, and the majesty and glory of the Redeemer himself, we shall never be able to discover the exceeding sinfulness of sin, which required a ransom of such inestimable value. And, on the other hand, until we see ourselves lost and undone, both by original and actual sin, and incapable of raising ourselves to newness of life, we shall never in earnest apply to Christ for help, nor value aright that great salvation which is in him. You complain of blindness, hardness of heart, and unbelief. O what delightful evidences are those complaints, that your heavenly Father is now convincing you of your lost and undone state by nature and practice, and that he is teaching you to set a true value on the undertaking of his dear Son, who invites all to come to him that labour with doubts and fears, and are weary and heavy laden with the burden of sin! You say that you *cannot believe*. I rejoice that you feel your inability; for undoubtedly a conviction of this is the first step towards obtaining true faith. You now experimentally know that faith is, as the Scripture declares, *the gift and the work of God*; from whom it must be sought in humble earnest prayer, and by whose Spirit it must be wrought in the heart. How different now are your sentiments from what they once were, or from those of the unawakened world around you! Were you to ask one who has the *form* of godliness without the *power*, if he has *faith?* the question would appear strange to him; he would perhaps be offended, and tell you confidently that he always believed. Were you to ask him, if he was ever weary and heavy laden with the burden of sin? his answer would probably be, that he thanks God he never did any thing so bad as to give uneasiness to his conscience: so blind is he both with regard to the state of his own soul and the spirituality of God's law. Whence is it, think you, that such a change has been wrought in you? The reason is evident. It is because Christ has chosen you to himself, and by his grace made you to differ from the world around you. O did you but know what terrors and sore conflicts! what blasphemous thoughts! what hardness of heart, many, who have told me their experiences, have been exercised with before they were set free by Christ, and under which I myself have at times groaned, you would not suppose your own case peculiar, but would see the kind hand of God in all his dealings with you. You have a gracious promise, that neither the world, nor death, nor hell, shall be able to pluck you out of the hand of Christ, your Saviour. Say, then, in the words of holy David, 'Why art thou cast down, O my soul? And why art thou disquieted within me? Hope in God; for I shall yet praise him who is the health of my countenance, and my God. Wait on the Lord: be of good courage, and he shall strengthen thine heart.' The faith of the strongest believers may be sometimes grievously attacked, and shaken, and ready to fail. Such seasons become doubly trying, when our evidences are at the same time clouded, divine consolations suspended, and communion with God interrupted. But however distressing these may be, they are a good sign of the existence of spiritual life, and of the exercise of spiritual senses. Whatever may be the nature of God's dealings with us, of this one thing we may rest assured, that he is good, the same yesterday, to-day, and for ever; and will be found always true to his covenant with his people. When, then, our faith is at the weakest, let us be careful not to let go our hold of the Saviour. The guilt of sin seems not the only thing that distresses you; you complain also of the deceitfulness of your heart, of frequent revoltings and wanderings from God. Do you not think that these complaints are the language of all who are brought out of the captivity of Satan into the glorious liberty of the children of God? Believe it, they are; and read, for your comfort, what severe conflicts even the apostle Paul himself had, as he tells us in Rom. vii. from verse 7. to the end; and I am sure, that whoever has any knowledge of the plague of his own heart, must earnestly cry out with him, 'O wretched man that I am! who shall deliver me from the body of this death?' But are these struggles with sin a proof that a person has *no* saving grace? Quite the contrary. They are a convincing evidence that he is born of God, and that the new nature is striving for victory over the old, which is sure to fight hard to attain the ascendency, and to give the soul much uneasiness before it will own itself conquered. The most advanced disciple in the school of Christ, will have cause to mourn over that corrupt nature which so continually fights against grace, and which even brings him into captivity to the law of sin. Be not discouraged, I therefore beseech you. You are fighting the good fight of faith, which has been done by every believer from the creation of the world to this present moment; and you have the same *Jesus*—the same Captain of Salvation present with you, and the same precious promises, that in the end you shall be more than conqueror through him who hath loved you, and redeemed you by his blood. Think, O think of Jesus on Mount Calvary. *There* did he satisfy, *completely* satisfy, divine justice. *There* the heavy blow which should otherwise have fallen upon us, fell upon his innocent head. The blood of the New Covenant is shed—it has made propitiation for our sins: that precious blood, far from crying for vengeance, like the blood of Abel, merits and demands, and obtains for us everlasting life. The reason why we do not hear our worldly acquaintances complaining of their corruptions is plain,—they are led captive by Satan at his will. They are ignorant of their disease, consequently careless of their remedy; they are under the dominion of sin; and though slaves to corruptions, yet they hug their chains. Is this the case with you? O no, blessed be God! from what you wrote me, I am sure it is not. You see yourself by nature a child of wrath, and that in you dwelleth no good thing; and you find in you a principle of grace making war against the natural principle of corruption which is in you and in every child of Adam; and this is an indisputable proof that you are quickened by the Spirit of God. You have no reason to doubt, therefore, that God is carrying on an effectual work of grace in your soul, and giving you an experimental knowledge of divine things, with which otherwise you could not be acquainted. I cannot conclude without again entreating you, my dear friend, to cast yourself entirely on the Lord Jesus. Trust him for the salvation you need, and while you do this you will never fail. It pleased the Father that all fulness should dwell in him, therefore go to him for all spiritual blessings."

Lady Glenorchy left Bath in the spring; and after making some stay in Edinburgh, according to her usual custom, went early in the summer to Taymouth. At this time, in addition to her domestic trials, she was visited with a very severe affliction, by the loss of her only sister, and which was much enhanced by the melancholy circumstances that attended it. Lord and Lady Sutherland had two children; Lady Catherine, born the 24th of May 1764, and Lady Elizabeth, who succeeded her father in the honours of Sutherland, and who, by marriage, is now * the Marchioness of Stafford, born May the 24th, 1765. Lady Catherine died on the 3d of January 1766. This event so affected her parents, that they left their seat, Dunrobin, in Sutherland, at which place it happened, and sought relief in the amusements of Bath, where they arrived much about the time that Lady Glenorchy left it. They sought relief; but they found it not. One affliction rapidly succeeded another. Soon after their arrival, Lord Sutherland was seized with a putrid fever, with which he struggled for fifty-four days, and then expired. The first twenty-one days and nights of this period, Lady Sutherland never left his bed-side, and then at last, overcome with fatigue, anxiety, and grief, she sunk, an unavailing victim to an amiable, but excessive attachment, seventeen days before the death of her Lord. Strange and unaccountable as the circumstance may appear, yet it is a fact, of which there

* January 1822.

can be no doubt, that her mother, Lady Alva, knew nothing of the death of her daughter for nearly three weeks after the event had taken place. The way in which she at last became acquainted with it was in itself particularly singular and affecting. Whilst she was hastening to her assistance, she happened to alight one day from her carriage at the door of an inn, on the road to Bath, where she saw two hearses standing. Upon inquiring whose remains they contained, she was told they were those of Lord and Lady Sutherland, on their way to the Royal Chapel of Holyrood-House in Scotland, for interment.

The cup of affliction, thus put into the hands of Lady Glenorchy, by her domestic trials, and by this painful bereavement, was full to the brim and running over: this led her to pour out her sorrows, as usual, into the bosom of her friend Miss Hill, from whom, in return, she received the following cheering communications:—

"*July* 10. 1766.

"O, my dear friend, what a mixture of pain and pleasure has your letter, which I have just now received, occasioned me! The effect which your illness has had upon me, shews me that I am too much attached to you. I feel my heart sinking within me, at the bare apprehension of losing you. May the Lord pardon me, and spare you to glorify him on the earth! I rejoice in the happy frame of soul in which you appear to be, patiently waiting the Lord's time for the removal of your troubles. Fear not, he will do it; and as you well observe, turn your present mourning into joy. But O I am almost at a loss how to advise you concerning the particulars you mention. I have laid the cause before God in prayer, beseeching him to direct you for the best, and to shew his will concerning you. Surely the weapons of a Christian should be always spiritual, and a Christian's adorning should be the ornament of a meek and quiet spirit, under the greatest provocations. Do not then, my friend, so far dishonour the profession you make of a follower of the lowly Jesus, and even act so contrary and wholly opposite to your own disposition and inclination, as to put on any appearance of ill-humour. This would be going out of the way of duty, and might provoke God rather to continue the affliction, than remove it. Besides, such a conduct and example might injure spiritual interest where you wish to promote it, and make what you say on religious subjects of no weight, as *that* religion will most naturally and justly be thought vain, which does not influence the temper and conversation. Rather continue to pour out your distress before the throne of God, nothing doubting but that the trial shall be removed when the Lord sees it requisite for the good of your soul. Your letter fills my heart with thankfulness to the ever-blessed God, who has thus wonderfully supported you, and shewn himself a present help in the time of your greatest extremity. Be not alarmed that you have felt those pains which are the consequences of natural affection; a want of them would have argued great insensibility. It would be, indeed, displeasing to God to mourn as those who have no hope; but he is far from forbidding us to weep over our departed friends. Did not our Saviour do the same?"

"*July* 26. 1766.

"I trust, my dearest friend, this letter will find you perfectly easy and composed under your late trial; and that having laid all your burden on the Lord, he has continued to support you under it. As this, however, was the chief subject of my last letter, I shall proceed to inform you of some particular circumstances relative to myself, in which you so kindly take an interest. Know, then, that since it has pleased the Lord, out of the abundant riches of his grace, for which I desire ever to magnify and adore him, to shew me the vast importance of salvation, and the absolute inconsistency of worldly pleasure with a life hid with Christ in God, I have been obliged to submit to some light crosses and trials from those who do not think of the nature and authority of the infallible word of God as I do, and who would persuade me that I am deceived both in doctrine and practice, and that all this strictness is unnecessary. Daily experience and observation shew me, that whosoever will be disciples of the crucified Jesus, must be thought particular, and many difficulties must meet them in their journey through life. Upon the whole, I have far more cause to be thankful than to complain; and I desire to bless the Lord for many privileges I enjoy, which others in my situation cannot possess. We know that suffering and war with this world form a part of our portion here. It is doubtless a great blessing to taste of the bitter cup of affliction in whatever way it may please our gracious God to send it; and I am convinced there is nothing outward more calculated to make us give up the world and its friendship, than to experience something of its enmity and malice. For my own part, I never have enjoyed such sweet and near communion with God in Christ, as after those seasons when I have been particularly called upon to bear my testimony boldly in the cause of my crucified Redeemer, which I have sometimes been under the necessity of doing, when a large party has been against me. But as truth is a powerful weapon even though wielded by a weak hand, I trust I shall never be ashamed of him who has bled and died for me. I see how dangerous it is to enjoy much of the favour of the world, whose smiles and blandishments might make us ready to take up our rest on earth, and abate our thoughts and desires after heaven. Opposition is certainly useful, and serves as an excitement to Christians in their journey towards Zion. Without it, many Christian precepts could not be put in practice. If we have not all manner of evil spoken against us, how can we bear contempt, and seek only the honour which cometh from above? If we have not persecutors, how can our suffering virtues be kept in exercise, and how can we love, pray for, and do good to those who despitefully use us? How can we overcome evil with good? In short, how can we know whether we love God better than life itself? It has been, I believe, an observation in every age of the Christian Church, and confirmed by experience, that when the Church was at the highest pitch of outward peace and prosperity, it was at the lowest in point of spiritual lustre; and that when it appeared in the greatest distress by cruel persecutions, and uncommonly severe sufferings, it was most abounding in sincerity, zeal, vigour, and grace. When the soul is most afflicted by outward trials, it is often most happy in the rich supplies of spiritual consolation and holy joy; and God speaks most peace to it when things seem to be most against it. I long to hear from you again, and to know how you bore this last misfortune, which I am encouraged to hope would have no violent effect upon you, as you were prepared for it, and had your mind stayed upon that Almighty God, whose hand has before been so wonderfully stretched out for your support. O what a blessing it is to have this God for *our* God, our steady unchangeable friend! Since he has done so much for us in times past, shall we not trust him for all that is to come, and leave every thing that concerns us in his hands, who bears us so much upon his heart, and who cannot mistake our true interest? In him is everlasting strength; therefore we may trust him, and wait upon him. O, my friend, shall we not confide in him, who is the Lord of all power, the Father of all mercies, and the God of love? Here, then, let us rest our minds; here repose all our trust and confidence; here our heavy burdened hearts may find rest, ease, and peace; safety and boldness; comfort and joy. Thus leaning on our beloved and our best friend, we shall praise him who is the health of our countenances and our God. On what besides can we depend for relief in times of trouble and adversity? All earthly things must fail: they cannot satisfy the desires of an immortal heaven-born soul. O may the Almighty Lord and giver of life and comfort, take us off from all confidence in any thing we are apt to trust to, either in ourselves or any creature, and enable us to look wholly to him who is the Lord our Righteousness and our Redeemer. You have certainly cause to rejoice in your afflictions, since they have been the means of weaning your affections from the world, and fixing your heart on the unchangeable things of eternity. Press forward, I beseech you press forward; the prize before us is of a most animating nature. Remember what Jesus suffered to obtain it, his dying agonies, his tender love. O how sweet is the name of Jesus! My dear friend, do you not see him to be your righteousness, your strength, your hope, your refuge, your confidence, your all? I know you do. Why then should any thing distress you? Strive after more full assurance that all shall work together for your good; and may we both employ the portion of time allotted us on earth, in the love and reverence of our great High Priest; and whilst we are raising up our most enlarged capacities to comprehend something of his ineffable greatness, let our longing hearts burn to be with him, that we may behold this all-sufficient Saviour as he now sits enthroned in light, angels, principalities, and powers, being made subject to him. O happy, happy time, when we shall, through grace, be admitted to fall before the throne, and join those heavenly hosts that day and night adore him without ceasing, and sing eternal Hallelujahs to his praise!"

Lady Glenorchy's health suffering much under the pressure of her great and complicated distress, change of air and scene was recommended to her, and in consequence of this she left home. This circumstance had occasioned, on her part, the suspension of her correspondence with her friend for some weeks, which Miss Hill thus laments.

"*August* 20. 1766.

"My heart is much weighed down on your account. It is a long time since I have had any letter from you, which gives me a thousand selfish fears concerning you; and my distress is greatly heightened by being told, a day or two since, that you were very ill. O my dearest friend, it is possible, if not probable, that we shall not be long together! Your race, according to human appearance, will be run first. If so, may the Lord give me grace to follow after you, and make me bow submissively under his hand when he takes from me one dear to me as my own soul. But O may God restore you for a comfort to your friends, bring you safe home to their longing arms, and make you the happy instrument of promoting his honour and glory amidst a crooked and perverse generation! I know you are in the hands of Jesus, and Jesus is good, wise, almighty. He will therefore dispose of you for the best. O then calmly look to him, and when the feebleness of your spirits prevents you crying out, 'My Lord and my God,' let your devoted, resigned, patient heart still whisper, 'Thy will be done!' O my much beloved friend, if God intends taking you to heaven, shall I wish it otherwise? Shall I, a foolish worm, turn again when he may see it meet to tread upon me? What! Shall I lament your happiness? O may the Lord increase my faith, bend down my stubborn perverse heart, and whatever may be his will concerning me in respect to one so dear to me, may he enable me to kiss the rod that smites, and to give glory to the hand that guides it! May God the Father, Son, and Holy Ghost, uphold and comfort you! I hope I shall not cease to pray for you; and I beg you to remember a sinful worm before the throne of grace, for such is your truly affectionate," &c.

[Aged 25.] Great as was Miss Hill's affection for Lady Glenorchy, her fidelity was equally so, as will appear by the following long but excellent letter.

" *September* 5. 1766.

" After many painful hours on your account, my dearest friend, I am at last relieved by your kind letter, which rejoices me more than I can express. I am truly happy to find that my fears are groundless, and that you are better; for indeed I gave way to the most alarming apprehensions, and as you might observe from my last letter, I was ready to conclude, that your race was very nearly run. But glory be to God, my hopes are again revived, though I dare not too much indulge them, that your days on earth may yet be prolonged to live to him, who has thus preserved you a monument of his mercy and goodness, and to be a comfort and blessing to your friends. But, my very dear friend, you must allow me to be free with you: Indeed my duty to my God, as well as to your soul, will not admit of my being otherwise, or of dealing deceitfully in matters of the highest consequence, particularly after the kind injunctions you have laid upon me to write without reserve. I am grieved that you had recourse to company in the time of your heavy distress, thinking therein to find that relief which can only proceed from God himself. Is it not in fact a distrust of God's power, of his willingness to help? Is it not dishonourable to him to seek other means of consolation than what he himself has appointed and promised to bestow? Undoubtedly it is, and every such unstable prop must fail, although for a short time it may seem to lend support. This is leaning on broken reeds instead of the Rock of Ages. Possibly for this cause the Lord has withdrawn the light of his countenance from you for a season, in order to show you the vanity of creature comforts, and that there is help only in him who is mighty, almighty, and the never failing staff of support. But be not discouraged, this I trust has been a useful lesson to you; let it teach you for the future to be continually looking to Jesus; his grace is sufficient for you, and no doubt the Sun of Righteousness will again arise on your benighted soul with healing under his wings. Live every moment upon the author of your salvation for present grace, believing in him for victory over sin, as well as for pardon of it. I know from dear-bought experience, that it will conquer me the very moment I cease to live on the aid of Jesus; it has conquered me again and again for want of constant dependence upon him; but it never did, nor can, while I feel weak and helpless in myself, and am depending on the Lord, that I may be strong in the power of his might. This abiding sense of my own helplessness, makes me desirous to cleave close to my Almighty Saviour. I would hold him fast and dare never let him go. "If," says Mr Romaine, "we got a clear view of Jehovah Jesus, the subduer of sin, it will be the most blessed sight we ever had in our lives. Leaving the past, having nothing to do with the future, my business is now with Jesus; whatever I meet with I go to his office, where salvation is freely dispensed by his almighty love, and I make use of that present need of his saving grace. Let us observe in some instances the blessedness of this living every moment as it comes by the faith of the Son of God. Having brought all my salvation matter to a point, I being a sinner and he a Saviour, I depend on him always to act as his name Jesus imports, and his office is to save me from my sins. He has saved me, by taking guilt out of my conscience, but not so as that it may not return; therefore *now*, as the minute goes on, I rely on his word, and call upon his faithfulness, and trust to his power to cleanse me from all sin; and while I do this, I have no guilt, I am free from condemnation. The blood of Jesus answers all the charges against me from law, and takes away all fear of justice, because it is on my side; as I am in Jesus, it is just in God to forgive me my sins. Thus you see how I keep guilt out of my conscience; I live upon Jesus, and depend on his blood and righteousness from moment to moment. If you say, 'I do so, but am sometimes discouraged because of the sins which I still find in me;' observe, I have to do with Jesus and none else in the subduing of sin. I could not save myself, nor could all the powers on earth, or all the angels in heaven, save me from one sin—that is the peculiar office of Christ; it is his crown and his glory. The free pardoner is the almighty conqueror of sin. In this matter my concern lies altogether with him, and I find all things are possible to him that believeth. While I believe I never fall: as I trust moment after moment, every moment I conquer. Suppose you have a bosom sin; it besets you, it conquers you, you fast and pray, and strive against it, you reason with it, and urge arguments of philosophy and morality, you try to frighten it away with legal terrors; but in vain, it mocks all your efforts, raging more violently, tyrannizing more wantonly: what will you do? Why *believe* it away, that is Gospel like. Set the Lord Christ upon it. He has said, 'Sin shall not have dominion over you.' Tell him you can do nothing in this work; but having his word for it that he will do all, you dare to trust him, and to leave him to fight with your besetting sin. Rest the matter here, and see what will be the consequence; as sure as Jesus is the Saviour you will come off conqueror. I am witness for him; whilst I was a poor legal creature, ignorant of sovereign grace, I tried every way I could think of, and only nursed my sin; but when I saw the free pardon of it through faith in the blood of Jesus, then I was enabled to trust him with the subduing of it, and by faith I had and have the victory. Thanks, all thanks be unto him who gives it! But when sin is once subdued, what then? It will the next moment be striving for power and dominion, therefore every moment we must look to and live upon Jesus." I shall make no apology for this long quotation. It is from a letter to a friend; and as I found it of some use to myself, I am in hopes it may be of the same use to you. And do you not, my dear friend, see this blessedness of living every moment upon the Lord? O he is a glorious complete Saviour! I would not only have you see it, but experience it in your own soul. I can wish you no greater happiness on this side eternity; for thus enjoying a free pardon, and gaining daily conquests through faith in the Son of God, we may look forward with comfort and joy to that blessed day when death shall put an end to all our sorrows. The more clear the pardon, the more complete the conquest; the more does the believer anticipate the happiness of being saved from sin, and therefore he waits for it, nothing wavering. It is the believer's happiness in all his duties to live by faith in Jesus; he does not perform them that he may be thereby saved, but being already saved, he meets his precious Saviour in the way of duty, and holds fellowship with him in the ways of his commandments; and this makes them not grievous, but a light and easy yoke. The power of Christ makes the hardest duty easy, and the love of Christ makes the bitterest affliction sweet. The believer lives like himself when the sense of imperfect services works aright, when it makes him carry them and lay them all upon the golden altar which sanctifieth the gift; and when he depends every moment and in every duty upon the righteousness and intercession of God his Saviour. O blessed life this! My dear friend, I would to God I knew more of it than I do! May we both press after it with earnestness!

"M. is greatly obliged to you for your kind inquiries after her. We have good reason to be thankful, not only for her recovery, but likewise for her illness, which it has pleased the Lord abundantly to bless to her soul; and I think I can safely say, she now with diligence pursues the road to Canaan's happy land, and will, I trust, be an ornament to the gospel of Christ.

"H. and R. are two shining lights in the Redeemer's cause. The latter is intended for the sacred and honourable office of a minister of the gospel, which I pray God he may adorn both by his preaching and living.

"We have lately met with a heavy blow in this parish by the death of our worthy minister, and we are now left as helpless sheep without a shepherd, although, blessed be God, Christ the good Shepherd is still over his little flock. All outward means of grace seem entirely shut out from amongst us, and I fear we shall be obliged to give up those comfortable weekly societies, which through the mercy of God we found useful towards strengthening the weak in faith, and awakening the secure and ignorant; but these meetings, you may imagine, did not fail to be called methodistical, and have been attended with great opposition. However, if they be the means of bringing any one to the knowledge of Christ, we have no reason to regard the malice of his enemies, who will always reproach those who take God for their chief good, and seek his love and favour above all things. Through mercy I continue well, but much harassed with perpetual company and visiting. These things ought to make one very watchful, otherwise they are sure to destroy all holy intimacy and communion with the blessed Jesus; but my circumstances are such that these kind of compliances cannot be avoided; and indeed it is necessary to keep up a civility with worldly people, which often tends to remove prejudices; though we should cautiously avoid all sinful diversions, and be careful that we are not hurt by their example, or abuse our Christian liberty in any matter. What satisfaction can those things, which the perverted will of man has made choice of, afford to a soul deeply sensible of its undone state by nature, and which is seeking salvation, and can rest contented with nothing short of the full enjoyment of Jesus Christ? Can the love and esteem of the world, can countenancing its follies and vanities, bring real and solid happiness to an immortal soul? It is impossible. How do the daily complaints of the most prosperous, the discontent of those who enjoy pleasure with unbounded sway, the frowning spirit within whilst every thing smiles without, plainly prove that the mistaken multitude seeks happiness where it is not to be found? Or even suppose these things should constitute happiness all the days of our life, yet when our sun declines and sets in death, what qualifications should we have about us for the kingdom of heaven? Alas! a proud, earthly, carnal mind is not meet for the company, the praises, the services of the eternal God. People often lull themselves into a false conceit of mercy, and of being admitted to heaven, notwithstanding their vain, worldly, and sinful life; but surely if heaven be the enjoyment of God, and the business of it his service, they whose hearts are far from him, who live without him on earth, who have no relish for spiritual food and nourishment, would find the sight of God to be appalling, and his service the most grievous slavery! May the blessing of God be with you. Adieu."

Lady Glenorchy, although in circumstances peculiarly unfavourable, was evidently advancing in religious knowledge, and growing in Christian experience. Miss Hill was anxious to promote the former, and to strengthen the latter; and for this purpose she not only conveyed doctrinal instructions to her friend, but opened to her the abundant stores of her own experience, and urged her with much earnestness to make the best improvement of each. An example of this will appear in her following addresses.

"*September* 30. 1766.

"It is a comfort to me, my dear friend, when I can retire from company, and write to you, which I am not always at liberty to do, although, from the frequency and length of my letters, you might reasonably conclude that my time is a good deal my own. I wish it was more so; but I am so circumstanced as to have few hours in a day uninterrupted, and those ought to be improved to the wisest purposes: but, alas! I find them strangely misapplied, and that even my best duties have need of the blood of the Lamb to cleanse them from sin. How many spend their precious time as if hours were insignificant things, and such as should never be accounted for! O, my friend, what have we to do upon earth but prepare ourselves for heaven! How indefatigable should we be in the pursuit of eternal life in this our only time of preparation! May the Lord pardon my past criminal sloth and negligence, and enable me to be more earnest in redeeming the time I have lost, and to improve every present enjoyment to my soul's eternal advantage! O that I could less regard the things that are seen, and keep my eyes continually fixed on the great eternal things unseen! But I fall wretchedly short of what I ought to be, and see continual need to be washed again and again in the blood of my crucified Jesus, which, glory be to free unmerited grace! cleanses from all sin. *Here* is my hope: this blessed hope I would embrace and for ever hold fast, as an anchor of the soul, sure and steadfast, which neither men nor devils can overthrow. O that

I could be driven more and more out of my miserable sinful self, and be found in Jesus, not having my own righteousness, but that which is through faith of him, for he it is who is the end of the law for righteousness to every one that believeth. May we, my beloved friend, receive him for our righteousness, and so believe in him that we may be justified by faith, and have peace with God through him. There can be no healing for our disordered souls but in his blood; no peace for our conscience but in his reconciling us to God; no satisfaction to our minds but in that most perfect atonement, which satisfies every demand of the law, and the strictest justice of offended Heaven. O none but Christ! Without him, what can the whole vast universe avail us? Compared with him, it is a mere nothing, less than nothing and vanity. If he is ours, what can we stand in need of that he will not be to us? My dear friend, may we never distrust the power or love of this exalted Saviour. May we not be faithless, but believing that Christ is our Lord and our God, who loved us and washed us from our sins in his own most precious blood; and may it ever be the delight of our hearts to be at the feet of Jesus, to cast all our burdens upon him, and to lean upon the beloved of our souls, and upon the promises of God in Christ!

'For us he lived,
Toil'd for our ease,
And for our safety bled.'

Oh what amazing love! which passeth knowledge! that he who knew no sin should be made sin for us, by whose stripes we a rebel race are healed. Even above our miseries are the mercies of our God. While by nature we wander like helpless sheep in the barren wilderness of this world, our tender compassionate

Shepherd is anxious to bring us back into his fold, into the fruitful pastures of his church. Whilst in this wilderness we can find no abiding city, within the pale of his church we may all find rest unto our weary souls. Though in ourselves we are utterly destitute of spiritual support, yet the flesh of Jesus is meat indeed, and his blood is drink indeed; and when his good Spirit applies the merits of them to our hearts, then have we true spiritual life abiding in us. Though our souls fainted within us while we wandered in the wilderness, yet Jesus, the God of all consolation, will refresh the fainting soul with his reviving grace, and will plenteously supply it with every thing that is good through the ages of eternity.

"The arm of our all-conquering Jesus is ever stretched over his flock, that little flock to whom it is the Father's good pleasure to give the kingdom. Are we babes? he feeds us with the sincere milk of the word, that we may grow thereby. Are we weak? In him have we strength, the Holy Spirit helping our infirmities. Are we growing up into the measure of the stature of the fulness of Christ? It is through the communicated power of the Holy Ghost that we are strengthened with might in the inner man, rooted in faith, and grounded in love. Thus are Christians supported, carried on, and encouraged, by his operations, who worketh in us mightily, whose office it is to sanctify all the elect people of God, that they may be meet for inheriting amongst the saints in light.

"You tell me you would not give up the knowledge you have of Jesus Christ the Redeemer for the whole world. O how did that single sentence rejoice me! You have found him precious, precious beyond all things, and will therefore, I am persuaded, hold him fast and never let him go. Those who experience any thing of the true knowledge of Jesus, and of the sweetness of communion with him, cannot but be earnest to increase that knowledge, and enjoy more of that communion. Now, in order to attain this, nothing is more useful than frequent prayer, and meditation on the revealed will of God, looking with an eye of faith to the Divine Author, and cautiously avoiding all such things as are apt to destroy in us a holy and devout frame of mind. For my own part, I find continual need of the greatest watchfulness, being unavoidably engaged in company, so that it is necessary I should keep a continual guard over myself, lest my spiritual interest should be hurt by any undue compliances; and, alas! I have but too much cause of humiliation, that my example tends more to the hardening than to the edification of my fellow-sinners. Your situation, my dear friend, is peculiarly dangerous, without public ordinances, and many other means of grace, and in the midst of worldly snares and temptations, and of all that can allure and draw the heart from the pursuit of its only good. You have great need therefore to watch and pray, keeping fast hold of him who is your strength, and whose grace and power are engaged to keep you in the narrow path which leads to glory. Hold on your way then, my dear fellow-pilgrim, and wax stronger and stronger in the grace which is in Jesus. Let no trials, no temptations, discourage you in that race you have happily begun. You know who it is that has promised that he will never leave you nor forsake you, even he that can fulfil in you the work of faith with power. Look therefore to him, that out of his fulness you may receive; apply to him with full assurance of faith, that you may obtain all needful supplies. Maintain constant communion with him, by keeping close to him in his appointed ways, praying always with all prayer and supplication in the Spirit, and watching thereunto with all perseverance; walking every moment in the sense of his nearness and presence, and thereby suppressing every rising corruption, quickened to every good word and work, and reaching forward to apprehend him in all his amazing fulness; and you may rest assured, that Jesus will redeem the believing soul from all its troubles. They that come to Zion shall have their mouths filled with songs of joy and gladness, and sorrow and sighing shall flee away. Jesus Christ said upon the cross, It is finished. Now, my friend, I want you to apply this finished salvation, I want you to look on it as wrought out for you; till you do this I know you will be continually perplexed with doubts and fears. Satan will strive to torment you with a thousand legal thoughts; that you are not good enough, that you must do this, or that, or the other thing. But tell him Christ has *done all*, and that it is *sinners* that are invited to partake of the benefits of his death and passion, and that, as a sinner, you are resolved to lay hold on him. Thus you will be sure to conquer; only *believe*,—all things are possible to him that believeth.—O! in what a safe and secure state are the lambs of Christ's fold, the sheep of his pasture. For them Jesus hath ascended up on high, he hath led captivity captive, has conquered and bound all their foes, and now reigns triumphant, having received all power, both in heaven and on earth. They can never perish;—'because I live,' says Christ, 'ye shall live also.' Do seek after a more full assurance of your interest in this exalted Saviour. I am certain you will not rest satisfied till you can in full confidence of faith call him your Lord and your God,—and what now hinders you from receiving him as yours? O what privileges! what comforts arise from the contemplation of a risen ascended Lord! There is none so unworthy but may come with boldness and confidence to him. O, what manner of love doth God bestow on his children, and all freely to the praise and glory of his grace! Surely the consideration of these things is enough to enliven and warm our cold hearts, and to make them glow with gratitude and love. These make sin so exceeding sinful, that an evil thought becomes loathsome and burdensome. These make the soul flee from evil, even the very appearance of it, as from the face of a serpent. These inspire life, spirit, and zeal, and constrain the children of God to walk worthy of him. O may we be monuments of the truth of these things in time and to all eternity!"

"*October* 20. 1766.

"O, my dear friend, there certainly can be no true peace, no solid happiness, till Christ is experimentally known in the heart, till we can see and feel that in him we have righteousness and strength; and this I earnestly pray may be the happy lot of us both. I must own, I am sometimes apt to be weighed down with legal fears; but I know they are dishonourable to the free grace of God, and therefore, as a sinner, the very chief of sinners, I am bold to lay hold on Jesus, as a poor sinking mariner would lay hold on a cord or plank within his reach, knowing that there is no other name under heaven by which I can be saved but Jesus Christ. He can tread down every enemy under his foot,—he is faithful and true. O may we ever trust in him in all difficulties, in all afflictions, in all distresses, hanging continually on him for grace and strength to withstand the crafty devices of that roaring lion, who goes about seeking whom he may devour, and striving to perplex and destroy the disciples of Christ, laying snares innumerable and temptations in their way. He would indeed soon accomplish their ruin were they left to combat with the arm of flesh, or left to themselves; but to Jesus they look, and to him they ascribe all their strength, who has undertaken for their security, and watches over them every moment. We are assured by the infallible word of God, that sin shall not have dominion over the soul that is staid on Jesus, but he will preserve it through his almighty power unto salvation. As the mountains are round about Jerusalem, even so standeth the Lord round about his people from henceforth even for ever.

"We have, since I wrote thus far in my letter, had a proof of the enmity of the natural heart to God and godliness, and of the unjust prejudices of worldly people against the true disciples of the blessed Jesus. My brother wrote a very handsome letter to the new minister of this parish, requesting that he would lend his pulpit the Sunday following to Mr S——, an intimate friend of his, and a gentleman of a most unexceptionable conduct and character, and firmly attached to the articles, homilies, and liturgy of the church of England. This preamble, my brother was in hopes would have prevailed on the minister; but to such a height did his prejudices against truth run, that he absolutely refused, concluding, because Mr S. was recommended by my brother, he must be an enthusiast, or in other words a methodist, and therefore would not suffer the ears of his congregation to be infected with his erroneous and delusive doctrine, though, blessed be God, many belonging to it are turned from darkness to light by means of that doctrine he is pleased to term erroneous and delusive. But no wonder the truth is thus derided,—the natural man cannot discern it,—it is foolishness unto him, neither can he know it, because it is spiritually discerned. As the pulpit at the parish church was refused to this minister, my father, with the greatest kindness and candour, told my brother, his friend should be welcome to preach in the chapel,—an offer my brother accepted with thankfulness; and accordingly he gave us one of the most faithful and judicious discourses I ever heard. It was taken from Isaiah xlii. 16. 'And I will bring the blind by a way that they knew not: I will lead them in paths that they have not known: I will make darkness light before them, and crooked things straight. These things will I do unto them, and not forsake them.'—A glorious subject, and full of consolation to those whose darkness was made light.

"I am in daily hopes of hearing from you, as you kindly promised to write me from the first place you rested in. Beware of new temptations from new scenes, and in all your journeys look at the great end of all—*eternity*. Look to Jesus for continual supplies of grace and strength,—he has promised and he will fulfil. Let no fresh doubts discourage you, no opposition drive you from that eternally blessed hope which is set before you; for opposition you will have from those who cannot see that friendship with the world is enmity with God. But outward opposition is not all; our own vile hearts within produce a continual conflict. We must fight or yield;—with ourselves against ourselves, is the sharpest battle. All within us is at enmity with Jesus. This you have experienced; and was it not a sight of the depravity of your own heart that first brought you to him? This, my dear friend, must, as long as you remain on this side heaven, keep you close to him. So long as we are in this tabernacle we do groan, being burdened. If ever we feel not this burden, we must be dead to God.

"May Jesus ever bless and protect you, my dear friend; and may the light of his countenance shine on your precious soul, and give you all joy and peace in believing. Remember to pray for your unworthy friend."

The winter of 1766 and 1767 Lady Glenorchy passed in the country, where she was not only deprived of the aid of religious friends and institutions, but exposed to the reasonings and objections of those who disregarded them. From the rank which she and her family held, she was obliged, not only to receive, for days and weeks together, the visits of the neighbouring nobility and gentry, but to repay them. From this circumstance she was exposed to much trifling conversation, which she found irksome, and which on the Lord's day she now believed to be sinful. She also began to experience the odium and reproach which usually follow conscientious, decided, consistent piety. Each of these particulars she communicated to Miss Hill, and requested her opinion and advice on them, which she obtained as follows:

"*January* 18. 1767.

"My dear Friend,—I rejoice that you have been enabled to resist the temptations so artfully and so industriously spread to draw you out of the path of duty, in the particular circumstance of visiting on the Lord's day; for though doubtless, as you justly remark, every day is the Lord's, and some portion of every day ought to be employed in religious exercises, yet that day being in an especial manner set apart by God for solemn attendance upon him, we ought on that day to rest from the common business and necessary employments of life, and not use *that* as common which he has set apart as sacred. May Almighty God give us grace so to hallow his Sabbaths here, that hereafter we may be admitted to the joyful celebration of the eternal sabbatism in his kingdom of heaven. I am not surprised that you are accused of hypocrisy and superstition. Nay, I should be surprised if you were not;—this is the common lot of all Christ's people, and a scriptural proof that they are chosen out of the world. Surely we may submit to bear a little reproach from the world for his sake, who for us was despised and rejected, and who for us humbled himself to death, even the death of the cross. In things indifferent, Christians do well to avoid singularity; but let us on no account follow the multitude to do any evil. Here the children of the Most High should by all means be singular; should distinguish themselves by a becoming zeal for their God; should set an example, and shine as lights in the midst of a perverse and crooked generation.

"I fear that when you return to London or Edinburgh, you will be encompassed with many trials, from such of your acquaintances, and perhaps even from your friends and relations, with whom you formerly mixed in the hurry and bustle of the world, who will wonder at the change produced in your sentiments. Opposition, however, we must expect to meet with, if we would be good soldiers of Jesus Christ. Now, my dear friend, since this is almost universally the case, let us strive, if we must suffer, to suffer for well-doing, and not give any just cause or handle to the enemies of the Lord to blaspheme; but watch over ourselves with a godly jealousy, that our outward behaviour may be consistent with our profession. As to introducing religious conversation into company, it is certainly very proper,—you must, in the most prudent manner possible, use the means, and leave the event in the hands of God; by such conduct the hearts of the most obdurate have been moved. Continue to be much in prayer to God, in whose hands are the hearts of all men. My humble petitions are constantly offered up in your behalf; I beseech him to undertake your cause, and to support you under all opposition; and O may he reconcile all those who are near and dear to you, to the peculiar doctrines of religion, and bring them to the knowledge of the true God, and Jesus Christ, whom he hath sent. When you, my dear friend, live in entire subjection to the gospel, giving no just occasion for blame or persecution, be not discouraged. You say you but too often give way to company to drive away thought, and relax the wearied mind. I will shew you a more excellent way; rather, my dear friend, have recourse to your God, your Saviour, your truest and best friend, who is always near to them that call upon him. I would not have you shut yourself up as a recluse; but I am sure you will find Jesus to be a present help in time of trouble, whereas worldly company will only serve to distress instead of relieving your soul; and this, my dear friend, you have more than once experienced. Trust Jesus, then, again and again. O pray! pray mightily that you may live more by faith on him; then will your life on earth be full of joy and peace—such joy and peace which passeth all understanding, and which it is not possible for the hearts of the ungodly to conceive.

CHAPTER V.

Lady Glenorchy in a bad state of health—Miss Hill writes her on this occasion—She goes to Bath—Miss Hill, afraid that her spiritual interest would suffer in that city, again writes her on that subject—She returns to Taymouth, and in a letter Miss Hill expresses her satisfaction, that she is now in a place more congenial to devotional exercises —At Taymouth, Lady Glenorchy receives visits from some clergymen, by whom she is benefited—Miss Hill writes to Lady Glenorchy, and adverts to this circumstance with pleasure—When Lady Glenorchy was on a visit at the Earl of Hardwicke's, where the change wrought upon her mind must have exposed her to trials, she receives a letter from Miss Hill, alluding to these circumstances, and giving at the same time an account of the death of Mrs Venn—Miss Hill writes to Lady Glenorchy, in which she mentions some interesting facts with respect to some of the younger branches of her father's family—Miss Hill suffers much from worldly acquaintances, and in a letter informs Lady Glenorchy of this—Lady Glenorchy attends meetings for religious purposes in Edinburgh—Letter from Lady Glenorchy to Mrs Baillie Walker—Lady Glenorchy indisposed—Letter from Miss Hill on that occasion—Miss Hill writes to Lady Glenorchy, giving an account of her own Christian experience—Lady Glenorchy in her religious feelings discovers a peculiar degree of sensibility—Miss Hill writes her on this subject—Lady Glenorchy more comfortable in her mind—Congratulated by Miss Hill, who gives a farther account of her own experience.

About this time Lady Glenorchy, who seems to have been in a very bad state of health, received the following letter from Miss Hill, in answer to one she had lately wrote to her.

"*February* 7. 1767.

"O, my dear friend, what words can express the grief that I now feel on your account! The letter I have just received from you but too plainly tells me, that I must not long expect to enjoy your friendship here on earth. How shall I give you up? My dearest friend, would to God I could be with you! Were I my own mistress, I would not be long without attending you in your distress. You should not be alone if I could be with you, nor suffer one pain if I could relieve you, or bear them for you. But what am I saying? It is good for you that you have been afflicted; such trials spring not from the dust, but are the appointments of an all-wise God, who intends them for your benefit. It is God, my dear friend, your unchangeable covenant God, who loves you with an everlasting love, who thus visits you. Happy, not wretched, is the person whom God correcteth; these chastenings shall yield the peaceable fruits of righteousness to them that are exercised thereby. Through much tribulation we must enter into the kingdom of heaven.—I must now lay down my pen, for I am not able to proceed. I would say much that occurs, and which, with the blessing of God, might be of use towards consoling you in your present situation; but my heart is too full to permit me to write, though I am something easier, and am brought to bow more under the mighty hand of God than when I first read your letter. My mother seeing my great distress, has been asking me the cause. I told her you was very ill, and that I had reason to believe I should never see you more: at this she seemed concerned, and expressed a regard for you, which indeed she has often done, but says she is surprised how I can make myself so miserable, and have so great an attachment to a person of whom I have seen so little; to which I only replied with tears, and could scarcely say, that though I had seen much less of you than I wished to do, yet I knew enough of you to make me love you most affectionately, and you had given me reason to believe you had few friends more dear to you than myself. How little does the world know of that heartfelt union which real Christians experience towards each other! I think my regard for you is established on so solid a foundation that it cannot be overthrown. Your being an heir of God, and joint heir with Christ—having undergone many very aggravated distresses—bearing these with Christian resignation and fortitude—having with unlimited confidence reposed them in my breast,—these are circumstances which greatly endear you to me; but these I cannot communicate to others, so they must wonder on. Few people know what real friendship is; sometimes I wish to know less of it; for truly it has many pangs, yet it has at the same time very many sweets and advantages.

"My friends here do not seem to approve of the Spa waters for me: thank God, I am by no means ill, though I am not well,—if I could see you, I think it would do me more good than all the waters and doctors in the world. But I have one Physician that can never fail me—so have you, my dear friend. Let us, then, both apply to him, and he will heal us as shall be most meet for us. O let us fly to him in every adversity, pour out our complaints before him, and shew him our trouble. When holy David was distressed, he thought upon God, the throne of grace was the place of his refuge: so may it be ours! *there* we shall find the Father of mercies and God of all consolation, ready to answer our prayers and to administer relief. He is able to give songs in the night of distress, to make the bones that sorrow and anguish have broken to rejoice. If he speak peace, who shall cause disquietude, or what shall destroy our tranquillity?—So soon as I hear from you, I shall write again. May Jesus preserve you every where, and fill you with that peace which passeth all understanding.—What a letter is this! I scarcely know what I have been writing; an aching heart, a weeping eye, and a trembling hand, make bad work upon paper. O my dear friend, blessed be God for Jesus Christ, he can wipe all tears from our eyes—to him I most earnestly recommend you."

Lady Glenorchy having left Taymouth, after spending some time with her mother, went to Bath unaccompanied by Lord Glenorchy. While *there*, Miss Hill wrote, and expressed her anxiety, lest her spiritual interest should suffer in a place so dangerous to the religion of young persons of rank and fortune.

"*June*, 1767.

"I had the very great pleasure yesterday of receiving your letter; but in the midst of the joy I feel on the recovery of your health, and the hope of seeing you soon, I grieve exceedingly at the distressed circumstances in which you appear to be, both spiritually and temporally. Would to God you could live more by faith on his Eternal Son! O pray, pray without ceasing, that he would give you that Spirit of adoption by which you may be enabled to cry Abba Father, and so reveal himself to you as to enable you to see and feel that your sins are blotted out by the reconciling blood of the Lamb, and that you are really engrafted into Christ, the living Vine. I fear that you are infected with a very legal spirit—nay, your letter assures me that you are so; and instead of living wholly on the finished salvation which is in Jesus, you are looking for some recommendatory qualities in yourself—tell me, is not this the case? It is this which bars your access to God, and renders you so dead, dry, and lifeless in duties, and, together with the temptations of Satan, makes you ready to doubt of the love and mercy of God to your soul. It is owing to this also that you are in the dark concerning your interest in Jesus, and all the benefits of his active and passive obedience which are offered to you. I know well how to pity your situation. It is indeed a trying one, but far from desperate, and abundantly more to be desired than that lukewarm security by which millions of souls are destroyed. He who has promised not to break the bruised reed, nor quench the smoking flax, will in his own good time help, relieve, heal, and comfort the soul that waits on him. May the Lord Jesus look upon you in mercy! may he not lay more upon you than he will enable you to bear! O may he lift up the light of his countenance upon you, give you strong faith in his merits and promises, a comfortable affiance in him in all your troubles, and the witness of his Spirit with your spirit, that you are a child of God; and though you now walk in darkness, yet, may you trust in the name of the Lord. May he who has in wisdom shewed you great and sore troubles, in mercy look down upon you and revive you again, that you may rejoice in him, and have knowledge of his salvation.

"I hope your stay at Bath will be short.—I cannot conclude without beseeching you once more to cast all your care upon the Lord. May you enjoy abundantly the blessed fruits of faith and union with Christ here, till you go to be ever with him."

In the month of July following, Lady Glenorchy seems to have returned to Taymouth, which, although she could there enjoy but few means of grace, Miss Hill considered as upon the whole a more favourable place for her in a religious point of view, because it exposed her to less temptation. To this effect she writes.

"*July*, 1767.

"I trust you will find the advantage of being another year at Taymouth, and that the Lord will more abundantly bless you with the immediate supplies of his grace and Spirit, as you are out of the way of means; for though they are the ordinary method in which he has appointed that he should be found, yet he does not confine himself to them. I see Satan has thrust sore at you, by endeavouring to draw off your trust and confidence in the Saviour of sinners. These are subtile arts and wiles by which he ever strives to distress the children of God, and he never fails to take advantage when we cease to rely every moment on the arm of Jesus, or suffer the world to catch us in its destructive snares. Our business is, in fact, every instant with Jesus. I would recommend to you to be much in prayer, and attend to the leadings, of divine Providence, who, I trust, will make your path of duty clear, not perhaps all at once, but by degrees, so that after you have been exercised with uncertainties for a season, you shall find that he is overruling all to bring about what he has already appointed for you. Commit yourself therefore to him, act so far as he affords you an opening, consult him step by step—follow closely the leadings of his providence. In the Lord's dealings with his people, there are usually a praying time and a waiting time. He often even brings a seeming death upon our hopes and prospects just before he is going to realize them, and thereby we more clearly see, and more thankfully acknowledge, his divine interposition."

[Aged 26.] The beautiful and sublime scenery of the wide extended domains of Taymouth, and of the surrounding country, has, for time immemorial, attracted the attention of strangers. Several of the clergy both of England and Scotland were then, as now, frequently to be found among those numerous parties, who, in the summer season, visited this delightful region. Those clergymen whose talents and character were known to, and approved of by Lady Glenorchy, she invited to the castle, and employed in giving family worship, and in preaching on the Lord's day, after canonical hours, to her household, and to as many of the neighbours as were disposed to attend. She had great pleasure in these occasional exercises of religion; and to one of these, from which she had derived peculiar satisfaction, Miss Hill refers in the following letter.—

" *September*, 1767.

" I am very thankful that the Lord has so abundantly blessed Mr M.'s ministry and conversation to you. May the impression dwell long on your heart, but remember, my friend, to look through all means to Jesus, without whose gracious presence every thing will be vain and unprofitable. I often think that your being in your present situation, has proved to you one of the greatest blessings that could have been conferred on you; since, perhaps, had you swam smoothly down the stream of prosperity, and drank more deeply into the cup of worldly felicity, you had not known Jesus, nor felt the power of his love upon your soul. When we are most easy and happy in things that are seen, the consequence too often is, an hearty acquiescence in present situations, and a total neglect of the things that are not seen; and the stupifying potion of worldly ease lulls the soul into a profound sleep, and into a fatal forgetfulness of that God and Saviour, whom to know is better than life, and at whose right hand are pleasures for evermore. It is said of Archbishop Usher, who enjoyed much uninterrupted prosperity, that he was on that account under sad apprehensions lest God had forsaken him, and given him over to a reprobate mind. He feared, because his heavenly Father spared the rod, that he hated the child."

Lord Breadalbane's first wife was Lady Amabella Grey, daughter and co-heiress of Henry Duke of Kent. The issue of this marriage was Henry, who died a few weeks after his mother at Copenhagen, where Lord Breadalbane was then in the capacity of ambassador from the British Court, and Jemima, who upon the death of her brother succeeded him under the title of Baroness Lucas of Crudwell, and Marchioness of Grey, and who, a few weeks prior to her father's death, had married the Earl of Hardwicke. With these relations, Lady Glenorchy always lived on the very best terms. Her first visit, however, after her avowed change of mind, must certainly have been very trying, and in some respects even unpleasant. Miss Hill, anticipating these circumstances, wrote her the following letter, in the close of which she gives a very interesting account of the death of Mrs Venn, wife of the late celebrated Rev. Mr Venn of Huddersfield, and author of the Complete Duty of Man.

"*October* 10. 1767.

"I fear the meeting with your friends at ———, will be a severe trial to you. I pray earnestly that our merciful Lord may give you strength proportionally to it, as well as for every thing he has prepared for you in your journey to the promised land. Here we have no abiding place, the rest is polluted, we are pilgrims and only sojourners, as all our fathers were;—let us then with vigour and activity pursue the narrow path, and make that speed which souls ought to do, who seek a city whose builder and maker is God. We are called to forsake all for Jesus—let us then listen to the small still voice directing us in our way, and let us steadily and resolutely walk in it, in spite of the opposition we must expect to meet with from an unbelieving world, our own corrupt hearts, and the temptations of the wicked one. Heaven, even an everlasting crown of glory, an inheritance among the saints in light, is the end.

"I send you an account of the death of Mrs Venn, which my brother received in an excellent letter from her afflicted husband, whose behaviour under his trial has been greatly blessed to his people, and been the means of convincing gainsayers of the reality of religion in his soul. Mr V. writes as follows:—'My dear wife was in a bad state of health for several months before her departure, but in the beginning of July her disorder lay greatly on her spirits, a thing perfectly unknown to her till that time;—this also was aggravated by the assaults of her spiritual enemy, for he was suffered to pour in upon her soul the most blasphemous suggestions, leading her to call in question the truths of Scripture, and even the very existence of God. To so great a height were these temptations permitted to rise, and the agony of her mind produced by them was so violent, that on the night of the first Sabbath of July, though there was a most tempestuous wind which rocked the house, she told me it did not even engage her attention, so much more horrible was the storm within. Indeed such were its effects upon her mind, that when she came down in the morning to breakfast, her very countenance expressed the vast disturbance of her soul. More or less of the same fiery trial she endured for some weeks; but in due time God heard her prayer, he set at liberty her tempted harassed soul—he put an end to the violent conflict, and gave her a blessing of grace which never left her, till it was swallowed up (there is no room to question) in the joy of the Lord. On the 27th of August the fever which was to carry her home made its appearance, and, at the very same time, my dear wife told Miss H. she had a manifestation from God her Saviour, more glorious than ever she had before experienced. In giving me an account of it, she said it was as clear and distinct an evidence in her soul of God's love to her, as if she had heard the Lord say, 'Thou art mine and I am thine, I have saved thee.' During the first seven days no danger was apprehended from the fever, but on the 5th of September some alarming symptoms began;—the day following she said, 'I am ready, I am willing to depart, I have so clear a view of my Saviour.' The next day she added, 'Jesus is so sufficient, I would have nothing to mix with him, nor do I want one single good work more.' On Tuesday, when the fever raged, she laid her hand upon the head of her most dear friend, Miss H. and said, 'O that I could take you up with me to everlasting rest!'* Upon observing the grief I was in, she told me I was so overcome and so unwilling to part with her, that she believed she should not be spared to me. Upon Mr R. asking her, whether she could not still bless God? O, said she, with a smile, 'now is the time for him to bless me;' meaning, the disease prevented all activity of mind, and rendered her entirely passive to receive the comforts of his love. Two days before her departure she desired Mr R. would not pray for her recovery, but for some mitigation of her pain, and an easy passage to her Lord. The last request was answered fully, for though her pain increased till she said, 'I think it is greater than I can bear;' yet the very last words she uttered were, 'O the joy, the delight!' I was in much pain, (after I knew we must part), for what she might suffer in the agonies of death; but in the midst of judgment upon me, a sinful man, my God remembered mercy, and spared me this additional weight to my burden, for she seemed insensible from six in the morning till a quarter past two, when only drawing her breath twice, somewhat longer than usual, she gave up the ghost, and left me suffering under the most grievous affliction, yet comforted with the most cheering, lively, and well grounded hope of her being in glory everlasting."

An extract from a letter of Miss Hill's, at this time, is worthy of insertion, not only as it contains some useful hints to Lady Glenorchy, but likewise as it exhibits an interesting view of the sentiments and conduct of some of the younger branches of the family of Hawkstone.

" *October* 20. 1767.

" We have just had a parting prayer with my dear brother, Rowland, who leaves us to-morrow. He proposes to see good Lady Huntington in his way to Cambridge, which, I trust, will be blessed to him, and that he will ever stand faithful in the cause of his crucified Master, whether he be admitted, as a minister of the gospel, to preach in his name, or not; but, alas! my dear friend, to such a deplorable apostacy is the world come, that young men who are steadfastly attached to the church, and live exemplary lives, can hardly get their testimonials signed for orders.

"I have just had a smart debate with N—— concerning *sects* and *parties*;—the cause of it was a most excellent letter, which my sister wrote to her, with congratulations on her birth-day, wherein she takes occasion to mention something of the necessity of a divine change of heart, and enlarges a little on the things of God, but in so proper a manner, that you would think it impossible that the least offence could be taken. The Lord enabled me to open my mouth with great boldness, (I trust with meekness also, for I am ever afraid of showing any thing of an improper spirit), and to give a reason for the hope that was in me. The Bible was brought in order to convince me of my errors, but not a text was produced which did not serve to overthrow the argument which N—— intended to support. I proved myself to be of the established church, and she a dissenter from it. Oh! may the Lord God bring good out of this;—but alas! so many have been the arguments, so great are the prejudices, that I have little hope left. My poor brother was attacked yesterday by some worldlings, and told he never could be easy, although he never was so happy in his life, till he got into their way again. Well, my dear friend, these things must be—May the Lord God make them as so many excitements to quicken us in our journey towards Zion. The cross of Christ is the Christian's glory, and blessed are all they that are thought worthy to bear it. I only fear that I dishonour my Master by being too much conformed to this world. Let us, my dear friend, joyfully embrace the all-perfect righteousness of the Lord Jehovah, so shall our justification be complete, and our services, although mere nothings in themselves, be accepted in the beloved. May the Lord God Almighty continually bless and preserve you; may he supply all your need according to his riches in glory by Christ Jesus!"

Although Lady Glenorchy suffered much from her worldly acquaintances in consequence of her attachment to serious religion, yet she was not singular in these sufferings. Her friend Miss Hill was also greatly exposed to them, and felt deeply under them, as appears from the following letter, which she at this time wrote to Lady Glenorchy.

"*December* 16. 1767.

"I have left two gambling parties, of whom I am pretty heartily tired, to write to you, an employment always agreeable to me. I have just been told that I am good for nothing, as I will neither play nor mingle in fashionable amusements. That I am good for nothing I know to my sorrow, and each day, each hour, shews the more of my own vileness, and sinks me lower than the dust to see my great unprofitableness; and when I consider how little my God and Saviour has been thought of or spoke of by me, I may with justice hide myself, and with shame and confusion cry, 'God be merciful to me a most ungrateful rebellious sinner!' Yet still Jesus follows the rebel with tender mercies and loving kindness; and it is only because his compassions fail not that I am not consumed, and not lifting up my eyes in torments. Blessed be God, he saves his people for his own name's sake, and that is the moving cause from first to last. His righteousness is highly and will be everlastingly exalted thereby; yea, his mercy, judgment, and righteousness, the attributes which he has always delighted to honour, and has made himself known by, will be glorified throughout the countless ages of eternity in the salvation of sinners, vile unworthy sinners in themselves, that it might be all of grace, and God thereby have all the glory. O what a salvation is this! how full of help and comfort! for it is founded on the everlasting love and glory of our never-changing God. O how completely miserable must they be under outward crosses and trials, who have not a God to fly to in time of trouble, and a certain hope that he will be their guide and counsellor in every time of need! Blessed be his holy name who has manifested himself to you, my dear friend, and given you experimentally to know, that each stroke with which you have been chastised was sent by a loving father's hand. No words can express what I feel of love and gratitude to him who has made you a partaker of the divine nature, and who with his abundant love drew you with his loving kindness out of the horrible pit of your sinful corrupt nature, and made you an heir of glory, washed you in his own precious blood, stripped you of your own worthless garments, and put on you his own best robe, his spotless righteousness, calling you his own, and uniting you to himself by the most indissoluble bonds! O what mercies are these! Join with me in praising God for the boundless ocean of his love! What shall we render to the Lord for all his benefits? All we can do, the sacrifice of our whole selves, is too little; yet Jesus will accept the mite, the free-will offering, however poor and mean. O let us from this moment begin to live to Jesus, our Friend, our Shepherd, Advocate, Surety, Saviour, Father, and our God; let us with all our might, with all our strength, begin to live to Jesus, that we may die to Jesus, and be for ever with him! Upon what a firm basis are the hopes of every believer built! Not a sudden thought, not a hasty decree, but the everlasting love of the great Almighty Jehovah, who so loved the world as to give his only begotten Son to die, that we might not perish, but have everlasting life. Behold what manner of love is this, for even now we are the children of God; and it doth not yet appear what we shall be, but this we know, that when Jesus shall appear we shall be like him, for we shall see him as he is, and be for ever in his presence, where is fulness of joy, and at whose right hand are pleasures evermore. And that all who by divine grace have been brought to flee for refuge to the hope set before them might have strong consolation, God has secured it by an everlasting covenant, ordered in all things and sure, confirmed with promises, with oaths, and sealed it with his own precious blood; and he that has not spared his own Son, but freely delivered him up to death for us, how shall he not with him freely give us all things.—O what cause have we ever to be giving thanks to this our Almighty deliverer! The Lord reigneth, let the earth rejoice, yea, let the multitude of the isles be glad thereof. He keeps and holds fast the infernal crew in chains of iron, restrains their cruel rage, sees their subtle plots against his feeble sheep, and baffles them all; he will make a hedge about them, and about their houses, and about all that they have on every side. O what a Father, Saviour, and Friend is here! How can we ever distrust his faithfulness, or harbour one unbelieving thought? Surely we may *trust* him where we cannot *trace* him, and adventure upon his bond although we have nothing in view! Can we fear he will ever leave or forsake his people when he has declared he never will? Can we suspect he will suffer them to fall a miserable helpless prey to their enemies? No, so long as he sits in heaven they must be safe and happy."

Lady Glenorchy diligently made use of every means which she thought were calculated to promote her spiritual improvement. Among others, she attended meetings for religious purposes, composed chiefly of ladies of rank and fortune; such as the Marchioness of Lothian, the Countesses of Leven and Northesk, Lady Banff, Lady Maxwell, Lady Ross Baillie, and many others. At these meetings the Rev. Mr Walker, at this time senior minister of the High Church of Edinburgh, and colleague to the celebrated Dr Blair, usually presided and conducted their devotions, and at the same time either expounded the Scriptures or delivered a sermon. At first it would appear they were held in the houses of one or other of these ladies. But in the course of time they were held in Mr Walker's own house, and were continued weekly by him to the close of his life. Of these meetings, which Lady Glenorchy uniformly attended when in town, and from which she received much pleasure and profit, she first makes mention in the following letter to a lady eminent for piety, a relation of Mr Walker's, who, in order to distinguish her from others of that name, was generally called Mrs Bailie Walker.

"My dear Madam,—I had not time yesterday to answer your letter as it deserved, and I am sorry that I cannot just now say all I wish upon the subject of it. I am not fond of controversy on any doctrine, and am every way unfit for it myself, being an ignorant creature, and having a confused manner of expressing myself. I will endeavour to see you very soon, and will send before in order that I may find you alone; and hope at meeting to convince you, that whatever our different sentiments may be on some points, yet our aim and desire is the same. And for my own part, I do not feel this alter my affection for those I believe to be the children of God, and whom I hope ere long to meet in a place where all discord and variance shall be for ever banished, and we shall then know what now we can only guess at. Lord Glenorchy and I have both been ill for a week past, which prevented my calling for you, and also for the other ladies of our meeting, which I beg you will tell them, as I have unfortunately an engagement on business this afternoon that will prevent my seeing you. If I had known of the meeting a day sooner I would have put off my engagement, but it is now too late. I hope next week to have the pleasure of seeing you all; and if Wednesday will do for Mr Walker, I beg you will ask him and all the rest of our friends for that day: if that be not convenient, any other day you please, only let me know which, that I may not be engaged. Be assured, my dear madam, that I take your writing or speaking your sentiments freely to me as a real proof of friendship, and hope you will tell me without reserve whatever you see or hear of me that you think inconsistent with my profession as a Christian, or hurtful to the interest of our common Lord. This will give me an opportunity of explaining my motives for any thing that may have given offence; and if they are not found sufficient, I hope through grace to be enabled to amend. I beg my compliments to your good husband, and am, with real regard, my dear madam, your sincere and faithful humble servant,

"W. Glenorchy."

In the beginning of this year Lady Glenorchy seems to have been again considerably indisposed; so much so, indeed, as to renew her friend Miss Hill's alarms about her, which she strongly and kindly expresses in the following letter.—

"*January* 1. 1768.

"Ever since I heard of your being ill, I have continually committed you to the Lord in prayer, beseeching him to give me a submissive heart to whatever is his will concerning you, and that as he has lent you to me, I may cheerfully resign to him his own whenever he shall see fit. But even now I find the struggle hard: it is easy to say, Thy will be done! but when the trial comes, to submit to it, to rejoice in it, as the hand of God, is utterly opposite to nature, and can be effected only by the mighty operation of his grace upon the soul. May the Lord work this grace effectually upon mine, then shall I count all things but dross for the excellency of the knowledge of Christ Jesus our Lord. I am ashamed of my fears and anxious thoughts, I would give them all to the Lord, and in all wait his power, that he may have the sure pre-eminence in my guilty soul. Let us be careful our whole heart is his, then may we say truly, It is the Lord, let him do what seemeth him good. My dear friend, you have frequently beheld death as ready at the door to take you; you have seen him, blessed be God, disarmed of his sting, and only as a friendly messenger to conduct you to your Father's house, after a weary painful pilgrimage. This will of course make your thoughts fixed more on eternity, where we must both shortly be, although our journey be somewhat lengthened. Reflecting seriously on this is not without its benefit, and will make us abundant in the work of the Lord, and it will make us contentedly suffer.

This being the first of a new year, I resolve, with God's grace and assistance, to begin to lead a new life. On looking back, what a mere nothing does the last appear,—departed as a tale that is told; and I, alas, have as much to learn as ever of spiritual-mindedness, and every holy virtue. O, how little have I done for Jesus! When I review the time that is past, and what a vain worldly life I have led, I am utterly ashamed and confounded; but this leads me to magnify and adore that almighty grace which receives the sinner freely: not for works of righteousness which we have done, but according to his mercy he saves us. May you, my dear friend, go on conquering and to conquer; soon will all temptations and trials of every kind be no more. But the more they assault us, the more let us cleave to Jesus, and by a continual application of his blood to our souls, we shall be enabled to pass the time of our sojourning here below in peace and joy, deriving our whole spiritual life, hope, and consolation, from that inexhaustible fountain of all good. May every rich blessing of God be poured down on you, my dear friend; and do not cease to pray for the most unworthy of all who profess the gospel of Jesus. To him be glory, now and for ever. Amen."

Miss Hill, from what we have seen, had evidently learned the gospel lesson to live by faith, and, in her letters, uniformly pressed the importance of this life on Lady Glenorchy. But, from the close of the following letter, it appears, that as the exercise of this grace, through human weakness and infirmity, may be disturbed, and for a season fail, even in those who have long been habituated to it, so it happened in her own experience.

" *January* 31. 1768.

" The more I see of the great mystery of godliness, the more I stand amazed, and am forced to cry out, O the depth of the riches both of the wisdom and knowledge of God, in contriving to bring the highest glory to all his attributes, and at the same time to bring fallen sinful creatures into a state of favour, grace, and peace here, and glory hereafter. How worthy is such a salvation of our God! How full of consolation to his people! Let us, then, my dear friend, put off the old man, with his corrupt deeds. Let us put on the Lord Jesus Christ, and draw near at all times with boldness to the throne of grace, that we may obtain mercy, and find grace to help in time of need. Let us plead our heavenly Father's promises in faith, nothing wavering; and let us live up to the high unspeakable privileges of the Lord's redeemed. I live, (says Paul), yet not I, but Christ liveth in me. Let us say the same; and let the life which we live in the flesh be by faith in the Son of God. Let us talk and think of Jesus, and thus let us go through this wilderness, leaning on the arm of our beloved; and soon, in spite of all the enemies of our salvation, we shall get into the wished-for haven, safely attain the promised land, and be put into everlasting possession of the kingdom prepared for us from the foundation of the world. O, then, let us not lose a moment, but haste to seek that better country. We have here no abiding place. Our treasure is in heaven; let our affections be there also.

" I find thinking of, and looking much into self, only hardens, deadens, and discourages; and speaking much of self feeds pride; for I can feel a spark of pride whilst talking of my own vileness, and be proud of being thought humble. O what an easily besetting sin is this, and under what specious pretences is it often masked! But thinking of Jesus animates; speaking of Jesus makes our hearts burn within us; looking to Jesus assimilates, transforms into his glorious image; and whilst believers make Jesus their all in all, they grow daily in humility, holiness, self-denial, heavenly-mindedness, and every Christian grace. O, my dear friend, thus may we pass victoriously through the wilderness of this world, till we fall asleep in Jesus, awake up after his likeness, and so be ever, ever with the Lord, to behold that glory which he had with his Father before the world began. O may the God and Father of our Lord Jesus Christ vouchsafe us frequent Pisgah views of the promised land, to animate our steps, and raise our faith; and may Jesus strengthen us so, that we may not tire nor faint on our way, but endure to the end, and be saved! Why should we doubt either his willingness or power to help us? his promise cannot fail, for the mouth of the Lord hath spoken it; and it is all owing to an evil heart of unbelief if we suffer ourselves to walk mournfully.

" I awoke last night with a load of guilt and uneasiness on my soul; and, ruminating on my state, I was tempted to believe all my past experience was a delusion, and that I had never in reality come to God by Christ. I knew it was in vain to argue with Satan or self, and therefore strove to cast myself wholly on the Lord, relying on his finished salvation, on the stability of God's covenant, the unchangeableness of his mind, the sure and lasting truth of his promises in Christ, several of which came with some degree of power into my mind, and I went to sleep again with much composure, although I rose this morning agitated, but reaped benefit from part of the 3d chapter of Malachi. O, my dear friend, pray for me, that I may ever have grace, in every hour of temptation and need, to lay hold on Jesus, in whom is righteousness that can justify the most ungodly. In him is fulness, how empty soever we are,—a fulness of merit always presented to God by Christ for our obtaining of that which at any time we want, whether it be wisdom, grace, righteousness, sanctification, or redemption."

Lady Glenorchy's temper was constitutionally both gay and firm, and when occasion required, it exhibited a boldness which no sense of danger could intimidate. In her religious feelings, however, arising, it may be, from a peculiar degree of sensibility, there was an incessant self-jealousy, which, though it did not produce what is termed a slavish fear or dread, had a direct tendency to produce what may be called a spirit of bondage, and which, like a cloud intercepting the rays of the sun, cast a sombre hue over the whole of her Christian exercises and experiences in private. This may be accounted for in various ways. She uniformly possessed very clear views of the spirituality of the divine law, and of the nature of that obedience which it required, in thought, word, and deed. As her integrity and fidelity in forming a judgment of herself were never seduced by self-love, she discovered in herself those imperfections which others, destitute of equal degrees of knowledge and grace, are often apt to overlook; and was always ready to acknowledge, that, as the Scriptures say, "In many things she offended, and in every thing came short of the glory of God." Hence, when she retired to her closet, and placed herself in the immediate presence of her Maker and her

Judge, she felt in an uncommon degree that her guilt was inconceivable. She thus became mortified and humbled to the very dust, and expressed her mortification and humiliation in the strongest terms. But although she had a firm faith in the Redeemer, in the virtue of his sacrifice, the fulness of his atonement, and the efficacy of his blood and cross to reconcile her to God, and from this experienced a well founded hope of a glorious immortality, yet, unlike her friend Miss Hill, she never was able to attain the happy art of habitually applying by faith to the blood of sprinkling, to remove every stain of guilt, as soon as contracted, from her conscience. Owing to this peculiar state of mind, her peace was often disturbed, and her spiritual comfort, like a winter's day, not absolutely dark, but gloomy, with a faint gleam of sun-light occasionally bursting through the cloud. This habitual spirit of jealousy with respect to her experience, accounts for many of the bitter things which she writes against herself in her diary, as will be afterwards observed.

Miss Hill was aware of these circumstances, and gave in writing the salutary advice which was requisite.

" *March* 1. 1768.

" I have just received your letter. Still on the complaining string, my dear friend! Will you still lend an ear to the suggestions of the enemy, who was a liar from the beginning, and not trust your soul on the faithfulness of God and his Christ? O away with all these complaints, these doubts, these fears, which keep your soul in bondage, and which will not permit you to possess joy and peace in believing. Were you really a hypocrite, depend upon it you would not be so uneasy under the apprehension of being one, nor would you examine your heart with that exact scrutiny you do. Take comfort then—live upon Jesus, trust to his almighty power and willingness to save, then shortly shall Satan be trampled under your feet as the accuser of the brethren. O labour after the full assurance of faith, that you may not be so continually poring upon yourself, instead of laying hold on the finished salvation which is in Jesus. May his grace ever be with you! remember he has said it is sufficient for you."

" *March* 11. 1768.

" As I had not leisure the last time I wrote to speak particularly of those doubts and fears which still harass your soul, I will now endeavour (with God's blessing and assistance) to suggest something which may tend to your relief. I know you will forgive me for reading part of your letter to a Christian friend of mine in this neighbourhood, who is a person fully taught in Christ's school; and as her experience and yours agree greatly together, I thought it would be a comfort to you both, to read her that part of your letter wherein you mention the state of your soul. She says, she has often been exactly in the same condition; and added, ' I am sure I can say I well know what that situation is, not only from my own experience, but from that of many others. I have thought myself the vilest hypocrite under the sun, and fancied I had never come savingly to Christ; and when I have endeavoured to apply the promises of God to my soul, Satan has tempted me to believe they did not belong to me, and made use of the very same method to distress me as he has done her: for in reading Owen on the Mortification of Sin in Believers, I was tempted to think myself the person described, and that I did wrong to speak peace to my soul when there was none with God. I was enabled, however, to wait patiently the Lord's time for deliverance; and looking to Jesus, now see him to be an all-sufficient Saviour, able to save to the uttermost all that come unto God by him.' This also is in general pretty much my own state; and though I cannot say I have any full assurance of my interest in Christ, yet I feel a comfortable hope that I shall certainly attain to it in the Lord's own time, and for which I desire to wait. What you say of yourself, my dear friend, gives me the sincerest pleasure, as I have no doubt of the reality of God's work upon your soul, from your being so fearful of healing slightly the wound which sin has made. You want a brighter discovery of the evidence to go upon, and are jealous and fearful of laying hold on the promise till you can see your way clear, and God justified in his dealings in thus freely pardoning. You have been truly convinced of sin; you are sensible of your need of Jesus; therefore let no doubts, no fears, distress your precious soul, which God has loved with an everlasting love. Behold the free grace of God, behold the purchase of it that it might be freely given to you, and the promise of it, and the tender of that promise to you! In Jesus is perfect righteousness laid up for your use. It is no presumption therefore; on the contrary, it is your indispensable duty, to lay hold of it, to plead it as a guilty condemned sinner, and in him to embrace the free pardon, the full acceptance which grace has provided for you. God has made him to be sin for us who knew no sin, that we might be made the righteousness of God in him. This God, too, is able to do exceedingly abundantly above all that you can ask or think. What can be more immediately calculated to give comfort to the most desponding soul than these words of the apostle? What now would you request of God?

You will say, 'to be saved from sins past, present, and to come; for more grace, more faith in Christ, and more desires after and love to him, that you may glorify him through life, and at the hour of death.' And think you, that the ear of him which is ever open to the supplication of his people, will be shut against you? O no, it is impossible! He hath graven you on the palms of his hands, he loves you with a love which passeth knowledge. It would be endless to enumerate all the soul-reviving passages of Scripture wherein God's love is represented. In each page of the sacred record there are traces of it; and we can only wonder, and adore, and cast ourselves upon the unfathomable depths of this love in every hour of distress and temptation. We are encompassed with enemies from within and from without, and great need have we to walk with the weapons of our warfare continually in our hand. We are tossed on the tempestuous billows of spiritual danger, and great need have we to cast anchor on the hope which is set before us, grounded on the love of God in Christ, as our sure defence and infallible help;—this is our privilege, this is our duty. The enemy is sure to direct his most violent attacks on those whom he thinks are most in God's favour. So much indeed is this the case, that it is very common for the children of God to be calling in question the evidences of their adoption, to fear that all their past experience is but a delusion, to have doubts about the truth of Scripture, even to imagine they have committed the sin against the Holy Ghost, and feel such horrible and blasphemous suggestions as to make them cry out by reason of the disquietness that is in them; and yet all these painful things are overruled to their advancement and joy in faith; for by these fiery darts they become acquainted with Satan's devices, and having been tempted themselves, are more able to administer consolation to those that are tempted. These assaults likewise drive them to examine more carefully that word which is able to make them wise unto salvation, that so their faith may stand in the power of God, and not in the wisdom of man, that they may be more earnest in prayer, watching thereunto with all perseverance. These temptations always tend to abase and humble the soul, to shew its natural vileness and helplessness, and thereby to bring it off more from leaning on self-righteousness, and to rely on Jesus, the rock of ages. In which case we may say with the apostle James, 'Blessed is the man that endureth temptation, for when he is tried he shall receive the crown of life.'

"As to my health, I beg you will not be uneasy about it. I am better; and O that every slight pain I feel may remind me that this is not my home, but that there remaineth a rest for the people of God in a better world, the inhabitants of which shall never say, I am sick. I rejoice to hear that you can boldly speak for Jesus in company. Go on conquering, and to conquer."

A few weeks after Lady Glenorchy had received the above communications, she seems to have been in a more than usually comfortable state of mind; and having written Miss Hill to that effect, received from her the following excellent letter, congratulating her on the circumstance, and offering her very sensible and sound advice as to her future conduct.

"*Good Friday,* 1768.

"I was thinking much of you, when your letter was brought me this morning; and, ruminating on the great things God had done for your soul, I could not but consider your state as happy, although in the midst of many outward distresses; and your letter has greatly increased my joy and thankfulness on your account, as it assures me of your coming more and more out of the captivity of nature, into the glorious liberty of the children of God; and that you are now enabled, not only to trust him, (which in itself is a blessed state), but also to rejoice in him, as the God of your salvation, for your present as well as future salvation.

" Heaviness may endure for a night, but gladness cometh in the morning; and when it comes after a long uneasy night, it is doubly welcome, and deserves a double tribute of praise and thankfulness. O be not wanting in that sweet duty of praise, from a sense of the divine goodness, love, and patience towards you; remember that you are brought from darkness to light, to shew forth the praises of him who calleth you, and that your feet are set at liberty to run with patience the race of prayer and praise, self-denial and obedience, which the Lord hath set before you. In order that you may go on comfortably and steadily for the time to come, I shall insert a few directions which were given to a Christian friend of mine, who long walked in darkness, but who afterwards lived much under the light of God's countenance, till it pleased him to give her the full vision and fruition of himself in glory. ' Live above earthly and creature comforts. Beware of flatness and lukewarmness; this, if not carried immediately to the Lord, ends in darkness and deadness. Value divine comforts above all things, and prize Christ above all comforts, that if these should fail, you may still glory in the God of your salvation. Let that which torments others be your happiness, that is, self-denial, and renouncing your own will. Be ready to yield with joy to every conviction of the Spirit of God. Be faithful to the present grace, and aspire after a continual growth. Live the present moment to God, and avoid perplexing yourself about your past and future experience, by giving up yourself to Christ as you are at the moment, and being willing to receive him now as he is, leaving all the rest to him, and you will cut a thousand temptations by the root.' Continue diligently to search the Scriptures—these contain an inexhaustible fund of comfort when opened to us by the Spirit of God. Otherwise, clear and plain as the sacred truths appear in themselves, they will be a dead letter to us, and we shall never truly know the mystery of godliness. Every day's observation is sufficient to prove, that all the most elaborate researches of human wisdom into God's word, are insufficient to lead us into the truth, unless the spirit of wisdom and revelation in the knowledge of Christ is given us. How often is that divine wisdom revealed to babes, whilst the wise and prudent are ignorant of it! May we ever come as poor blind sinners to a throne of grace for light and understanding; then, although strait is the gate, we shall assuredly find it, and though the way be narrow, we shall not turn aside to the right hand or to the left. Let self-righteous ceremonial formalists stay themselves upon a round of unmeaning duties, and rest in a righteousness of their own imaginations; but we will make mention of thy righteousness, O Lord, even thine only;—contented to be saved by rich free grace, we gladly embrace the offered gift, and glorify that wondrous love, that raises us from children of wrath to be the heirs of heaven."

That the reader may have some view of the state of religion in Miss Hill's own mind, and the nature of her own Christian experience, it may not be unacceptable to add the following extract from one of her letters to Lady Glenorchy.

"*Easter Sunday*, 1768.

"I have this day been commemorating the love of Jesus at his table with a hard and stony heart, which neither the remembrance of his cruel sufferings, nor his victory over death and the grave, could melt. O, when shall this torrent of sin and corruption, so offensive to the God of all purity, be done away? When shall I arise with Christ in the spiritual resurrection, and be so vitally united to my living head, as to be one with him by a growing conformity to his likeness? Come down, thou eternal Jesus, into my heart, and sit as a refiner's fire and as fullers' soap,—burn up all the corruptions of my nature,—wash away the guilt and stain of sin, and set my feet upon the rock of everlasting ages! Surely this is a season which should, above all others, fill the believing soul with joy, the heart with praise, and the tongue with thanksgiving, since the resurrection of Jesus from the dead is the alone foundation on which our everlasting hopes are built. We are thereby assured, that God is well pleased with his Son's undertaking, and satisfied with his one oblation. The majesty of heaven cannot now but be reconciled to those who plead the offering of his Son, for in him mercy and truth are met together, righteousness and peace have kissed each other. Whatever before was interruptive of our peace is now removed, and we have the most satisfying grounds of never-ending consolation in a crucified risen Saviour, who has triumphed over death, broke its iron bars asunder, and cast away all its cords. O for grace to rise from the death of sin to a life of righteousness, that we, having part in the past resurrection, may not only escape the second death, but see the eternal joy of his salvation! Alas! my dear friend, I am utterly confounded when I review my unprofitable life and conversation, and see any thing of that hidden mystery of iniquity in my own heart;—but blessed be that inexhaustible fountain of divine grace, which wants no legal performances or qualifications of mine to make me a fit object of mercy. O what wondrous love was that which plucked us as brands from the fire, awakened us to see our danger, and showed us that the Lord had laid help on one that was mighty, and not only mighty, but willing to save! I have more hopes with regard to the spiritual state of my friend, Mrs ——, than I had. Her situation some time ago makes it appear evident to me, that the Lord has thoughts of mercy towards her soul, although at present I do not see those marks of conviction in her I wish to see. In an illness she had some time ago, in which she suffered the most excruciating agonies of pain, without the smallest appearance of her recovery, and during this time of great extremity her husband grudged her common necessaries,—amidst these, and many more distresses which I will not now repeat, the concerns of her soul were uppermost in her thoughts. Death would, indeed, have been a welcome messenger to have delivered her from her torture; but, alas! she feared his sting, and shrunk back at the thoughts of his advancing, and assured me, that her outward trials were not to be compared to the desponding thoughts that were within her. An offended God, a broken law, stared her in the face; the uplifted arm of justice she saw ready to fall upon her, and sink her into the bottomless pit, and made her earnestly cry for redemption through the blood of Jesus. 'O,' said she, 'could I but get the least glimmering hope of my salvation, how glad I should be to die! but all is darkness, horror, and despair within me.' Then would she pray with the utmost ardency, that Christ would reveal himself to her soul, give her some token of his love, and not suffer her to continue under such dreadful apprehensions of God's wrath. This she did for a long while without receiving any answer of peace; but at last the Lord lent an ear to the voice of her groaning, and although she was so ill and weak before, as not to be able to move in her bed without help, she now raised herself suddenly up, in an ecstasy not to be expressed, clasped her arms, and with great vehemence said, 'O, he is come, he is come; Jesus is come indeed! let me embrace him, let me hold him fast and never let him go. What raptures do I feel! how is my soul filled with ecstasy! I have the fullest assurance of my salvation, and desire to depart and be with Christ.' These extraordinary comforts by degrees abated, (perhaps God seeing they were more than her weak frame could bear), and were succeeded by a sweet and delightful calm, in which she lay waiting with a hope full of immortality for her dissolution, which according to all human appearance was very near; but it pleased God to raise her up for fresh trials, which, I will still hope, are only to try her as gold is tried in the furnace, and that she may be purified. She frequently speaks of the above experience, and says it has left a strong and abiding impression.—I am sorry for your situation, having none to whom you can open your heart concerning the things of God; but he is ever near to hear you, and you may unbosom yourself to him with a certainty of redress in every hour of need. The post waits, so have only time to entreat you to be faithful,—be bold to follow the leading of the Lord. Be steadfast in faith, and all will be well."

CHAPTER VI.

Practice of keeping a Diary commended—Lady Glenorchy follows that laudable custom—Extracts from her Diary, from May 11. to July 19. 1768.—Letter from Lady Glenorchy to Lady Maxwell—Uniformly takes notice of her Birth-day; and on the first recurrence of it in her Diary, gives a particular account of her Conversion—Lord Glenorchy sells Sugnall—This circumstance carries Lady Glenorchy to England—Diary thereby interrupted—Lord Glenorchy purchases Barnton—Extracts from Lady Glenorchy's Diary from August 1. to September 2. 1769.—Usefulness of keeping a Diary further confirmed, by another Extract from her Diary—Still exposed to many trials—Much benefited by Lady Maxwell—Extracts from Diary, January 27—31. 1770.—Lady Glenorchy procures St Mary's Chapel as a place for public worship—Circumstances connected with this event—Extracts from Diary, from February 2. to February 18. 1770.

The practice of keeping a Diary, or daily account of Christian experience, and interesting occurrences, has, it is well known, been in all ages common with religious characters. This practice, when conducted with prudence and discretion, is certainly attended with many advantages, both to the individual writer, and to Christians in general. The individual writer is enabled to review the nature of God's dealings towards him, the dangers to which he has been exposed, the sins which have been more easily besetting him; and from thence learns how to avoid the one, and overcome the other: his different graces are brought more conspicuously into exercise, and the influence of true godliness is more habitually felt; and Christians in general are, by perusing them, often instructed, strengthened, and comforted, in their pilgrimage through this world.

At what time Lady Glenorchy began to keep a Diary is not certain; but from circumstances, it would appear to have been about this period, perhaps somewhat earlier. She frequently corrected and transcribed her papers, especially such as she wished to preserve, and wrote them on a fine quarto page, with a large margin, ruled off at the top and bottom, and on each side, by a red line. Two-thirds of her Diary are nearly written in this manner, apparently taken from a scroll, and entitled 'Extracts from the Diary of ————.' The remainder is contained in a book of coarse paper, interlined and blotted, and evidently not intended to be seen in that shape by any eye but her own, and which she seems not to have found leisure to transcribe. It is probable, that the Diary which she kept during the first part of her religious life had been destroyed by herself. From the view which Miss Hill's letters give of her experience, it is likely she judged it not requisite to preserve it; and to this conjecture we are led from this singular fact, that the Diary which exists commences but a very short period before that part of Miss Hill's correspondence with her ceased, which, as we have before said, Lady Glenorchy thought fit to preserve. Neither is it unlikely that the existence of her Diary was the reason why she did not think it necessary to transcribe any more of her friend's letters: this circumstance accounts for the very abrupt manner in which it begins. Lady Glenorchy had by this time acquired courage not merely to defend her own religious opinions, but even to animadvert on those of others which she thought to be erroneous.

The steward, or factor as he is called in Scotland, of the Breadalbane estates, usually lived at Taymouth during the time that the family resided there. He was the proprietor of a neighbouring ancient family estate, and a gentleman of great talents and learning. With this gentleman Lady Glenorchy ventured to argue; and, as is not unfrequently the case in disputation, unfortunately lost her temper. She had too much good sense and religious feeling, however, not to be aware of the great impropriety of this, and too much integrity and candour not to confess it. Hence, on the 11th day of May 1768, her Diary thus begins.—

EXTRACTS

FROM THE

DIARY OF LADY GLENORCHY.

May 11. 1768.—This morning I awoke with a great desire to praise God for his mercies; but my lips were sealed, I could not utter what I felt.—At breakfast, I renewed the argument upon faith with Auchalladear, and was led away by the impetuosity of my temper to say what I did not at first intend, and some things that savoured too much of Antinomianism. In the course of the argument, I felt much carnal pride and self-applause in my heart, and I did not apply, as I ought to have done, to the Holy Spirit for his assistance. This I take to be the reason why I was left to fall into error. After this, I walked out to the place which I have chosen for my morning devotions. My mind was much disturbed in reading the word: I was in great darkness, but it pleased the Lord to enable me to utter my wants to him, and to pray fervently, with many tears, for myself and all my friends. After this, in walking home, I sung part of the 71st psalm, and felt much joy and comfort in the latter part of it, from the 20th verse:—

Thou, Lord, who great adversities
And sore to me did show,
Shall quicken, and bring me again,
From depths of earth below, &c. &c.

After dinner, I met with a sore trial of patience, and here (from not looking to Jesus for help) I felt most sadly. I lost temper, and said many bitter things. I recalled to mind all my former grievances, repined at the will of God, and thought my case uncommonly hard. In short, the Lord left me to my own proud heart; and I sinned greatly. This has cost me many tears. Lord forgive me this offence, and wash it away in thy precious blood.

I this day resolve (with the assistance of the Spirit) to watch over the first risings of passion, and to pray daily for the grace of a meek and quiet spirit, and above all for humility, in which I am greatly deficient. This has been a day of many errors and infirmities. Lord, if thou shouldst mark iniquity, who could stand before thee? but with thee there is mercy, and plenteous redemption. O clothe me with the righteousness which cometh by faith from Jesus; for all my righteousnesses are as filthy rags: even my best duties are stained with sin. My trust is in thee, O Lord; let me never be confounded.

May 16.—This day I came home from a visit at Dunkeld, where I have spent three days very unprofitably, and wasted the precious time given me to work out my salvation. I there fell into a sin that most easily besets me, which is seeking the praise of my fellow creatures, more than the approbation of God. Although I had opportunities of worship evening and morning, yet my thoughts wandered, and I could not apply my mind to any thing that was good. The world and sin got possession of me, and corrupt nature led me captive. I often groaned under the oppression, and lifted up my cry to my Redeemer for help, but could not obtain relief; my sinful heart separated me from God. O remember not against me these three mispent days, most merciful Father; but blot out my numberless transgressions, by the precious blood of the Lamb; raise me up and set me in a straight path; stablish, strengthen, and settle me in the faith, and uphold me with thy free spirit.

I resolve, by the grace of God, to stay as much at home as possible for the future, and, when abroad, to set a watch over the door of my lips, that I offend not with my tongue; likewise, to mortify this desire of admiration and love of the world. O Lord, grant me thy assistance; lead me by thy Spirit, create a clean heart within me, and deliver me from the temptations of the devil, the world, and the flesh.

May 17.—I awoke this morning in a holy frame, desirous of living to God; but, alas! it was as the morning dew, it soon passed away. I read the word carelessly, and found no benefit from it. I lent an ear to flattery, and on hearing that a person had expressed a good opinion of me, I sought to increase it, talked too much, and uttered words of vanity. Upon the whole, I have spent this day most unprofitably.—O when shall I begin to live to thee, my blessed Lord, who so freely gave thy precious blood for me! I am ashamed and confounded when I think on my sins. I am a vile creature, unworthy of the least mercy. Blessed be God, who hath opened unto us a fountain for sin and for uncleanness. O wash me, good Lord, and I shall be whiter than snow!

I have met with a trial of patience to-day: but I need the rod—I know that the Lord sendeth every affliction for my good. Thy will, not mine, be done, O Lord!

June 10.—Many have been the sins and vanities of near a month past, and little good done. Blessed be God who hath sent Jesus Christ to be a propitiation for sin; in him only can I hope for mercy: "In me dwelleth no good thing," Rom. vii. 18. I have broken God's righteous law in every particular, and cannot have the least hope of salvation by works; for my best duties are defiled by sin. The sins of one day are enough to ruin me for ever. O gracious God, look upon me in thy beloved Son, and save me for his sake; for he has borne my transgressions, and was wounded and bruised for mine iniquities: he has fulfilled the law for all those who believe on him, and all believers are justified from all things. Lord increase my faith!

I have been in great darkness for some weeks past, and have had little comfort in prayer. This, I believe, is greatly owing to negligence in that duty, and allowing a slothful spirit to prevail, and to prevent my frequenting a throne of grace. I resolve, by the grace of God, to be more frequent and importunate in prayer, and to retire often for that purpose.

Lady Glenorchy did not make daily entries in her Diary. Days and weeks, and even months, sometimes elapsed between these, which she herself takes notice of, and accounts for, ascribing it to company, business, journeys, and illness.

June 17.—I have gained but little ground in my spiritual race, and have more than once been in danger of having my resolutions overthrown by the worldly counsels and arguments of a near relation. Thanks be to the Lord, who enabled me to bear my testimony boldly for him, and set my face against those who opposed the way of salvation.

O merciful Lord! who hath out of thy great goodness opened my eyes, and brought me from darkness to see this great and marvellous light, even thy beloved Son as the Saviour of sinners, open in like manner the eyes of this person, and bring every thought of her heart into subjection to Christ, that she being found in him, may, through the merits and atonement of his blood, obtain everlasting life!

For some days past, the Lord hath blessed me with the company of a friend, who seems desirous of working out her salvation. A godly companion is a great blessing. Lord make me duly thankful for it: enable me through grace to be faithful to her soul, and help her all I can in her Christian course. Lord, work with us and for us—we can do nothing of ourselves!

The person mentioned in the above extract, but not named, was Lady Maxwell, the friend of Mr

Wesley, who ceased not through life to aid her by her prayers, her counsel, and her co-operations. They differed widely on some religious topics, and in their opinions of certain religious characters; yet they were inseparable friends, bound together by the indissoluble ties of Christian affection and esteem.

The incessant crowds of company to which Lady Glenorchy was unavoidably exposed, both in town and country, were very harassing to her feelings. She was compelled to hear remarks and sarcasms hostile to religion. These, as might be expected, made at times an unpleasant, though happily but a feeble impression on her mind, and which the devotional exercises of the closet, by the blessing of God, speedily removed. Of the unpleasant effects of company and conversation, she thus speaks in her Diary, and in the following letter to Lady Maxwell.

July 19.—I have had many struggles for a month past with coldness of heart, spiritual pride, and worldly thoughts. I have been sorely vexed with arguments of others against the doctrine of Jesus, and have sometimes been made to call in question the soundness of my religious opinions; but thanks be to God, he hath delivered me. Yesterday, for a moment, I saw my salvation complete in Jesus, and the Father reconciled to me through him. This day my mind enjoys perfect peace. Grant me a heart, O Lord, to praise thee for the marvellous things thou hast done to my soul.—All blessing, and honour, and power be unto thee, O Lord God, and unto the Lamb, for ever. Amen.

The following is part of a letter from Lady Glenorchy to Lady Maxwell.

"My dear Madam,—After finishing three long letters, it will be a relief to my spirits to begin one to you. I have often found an hour's conversation with you act as a cordial; perhaps writing may also help to dispel the cloud of cares and fears that hang over me this day. I am sure a letter from you would,—and who knows but the post may bring me one this evening? Since I came here, I have endeavoured to bestir myself a little in my family, and put the house in order for the crowd of company I expect, and this has left me less time than usual to look inwards; yet, blessed be God, I feel rather more composed than when in Edinburgh. I begin to have more stability of mind, and more confidence in God, that he will perfect the work he has begun in my soul. I can discern at times the workings of faith striving with unbelief; and I have no doubt that the Lord will get himself the victory. He is now shewing me by degrees the numberless evils and corruptions of my heart, specially that worst of evils, unbelief. He shews me the necessity of conquering this, and gives me the desire to fight against it daily. I therefore am persuaded I shall come off more than conqueror.

"The company I expected on Saturday are not yet come, so I got most part of yesterday to myself.—We had sermon in the dining-room last night. Lord B—— was present, and nearly forty servants and others. Mr M'—— gave us a good discourse and a seasonable application. He spoke the truth boldly, and I would gladly hope it did not all fall to the ground."

Lady Glenorchy, like many other excellent persons, observed her birth-day with serious and devotional recollections. Her reflections on the first of these days, taken notice of in her Diary, will be read with peculiar interest, as in these she gives a full account of her religious sentiments from her earliest days, and also of that happy change in her views and conduct which produced in her an entirely new character, the eminent worth of which continued to unfold itself more and more to the end of her life. On the 2d of September this year, she writes as follows.

[Aged 27.] *September* 2.—I desire this day to humble myself before God, and to bless him as my Creator, who called me into being from the dust of the earth; who hath been my preserver in the midst of many dangers; and who hath, ever since my birth, loaded me with tender mercies and loving-kindnesses. But above all, I would bless his holy name, that he hath not left me in the state of alienation from him in which I was by nature, but that he hath of his free grace and mercy brought me out of darkness, and shown me the glorious light of his gospel, and caused me to hope for salvation through Jesus Christ. Many a time was he pleased to convince me of sin in my early years;—but these convictions were as the morning dew that soon passeth away. A life of dissipation and folly soon choked the good seed. Carnal company and diversions filled up the place in my soul that was due alone to God. The first twenty years of my life were spent after the fashion of this world. Led away by vanity and youthful folly, I forgot my Creator and Redeemer; and if at any time I was brought by sickness or retirement to serious reflection, my ideas of God were confused and full of terror: I saw my course of life was wrong, but had not power to alter it, or to resist the torrent of fashionable dissipation that drew me along with it. Sometimes I resolved to begin a godly life,—

to give all I had in charity, and to live only to God;—but I was then ignorant of God's righteousness, and was about to establish a sort of righteousness of my own, by which I hoped to be saved. God was therefore gracious in letting me feel how vain all my resolutions were, by allowing me to relapse again and again into a life of folly and vanity. My ignorance of the gospel was then so great, that I did not like to hear ministers preach much about Jesus Christ: I saw neither form nor comeliness in him, and thought it would have been more to the purpose, had they told us what we should do to inherit eternal life. My idea of Christ was,—that after I had done a great deal, he was to make up the rest: This was my religion! How marvellous is thy grace, O Lord!. to pardon such a worthless creature, who thus depreciated thy great sufferings and meritorious death, and endeavoured to rob thee of the glory which belongs to thee alone.

But this was not the only way in which I tried to rob God of his glory. I claimed great merit in the patience with which he enabled me to bear the severe trials and afflictions he was graciously pleased to send upon me, to bend my stubborn heart to his yoke. I thought I had not deserved such a lot;—and thus I secretly rebelled against the good will of the Lord. About this time I got acquainted with the Hawkstone family—some of them had the reputation of being Methodists. I liked their company and conversation, and wished to be as religious as they were, being convinced that they were right; but I still loved the world in my heart, and could not think of secluding myself from its pleasures altogether. I would gladly have found out some way of reconciling God and the world, so as to save my soul, and keep some of my favourite amusements. I used many arguments to prove that balls, and other public places, were useful, and necessary in society,—that they were innocent and lawful, and that the affairs of life could not go on well without them. The Lord, however, followed me with convictions. My own thoughts became very uneasy to me, the burden of my misfortunes intolerable. My health and spirits at last sunk under them, and for some time before I left off going to public amusements, (where I appeared outwardly gay and cheerful), my heart was inwardly torn with anguish and inexpressible grief. The enemy now suggested to me, that I had no resource left, but to give myself up entirely to the gaieties of life, and seek consolation in whatever way it presented itself, without paying any regard to those maxims of wisdom which hitherto had kept me within some bounds. To the best of my remembrance, it was the very same night in which this thought was suggested, that I was seized with a fever, which threatened to cut short my days; during the course of which, the first question of the Assembly's Catechism was brought to my mind,—What is the chief end of man? as if some one had asked it. When I considered the answer to it, To glorify God, and enjoy him for ever, I was struck with shame and confusion. I found I had never sought to glorify God in my life, nor had any idea of what was meant by enjoying him for ever. Death and judgment were set before me,—my past sins came to my remembrance. I saw no way to escape the punishment due unto them, nor had I the least glimmering hope of obtaining the pardon of them through the righteousness of another. In this dismal state I continued some days, viewing death as the king of terrors, without a friend to whom I could communicate my distress, and altogether ignorant of Jesus the friend of sinners. At this time the Lord put it into the heart of Miss Hill to write to me. I received her letter with inexpressible joy, as I thought she might possibly say something that would lessen my fears of death. I immediately wrote to her of my sad situation, and begged her advice. Her answer set me upon searching the Scriptures, with much prayer and supplication that the Lord would shew me the true way of salvation, and not suffer me to be led into error. One day, in particular, I took the Bible in my hand, and fell upon my knees before God, beseeching him with much importunity to reveal his will to me by his word. My mouth was filled with arguments, and I was enabled to plead with him, that as he had made me, and given me the desire I then felt to know him, he would surely teach me the way in which I should walk, and lead me into all truth,—that he knew I only wished to know his will in order to do it,—that I was afraid of being led into error; but as he was truth itself, his teaching must be infallible. I therefore committed my soul to him, to be taught the true way of salvation. After this prayer was finished, I opened the Bible then in my hands, and read part of the third chapter of the Epistle to the Romans, where our state by nature, and the way of redemption through a propitiatory sacrifice, are set clearly forth. The eyes of my understanding were opened, and I saw wisdom and beauty in the way of salvation by a crucified Redeemer. I saw that God could be just, and justify the ungodly. The Lord Jesus now appeared to me as the city of refuge, and I was glad to flee to him as my only hope. This was in summer 1765. Since that time I have had many ups and downs in my Christian course, but have never lost sight of Jesus as the Saviour of the world, though I have often had doubts of my own interest in him. I can safely say, that I would not give up the little knowledge I have of him for any thing on earth. And although I have already suffered reproach for observing his precepts, and shortly expect to be scoffed at by all my former acquaintances, and to have my name cast out as evil, yet I rejoice in that he thinketh me worthy to bear his cross. And I now beseech thee, O Lord, to accept of my soul, body, reputation, property, and influence, and every thing that is called mine, and do with them whatever seemeth good in thy sight. I desire neither ease, health, nor prosperity, any farther than may be useful to promote thy glory. Let thy blessed will be done in me, and by me, from this day forth. O let me begin this day to live wholly to thee. Let thy grace be sufficient for me, and enable me to overcome the world. And to thee be ascribed the honour and glory, now and for ever more. Amen and amen.

About this time Lord Glenorchy sold his maternal patrimony of Sugnal. This event naturally called the family to England, and the final abandonment of such an ancient mansion must have occupied a considerable portion of Lady Glenorchy's time, and given her much employment. This will account for the neglect of her Diary, from the date of our last extract, for almost a whole year.

When Lord Glenorchy sold Sugnal, for which he received between forty and fifty thousand pounds, his lady, it should seem, felt a very great anxiety that some suitable place of residence in lieu of it should be purchased near Edinburgh, probably with a view of enjoying occasionally a retreat in the country when tired with the bustle of a large city, and that she might also more effectually carry on some plans that she had formed for advancing the interests of religion. The estate of Barnton, about four miles distance from Edinburgh, at that time the property of the Duke of Queensberry, was then in the market, and she persuaded her lord, although not without some difficulty, to purchase it. Of this, together with the desirable state of her household, with much thankfulness she takes notice.

August 8.—Great cause have I to bless God for shewing mercy to my family. Sixteen of them were communicants last Lord's day; and, unknown to me, they have set up worship among themselves. O that I may never cease to pray for them, and for myself, seeing how graciously the Lord has granted the desires of my heart concerning these poor people, who a year ago were wallowing in sin, and now are every one seeking the Lord. O for a tongue to praise him who worketh wonders, and by his great power brings life out of death. Bless the Lord, O my soul, and forget not all his benefits!

August 9.—This morning I received accounts of the purchase of Barnton, in which I was much interested. I had prayed the Lord to accomplish it if for our good, and I rested on this, and looked to him for success; though, from weakness of faith, I took one step in it myself, which gave me much uneasiness afterwards. But blessed be the Lord, I have not been punished as I deserved. What a dead creature must I be, to feel so little gratitude for the innumerable mercies that follow me every day of my life. O Lord, thou canst change this heart, and I believe that thou wilt, for I long for a renewed spirit; and this longing doubtless is from thee. Thou satisfiest the desire of every creature that seeketh thee. Thou wilt not quench the smoking flax. O kindle it up into a flame of love and gratitude, for all thy goodness to me the poorest of thy creatures.

On the return of her birth-day she thus writes:—

[Aged 28.] *September* 2. 1769.—I desire to begin this day with praise unto thee, O most holy and gracious Lord God, for my creation, and preservation unto this hour, notwithstanding my numberless sins and provocations; and I desire to renew the dedication of myself to thee, which is my bounden duty, and glorious privilege.

I beseech thee, O Lord Jesus, to pardon my past sins, and to seal this pardon on my heart. Thou knowest that I desire to give myself up wholly to thee, in soul, body, and spirit. Take me, Lord, and make me what I ought to be. Let thy will be accomplished in me, in whatever way seemeth good unto thee.

This year I have been taught many things:—That I know nothing as I ought, but am yet ignorant of God, myself, and the things of eternity. That saving knowledge is not to be learnt but from the revelation of the Spirit, who alone can teach us all things, and open to us the mysteries of the kingdom of God. I conclude that the Lord has begun a good work on my soul, because the first operation of the Spirit is to shew us our darkness and ignorance, to point out to us the great prize set before us, and to give us a longing desire after it. This is my present case, and I hope the Lord will grant those desires he has put into my heart. I have learnt that points of controversy are to be avoided as much as possible, and that the best way of bringing men to the acknowledgment of the truth, is to alarm their consciences by the view of their actual sins, and the fear of death and judgment. When this is done, then point out to them the Saviour of sinners.

In adverting to the circumstance of Lady Glenorchy keeping a Diary, we formerly noticed the very great benefit accruing to the individual Christian by such a habit, particularly as, by recalling the manner of the Lord's dealing with his soul, he is often improved and strengthened, and made to observe the loving kindness of the Lord whilst he traces the operations of his hand. This advantage Lady Glenorchy herself experienced; and in the following extract, which is the only remaining entry in her Diary for this year, she thus mentions the advantage she derived from the practice:—

October 11. 1769.—This day, upon perusing some past experiences, I find that the Lord has been pleased to shew me by his Spirit more of the hope of my calling than I saw at this time last year. I understood to-day some things that appeared dark and disagreeable to me then. From this I infer that I have more light, though I feel my darkness more sensibly, and long more to be delivered from it. I desire to bless God for having enabled me this day to contribute both to the spiritual and temporal relief of a poor person. This I consider as an answer to a prayer put into my heart this morning, that I might be made useful. I have observed, that prayer when fervent is generally speedily answered. The Lord by his Spirit first gives the prayer for the blessings he means to bestow, and then grants them. This he does, that all may be of grace. Blessed be his name for ever and ever!

Lady Glenorchy spent this winter in Edinburgh, and remained there till she went to Taymouth in the middle of summer. Like every other Christian, especially in the higher walk of life, Lady Glenorchy found herself exposed to many trials and difficulties arising from her connexion with the world. She derived great comfort and assistance, however, under these circumstances, from the counsel and kindness of her pious friend Lady Maxwell, who never failed to give her the full benefit of her experience in the school of Christ. Of this state of her mind, and the benefit she received from Lady Maxwell, she thus wrote in her Diary :—

Saturday, January 27. 1770.—Many hours, days, weeks, and months, have passed away unobserved, in which I have received distinguishing blessings with a cold, dead, ungrateful heart. O how can I sufficiently extol that mercy that has permitted me to live, and has not cut me off in wrath long ere now! My mind has of late been distracted with various opinions insensibly imbibed from others, which have drawn me away from the simplicity of the gospel, which have led me to depreciate ordinances, and to seek a useless speculative life. Blessed be God, who has in Lady Maxwell raised up for me a friend in this time of need, who has been the instrument in his hand of bringing back my soul into a plain path. She is indeed one among a thousand. Of all I have ever known, she is the most upright Christian. Bless the Lord, O my soul, for this excellent gift of Heaven! A faithful friend, a counsellor in the ways of God. Ever since my first interview with her, the Lord has been pleased to shew me gradually from whence I have fallen, and has led me back to that singleness of heart, with which he enabled me to set out some years ago. I have of late sought God more frequently by prayer. My heart grows more dead to the world. For some days past I have been enabled to pray with some degree of fervency, and have wrestled with God for a blessing. Most part of yesterday I spent in reading and prayer; and this morning I felt peace in my soul, although not much liberty in prayer. I was led to plead with God that he would enable me to follow Christ whithersoever he would, through good report and evil report, and even to suffer for his sake if he saw meet. I wept before the Lord, and felt a comfortable hope that he was indeed willing to save me. I was also overwhelmed with shame and confusion, when I considered my unworthiness in his sight. This evening I heard an excellent sermon on the second petition of the Lord's prayer. I can say with my whole heart, I desire that the kingdom of God may come, in every sense. I thought the preacher had been told my case, so applicable were his prayers and sermon to the state of my soul. O merciful and blessed Jesus! let thy kingdom come now into my heart. Reign thou there for ever! Subdue all thine enemies in me, and perfect thy will in and by me, in whatever way seemeth best unto thee. Amen.

Sunday, January 28. 1770.—This morning I awoke in a dead insensible frame;—after much wrestling I got some freedom in prayer for near an hour. But O how imperfect are my best prayers! Lord pardon the sins of my holy things! I went out to church in a dull frame, found little comfort, and with difficulty attended to what I heard. I found some consolation in singing the 43d psalm from the 3d verse:—

O send thy light forth and thy truth ;
Let them be guides to me,
And bring me to thine holy hill,
Even where thy dwellings be, &c. &c.

I then went to see a friend in distress: I was enabled to deal faithfully with her. I went again to church, and heard an excellent sermon from Mr Plenderleath, to which my mind assented, but my heart was not affected; and since I came home, I have been wholly dead to spiritual things. The word I have heard to-day seems as water spilt upon the ground; no traces of it remain. O let it not rise up against me to my condemnation! O when wilt thou come, Lord, and take full possession of my soul, and subdue thy enemies! My soul longeth for thee, O come quickly!

This evening I have had a trial of patience. The Lord was pleased to give the spirit of meekness, and thus to soften the heart of him who reproached me. Love and mercy follow me continually, yet still I am an insensible slothful creature. O Lord, forsake me not, but continue to draw me, and compel me to come to thee; deliver me from indwelling sin, and a careless spirit. Let me love thee, and serve thee with a child-like spirit.

Monday, January 29. 1770.—This morning I was very lifeless in prayer and reading. Wandering thoughts are a torment to me. This day I allotted for returning the visits of my ordinary acquaintances. After prayer to God, that he would enable me to be faithful, to keep me from conforming to their vain conversation, I set out. But, alas! how little have I observed this. At the first place I went to, I was enabled to speak freely against the prevailing dissipations: at the second, I could only get in one moral reflection. In my next two visits, I had no opportunity of saying any one thing profitable. Upon the whole, I find much visiting hurtful to the spiritual life, and I wish to give it up. Lord, thou knowest how my heart longs to be separated from vanity, and to live wholly to thee: O grant that I may live every moment of my life to thy glory!

Wednesday, January 31. 1770.—Last night I was enabled to wrestle with the Lord in prayer for about half an hour, with many cries and tears, and to plead with him for a blessing. Yet I am still in darkness; my prayers this morning have been formal and dead; and I find no comfort in the scriptures I read. Lord, what shall I do to be saved? O have pity upon me, and cause thy face to shine upon my benighted soul! turn away thine anger; blot out my transgressions; and wash me in the fountain opened for sin. Sanctify me by thy Spirit, and lead me in the right way to thy everlasting kingdom. I have spent this afternoon in talking with Miss B—— on religious subjects, endeavouring to lead her to devote herself wholly to God; but whilst I spoke to her, I myself was cold and dead. In the evening I spent two pleasant hours with Lady Maxwell, and was strengthened in the ways of holiness.

The deep hold which religion had upon Lady Glenorchy's mind, made her zealous to promote it, and to devise plans for that purpose. In union with her friend Lady Maxwell, and probably at her suggestion, she formed the design of opening a place of worship, in which ministers of the gospel of every denomination who held its essential truths might preach:—a scheme which, however fair it appeared in theory, was soon found to be impracticable. With this object in view, she hired St Mary's Chapel, in Niddry's-wynd, originally a Roman Catholic chapel, but then and now the Hall of some of the Corporations or Companies of the Tradesmen in Edinburgh.

Prior to opening this place of worship, she informed Mr Walker of her intentions, who expressed his decided disapprobation of the measure, and dissuaded her from attempting its execution, declaring, at the same time, his determination to give her no aid. She found, however, an adviser more accommodating to her views in Dr Webster, one of the ministers of the Tolbooth church, a clergyman of great abilities, and the projector and first administrator of the fund for the provision of an annuity to the widows of ministers of the Church of Scotland. The polished manners, and fascinating conversation of this clergyman, made his society much courted by all sorts of persons, but especially by those of rank and fortune. Dr Webster was an avowed Calvinist of the higher class, but very liberal in his sentiments and conduct to those who differed in opinion from him. He was, from the time Lady Maxwell became decidedly serious, her intimate friend and adviser, as well as pastor, and usually attended her on the evening of every Lord's day to Mr Wesley's chapel, then in the Calton, which was built some time before. The religious meetings to be held in St Mary's Chapel, appear to have been regulated by a plan laid down by Lady Glenorchy and Lady Maxwell, with the assistance of Dr Webster; and divine service was intended to be performed by Presbyterians, Episcopalians, and one day in the week by Mr Wesley's preachers. The chapel was not to be occupied in canonical hours; but there was worship in it on the Lord's day at seven in the morning, in the interval between the morning and afternoon services in the churches, which was then much longer than now, and in the evenings, and in some of the evenings of the week days. To this institution and its concerns, some short references are made in the Diary.

Friday, February 2.—This morning I lay long in bed, having a headach. Devotions were slurred over in a slothful manner. I had two hours' conversation this forenoon with a minister about the chapel. He disapproved much of attempting to reconcile sects and parties, by bringing them to preach alternately in one place: he said it would give great offence, and used many arguments to dissuade me from my plan; and concluded by saying he could not preach in it, if the Episcopal forms were ever allowed there. Upon which I told him, that since both establishments refused me assistance, he must not be surprised if I asked the Methodists next.

Monday, February 5.—For two days past I have had no time for writing; my trials have been great. The Lord knows what I have suffered. This morning I met with Dr Webster at Lady Maxwell's, to consult about the chapel. It is determined that I am to seek an English Episcopal minister to supply it; and to give one day in the week to the Methodists. Lord, provide thou one after thine own heart! I paid a visit to-night to Lady G——; and although I wished to say something to edification, could get no opportunity, and so passed an hour unprofitably. O Lord, thou knowest the desire of my heart is to glorify thee at all times; open thou the door to me, and give me a tongue to magnify thy name!

In many Diaries, the reader is presented with all that is fair and commendable in the writer's spirit and conduct, and with nothing more. Lady Glenorchy's Diary, on the contrary, bears evident proof of its having been a full as well as faithful record of what she thought, and felt, and did, whether it was pleasant or painful, or whether it tended to place her temper and conduct in a favourable or unfavourable point of view. The quotations which will next appear, illustrate the truth of this remark.

Tuesday, February 6.—This has been an uncomfortable day. When on my knees this mòrning, a crowd of vain thoughts broke in upon me: ashamed to continue in that posture, I got up and walked about the room in great distress, and before I could return to prayer, was sent for, and the whole day has passed in worldly business, till five—when I went to our meeting, at Mrs Walker's. I have had several severe trials to-day, and not my usual consolation of pouring out my complaint to God. O that he would take compassion on me, and deliver me from my sins and this present evil world! I would willingly depart and be with Christ.

Thursday, February 8.—This being the fast-day in the parish church, Canongate, I got up early, and besought the Lord to sanctify it to my soul. I endeavoured to recollect the sins of my life, and spread them before the Lord, that he might blot them out by the blood of the covenant, and renew me by his Spirit. I did not feel them as I ought, neither did I abhor myself, although I knew I was very sinful in the sight of God. O when wilt thou give me the victory over myself!—I went to church, was very dead under the preaching of Mr B. in the forenoon; and notwithstanding my desire and prayer to be more benefited in the afternoon, by Mr Plenderleath's discourse, was still dead, and felt a heaviness on my spirits, and fears of not being worthy to come to the Lord's table. I have now been pouring out my complaint to the Lord, and crying to him to help me, and deliver my soul; but have no answer to my prayers. Yet still will I wait upon him. To whom can I go but unto thee, blessed Saviour; thou only canst deliver and give me peace. I have chosen thee for my portion, I have counted the cost. I desire to be wholly thine; to follow thee whithersoever thou mayest be pleased to lead me. Only do thou grant me an interest in thy redemption, and sanctify me by thy truth, that I may glorify thee in soul and body in this world; and when thou hast no more use for me here, receive me into thine everlasting habitations, to dwell in thy presence for ever. Amen!

Friday, February 9.—This morning I was much comforted by a visit from Mr Plenderleath; he stayed two hours, and exhorted and prayed in the family. He seems full of love to God and man. My heart warmed towards him. I felt much sweetness of spirit, both while he was here and after he was gone; it seemed as if the Lord was present with us—and surely he was, since we were met in his name. How different the afternoon!—my usual trials; my affections cold, my thoughts confused—unable to pray or meditate. I have written to a friend who is a bigot, to exhort her to love and charity. I have also spoken a few words of exhortation to a servant; but after all, I must set this down as an unprofitable day, and pray that it may not be remembered against me in judgment.

February 10.—After prayer and reading this morning, I was thinking on my trials, when the Lord was pleased to shew me that they proceed from the malice of his enemies, who rage violently when likely to lose their prey. This accounts for my trouble increasing when I get nearer to the Lord. This plainly appears from the nature of my trials, as they tend to make me weary of religion, and to comply with the world for present ease. But art not thou, O blessed Jehovah, stronger than the enemy? Thou art able to preserve me. Unto thee I flee for protection and strength in the hour of temptation. Unto thee do I commit my soul.—This afternoon I was enabled to continue some time in prayer. I endeavoured to lay hold on the Lord as my righteousness and my intercessor. I solemnly gave myself to him, and besought him that I might not rest short of any of the privileges of his people; but that he would purify my soul, and bring it to as great a degree of conformity to his image and will as was possible in this life, whatever I might suffer. I desired him alone as my portion, and took him to witness that I was willing to forsake all things for his sake. I went in the evening to the meeting, and found some access to the Lord in singing the first hymn, and in prayer. In my way home, I put up a prayer, which was answered. My trials this evening were more severe than common; I have reason to bless God for the composure of spirit with which I have been enabled to bear them. Thy mercies, O God, are infinite! O that my heart was more grateful!

Communion Sabbath, Edinburgh, February 11.—I had broken rest last night, with the thoughts of the ensuing solemnity, and had some hope that this day would be the time of deliverance to my soul. In the morning I besought the Lord to confirm this hope, and went to church with some degree of comfort in that view. But, alas! I did not find him whom I sought. My mind was distracted with impatience, and I returned in great distress from the table. Being much dejected, I said to myself, will the Lord hide himself for ever? will he be favourable no more?—At that instant Dr Webster began to serve a table, with these words, " Perhaps some one is saying, will the Lord hide himself for ever? will he be favourable no more? Let such take comfort; the Lord is nigh, though you perceive him not: he will yet come, though not now," &c. At this moment I felt that the Lord was nigh, and that he gave a persuasion that he would visit me in his own time. My heart replied, it is well; let the Lord come in his own time, I will still wait on him and put my trust in him. I had at different times some sweet intimation that he was near, and that my prayers were heard; and could with confidence say, I have chosen the Lord as my portion, and desire no other. I saw the beauty of this choice, and could say, Lord, thou who knowest all things, knowest that I desire to love thee above all. Much cause have I to lament over wandering thoughts and hypocrisy, that mixes in all my duties. O that the Lord would deliver me from them!—I have to remark this day, an answer of a prayer I put up when at the Lord's table. Glory to God for this and all his mercies!

Monday, February 12.—I heard an excellent sermon to-day from one I was prejudiced against. From this circumstance I would learn to despise no man, for the Lord can make use of any man to convey instruction to others. This evening I went to see a dear friend, when I uttered many idle words, and repeated a conversation to the prejudice of another, trying to raise myself at their expense. May this be a warning to me, and teach me to set a watch before my mouth, and to keep the door of my lips, even when with a bosom friend.

Tuesday, February 13.—An unprofitable day.—I had no time in the morning for reading and serious prayer. Company most of the day;—tried to pray before dinner, but could not to any purpose. I have been very miserable all day under the slavery of the world;—wishing to be released from vain company. Lord, pardon the sins of this day!

Wednesday, February 14.—Worse, if possible, than yesterday. Dined out in a large company—paid visits in the evening—was much indisposed in body, and my whole soul sick. The bondage of the people of the world grows daily more insupportable. I must give them up in order to be happy. Without God, this world is a miserable place; I will, therefore, take him for my portion.

Thursday, February 15.—Carried Miss B—— to see Lady M——; found myself a little enlivened by her conversation; brought Miss B—— home with me, and endeavoured to stir her up to more devotedness of heart to the Lord; but while speaking to her, I felt need myself of instruction. Carried her in the evening to the meeting, and was somewhat refreshed there.

Sunday, February 18.—This morning my devotions were cold and languid. I went to church and heard sermon; I came home much dissatisfied with it and with myself. In the afternoon I heard Mr Gibson of St Cuthbert's, on our Saviour the light of the world; but got little benefit. I lamented my case before the Lord, but got no comfort. I have neither light nor faith at present, and am afraid of falling again into the world. My life is bitter; I know not what will become of me, if the Lord does not take compassion on me, and deliver me from my present spiritual bondage.

Sunday Evening.—Upon taking a review of last week, I find I have lost ground, and am farther from the mark than when I began. I see several causes of this:—viz. want of watchfulness after the sacrament, which is a time in which the enemy is always most busy to draw away my soul from God. I therefore resolve, through God's grace, if ever I have another opportunity, to double my diligence in prayer, after partaking of that blessed ordinance. I have been more engaged in company than usual. This is a snare to the feet, which I pray God I may be enabled for the future to avoid as much as possible. I have been very much afflicted to-day with a suggestion from the enemy of souls, that it was in vain I sought the Lord, seeing I got no answer to my prayers; that it mattered not what I did, for the Lord would not come the sooner. Blessed be God, I saw it was a temptation and did not yield to it. No, I will wait on thee, O blessed Jesus, in a way of duty, knowing that it is in the use of the means that thou art most frequently found; and as thou hast given me this light, if I follow it not, I thereby cut myself off from all hope of finding thee. The Lord hath said, Seek and ye shall find,—ask and it shall be given. What a gracious command is this! No limitation; we are commanded to come, and ask whatever we will. Lord, I beseech thee, give me a new heart to love thee, to praise thee, to glorify thee. I beseech thee to give me a lively faith—to fill me with the Holy Ghost—to sanctify me wholly—to unite me unto thee, and make me partaker of thy holiness—to preserve me unspotted from the world—to blot out all my transgressions—renew me after thy image, and save me to the uttermost. Employ me, if it be thy will, in promoting thy glory on earth, and when thou hast no more to do with me here, take me to thyself to enjoy thee for ever. I beseech thee to grant thy salvation also to all with whom I am connected;—my husband, parents, friends, acquaintances, and servants. Grant that all my household may receive thy blessing, and believe on thee to the saving of their souls. I beseech thee also for thy church. Pour out thy Spirit on thy ministers. May they be messengers of peace to many souls. May thy kingdom come with power to this land. I beseech thee also for the poor ignorant heathen. O send thy gospel unto them, and cause thy light to arise on the dark corners of the earth. Have compassion on those who are under delusion and superstition; open their eyes and cause them to repent, and turn to thee, the living God, from idols. And finally, O Lord, grant that thy will may be done on earth as it is done in heaven. Let all men praise thee. Let every thing thou hast made rejoice in thee, thou Creator and Redeemer. For thine is the kingdom, and the power, and the glory, now and for ever. Amen.

CHAPTER VII.

Lady Glenorchy establishes family worship in her house—Extracts from Diary from February 19. to March 4. 1770—Plan of conducting worship in St Mary's Chapel not approved of by many religious characters in Edinburgh—Extracts from Diary from March 7. to May 7. 1770—Lady Glenorchy becomes acquainted with Mr Wesley—Is urged to join his Society, which she declines—She occasionally hears his preachers—Extracts from Diary from May 12. to June 3. 1770—Lord Glenorchy gets possession of Barnton—A great many workmen employed in embellishing it—Lady Glenorchy erects a chapel there—Much good done by this means—Extracts from the Diary from June 4. to 19. 1770.

It is abundantly obvious, that the regular worship of God in the family, is in every case of the greatest importance to the interests of religion, and more especially so when there happens to be a very numerous household. Of this truth Lady Glenorchy was deeply sensible. Circumstanced as she was, however, the introduction of this excellent practice into her family was a work of no small difficulty. Nevertheless, to a person of her integrity, piety, and decision of character, all things, if seen to be duty, are possible. Hence, at this time she actually accomplished the desire of her heart, and raised an altar to God in her house, the pure flame of which was never afterwards during her whole life extinguished, and around which, every morning and every evening, fervent prayer and grateful praise ascended to the God of the families of the whole earth. This event she records in her Diary with much humility and thankfulness. She also occasionally had a sermon delivered in her drawing-room at the Abbey of Holyroodhouse. Yet she laments with great feeling the little progress she made in the divine life, in the midst of this and many other means of grace which she enjoyed.

Monday, February 19. 1770.—This day I have felt more life in my soul than for a week past. Lord Glenorchy told me this morning that he would allow me to take a chaplain into the family as soon as Lord Breadalbane was gone. I went to Lady Maxwell, and sent for Mr Middleton, and invited him to come and officiate as chaplain during the absence of Lord Breadalbane. At that time I felt myself in the spirit of devotion; but on coming home I found a friend there who has often been a snare to me. Being very agreeable, with her I entered into idle conversation; and although my conscience frequently checked me, yet I went on till after tea. Thus did I knowingly trifle away time against conviction, which brought darkness on my mind. O when shall I live wholly to God!

Tuesday, February 20.—I prayed this morning for help to be faithful through the ensuing day. In some measure this has been granted. I paid two visits this morning, where I was enabled to speak boldly for the truth. Before dinner, I spoke seriously to a person of whom I have hitherto been much afraid. Had company to dinner, and did not feel ashamed of owning my singularity. I went in the evening to the meeting, and heard a good sermon on these words, "Lord, help me." It was very suitable to my case—in every thing I need his help. Without it I must quickly perish.

Thursday, February 22.—I got up early for prayer. Spent some time in it, but had little comfort. Went out to visit, and providentially called at a place I did not at first intend, where I met with Mr Thomson, whose conversation was blessed to me.

Friday, February 23.—Went to Lady Leven, where a proposal was made for printing some small tracts, to shew the evil of indulging a party spirit; also to reprint Professor Frank's Nicodemus. Afternoon I went to meet Mr Thomson at Lady Maxwell's. I was much pleased with his conversation—he observed, that the farther we advanced in divine knowledge, the more we see our ignorance, because every step we get on shews us that there are greater degrees yet to be attained. After he was gone, Lady Maxwell asked me to pray with her, which I refused, and have been much distressed ever since I did so, as I perceive now I am more desirous of appearing well before my fellow-creature than before God. Pride and false shame abash me. I have asked the Lord to give me courage to pray with others.

Saturday, February 24.—I began this day by praying that the Lord would enable me to walk up to the light he had given me. I saw my danger if I persisted in neglecting to comply with what he demanded, particularly in praying with my friends, and instructing my servants. I am determined in his strength to comply, let it cost me what it will, and to humble myself, and appear weak and mean in the sight of others, rather than forfeit the love of God, grieve his Spirit, and stifle the convictions of conscience. Accordingly, after prayer for assistance, I called one of my menservants, whom I judged most ignorant. I spoke some time to him on religious subjects. I then went out to see a Christian friend. I prayed first to be enabled to pray with her, which after some conversation I did, and found liberty of expression beyond expectation. I found, that in keeping the command, and following the teachings of the Lord, there is a present reward. After this I had two opportunities given me of speaking freely, without fear or shame, for the cause of religion. After tea I went to the chapel, and heard an excellent sermon on following Christ and denying self; that is, being denied to sin, the honours and friendship of the world, and all confidence in the flesh. I cannot but observe, that Satan begins again to-day to assault me as formerly, by stirring up some to teaze and vex me; but I dare not repine at this, for when the Lord prevails over my slothful temper, and enables me to be somewhat active for him, the enemy rages with most violence against me. I hope this night I have learnt to take up my cross, deny myself, and follow him. May he enable me to possess my soul in patience, to bear all things, and forsake all things, for his sake. O blessed Jesus, who would not willingly give up all things for thy love? What must their joy be who are blessed continually with the light of thy countenance, when I, even the poorest of thy creatures, sitting in darkness, feel unspeakable comfort in obeying thy commands?

Sunday, February 25.—Went to church, and heard a good lecture and sermon. Came home, and spoke with a maid-servant. Endeavoured to stir her up to more diligence to make her calling and election sure. Afternoon, heard Mr Plenderleath on the Shunamite,—a delightful sermon. I came home, and had sore trials of patience during the whole evening. Lord, withdraw not thy help from me one moment! Support me under these afflictions, till thou hast answered all thy loving purposes by them. I commit my soul to thee; thou knowest what it stands in need of to purify and subdue my evil temper. Let all thy will be fulfilled in me. Save me to the uttermost, and glorify thyself in me. Amen.—I have spoken with two of the servants to-night, and find that one of them wishes to follow the Lord.

Monday, February 26.—I was employed all the morning in the country. My soul feels much oppressed with the things of this world.

Thursday, March 1.—Mr Middleton came home and began family worship. I had some spiritual conversation with him. Found great comfort in considering his coming as an answer to prayer.

Friday, March 2.—After prayer in my family I went out to see my mother. Ventured to speak to her on religion. Came home to meet Dr Webster and Mr Thomson. Was interrupted in a useful conversation by Lady G——, who came to ask me to a ball; —was enabled boldly to state my reasons against it. After tea, preaching in the great room by Mr Thomson—the servants were much pleased. This day I have enjoyed many privileges; but hast thou profited, O my soul? Alas, how cold and dead I yet am, notwithstanding all these means of grace! Lord, quicken me, and impart saving faith and knowledge to my dark ignorant mind!

Saturday, March 3.—I spent the day in reading, writing, and talking of the things of God; but alas, in how cold and unprofitable a manner! My heart is not yet right with God. I continually lose a sense of his presence, and speak of him as of an absent God. I am formal and hypocritical in family duty, and appear devout, while my thoughts wander.

Sunday, March 4.—Last night I prayed for health to attend on public ordinances this day, and was heard. Mr —— preached in the morning upon these words: "Having a form of godliness," &c. a good sermon. In the afternoon we had an excellent sermon from Mr Plenderleath on the sufferings of Christ. My soul was not so much quickened by it as it ought; yet I could not help shedding tears to see with what indifference it was received by those who call themselves followers of that divine Redeemer, who suffered so much for them.

Wednesday, March 7. 1770.—This day St Mary's Chapel was opened for preaching the gospel. Ministers of every denomination are to be admitted, who have a sincere love to the Lord Jesus Christ and the souls of men, and who preach the doctrine of justification by faith alone. Mr Middleton* preached this day from Ephesians ii. 8. "For by grace are ye saved through faith; and that not of yourselves, it is the gift of God."

* St Mary's Chapel was opened, on the plan formerly mentioned, by the Rev. Mr Middleton, author of "The Lives of Eminently Pious Women," and one of the six students who, a year or two before, had been expelled from Oxford for attending private religious meetings, and who, having received orders in the Church of England, officiated at this time in a small Episcopal Chapel at Dalkeith. The different opinions of the persons employed in officiating in this chapel, never could in the nature of things coalesce; and although the congregations were large, and good was done to individuals, the design being in Scotland altogether novel, met with much disapprobation from the religious public; and their remarks, as it often happens on such occasions, either from levity, thoughtlessness, or prejudice, were neither kind nor just. These expressions of

I have been much distressed to-day with a weak body and an unbelieving heart. I laboured under anxiety that good might be done, and at the same time was so much distressed by the fear of man, that I got no good by the sermon myself. In the evening I wrote an addition to a little book against vain amusements.

Thursday, March 8.—I received a visit this morning from Mr ——, and had a long conference with him about Mr W—— and public places. He seems deeply prejudiced against Mr W——; thinks he is stealing in Arminian doctrines into the country, and sapping the foundation of our faith under the pretext of greater sanctity and strictness than others. As to public places, he seems to have little light upon the evil tendency of them,—makes distinctions,—condemns some as bad,—thinks others lawful if not carried to excess. I ventured to oppose him, and to maintain the evil nature of them all; and he seemed to listen to what I said on the subject, and although we did not agree in every thing, yet we parted good friends. This evening I read some of Mr W——'s sermons on Matth. v. I think he carries the doctrine of perfection too far, and I wish he had laid the foundation, even Jesus Christ, before he began to build. He showed me, however, that I cannot make myself a Christian, and sent me to my knees to beseech the Lord to teach me, and to preserve me from being deceived.

Saturday, March 10.—I received an account of another person's having been benefited by Wednesday's

dissatisfaction, together with her other trials, temporal and spiritual, deeply depressed Lady Glenorchy; but, following the example of the Psalmist David, she waited on God, and prayed that integrity and uprightness might preserve her; and she was preserved.

sermon, which filled me with gratitude to the Lord, for having made me instrumental in this way of bringing souls to him. It stirred me up to seek those blessings that others had received, and I spent some time in prayer with a degree of comfort and hope.

Tuesday, March 13.—I am still in trouble of mind and in outward afflictions. The Lord knows what is necessary to purge away my dross. Be it unto me even as thou wilt! This evening I was refreshed by a sermon at the meeting; I feel more comfort there than any where else, and am more stirred up to forsake all and follow Christ.

Thursday, March 15.—The Lord has been pleased to make this a refreshing day in his courts. Mr —— preached this morning on the necessity of the teaching of the Holy Ghost. The word came with power to my soul. I was convinced of having too much neglected to seek the influence of the Spirit, and of having trusted too much to my own strength. I also saw, that the Lord has begun a good work in my soul, and was made to believe, that he will perfect that which concerns me. I returned home with joy and peace in my mind. In the afternoon I went to church, and found great joy in singing Psalm cxxx.

> "Lord, from the depths to thee I cried,
> My voice, Lord, do thou hear;
> Unto my supplications' voice
> Give an attentive ear," &c. &c.

My soul rejoiced in the Lord, and I felt the power of his presence. I passed part of the afternoon at L—— M——'s with Mr In—s, in talking of the things of God, and went in the evening to the chapel, where the Lord confirmed my joy, by seeing he had accepted that service by the crowds that attended, and the power that accompanied the word preached. At night I found great freedom in prayer. On the whole, I can say that one day spent in the courts of the Lord is better than a thousand elsewhere.

Friday, March 16.—How fickle and uncertain are our best frames!—Blessed be God, although *we* change, *he* never does. This morning I waked in a dead frame; had no comfort all day. Worldly affairs crowded in upon me—I felt quite miserable, and could not but look towards the Lord for deliverance.

Sunday, March 18.—Still much troubled in mind. I went to church, was very dead and insensible under the sermon—full of wandering thoughts. I saw myself every way a sinner, unfit to approach the Lord's table; yet durst not stay away, and was always in hopes that the Lord would break the clouds of unbelief. I sought him earnestly, but I found him not; every body seemed happy in him but me. At night I was somewhat comforted by Mr P——'s sermon. I saw I was very sinful in having hard thoughts of Christ.

April 8.—I resolve this day to set out anew, in the strength and in the name of the Lord, in the path of duty—to miss no opportunity of waiting upon him; and for this end, I intend to get up at six every morning, and sooner if health permits. To spend two hours in reading and prayer before family worship—also to preserve a serious frame of mind through the day—to set a watch before the door of my lips, that I may offend not in speaking upon vain subjects; and not to be ashamed of the truth before any one whatsoever, but to speak to all about their eternal concerns. To possess my soul in patience, meekness, and silence, under the trials I may meet with. To spend some time before dinner in prayer, also before or after supper, and in meditation and writing down the work of God on my soul through the preceding day. O Lord, grant me thy grace to enable me to observe these things faithfully. Without thee I can do nothing!

April 9.—I got up at half an hour after five, had some liberty in prayer for near an hour, and a little light on the scriptures. I resolved to spend the day according to the plan laid down yesterday, but was prevented by unexpected occurrences. This evening felt the corruption of my nature very strong, in being inclined to anger under a trial of patience. I am yet far from having a meek and quiet spirit, and have a fearful and unbelieving heart. Lord, deliver me from the bondage of sin, for thine own name's sake!

April 11.—This has been an unprofitable day; much worldly business—little done for God. Yet in all my worldly affairs I feel a desire after him, and a weariness of every thing that does not tend to his service.—Blessed be God for this.

April 18.—Many tongues are let loose against me. The godly, in particular, have spoken bitter, and imagined false things of me. At first I was greatly hurt at this, lest I should have given any cause for it, and that I was not suffering the reproach of Christ, but bringing reproach on his name. But now I see this storm as coming from the enemy, whose kingdom is shaken, and therefore will leave no stone unturned to put a stop to our proceedings. I have examined my own heart, and the conduct of those preachers I have countenanced, and can say before God, that I believe we are sincere in wishing to advance his kingdom, and to win souls to Christ; and to endeavour as far as possible to promote that purity and simplicity which the gospel teaches, but which the world will always oppose and ridicule, being contrary to its maxims and customs. Our desire is to bring poor sinners to Christ, to receive the forgiveness of their sins and eternal life, in order that they may glorify God here, and enjoy him for ever. O Lord, thou only knowest the heart of man! Search me and try me; see if there is any concealed pride, self-love, or any view derogatory to thy glory, in what I have done: Remove it, O Lord, for thine own name sake, and let me be humbled for it before thee, and before the world if thou seest meet. Lead me in the narrow way that leadeth to everlasting life; keep my feet from falling, and let me not become a snare and stumbling block to any of thy children. Grant me patience to bear with meekness the strife of tongues, and enable me to return good for evil. Let me not only pray for my enemies, but love them, and do them every kind office in my power, for thy name sake.—Lord, thy love is all I want!

Thursday, April 19.—The fast-day at Leith.—The whole day has been spent in religious exercises and conversation; yet what does this avail if the heart is still unrenewed? if the soul is in a state of unbelief, and under the wrath and condemnation of God? All I can say for myself is, that I desire to be wholly thine, O Lord—to believe in thee, and to love thee above all. Perfect in me the work thou hast begun!

Friday, April 20.—I met with Mr Wesley, and had much conversation with him. He appears to be a faithful zealous minister of Jesus, and to have a single eye to the glory of God. I believe him to be sound in all essential doctrines.

Sunday, April 22.—This day I have once more presumed to sit down at the Lord's table, full of hopes and fears. I saw my great unworthiness, but endeavoured to look to him who alone is worthy. I took the bread and wine as pledges of my union with Christ, and devoted myself, soul, body, and spirit, to be for ever his. Lord, remember, I beseech thee, thy gracious promises to those who seek thee, and come to thee. Keep thou my soul, and preserve me amidst the numberless snares and dangers that surround me. Let not mine enemies triumph over me, for in thee alone do I put my trust!

Monday, April 30.—Since Wednesday I have been in great distress of soul at times, from being convinced of the sin of unbelief. I am grieved to think of living day after day in rebellion against God. I see that without faith it is impossible to please him. Lord, help mine unbelief! I have seen more of my own evil heart than usual, and more of the purity required in a Christian. I see that the generality, nay, almost all professors of the gospel, fall greatly short of their privileges. I can mourn over the sin of the world, and wish to tell every creature of their danger, but have not yet the power. I see in some measure the beauty of holiness, and wish to be conformed to the image of Christ. Upon reviewing the last month, I think I have rather increased in self-knowledge; for which I desire to bless God, and pray that he may carry me on, and perfect what he has begun in me.

May 4.—Last night I was somewhat refreshed by hearing a sermon on the reign of grace; but these revivals are short-lived. One cause of my instability in holy things, is the vanity of objects with which my imagination is crowded. This may be attributed partly to the dissipated life I formerly led, and partly to the hurry I am obliged to be in continually, from the peculiar situation in which I am placed. It is seldom I can obtain half an hour's quiet in a day, and am necessarily obliged to hear and think on a variety of worldly things, so that my mind is tossed to and fro with cares, fears, and troubles, outward and inward; and no sooner am I composed to think of my eternal concerns, than a very different subject is immediately intruded upon me. I can see no remedy for this, but must patiently wait the Lord's time for deliverance. He knows my distresses, and he only can deliver me from them, or support me under them. He knows that my heart's supreme desire is to live wholly to his glory upon earth. I do not perceive that I wish for any thing but his love, and to approve myself to him in well-doing. He has enabled me to give up my name, and the approbation of the world, for his sake, and I cannot see that any creature divides my heart with him. Lord, I appeal unto thee, if I would not willingly part with all for thy love! If there is any unseen improper attachment to the creature in my heart that keeps it from thee, do thou root it out; and take thou my whole heart, such as it is. Make it what it ought to be, and keep it faithful.

May 6.—Yesterday was a day of retirement. I found comfort in reading and prayer, and was enabled to write out portions of the Scriptures with some degree of light. It was like the day dawn upon my soul. In the evening the sermon was refreshing, and came like rain to the parched ground. I found myself on the threshold of heaven, but did not get in. This morning I got up before five, prayed with some liberty for near an hour. At seven I went out and heard the end of Mr Thomson's discourse; it was pleasant to my soul. I see all things ready; the Lord is willing and able, but there is yet an inability in me: what that is I cannot discover: I think I am willing: Lord, do thou search and try me! The sermons in church to-day have come home with unusual power to my soul. I feel a clearer conviction of eternity, and of the nothingness of time. I wish to live wholly to God. I have not done so hitherto, and am impatient under my failings and short-comings.

Monday, May 7.—I got up early, spent two hours in reading and prayer before family worship;—find early rising a great help to me, it lays a foundation for the practice of the whole day. We err greatly in praying seldom; for the oftener we pray, the nearer we get to God, the stronger we grow, and the more we shall love to pray.

During Lady Glenorchy's former temporary residences in London, various clergymen of eminence were introduced to her, and among others Mr Whitefield, of whose zeal, abilities, and general character she highly approved. Mr Wesley she had not seen, never, as the Author believes, having had any acquaintance with any of his friends there, and not being in Scotland when he previously visited it. That countenance, however, which Lady Glenorchy gave at this time to the Wesleyan preachers, naturally brought about her acquaintance with Mr Wesley himself, who was now in Edinburgh. He and his friends had previously wished her to join their Society, which she declined; for although she esteemed them, and wished them well as good men, and as labourers with others in the great vineyard of the Lord, she never could adopt their peculiar opinions. Mr Wesley had at this time repeated interviews with her, and twice or thrice in company with Dr Webster, who always heard Mr Wesley when here, as well as occasionally his preachers. Probably at the desire of Lady Glenorchy, Dr Webster had a conference with Mr Wesley, in her presence, on some of those points of doctrine in which they principally differed. The effect of this discussion was, that she was confirmed in her orthodox opinions. She still, however, continued occasionally to attend his chapel, and to employ his assistants. About the time that the above circumstance occurred, it appears that Lady Glenorchy continued to suffer much in the course of her spiritual warfare; and although she experienced a great deal of the hardships of it, yet she not only persevered, but had the happiness to gain some considerable ground. Hence she thus writes in her Diary:—

May 12.—For some days past I have had a sense of my unprofitableness; when I would do good, evil is present with me. I still labour under corruption of heart; and although I have as much spiritual light as shews me the emptiness of the world, and the necessity of faith, yet I still want the witness of the Spirit to testify in me that I am Christ's.

This morning the Rev. Dr Webster and Mr Wesley met at my house, and had a long conversation together. They agreed on all doctrines on which they spoke, except those of God's decrees, predestination, and the saints' perseverance, which Mr Wesley does not hold. After Mr Wesley was gone, Dr Webster told me in a fair and candid manner wherein he disapproved of Mr Wesley's sentiments. I must (according to the light I now have, and always have had, ever since the Lord was pleased to awaken me) agree with Dr Webster. Nevertheless I hope Mr Wesley is a child of God. He has been an instrument in his hands of saving souls; as such I honour him, and will countenance his preachers. I have heard him preach thrice; and should have been better pleased had he preached more of Christ, and less of himself. I did not find his words come with power to my own soul. I desire to bless God for having enabled me in some measure this day to be faithful to the convictions of his Spirit. O that I may daily receive more strength and courage, to be accounted a fool for Christ's sake!

Sunday, May 13.—I have spent this day in the courts of the Lord. Consider, O my soul, what thou hast heard, and how many will rise up as witnesses against thee if thou hast profited nothing thereby. Salvation has this day been freely offered thee. Thou hast seen and confessed the beauty of holiness, and of a life devoted to him who gave it, and thou hast been convinced there is no happiness elsewhere. Come then to Jesus, give thyself up without reserve to him. Lord Jesus, I come to thee to receive this great salvation! I think I am willing to receive thee on thy own terms. If my heart deceives me in this, thou knowest, and thou canst make it willing. Come thou, and set up thy throne in my heart, subdue every enemy that is there, and make me wholly thine. Grant me the gifts of repentance and faith, thy Spirit to guide and sanctify me, and the efficacy of thy blood to atone for all my past sins. Save me to the uttermost, and let me not rest short of thy complete salvation. Come quickly, Lord Jesus! Amen. So be it!

Saturday, May 19.—I got up early, spent some hours in prayer and reading. L. E. came to breakfast. I was enabled to speak freely to her, to confess the truth, and, after a severe struggle, asked her to join with me in prayer. Afterwards I went to church in the afternoon and evening. The Lord shewed me several evils in my heart, particularly resting in duties, and not having a single eye to God. I would gladly have spent this night in prayer, but my body is weak, and requires rest.

Sunday, May 20.—I rose early, had great freedom in prayer, and was enabled to wrestle with cries and tears that the Lord would meet me this day at his table, and set my soul at liberty. I felt little power in the sermon; but found much liberty in prayer when going to the table, and praised the Lord for the great blessings he had spread before me. I felt a consciousness of his presence, and a sweet intimation that my prayers were heard. I took the bread and wine as pledges of his love, and as an earnest of what he would do for me. This hope was afterwards confirmed to me in private prayer. I was sensible of the Lord's loving-kindness and designs of mercy towards me. Though

I could not say he gave me the full assurance of faith, yet I believe he will work faith in me with power. I have found him drawing me on to seek after him. O bless the Lord, my soul, and forget not this day's mercies! His hand has also appeared in outward Providences—keeping off outward troubles that might have disturbed my mind. My prayers have been answered even in lesser matters. O how gracious is the Lord to those who seek him! Surely he will be found of all who seek him in sincerity; therefore will I wait on the Lord, and follow on, that I may know him.

Monday, May 21.—I got up at five, and had great liberty in prayer. I perceive the Lord is shewing me more and more of my own vile heart, and strengthening my trust and confidence in him. I find the besetting sin of my heart is the love of praise and esteem. I am full of pride, self-conceit, and a slothful spirit; still ashamed of the gospel of Christ; apt to judge rashly of others, and overvalue myself. I feel averse to many known duties, viz. reproving sin; admonishing others; praying with my friends; instructing my servants. I am addicted to vain wandering thoughts in prayer. I see a great deal of corruption in my heart, and feel utterly unable to remove any part of it. I have therefore spread it before the Lord, and put my case into his hands. I am persuaded he is able and willing to cleanse and purify me. I look to him for faith to conquer the fear of man, and to bring peace and health to my soul. He is exalted a Prince and Saviour, to give faith and repentance to a guilty world. I have asked them, and he will not deny them; therefore will I look for an answer of peace, and wait the accomplishment of his promise. I have also seen the danger I now am in of being assaulted by those temptations I have formerly felt at coming from the Lord's table. Nothing but cleaving to, and continually looking to the Lord, can keep me from them. I have sought power to do this; and hitherto he hath helped me.

Wednesday, May 23.—I spent most of this day in reading and prayer; felt a conviction that I was idle, and that Christians should be employed in doing good to others as well as to themselves.

Friday, May 25.—I see there is no being almost a Christian. Christ must be all or nothing. O that I may be swallowed up in him, and dead to the vain world!

Saturday, May 26.—I determined this day to set out anew, and to struggle to get loose from this vain world. But, instead of this, my whole morning was taken up with visitors, and I had no power to speak faithfully to them. They were professors, but dead ones, and I could find nothing to say to them. At night I went to the chapel, and heard Mr T———. He spoke to my heart; I was convinced of my unfaithfulness, and was ashamed before the Lord. At my return home I met with a great trial, which sent me to prayer; and there I found again somewhat of that confidence and hope that was like to perish through my negligence. I find trials are needful: when all things go smoothly, I sink into insensibility. O, how good is the Lord thus to chastise my folly, and bring me back to himself, the centre of all happiness.

Sunday, May 27.—I got up early, and went out at seven to the chapel, and was somewhat revived by the sermon. At ten went to church, where I heard two excellent sermons from Mr S——th, accompanied with more life and power than any I have yet heard in the church. I was led to pray much for a blessing on them, both while there and since I came home. Surely the Lord was present, and I trust the word was the savour of life to those who heard it. I was filled with joy at the precious truths he so clearly explained, and with horror and grief when I thought of those who might reject the free offer made them of life and salvation in Jesus Christ. My desires for a blessing to the people were fervent. I do not remember having ever been so deeply engaged in hearing in this church. I look back with shame and grief on the loss I suffered last week, which may be attributed to mixing with a company where God was not in all their thoughts. What a dreadful enemy is the world to religion! Its maxims and customs are altogether opposite to true Christianity. I see no safety but in coming out from among them, and being separate; yet my situation does not allow of this—it would bring reproach on the Christian name. Surely the Lord knows my case, and can direct me; he can save me in the world, or deliver me from it: he has taken my heart in some measure out of it. Its pleasures, honours, and riches, are become a burden to me; they are the greatest load I have: and I can truly say, I would gladly part with them all for the knowledge of Christ Jesus, and my interest in his salvation.

Sunday, June 3.—Last week I passed through a variety of trials, temptations, fears, hopes, and businesses. I had not time to write the state of my soul, yet I can see that the Lord is carrying on his work; "through waves, clouds, and storms, he gently clears the way." He is every day shewing me more of my own vile heart. A self-righteous spirit is ever present with me, prompting me to rest in duties performed, and expect rewards. As long as this is my state, how can I expect to be justified by the blood of Jesus? It is those who see themselves wholly undone without him, that are fit objects of his compassion. I see also that it is my own evil temper that renders my present situation disagreeable; for it is not in the power of man to give real uneasiness to a soul that seeks its happiness only in God. I see I am unfaithful to the grace and light given me; how then can I expect to receive more? I am called to a high calling, the Lord would have me stand forth as a witness for him; yet, instead of obeying, I shun the cross, and am ashamed to speak for him. This morning I got a view of the sin of neglecting any opportunity of speaking seriously to those I meet, and was convinced of the great importance, not only of making my own peace with God, but pressing others to do so. All things appeared as dross and dung, when compared to the love of God shed abroad in the heart. I felt then able and willing to speak to every body; but this frame is now gone.

The purchase of the estate of Barnton, as we have seen, was to Lady Glenorchy an object of considerable interest, as she conceived she obtained it in answer to prayer. Lord Glenorchy had by this time got possession of it, and a great number of workmen were employed in its improvement, and in preparing it for the reception of the family. Had Lady Glenorchy foreseen, what in truth soon happened, that this spot was destined to be the place where the most expeditious and best aid, temporal and spiritual, was to be procured for her lord in his last moments, and in which she was to find an asylum for her widowed state, she could hardly have felt or acted otherwise than she did upon her first going there. In company with her friend Lady Maxwell, she solemnly implored the divine blessing upon it, and the works carrying on there, and she dedicated them to the service of God. Following up this principle, she employed persons from time to time to preach to the workmen. A chapel accordingly was afterwards built, attached to the house, in which, whilst she was resident there, divine service was performed generally every Lord's day, after the service in the parish church was closed, and sometimes of a week-day evening; and even during her absence this duty was occasionally performed. This practice was continued till she sold the property, a little before her death.

The providence of God seems to have remarkably blessed this effort of Lady Glenorchy to promote the interest of religion; for many persons were known to have dated their first serious impressions from attending divine worship in the family and the chapel.

The service of the chapel was usually conducted by her domestic chaplains, among whom are numbered men who were afterwards destined to attain no small degree of eminence in the church, as Mr De Courcy, late rector of a parish in Shrewsbury, the late Dr Balfour of Glasgow, the late Mr John Russel of Stirling, Dr John Campbell, at present one of the ministers of the Tolbooth Church, Edinburgh, and the late Mr David Black of Lady Yester's Church, Edinburgh, and others.

Amidst all these attentions to spiritual matters, and this deep concern for the glory of God and the good of others, Lady Glenorchy seems to have been much cast down, and greatly harassed by the power of temptation. Accordingly she says—

Monday, June 4.—I was much oppressed in spirit this morning, with a view of my own dead soul, and the state of my family, who seem to decline of late. I got up, and prayed for them, and spoke to two servants closely, and with some degree of life. In the evening I went to Barnton with Lady M——, Mr T——, and Mr H——; had a word of exhortation in the great room to the workmen, and then one of the ministers prayed and solemnly dedicated that house and all that belonged to it to the Lord. O bless the Lord, my soul, for this and all his benefits! I heard to-day that Mr Wesley has found a religious schoolmaster for me;—this is also the Lord's doing, and the answer of prayer. O what am I that thou shouldst thus care for me?

Tuesday, June 5.—I was much affected this morning with the Lord's goodness to me in answering my prayers,—also in giving me the comfort of some pious friends.

Friday, June 8.—I was all this morning in my room, reading Alleine's Alarm, and praying over it.—I remember a friend of mine forbade me, three years ago, to read such books, saying they were legal, and set me a-poring over myself, instead of looking to Christ. I unfortunately took this advice, and thus have healed my wounds slightly; and said peace to myself, before I was thoroughly convinced of sin. The wall which has been daubed with untempered mortar, is now coming down. My breaches appear, and I find I am a poor, vile, abominable sinner at this day, continually offending God;—at times I am so miserable, that I am ready to give all up. I went to-day to Barnton, and had preaching again in the great room, to about seventy of the workmen and labourers: the text was Matthew xxiv. 44. "Therefore, be ye also ready; for in such an hour as ye think not, the Son of Man cometh."—I felt very happy in procuring them this instruction, and was perhaps too much lifted up; and the Lord permitted me to be assaulted by a grievous temptation in my way home, which filled me with grief and horror at the depth of sin which I perceived in my heart, and the little power I have over it. If the Lord did not restrain me, I should surely bring great reproach on his name by outward sins also. I cannot think that any one, who has heard and believed the gospel, is so vile as I am. But, O blessed Jesus, didst thou not cast seven devils out of Mary Magdalene?—speak the word, and I also shall be delivered.

Friday, June 15.—I find it always a loss to my soul when I neglect to write, as I have done for a week past. I grow careless, and forget at what a distance I yet am from God. I have heard many excellent sermons this last week, and have been in various frames. Yesterday I had a sweet persuasion that I belonged to God, and should live to praise him.—This morning a young woman called upon me, by her father's desire, that I might speak to her about her soul. She was an utter stranger to me, and I felt ashamed and averse to speak to her. Sensible how unfit I was to speak to her as I ought, I begged of God to help me, and to put words in my mouth;

and I may truly say he opened my lips. Bless the Lord, O my soul, for this. Make thine own word, which thou gavest me to speak, effectual, O Lord, to the conversion and salvation of this poor soul!

Monday, Jnne 18.—I got once more to Barnton, where Mr H—— preached to the labourers, from Isaiah lv. 6, 7. "Seek ye the Lord while he may be found: call ye upon him while he is near. Let the wicked forsake his way, and the unrighteous man his thoughts; and let him return unto the Lord, and he will have mercy upon him, and to our God, for he will abundantly pardon."—Some of them were affected. I have seen much of the goodness of God this day in interposing in my behalf when I returned home; and although I had, by my exceeding great unworthiness, deserved to suffer, yet I was saved from the trials I feared, and at the same time my heart was humbled by pain of body, which I have ever found a needful medicine to my soul.

CHAPTER VIII.

Lady Glenorchy at Taymouth—Is an eminent example of diligence in business, united with fervour of spirit—Grows in the divine life—Makes her will, and appoints Lady Maxwell executrix—Extracts from Diary from July 10. to September 30. 1770—Letters from Lady Glenorchy to Lady Maxwell—Lady Glenorchy returns to Edinburgh—There enjoys the means of grace in great abundance—Account of her religious experience—Extracts from Diary, from October 26. to December 31. 1770.

Lady Glenorchy in the end of June went to Taymouth, and remained there till the beginning of October following, managing the domestic affairs of that great and magnificent establishment. This was an employment which might be thought, considering her age, (for she was not yet twenty-nine), the delicacy of her constitution, and the bad state of her health, would have fully occupied the whole of her time and talents, and left her little leisure for any thing else; yet, in reading her Diary at this period, one might be led to suppose, that early and late, and all the day long, she was only employed in works of piety and benevolence. She certainly was a most eminent example of diligence in business, united with fervour of spirit in serving the Lord. Still she was not satisfied with herself, or what she did. She thought she never could do enough; and what she did do, she considered as stained with most mortifying imperfection. She was always striving to do somewhat more, and praying fervently that she might do it better. Considering her circumstances, her youth, her rank, her wealth, her power, her trials, and the society in which, although reluctantly, she was obliged to mingle, and the very strong allurements to which she was exposed, her activity, her humility, her spirituality, and her fidelity, were truly surprising, and pointed her out as a wonderful and admirable monument of the grace of God. The truth of this remark will strikingly appear in the following extracts from the Diary, and letters which she wrote during this period to her friend Lady Maxwell. The intelligent reader will observe, too, in these extracts, how very much Lady Glenorchy's practice of writing a Diary tended to promote and strengthen the divine life in her soul, particularly from the account she gives of her experience on the return of her birth-day this year. Notwithstanding that self-abasement still continued, and in fact ever did continue to be a strong feature in her character, she evidently acknowledges herself to have made decided advances in her spiritual life. Her graces seem to have been improved, and her resolution of doing good greatly confirmed. This will appear to much advantage, if we attend to what passed in her mind, when, from the circumstance of her making her will, and appointing Lady Maxwell her executrix, she conceived herself to be on the very borders of eternity.

July 10.—I have been prevented, by the hurry of removing my family to this place, from continuing my Diary. I feel I am losing ground fast, and resolve through grace to set out afresh in the Christian course. Gracious Lord, grant me thy strength; undertake for me; turn thou me, and I shall be turned; draw me, and I will run after thee.

July 11.—I awoke this morning with great longings after Christ, and desires for perfect conformity to his image, and resolved to live to him through the day; but no sooner did I go into company, than my thoughts were dissipated. After breakfast I got some little revival by prayer. The rest of the day I spent in work, and hearing the life of Mr Hogg read. I feel condemned at having done nothing for the souls of my fellow-creatures, nor having redeemed much time for prayer. Lord help me, for I am weak!

Sunday, July 15.—For some days the Lord has been pleased to visit me with sickness—blessed be his name for this. I had great need of correction. Alas, I fear I stand still in need of much more. But did not Christ come to seek and to save those who were lost? Did he not die for the ungodly? Surely then he came to die for me, to save me;—this is my hope. O that thou wouldst now witness this truth to my soul by thy Holy Spirit, and cause it rejoice in thee, my God and Saviour!

Sunday, July 22.—This week past I have lived an inactive life, yet the Lord has given me some few opportunities of speaking for him, and of relieving the bodily wants of the poor. He has also delivered me from temptation. I observe, that by prayer we may obtain all things consistent with the will of God. I have found it to be so this week.

July 24.—Last night the Lord was pleased to give me a sight of my great distance from him, and my sloth and negligence in seeking him in a way of duty. He hath shewn himself to me to-day as a prayer hearing God. I asked power to speak to a person of distinction about his soul, and was enabled to do so, and to give him a book. I was enabled to bear my testimony to the truth, to him, and to several others during the course of the day. This evening six of my servants have met together to pray for the rest.

Sunday, July 29.—Yesterday I was ill in body, but much refreshed and comforted by the coming of the Rev. Mr J.—— He preached this day. I was led to be much in prayer for a blessing to the people. In the evening he preached again in the dining-room; the power and presence of the Lord seemed to be with us, and my dead heart felt in some measure the force of what he said. I was condemned, and roused, and strengthened to speak boldly for God to my company during the rest of the evening. I find the more I speak of God, the easier it is, and the more opportunities I get of doing so. O that I could praise the Lord for all he has done for me! But instead of this, I grow impatient under the remainder of sin, and am in danger of thinking hard thoughts of God. I would be set free all at once. Self still reigns in me, else I should submit to his time and way, and be found patiently waiting for him in the use of the means he has appointed. O Lord, when, how, and what thou wilt!

Thursday, August 2.—This being a fast-day, I got up earlier than usual, and spent two hours in humbling myself before the Lord, and imploring that faith without which it is impossible to please him. I likewise asked strength to perform a difficult duty, which he has enabled me to do this afternoon. I have found great benefit from being much in prayer this day, and have a comfortable hope that the Lord will receive me, and enable me to live to his glory.

Friday, August 3.—The Lord has heard me this day, in giving me power to speak to several poor souls. I find he is always willing to impart strength for duty when we are willing to perform it. I received an account of the illness of a dear friend this night. I find I have not so much resignation to the will of God as I ought. I have prayed for it, and committed my friend to the Lord. I desire to see God as my only portion!

Sunday, August 5.—Very dead in prayer this morning, although not without hope that the Lord would revive me. I went to his table, and sought him; and though I felt no assurance of his love, yet was enabled to cast my soul upon Jesus, and to look to him for complete salvation. I was led to pray much for the people; and think the Lord will visit this country.

Monday, August 6.—I went out this morning to the fields, at seven o'clock, in great deadness of soul, to pour out my heart, and to cry to the Lord. I took all around me to witness that I consented to be his, and committed my soul to him. And now, O my God, I would again beseech thee to accept this free-will offering of my soul, body, and spirit! I have none in heaven but thee, and there is none on earth that I desire besides thee. I would give thee my whole heart, but I am unable to do any thing of myself. I therefore beseech thee to come this day, even now, Lord Jesus, into my soul, and reign thou there king for ever! Subdue all thine enemies in me, and make

him, that the glory may be his. When we are very dead, then ought we the more to strive to pray, for this is the time of greatest need, and it is then the Lord is most ready to hear.

Monday, September 10.—Having (through grace) got a sight this morning of my late unprofitable walk, I prayed to be made useful to others this day, and obtained faith that my prayers would be answered. I set out from my bed-chamber in the name of the Lord, trusting that in his strength I should be enabled to speak to as many as came in my way. My prayer was heard. I have spoken with seven persons this day about their souls,—one of whom was a young gentleman, who received what I said with much kindness, and thanked me for it. I felt joy at having been faithful to his soul, though I have much reason to blush at the imperfect manner in which I at all times speak of the Lord. But he knows my weakness, and will, when he sees good, give me the power of utterance. He first gives the willing mind, afterwards the power. O what comfort is there in looking back upon a day spent for God, and dedicated to his service through the blood of Jesus, which cleanseth from all our imperfections and infirmities!

Tuesday, September 11.—I desire this day to set to my seal, that God is a prayer-hearing God, and that it is our unfaithfulness and unwillingness that cause our great unprofitableness. I prayed this morning for three things which I found myself wholly unfit for, yet saw them to be duty; and the Lord cleared my way, put strength in me, and brought me off more than conqueror; I had many struggles and temptations, but the Lord got himself the victory. O that this may encourage me to put my trust in him, and to go on conquering and to conquer!

Friday, September 14.—I got up earlier than usual this morning to spend some time in prayer, but before I got on my clothes met with a trial of patience which overcame me. I fell into pride, self-conceit, and anger. I several times asked help of God, yet continued sinning against him. Surely the Lord, by permitting this, intends to show me my own heart; perhaps I have been full of spiritual pride, and he takes this way of laying me in the dust, and causing me to abhor myself. Yes, Lord, I do abhor myself for sinning against thee. O let me become still more vile in my own eyes, that I may be more earnest to obtain the blood of sprinkling, to cover my sins from thy sight, and to wash me from all iniquity. O let this morning's fall be a warning to me, to watch and pray continually, lest I enter into temptation. Give me that charity that beareth all things; and suffer me not to murmur at the trials thou hast in mercy sent me; but let me ever remember that I have deserved hell, and that it is of thy tender mercies I am not consumed. Since writing the above, I went out into the fields to humble myself before God, (after having confessed my fault to two friends, in order to be revenged of my proud heart). I went into a summer-house, and there poured out my heart with many tears before the Lord, and at length obtained peace, but could not be reconciled to myself. In my way home I embraced several opportunities that offered of warning others of the evil of sin. I endeavoured to explain to them the nature of it, the original depravity of their hearts, and the way of salvation by Jesus Christ. O what love is this in God, to employ such a poor sinful wretch as

I am in speaking for him! I received a letter this morning, telling me of a tradesman's daughter having been awakened by a conversation I had with her before I left town. Glory be to thee, thou Almighty Lord, who out of weakness ordaineth strength!

Saturday, September 15.—I spent some hours this morning in reading and prayer. I begged of God to employ me in his work through the day; but could not recollect any person in this family or place that I had not spoken to. I was afraid I should be idle; but the Lord provided work for me when I least expected it. Two or three persons came to me from a distance about business, to whom I gave books, and spoke about their souls. One woman wept, and seemed much obliged to me. My travelling bookseller coming this way, brought me a supply of books. I went out in the carriage, and called at several houses, where I dispersed many of them. I had also some opportunities of relieving the temporal wants of a few of these poor persons. What joy does it give one's heart to relieve the indigent members of Christ! Surely all that the world calls pleasure is not to be compared to it. How blind, how stupid is man,—always seeking happiness, yet neglecting the only way in which it can be obtained. Did he once know the pleasures of religion, he would soon quit the poor, empty, insipid vanities of this world.

Sunday, September 16.—Upon reviewing my life last week, I cannot but give glory to God, and bless his name, for carrying on his work in my soul, and calling me to experience his power in working in me both to will and to do of his good pleasure, and, lest spiritual pride should take possession of me, has permitted me to fall into temptation, that I might see my own vileness, and his mercy and loving kindness in raising me up to more diligence, making me more watchful, and shewing me that my only safety is in continual dependance on him. O my soul, bless God thy Lord,—forget not his benefits. Surely I am the most ungrateful of all his creatures. What am I, O Lord, that thou shouldst thus regard me! O let me ever keep in remembrance thy mercies and my unworthiness; let my song be, Grace, grace, free grace to the chief of sinners. Thou art found of them that sought thee not, and art merciful to the evil and unthankful, that thou mayst have all the glory, the honour, and praise, for ever and ever. Amen. So be it.

Thursday, September 20.—Since writing the above I have been indisposed in body, and much oppressed in spirit. Unable to pray, my thoughts wandering and unfixed. The Lord hath hid his face from me, and my soul is troubled. O when wilt thou revive me? When shall my soul rest in thee? Lord, search me and try me; bring forth all thine enemies and slay them; let not a thought live in my heart that rebels against thee.

Sunday, September 23.—I rose early this morning to seek the Lord, and after struggling some time with temptations, I at last got some measure of the spirit of prayer and faith to say, "Lord, I believe; help thou mine unbelief." I have besought the Lord to shew me whether or not I am in a regenerate state. Surely I am not an enemy to God, since it is the prevailing desire of my soul to know him, and to bear his image. Sin is the burden of my life. I groan to be delivered from it. I find no pleasure in any thing that does not tend to the glory of God. I look upon every moment as lost that is not spent in reading, hearing, or speaking of the things of God. My views in this world are now confined to a life of conformity to his will, and obedience to his laws. I perceive sin in many things now, which formerly appeared innocent to me; and duties which then appeared unattainable, I am now enabled to perform. These things convince me that the Lord is carrying on a work of grace on my soul, and that he hath thoughts of mercy towards me. Suffer me not, I beseech thee, O Lord, to be deceived in this; but if I am thine indeed, shine upon thy work, and witness it to my heart by thy Spirit. Or if I am still an alien, in a natural state, O let me not continue so, but convert my inmost soul. Bring me out from the bondage of sin and Satan, redeem my soul, and shew unto me the way of salvation. Reveal Christ in my soul, and glorify thyself in saving a miserable sinner!

Monday, September 24.—I rose early, and besought the Lord to enable me to live this day as if it were the last day of my life, and to make me useful to others. I found much desire after Christ, and some liberty in prayer; and surely my prayers have been heard and answered, for I have had an opportunity of speaking to nine or ten people with some degree of earnestness, and a clear conviction of the truth of what I said. May the Lord bless it to their souls! Without this, it will be as water spilt upon the ground.

Tuesday, September 25.—This morning the Lord enabled me to pour out my heart before him, and to wrestle in prayer, with many tears, for nearly two hours, not only for myself, but for all men,—for the church, my friends, and every one of my family by name. I found liberty to plead with strong cries and tears for my mother, and I trust in the Lord that she will come to acknowledge the truth as it is in Jesus.

Wednesday, September 26.—This morning I was enabled to give my first thoughts to God. I asked for the spirit of prayer this day. My soul was cold and dead all this morning, but before dinner I got a view of my great unfaithfulness, and my negligence in not wrestling more for a lively faith, which alone can save the soul. Mr Andrew Gray's Sermons were blessed to me, and shewed me much of my own heart. I determined to spend the afternoon in seeking the Lord, but my prayer was lifeless. I could only cast my soul on the Lord; he can and will save it. I cannot doubt of this, for he hath given me to hunger and thirst for all his salvation. Surely he will come, and will not tarry.

Friday, September 28.—I have this day had a long (and a too warm) debate with Mr Middleton, about the doctrine of assurance. He says he dare not preach it; and that those who say they know their sins to be forgiven, are deluded. I affirmed, that the knowledge of the pardon of sin naturally flowed from faith; for a man that hath faith, knows that he has it; and that those who have it, are pardoned and justified in the name of the Lord Jesus: their transgressions are blotted out, and they have joy and peace in believing, &c. Blessed God, remove darkness from our minds; reveal unto us what thou wouldst have us to believe; teach us what is needful for our salvation; and suffer us not to wander into error; but lead us into all truth, for thine own name's sake. Thou art truth.

Saturday, September 29.—More and more confirmed in the doctrine of the knowledge of remission of sins in this life. I find Calvin, John Knox, Rous, all mention faith as a sure trust and knowledge of forgiveness through the blood of Jesus. Calvin makes this knowledge of pardon of the essence of faith, and the motive to love and obedience.

Sunday, September 30.—I waked this morning with a conviction of my great ignorance of God, and distance from him. I see my distress proceeds from the weakness of my faith. At times I have peace, and never lose hope of receiving faith. But I cannot be established till the Lord give me the witness of the Spirit. I have gained last week some self-knowledge, and see a tendency to passion and impatience that I did not know of before. Lord, give me a humble heart.

Lady Glenorchy to Lady Maxwell.

" My dear Madam,—I have been much distressed, since I wrote to you, with company to whom I had not the power to be so faithful as I wished, and saw to be my duty. I feel exceedingly condemned for not speaking more boldly to them, and my own soul has suffered loss by hearing all their carnal conversation for four days. My friend, Miss Hill, came yesterday, which is a comfort to me. How good is the Lord to send me a helper, when I stand so much in need of one! She is grown in self-knowledge since I saw her, and sees it as her privilege to be wholly devoted to God. I trust we shall be faithful to each other, and to those around us. But, my dear madam, you must really continue your friendly admonitions and counsels, and tell me all you have seen amiss in me since the Lord was pleased to give me the comfort of your acquaintance. This is an act of friendship I demand of you, as an evidence of the faith you profess; it is a precept of the gospel which ought to be observed, however disagreeable it may be to flesh and blood. I think I can bear to be told my faults; I wish to know them, that I may spread them before the Lord, and ask his grace to conquer every thing that would separate me from him. If I know any thing of myself, I wish to be wholly his without reserve; and it is my greatest grief that I perceive every day more and more the distance I am from that mind that was in Christ, &c. O that he would speak the word, and I should be whole. I can truly say, my soul longeth for his salvation. Help, my dear madam, with your prayers. I have time for no more just now. May the best blessings of the Lord Jesus rest upon you. Farewell."

"*July* 22. 1770."

Lady Glenorchy to Lady Maxwell.

"My dear Madam,—Your question is of the utmost importance; and it is not my interest to deal deceitfully with you in answering it. My soul does not prosper; I have suffered already from that contagious air you mention, and feel myself falling into a lifeless inactive spirit: my thoughts are dissipated; my religion lies floating in the head, and my heart is not impressed with that deep seriousness and holy desire after communion with God that I have formerly felt; in short, I am declining fast, under the power of temptation, and in the utmost danger of getting altogether into a carnal spirit. I therefore beg you will write me whatever is most alarming; try to rouse me up to a sense of my danger. Your words are generally blessed to me. O that the Lord would now put it into your heart to say something that would reach mine, and pierce me to the quick! for I am as one asleep on the top of a mast—in imminent danger of falling into eternity. I have been confined with a fever of cold since Monday.; the fever still continues, but so slight, that I have got up to write; yet who knows but this may be a messenger to call me hence! Miss Hill, in some respects, is a help to me, yet in others I feel worse since she came, as I am inclined to spend too much time with her, and less in my closet. O, my dear madam, what a cordial an hour's conversation with you would be to my dying soul! I am now going to settle all my worldly affairs, and shall leave you my sole executrix. You know my intentions, and I doubt not will fulfil them. I feel my mind quite easy in leaving all I have to you: I hope I shall live to execute it. My body is at present so weak, that I must give over writing for this day, and will only now add my repeated request, that you would be free with me, and write me, as often as you can, every thing that will tend to stir me up to more fidelity towards God and man. Surely none ever misimproved so many mercies as I have done; none will deserve so much punishment; and yet, when I think of the love of God, I cannot fear. I see him ready to forgive, already reconciled in Jesus; yet still I cannot love him and serve him as I ought. What strange perverseness this! My heart is ready to break when I think of its ingratitude! May the Lord be your sun and shield now and for ever. Yours, affectionately, W. G."

"*Saturday, August* 14. 1770."

"My dear Madam,—Your letter last night was a very great comfort to me in many respects, both as it told me you were better, and in the country, which I much wished you to be, and also, as you gave me a direction for you. I have been very much distressed with the apprehension of losing you; and have seen by this how much my heart is still attached to creature-comforts. A number of people here have added greatly to my trouble, as I could not tell them the cause of my grief, none of them being acquainted with you, nor enough acquainted with the nature of Christian friendship to understand all I felt at being left behind you in this perverse world. After several days of hard struggling and wrestling for submission to the divine will, I did at last obtain some measure of resignation, and was enabled to bless God for the comfort I had enjoyed in your company, of which I surely was utterly unworthy. I left it to God to continue or withdraw this blessing, as seemed best to him. I would gladly hope the Lord has yet much to do with you here; and rejoice at your present situation, as you will have many opportunities of speaking for him in the country, which you could not have in town. I have reason to be thankful for those given me every day among the poor, who come for medicines for the body, and, when the weather permits, I go out to the fields, or into their houses, and attempt to speak for God; but, alas! what reason have I to blush at the weakness and ignorance with which I speak of divine truths. Miss H. is willing to help me, but the country people do not understand her. I find the attempts I make to awaken others the best means of keeping my own soul alive: were it not for this, I believe I should grow dead to every thing. The company that is with me have no relish for these things: when I speak to them they seem to approve; but no impression is made. Mr Gillies, from Glasgow, was here yesterday, and I was much refreshed with his conversation, as also with seeing Mr M'Nab, on his return from Strathfillan, where he preached several times, and was well received. I hope the Lord is beginning to work among us. I went to-day to a neighbouring church, where the sacrament is to be given to-morrow, and had a great deal of conversation with some country people in the church-yard, who spoke experimentally of the things of God.

It is surely your duty to use every means for your recovery. I make no doubt of the love of God to you in this severe illness; it is sent to purge away the remaining corruption of your nature, and bring you into nearer union with himself. And what a blessing it is in this view! O what can we desire but this union! My heart is often like to break with longings to know God in Christ, and to be swallowed up in him. I have no doubt of my attaining this: he has given me the desire; he is faithful, and he will surely satisfy my soul with his complete salvation. I could write many sheets to you were I to indulge my inclination, but I fear tiring you; so will only add, that I am, with sincere affection, my dear Madam, your obliged friend and servant, W. G."

"I have the comfort to tell you, that there is a great appearance of a change in the heart of my father-in-law. I know not how to ask you to write, and yet I am very desirous of hearing often from you.

"*Saturday, August* 21. 1770."

Lady Glenorchy to Lady Maxwell.

"My dear Madam,—I received your letter last post, and hope I shall never be so far an enemy to myself as to think your friendly cautions or advice too free. Indeed so far from this, I think you are not free enough; and I should take it very kind were you to tell me my faults without ceremony, and shew me where I fall short of that entire devotedness to God, to which I long to attain. Alas! I am far from it as yet. But at times I can see it as a privilege, and desire it with my whole heart. I have of late seen much of the meaning of the Lord's dealings with me, and must acknowledge that all his dispensations are mercy and love. I have met with an old book, which I think has been blessed to me. It agrees so entirely with my own view of things, that I am more and more confirmed in the desire of seeking the knowledge of God in my own soul as the only real good. It has also shewn me that I am indeed seeking the Lord, and therefore I know I must find him if I follow on to know him. I rejoice to think I shall once more meet you in the flesh. Miss Hill and I set out next Monday. This we owe to the loving kindness of the Lord, who has made the way clear, and got me permission to go with her to Edinburgh. We are to be at Lord Leven's by the way, so it will be Friday or Saturday before we reach Edinburgh. I wish much you should see M. H. as I think you may be of use to her, and I hope you will find her a sincere seeker of the Lord. I wish you would send a note to the Abbey, to let me know where you are when I arrive; and when and where we can see you, as she will stay but a few days in Edinburgh. I will not now take up more of your time, as

I hope so soon to see you, only I beg you will take care of your health for the Lord's sake, that you may be more able for his service. O that we may be enabled this winter to be all for him! And may he manifest his power in our weakness, and cause us to bear much fruit to his glory! With much affection, I am, my dear Madam, yours, W. G."

"*October* 11. 1770."

In the end of October Lady Glenorchy was alone in Edinburgh, to which place, as we have seen from her letter to Lady Maxwell, dated October 11. of which we have given an extract, she, with the consent of Lord G. had accompanied her friend Miss Hill in her return to England, who had spent the summer and autumn with her at Taymouth. At Edinburgh she possessed the means of grace and religious society in great abundance; and she both diligently used them, and improved by them, notwithstanding her almost constantly writing bitter things against herself; for at the end of the year, when she took a review of her past experiences, she admits she had made considerable progress in religion. There can be no doubt that at this time Lady Glenorchy knew the truth as it is in Jesus; that the only way to obtain pardon and acceptance from God is by the blood and righteousness of Christ; that in this she sincerely believed and trusted; and that she shewed the strength of her faith by the entire surrender of herself and of all her talents to the service of God. But one thing, which we formerly adverted to, essential to habitual spiritual comfort, she lacked, which was the witnessing of the Spirit with her spirit that she was a child of God. This privilege indeed God bestows or withholds according to his sovereign pleasure; and as she herself sometimes thought, he perhaps withheld it from her to keep her humble and lowly in spirit. The soundness of her state before God at this period must, to every Christian acquainted with the truth and with the ways of Providence, be evident; and as she persevered in the faith and holiness of the gospel to the end, she gave full proof of her election of God; but still, for want of this precious gift, she went mourning, more or less, all her days. Hence she thus writes:—

Edinburgh, Friday, October 26. 1770.—I have been obliged to discontinue my Diary, being on a journey, and much hurried. I feel my soul somewhat revived by hearing the gospel preached. I see my great distance from God, yet still hope in him that he will perfect the work he hath begun.

Friday, November 2.—Last night and this morning I have been much oppressed in spirit with a sense of my deadness and want of the experimental knowledge of Christ. I was enabled to lay my case before God, and plead with him. I appealed to him if I desired any other portion in time or eternity than Christ. I renewed the dedication of myself to him, and took him to witness that I gave up my soul to him, and would trust in him; and if I perished, it should be at his feet. I desired to be made whatever he would have me to be, and that every thing might be rooted out of my heart that opposed his will.

Sunday, November 4.—This morning my soul seemed void of spiritual life, yet I got some comfort in family prayer and in church. After I came home I had occasion to pray with a person in distress, and found great comfort, both in this, and afterwards in private.

The love of God was shed abroad in my soul; my mouth was filled with praise. I could not utter what I felt. The goodness of the Lord appeared infinite to me. In the afternoon I heard Mr Walker, and was refreshed by his discourse. I saw the sinfulness of unbelief, and strove to believe, and got power to do so, but in so faint a degree, that I dare not yet say I have assurances of faith, although I cannot doubt of God's love: every thing testifies it, all his ways are mercy and love to me, even to me. Lord, I beseech thee to confirm my faith, enable me to abide in thee. Seal my peace, and make me thine for ever. I renounce all other Lords. I desire to take thee as my only portion from this time forth and for ever more! W. G.

Tuesday, November 6.—Yesterday morning I got great liberty in prayer, and was led to ask for victory, in particular, over wandering thoughts, which have been a great hinderance to me in duty; and in some measure this was granted. But afterwards, worldly business occurred, a slothful spirit crept in upon me, I neglected private prayer through the day, and when night came, my soul was as dead as ever. In the forenoon I was enabled to pour out my soul to God, my Saviour, with some degree of confidence of being heard. I solemnly devoted my soul and body to the Lord Jesus without reserve. I told him all my desire, and I believe he heard, and will give it me. I asked to live to his glory upon earth, and to die bearing my testimony to the truth of his gospel, recommending him to others, and praising his name with my latest breath.

Thursday, November 8.—This being the fast-day before the sacrament, I got up early, and confessed my sins unto God, beseeching him to blot them out for Christ's sake. After this I went to church, hoping to get my pardon sealed there. The sermons were excellent, and my judgment approved of them; but the word did not affect my heart. I was left to wrestle with sin and corruption. After sermon, I went to see Lady M——. She asked me to pray with her—I consented, and felt very much ashamed of appearing so weak and contemptible as I must have done in her eyes, forgetting that God only is to be feared and had in reverence by those that draw nigh unto him. When I came home, I got liberty to pour out my soul in secret to God, and saw that all my trouble through the past day had been the answer of prayer; for I had asked of him in the morning to humble me in my own eyes, to shew me the corruption of my heart, and to enable me to mourn for it. And it has indeed been a day of humiliation to me; I never appeared more vile in my own eyes, or was more desirous of converting grace.

Saturday, November 10.—I prayed much this morning, for a blessing at church. Mr Spiers's text was Isaiah xxxiii. 17. "Thine eyes shall see the King in his beauty: they shall behold the land that is very far off."—I believed the word, and rejoiced in the hope that mine eyes should see the King in his beauty; and I was much comforted and confirmed in the expectation of receiving a blessing to-morrow. Mr S. bade us expect great things: I did so; and have spent the evening and part of the night in prayer for a blessing on the ordinance to-morrow.

Sunday, November 11.—I waked early this morning, and spent some time in prayer. Went out to church;

but was no sooner there than my soul was seized with stupor, and my body so uneasy that I could not attend to the sermon. I felt unfit to go to the table of the Lord; and though my conscience could give a good answer to all the marks Mr P—— gave of those who were invited to partake of the ordinance, yet unbelief strove to keep me away. I waited long to hear if any minister would speak to my case, and give me encouragement to come. At length Mr Spiers called upon the weary and heavy laden to come to Christ, who waited to be gracious. On hearing which, I got up, thinking I was called; but could not get forward to that table on account of the crowd. Meanwhile, a minister I did not know stood up to exhort, and described my case so exactly, that every word seemed spoken to me. My heart was then overwhelmed,—I could hardly contain myself. I went forward to the table in faith; and when he said, "I now deliver you the seal of the covenant," my heart replied, Lord, I receive it, and do believe I am now in thy covenant. Now, Lord, remember thy covenant, and suffer me never more to depart from thee.

Saturday, November 24.—I found much liberty in prayer this morning; my hopes are revived. I have been enabled to speak faithfully, and to confess Christ to a man of learning who came this day to see me. In the evening I heard a good sermon, on the almost Christian. My conscience bore me witness to many marks given of the real Christian, and I came home rejoicing in hope of the favour of God.

Sunday, November 25.—I found much comfort this morning in reading and praying over the 31st and 32d Psalms;—found liberty of access to God in prayer.

I heard Mr Walker this morning, and Mr Erskine in the afternoon, bear their testimony against the horrid and blasphemous farce that was acted last night in this place. O that the impression these solemn discourses have made on my heart this day, may never be effaced! May I stand forth boldly, as a witness for a despised and crucified Saviour, in the face of men and devils! I have repeatedly and solemnly taken the Lord to be my God—O that I may no longer be ashamed to confess him before men, but bear my testimony in all things to his truth and faithfulness, whatever may be the consequence. Come Lord, seal me thine for ever!

Saturday, December 1.—I found comfort this morning in hearing the experiences of a Christian, who came to see me. I find my case is not singular; others feel the same load of sin that I do. I attempted today to visit a poor person who was sick, but was denied admittance; this was a disappointment to me, as it has been much upon my mind lately, to visit the sick as a Christian duty. What cause have I to blush when I think how little I have done to-day for God! I cannot doubt of his love, yet I do not feel its constraining power, else I should redeem more time for his service.

Sunday, December 9.—Last week I have been much engaged in company with the people of God. I find their conversation very pleasing to me, but very dangerous; for instead of being humbled by seeing how far short I come of the least of the saints, I am led into self-seeking; and while I should be learning wisdom from them, I am trying to give them a good opinion of me. Alas! did they see my heart, as God sees it, they would rather fly than seek my company.

Monday, December 10.—I went this morning to visit some people of fashion, and was enabled to speak to them of the things of God. This I believe to be the answer of prayer.—Afterwards, I visited my school, and found the poor children singing a hymn. My heart was filled with joy and gratitude to the Lord for having made me the instrument of bringing these poor souls to sing his praise. After dinner, I went to visit a near relation, and soon fell into a worldly spirit, and said not a serious word;—came home with guilt upon my conscience. I find I want that deep seriousness which can alone preserve me from the contagion of worldly company.

Tuesday, December 11.—This morning I received a visit from two young ladies, to whom I was enabled to speak freely against the fashionable follies, and pressed upon them to examine their own hearts, to see if they experienced the influence of the gospel, or had any saving knowledge of the truths of God. After they were gone, I felt deeply ashamed before God for the poor manner in which I had spoken of him, and feared having talked of things I did not experience myself. I got a clear view of the evil of sin, and never felt it so deeply, nor such a burden before. I wrestled long with God in prayer, and got power from him to keep my heart and tongue through the day. My fears of hypocrisy were also removed, and I believed that this was indeed the Spirit of God convincing me of sin, and carrying on his work upon my soul, giving me a sight of my backslidings and shortcomings. My soul longed to employ this whole evening in prayer, and I got it partly accomplished. I find the spirit is willing, but the flesh weak.

Wednesday, December 12.—I spent most part of this morning, till twelve o'clock, in prayer, and found my soul longing and thirsting after the experimental knowledge of Christ. Afterwards I had some edifying discourse with Dr Erskine, which was interrupted by visitors. I was enabled to continue to speak before them of the things of God, and we were all refreshed, and I hope profited. When they were gone, I found it needful to ask the Lord to pardon the self-seeking and spiritual pride, which I discovered in my own heart. I was then led out to praise the Lord for his goodness, and to pray that he would impart grace to all men, that every thing that he had made might praise him for ever.

Dr Erskine says, that a general acquaintance, even with good people, is a loss to a Christian,—it takes up much of that time which ought to be employed in communion with God, and bestows it on the creature. This is certainly true; I therefore resolve, through grace, to give up all needless and useless visits, and redeem more time for private devotion. In this way my faith will be strengthened, and then I shall not be so easily hurt when I go out among others. I find I have not yet attained an appropriating faith in Christ as my Saviour;—I see my need of him—my heart is like to break at times for longing for him—I think I am willing to part with all, even life itself, for his love: But by and by my soul grows dead,—a crowd of useless impertinent thoughts break in upon me like a flood without my consent, and hurry me away I know not whither. This often happens when I am at prayer; and when I discover the treachery of my enemies, who have thus unawares got possession of me, I cry aloud to the Lord for help, and he delivers me. O for a steadfast faith, to cleave continually to the

Lord. Then should I be more than conqueror! Lord, grant me this faith.

Thursday, December 13.—I found liberty in private prayer this morning, but great wanderings in family worship;—the enmity of the natural heart was strong, and there was a great struggle between the old and new nature within me. I felt great deadness in speaking to some people about their souls this forenoon, yet the Lord carried me on, giving me something more to say, when I thought I had not another word. Alas! I am very dead and of a careless spirit. I do not mourn after Christ as I have done for some days past. I tremble lest I should again fall into a false peace. O blessed Jesus, suffer me not to find comfort in any thing short of thy love, revealed to my soul by the Holy Ghost!

Friday, December 14.—I spent this morning in reading and prayer, and found liberty to cast my soul on Jesus, and trust upon his word both for present and future mercy. I have cause to praise the Lord this day for ordering all things well that concerneth me. Lord G—— arrived from the country. I received many comfortable letters from absent friends. O how comes it that so many show kindness to such a poor worm as I? What cause have I to bless him who turneth their hearts towards me!

Sunday, December 16.—I went this morning to Leith to hear Mr A. Hunter, and found much comfort in hearing him preach from these words,—"To those that believe he is precious." His prayers and sermon came with power to my soul. I felt a secret witness within me, that the marks he gave of true believers applied in some measure to me. Since I came home, I have met with a severe trial, which sent me to a throne of grace with strong cries and tears. The Lord enabled me to plead with him for perfect submission to his will, and he gave me power to rejoice in some measure in this trial, as the way he hath appointed to mortify my corruptions, and to subdue his enemies in my soul. I cast my care upon him, and he hath sustained me, and caused me to look forward with joy to the glorious appearance and second coming of Christ,—to that happy period when all sin and sorrow shall for ever cease, and I shall behold him, and be transformed into his image, and rejoice in his presence for ever more. O blessed trials! happy afflictions! since they bring me nearer to God, and give me clearer views of him for whom my soul longeth.

Sunday, December 23.—I have been confined all last week with a cold, and also attending Lord G. who has been ill. I have had little leisure for reading, meditation, or prayer; no Christian companions, nor any person to whom I could speak of the things of God, and my own soul in a dead and uncomfortable frame. At times I have got liberty to pour out my complaint to the Lord, and found some comfort in weeping in secret for my own sins and the sins of others. I have also had refreshing letters from friends at a distance; yet, upon the whole, it is not with me now as in former times of sickness. I am confused, and my thoughts are dissipated. I long for access to God; I groan after him, but cannot get near him. O merciful Jesus! thou who knowest my inmost soul, and canst read the secret desires of my heart, have pity upon me! Grant but the crumbs which fall from thy children's table,—remove whatever hinders my intercourse with thee.

I desire only thy love,—take whatever else thou wilt from me,—take health, friends, fortune, reputation, or even life itself,—only let me be assured of an interest in thee, and of the eternal enjoyment of thee, in the world to come!

Sunday, December 30.—All last week I was confined to my room with sickness, and greatly oppressed in spirit with outward trials, and no inward comfort. I have had little time for prayer; and when I had, my mind was so confused and dissipated, that I was a terror to myself. I have been led to doubt if ever I was awakened. The Lord's dealings with me are very mysterious. I cannot see why he hides his face from me, but I trust it is for my good. I will still hope in his word, that those who trust in him shall never be ashamed, and they that seek him shall find him; and though I am yet in darkness, yet will I hope and wait on him till he sees fit to bring me to light. Why art thou cast down, my soul? Still trust in God, for I shall yet praise him.

Monday, December 31.—Another year is gone, and where art thou, my soul? What shall I render unto thee, O Lord, for thy long-suffering kindness and forbearance with me? Hadst thou cut me off in my sins I could not but have justified thee: But thou hast prolonged my day of grace;—still there is hope—still thy Spirit strives with me, and carries on thy work, thy marvellous work, in my soul. Thou art refining me in the furnace of affliction, that I may come forth like gold. I see thy hand in all my trials. They are necessary to my soul,—I could not do without them. Lord, I would submit in all things to thy will. I commit my soul wholly to thee. Do with it whatever is most for thy glory!

This year I have gained a deeper sense of the evil of sin, and seen more of the depth of corruption in my own heart. I have seen more of the vanity of the world, and am become (through grace) more dead to it. I have got more courage to speak for God, and less fear of the reproach of men. I have spent more time in prayer, and have been enabled to pray with others. The Lord has blessed some attempts I have made for the conversion of souls, and I hunger and thirst more after Christ; yet the light has not shone so powerfully upon my own soul as I have experienced it formerly. The Lord hides his face from me, and I am troubled; I mourn after him,—it has been a sorrowful year to me in this respect. But blessed be his name for the mercies and privileges bestowed upon me, and that he still keeps me waiting upon him, and trusting in his word.

CHAPTER IX.

Lady Glenorchy's zeal leads her to go lengths which unnecessarily expose her to trials—This remonstrated against by her Christian friends—Rev. Mr Gillespie's letter to Lady Glenorchy on the subject—Admirable letter of Mr Walker on the same subject—Lady Glenorchy's influence over Lord Glenorchy—Mr De Courcy appointed minister of St Mary's Chapel—Letter of his to Lady Glenorchy—Extracts from Diary January 6. to February 2. 1771—Lady Glenorchy's letter to Lady Maxwell—Extracts from Diary from February 7. to 12—Letter from Lady Glenorchy to Lady Maxwell—Extracts from Diary.

The reader will no doubt have observed, by the extracts already made from Lady Glenorchy's Diary, that she considered it a duty incumbent on her to recommend and enforce, not only by her example, but also in her conversation, the practice of religion upon every one, great and small, to whom she had access; and if she happened to neglect any opportunity of this kind which occurred, she viewed and lamented it as a sin of omission, which heavily burdened her conscience: and hence she studiously sought occasions to perform these services. These services, however, were not confined to persons in her own family, or of her own rank and station in society. She was in the practice of going among the lower orders, especially in the country, and in the course of her journeys, and speaking to them respecting the state of their souls. This, as might be expected, did not always succeed. Indeed, it not unfrequently exposed her to very unworthy treatment, unsuitable to her rank. These circumstances, and other peculiarities connected with her Christian zeal, were observed by some of her friends not without a considerable degree of uneasiness and regret, and produced some attempts to open her eyes to the impropriety of it. Accordingly, a very interesting and sensible letter on this subject, though directed to a lady in general terms, yet evidently intended for her use, was written by that very apostolical man, the Rev. Mr Gillespie, justly considered as one of the most able casuists of his day, and who had himself been deprived of his living of Carnock, for his zeal and fidelity in the cause of truth. This letter was communicated to her; and a copy of it, taken by herself, is still in existence. Another letter, of which she frequently spoke, even to the close of her life, with great approbation, and the original of which was found amongst her papers, was written and sent to her by her judicious faithful friend and pastor Mr Walker. It is, as might be expected, marked with all the good sense and elegance, as well as piety, for which he was so eminently distinguished. As these letters are both excellent in themselves, and have a relation to the situation of Lady Glenorchy at this time, they shall be inserted, and are as follow.

Letter of Mr Gillespie.

" Dear Madam,—The doubtful point on which your conscience wants satisfaction, is a weighty case. Resolution of it is to be humbly sought of from the Lord by prayer, and searched for in the blessed Bible, —a rule both perfect and infallible. That our hearts are deceitful above all things, and desperately wicked, appears by the divine declaration. Hence it is both difficult to discern duty in certain circumstances, and to practise it aright. The warm affections of young Christians are apt to carry them too far in some things, although with the best design. It is no less the will of the Great God and Saviour, that we be wise as serpents, as well as harmless as doves. Want of proper caution may hurt the religion of Jesus as much as insincerity and craft. Christ's disciples are sent forth as sheep in the midst of wolves. This calls for the greatest care and circumspection. Dependance on the Lord is to be exercised, that one may not hurt his interest, and prejudice those against the ways of their God who are otherwise minded. Christ appoints "that pearls be not laid before swine." The pearls of the things of God are not to be laid before persons in conversation, who are known to have the spirit of scorners of these great and glorious things, and to be disposed to make a bad use of what is ever so well intended, however well it may be expressed. The pearls of reproof and rebuke are not to be cast before swine, those who are daring in sin, and obstinate in evil ways, lest they trample them under their feet, contemn them, turn again and rend the reprovers, and hurt them in character, or at least wound their spirits, in place of profiting by the reproof. To administer a suitable rebuke to reach the end desired, requires much spiritual wisdom, prudence, and Christian temper. Without these, it is like to do more hurt than good. There are evil times of general corruption and danger, when, though persons in public office must speak, private believers who are prudent, as exercises of spiritual prudence, ought to keep silence, because it is an evil time, and persons are become incorrigible. Amos v. 13. 'Therefore the prudent shall keep silence in that time; for it is an evil time.' Holy silence in some instances does more service to religion than any thing said, how suitable, how seasonable soever it may appear to be. Lamentations iii. 28, 29. 'He sitteth alone and keepeth silence, because he hath borne it upon him. He putteth his mouth in the dust, if so be there may be hope.' Christianity is true wisdom. Job xxviii. 28. 'And to man he said, The fear of the Lord, that is wisdom, and to depart from evil is understanding.' The religion of Jesus both requires us to attain prudence and to practise it. It teaches that there is a time to keep silence, and a time to speak, Ecclesiastes iii. 7. It directs when to speak in confessing Christ before men, and when one should keep silence in obedience to him. Rashness and imprudence are not only natural weaknesses, but moral evils. Ecclesiastes v. 3. 'A fool's voice is known by the multitude of words.' Christ kept silence when falsely accused, so that his unjust judge marvelled. Matt. xxvii. 13, 14. 'Hearest thou how many things they witness against thee? And he answered him never a word.' We must have a warrant from the Lord's word, a clear call in Providence in connexion with the Bible, and in subordination to it, for what we do, else it is not done in faith. If not in faith, so far are we from having reason to expect any good from it, that it is indeed sin. Romans xiv. 23. 'For whatsoever is not of faith is of sin.' I am, dear Madam, yours," &c.

"*January* 1771."

Mr Walker to Lady Glenorchy.

"*January* 2. 1771.

"The manner in which your Ladyship was affected on Friday last, has left a very deep impression on my mind. Your spirit is by far too strong for your body; and yet such is the human constitution, that the spirit cannot hurt the body without impairing its own vigour, while it disables the instrument in, and by which it must necessarily act. I can easily perceive that you have more sensibility than you are aware of. You had laid your account with the persecution of the world; and it is my real opinion that you are invulnerable on that side: one that can despise its smiles, must certainly be superior to its frowns. But your heart has already told you, that it is not equally fortified against sufferings from another quarter. When the purest intentions, when the most generous and disinterested schemes of usefulness, (for in this light all your aims and operations have invariably appeared to me), when these do not meet with the approbation and support of those who acknowledge the same Lord, and are engaged in the same cause, especially when you apprehend that such begin to look upon you with a jealous eye, and are become cooler in their love, and more reserved in their confidence,—then, your Ladyship will confess that your heart receives a wound which pains it very sensibly. This is a trial which perhaps you did not reckon upon, and might have wished to escape; and yet I have no doubt, that even this is one of the many well chosen ingredients, which your wise and tender-hearted Physician hath selected, and ordained to work together for your good.

"It hath pleased God to form you by his Providence and grace, for important services in his spiritual kingdom. But he hath not left you to chuse either your station or your work: In both these particulars your resignation to his will must be entire and unreserved. When I had the honour and happiness to be first acquainted with your Ladyship, you seemed to move in a sphere, in which I thought you could not fail to be eminently and extensively useful. I then

beheld, what I had long wished to see, one who might have been seated as queen in Vanity Fair, and even courted to ascend the throne, nobly preferring the pilgrim's staff to the sceptre, and resolutely setting out on the wilderness road to the celestial city. In this amiable light I still view you with pleasure, though I cannot help suspecting, that an over-anxiety to shun the dangerous pits on the left hand of the narrow way, hath rendered you less attentive than was necessary to some openings on the right hand, which ought likewise to have been avoided. My plain meaning is, that Lady Glenorchy, through an excess of self-denial, hath for many months past been employing that activity in the open fields, which, before this time, might have enlightened, warmed, and adorned some of the principal apartments in the house.

"I am far from thinking that your labours of piety and love have been fruitless; but I seriously believe that their fruit would have been more abundant within your proper sphere.

"The most ornamental parts of your character as a Christian, and those which are the most demonstrative of the power of godliness, can make no impression at all upon the lower ranks of people. Your condescension may gratify them, your liberality will certainly profit them, and your advices, thus accompanied, may penetrate deep into their hearts. But how can such persons estimate your renunciation of those alluring pleasures, with which they are altogether unacquainted? You work at present with less than half the strength with which God hath armed you. The only weapons you can employ, are your station and fortune, and these, at the age of threescore years and ten, will serve you just as well as in the bloom and vigour of youth. There are other weapons in your possession, altogether peculiar to your season of life—weapons of a finer polish and keener edge, which, if properly applied, will do more execution in a very short time, among persons of rank and education, than all the ponderous artillery of title and opulence will be able to perform, for many long years, among those inferior classes to which your attention is at present almost wholly confined. In short, my Lady, were I an enemy to the cause for which you contend, I should certainly wish to encounter you at the very spot you have chosen, and would give you no more opposition than might suffice to amuse, and detain you where you are, and prevent your removing to more advantageous ground. You not only want auxiliaries who cordially love you, and would reckon themselves happy in contributing their aid, (though they are unwilling to accompany you in the levelling scheme), but you even want room in that narrow field, for bringing into action some of the best of those forces that are properly your own. I know with what regret you look back upon the time you spent in Egypt. At present, it appears to you an awful blank—a mere vacancy in life, or something worse; and I readily admit, that had you been suffered to live and die there, both your time and your soul would have been lost irrecoverably. But now that you have got to the Canaan side of the Red Sea, I would have you to know, that the time you reckon lost may not only be redeemed, but even serve to enrich the many years of real and useful living, which I trust are in reserve for you.

" Why did the Lord give you favour in the sight of the Egyptians, so that they lent unto you such things as you required? (Exod. xii. 36.) Was it that you should throw them aside into some dark corner, and hide them as if they were stolen goods you are ashamed of? No, madam, give me leave to tell you, they are lawful spoil,—you are become the rightful possessor of them; and the great Proprietor who hath put them into your hands, expects and requires that they should be consecrated to his service. And however your Ladyship may despise them, I dare venture to assure you, that you have not one useless trinket in your custody. Not the onyx stones only, and the bracelets, and jewels of gold, but the silver and the brass, nay, the smallest parcel of goat's hair, or fragment of Shittim wood, that you picked up in the house of bondage, may all be employed in rearing up the tabernacle, or in some work that pertains to the sanctuary of God.

"You know the history of Moses. In the account given by himself, which is short and modest, he passeth over every thing that befell him from his adoption by Pharaoh's daughter, till it came into his heart to visit his brethren, when he was full forty years old. But Stephen, in his defence before the Jewish council, took notice of some particulars in that first period of his life, which Luke the inspired historian hath thought worthy to be left upon record, viz. "That he was exceeding fair; that he was learned in all the wisdom of the Egyptians; and mighty in words and in deeds." Now, can your Ladyship really suppose, that all these natural and acquired advantages, his form—his literature—his elocution—his magnanimity and prowess, were mere superfluous embellishments, which contributed nothing to qualify him for the high office he afterwards bore in the church of God? You must be sensible, that upon this supposition the marvellous train of providences, which introduced him into the court and family of Pharaoh, would have neither voice nor meaning. For it is evident, that Moses would have been as safe, or rather more safe, because less formidable, under the homely appearance of a clumsy awkward common Jew, than the figure and splendour of an accomplished prince. And I cannot help thinking, that if his courtly education and breeding had not been intended by God as means of preparation for future services, he would have been as profitably employed in making bricks with his kindred slaves, as in acquiring all the wisdom and learning of the Egyptians.

"It hath long been my opinion, and I am every day more confirmed in it, that as the timber and stones which were employed in building the temple at Jerusalem, were prepared (at least in part) by Tyrian artificers, in the mountains that produced them; so, many of the materials of the spiritual temple, though squared, perhaps, and hewed by unhallowed hands while they remain in their natural inanimate state, do nevertheless, even then, frequently receive that shape and fashion, whereby they are adapted to the several places they are destined to occupy in the house of God, when, by the Spirit of life entering into them, they become lively stones through their union with that living stone chosen of God, and precious, which is at once the foundation and the head of the corner, (1 Pet. ii. 4, and 5.

"I can assure Lady G. that her projection is too prominent for a low situation. The carving bestowed upon her is a plain indication that she is not to be laid at random, like a rubble stone in the building, merely to fill up a vacant space; but that a station is prepared for her at a great distance from the bottom, to which her dimensions are exactly proportioned, where God's workmanship will be displayed with more attractive grace, and where she will moreover escape many of those coarse and fretting rubs, to which, though *undeservedly*, yet, forgive me to say, she is at present, in some measure, *unnecessarily* exposed.

"I have not the smallest doubt that the all-wise, the all-gracious, and all-powerful Architect, who hath been pleased to form her for himself, to shew forth his praise, will in due time place her where she ought to be. That the time may be at hand, is the earnest wish and prayer of your Ladyship's faithful servant,

"ROBERT WALKER."

Both in her temporal and spiritual affairs, Lady Glenorchy commenced this year in circumstances which alternately depressed and comforted her. There was one event which in a peculiar manner perplexed and agitated her for a season, but which nevertheless at last terminated agreeably to her wishes. It is worthy of notice, that notwithstanding Lord Glenorchy's temper was peculiar and unpleasant, such was her influence over him, that there was no object of importance which she wished to gain, that she did not accomplish, and that too with his entire approbation. St Mary's Chapel had now been open ten months. The ministers of the Establishment refused to preach in it on account of the admission of Mr Wesley's preachers, who by no means pleased the taste of the people. A young clergyman of the Irish church, the Rev. Richard De Courcy, of the very ancient and noble family of Kingsale, a gentleman of very good talents, acquirements, and manners, and a very able preacher, was recommended by Miss Hill to Lady Glenorchy as a person well adapted to supply the place of domestic chaplain, and to preach in St Mary's Chapel. With Lord Glenorchy's consent, proposals were made to him to undertake these duties, which he accepted, and expressed his acceptance in the following well written terms:—

The Rev. Richard De Courcy to Lady Glenorchy.

" Madam,—I acknowledge, with many thanks, the honour of your Ladyship's letter transmitted to me by Miss Hill. Before its arrival, my mind was held in anxious suspense, concerning the path in which the Lord would have me to walk. For, upon the death of that eminent minister of Christ, and my honoured and dear friend, Mr Whitfield, proposals were made to me by his trustees to settle among his people in London. But as I had previously accepted your Ladyship's invitation to Scotland, and nothing remained to confirm my engagement but Lord Glenorchy's acquiescence in the matter, and as that circumstance has turned out favourably, I have put by the proposals of Mr Whitfield's trustees, clearly discerning that Providence concurred to point me, as with a sun-beam, to the north: and now, sensible of my extreme weakness, and entire dependance on infinite wisdom and strength, my heart ardently crieth to the Lord, " If thy presence go not with me, carry me not up hence." May your Ladyship find freedom of access to the throne of grace in my behalf, and often recommend me in your petitions to our common Saviour! and may the great Prophet of Israel point out to your Ladyship, and his most unworthy servant, such means as will prove most effectual to the spreading among all, the sweet savour of Jesus's precious name!

Nothing could yield me greater satisfaction than to find, that your Ladyship's sentiments and mine so perfectly harmonize respecting the non-essentials of Christianity. For, indeed, it is lamentable to see how the Church of Christ is rent by the party debates of bigotted professors, who, while contending for the shadow of religion, let go the substance; and it is equal matter of concern, to behold the Laodicean indifferency of some, who would be thought to contend for the faith once delivered to the saints, and who nevertheless suffer it, unconcerned, to be trampled under foot of every species of opposers to the truth as it is in Jesus. What, therefore, I humbly apprehend to be most difficult, especially for a minister of the gospel, is, to preserve a happy medium between an overheated zeal for the truth itself, and a remiss connivance at error. There are certain points which are of no more consequence to the fundamentals of Christianity, than the fringes annexed to the Israelites' garments under the law. These are not worth a moment's contention. But there are other particulars which affect the garments themselves, or rather that which they prefigured; I mean the robe of Christ's righteousness. Here, I humbly suppose, a minister is to exert all the gifts the Lord hath conferred on him, to the overthrow of every thing that stands in competition with the finished salvation of Emanuel. And yet, even upon this subject, as upon every other, I would desire to speak with all meekness of wisdom, long-suffering, and forbearance, well remembering what a long time it was, before my own ideas were adjusted on this momentous point; and while the Lord enables me to make faith in the Redeemer's righteousness the ground-work of all evangelical obedience, I hope I shall also inculcate those fruits of righteousness and true holiness, which are inseparably connected with that blessed operative principle, whereby the heart is more and more transformed into the lovely image of Jesus, and rendered a meet partaker of the inheritance of the saints in light. But being still deeply sensible of my ignorance, and how much I stand in need of being taught by all the Lord's people, I shall gladly receive instructions from your Ladyship.

On Monday the 31st instant, I shall (by divine permission) leave Shropshire; but am afraid I shall not be able to set out from London, for the north, sooner than the middle or close of January. However, your Ladyship shall know the day when I set out, and may be assured I will delay as short a time as possible.

In the mean time, praying the Lord abundantly to prosper this and every future effort of your Ladyship, to espouse the insulted but glorious cause of the despised Nazarene, I have the honour to be, with all respect, Madam, your Ladyship's most humble and most obedient servant, RICHARD DE COURCY."

When this arrangement became known, some ill-disposed person endeavoured to prejudice Lord Glenorchy's mind against Mr De Courcy, and to persuade him not to admit him into his house. This attempt, however, as is not unfrequently the case, produced an effect diametrically opposite to that which was intended. Of this a very interesting account will be seen in the following extracts from Lady Glenorchy's Diary, and in a note or two to Lady Maxwell.

Sunday, January 6. 1771.—I am ashamed when I look back upon the last week, to think how slothful I have been. Instead of making progress, I am on the decline; my spirits and health bad; my mind sorely distressed; I cannot get at any certainty about my state. Sometimes I think I believe, and at other times think I know nothing about religion. I am tossed to and fro with the different opinions concerning faith, and have been hurt by reasoning about it in my own mind, instead of actually believing in Jesus, which would at once put an end to my doubts and distresses.

Wednesday, January 9.—This day I mentioned my case to Mr T——, who said, that he had no doubt of my having been awakened by the Spirit of God, and having received faith; but that I still had not the abiding witness of the Spirit, which alone could give me constant peace, and establish my soul. That this I ought constantly to seek, and expect according to the promise.

Upon examining coolly the work of God upon my soul, I cannot but acknowledge that my heart is in some measure changed; my desires and affections are placed on spiritual things; almost every action of my life now proceeds from a desire to please God, and with a view to eternity; whereas, a few years ago, my views terminated in earthly grandeur, worldly applause, and pleasing myself. This change can be wrought only by faith of the operation of the Spirit of God. I will therefore acknowledge with gratitude thy mercy, O Lord, in bringing me forth from the captivity of sin, and renewing my nature by the Holy Ghost. This is the work of thy power; and thine be the glory for ever. Perfect the good work thou hast begun, and suffer me not again to doubt of thy love to my soul.

Sunday, January 13.—Upon a review of last week, I find that I have given way to a slothful inactive spirit, and have not been diligent in the Lord's work; yet, blessed be his name, I have come to some knowledge of my state, and now see somewhat of the meaning of last year's painful experience. The Lord is trying the faith he has given me. I have had outward trials and inward temptations; the use of means, without feeling comfort from them; cruel mockings from near and dear friends,—at times kindness shown me to allure me from the right path. Hitherto (through grace and strength imparted) I have stood unmoved. In my last illness I was tried with a careless and dead spirit, which seemed to me the greatest of all afflictions; but blessed be God, I believe all these things are working together for my good, and I will trust in the Lord that he will bring me out of the furnace purified from the dross of sin, and more alive to serve him. O my God, carry on thy work in my soul, in whatever way is most for thy glory and my complete salvation. Strengthen my faith, subdue my corruptions, quicken my soul more and more by thy Spirit, and grant me the comfortable assurance of thy love; and may that love constrain me to live every moment of my life to thy glory,—not seeking my own will, but to do the will of thee, my heavenly Father. Amen!

Monday, January 14.—This morning I resolved, through grace, to live this day to the Lord, and besought him to give me zeal and activity in his service. But, alas! upon review of the day I find nothing done. In the evening I was much tried by an outward cross—felt inclined to anger. My soul is distressed about an affair in which I do not see the path of duty plain. Lord, send forth thy light and truth to be my guide,—shew me thy will, and give me power and grace to comply with it!

Wednesday, January 16.—How shall I tell of the mercy of God my deliverer! O that my soul may never forget his goodness! When I was in trouble I cried unto him, and he answered me,—he delivered me speedily. This evening, after a severe trial, on account of the person I expect from England in two days as chaplain, and being told by Lord G—— that he should not be permitted to enter the house, I went to prayer and cried to the Lord for help. Before I got from my knees, Lord G—— came to my door and asked admittance;—with fear and trembling I opened it. He came in and threw a letter upon the table, and bade me read it. It was an anonymous letter, informing him of some circumstances relating to Mr De Courcy, which tended to exasperate him more, and seemed written with a view to make dispeace in the family. My heart sunk within me when I read it. I stood in silent suspense, expecting the storm to burst with redoubled violence, when to my unspeakable surprise he said, "I now see that I have been the tool of Satan, when I opposed the coming of Mr De C——; this letter shows it me,—here the cloven foot appears; but the writer of it shall be disappointed, for I shall not only receive him into my house, but do every thing in my power to encourage him in his work, and will countenance him myself." O how wonderful is the way of the Lord to bring about the desire of his people, by those things that seem most opposite and unlikely to effect it! How clearly does his hand appear in thus interposing in the time of my extremity! O that my heart may ever retain the sentiments of love and gratitude, which so singular a providence in my favour ought to inspire!

Thursday, January 17.—I went this morning to visit a poor dying woman,—got power to speak to her, and to encourage her to trust in the Lord. She was in great pain, and had lost clear views of Christ. She complained of not being able to pray, or to attend to prayer, and said, " O, it is a great thing to be a Christian." I was much affected with her distress, and could with pleasure have attended her all day. I saw it was a privilege and duty to visit the sick.

Saturday, January 19.—Lord B—— very ill. I sent and begged the prayers of the faithful for him; got liberty in prayer for him myself. Received a letter from Mr G——, in the name of the majority of the Tottenham Court congregation, begging me, for the sake of the general interest of religion, to relieve Mr De Courcy from his engagement to come to Scotland. Lord direct me to do what is most for thy glory. Thou knowest this is what I wish to promote. O send forth thy light and truth to guide me!

Sunday, January 20.—Not well in body, and much oppressed in mind. I heard a good sermon to-day on the doctrine of election, to which I heartily assented—the arguments were unanswerable: I cannot but regret that any oppose this Scripture doctrine. I heard another good sermon in the afternoon, to which my mind assented; but, alas! my heart was dead. In the evening, after much wrestling with a cold lukewarm heart, I at length got access in prayer, and was pouring out my soul before God with some liberty, when I was interrupted. But blessed be God for the few minutes I enjoyed in prayer. Lord, I am not worthy of the least of thy mercies!

Wednesday, January 23.—This day I will endeavour, in the strength of the Lord, to set out afresh to run in his ways. Lord, thou knowest I can do nothing of myself. Give me strength, I beseech thee, to do this. O let thy whole will take place in me!

Since writing the above this morning, the Lord has graciously enabled me to visit a poor sick person, and opened my mouth to speak and to pray with her beyond expectation. O that I could praise him for his goodness, in hearing my cry, stirring me up to more diligence, and awakening in me again the desire of living in all his commandments! Glory be to thee, O Lord, for ever and ever!

Thursday, January 24.—I got up early this morning, and felt comfort in drawing near to God. I found time to write a letter to a poor sinner, and to speak to two women about their souls. I went in the evening to Mr Walker's, who spoke from Romans viii. 30. "Moreover whom he did predestinate, them he also called; and whom he called, them he also justified; and whom he justified, them he also glorified." I got a sight of my great darkness and ignorance, and was humbled under it. The Lord graciously interposed in my behalf upon my coming home, and saved me from a trial. Glory be to his name!

Friday, January 25.—I got up this morning in a very dead frame. After breakfast I went out, in hopes of meeting with some poor person to whom I might be of use. After walking some time I met with a poor man, who was carrying his two little sick children to give them the air. I asked him some questions, and found he was an experienced Christian; upon which I walked some time with him, and found his conversation very profitable. He seemed perfectly happy and contented, notwithstanding his great poverty, having Christ for his portion; and it was with difficulty I could persuade him to take the small sum I then had in my pocket.

This evening I was refreshed by receiving letters from Lady H—— and Hiss Hill; and must here remark, that the Lord in his providence gave me an answer to prayer this afternoon. And I do not remember that I ever applied to him in any difficulty, and trusted in him for help, that he did not hear, and bring the matter about in the best way for me. Glory be to his name for this! Wherefore do I ever doubt?

Saturday, January 26.—This evening a dreadful fire broke out in town—it is an awful sight. Lord, help us to make the suitable improvement of it! If this is so terrible, how should I haste to escape from those flames which shall endure throughout eternity! Three people perished in the ruins. O Lord, make us thankful for thy preserving mercy!

Sunday, January 27.—I got freedom to pray to the Lord for faith, and for his presence in the sanctuary. I heard a good sermon, and in some measure felt it. I went and saw the fire. I afterwards went to Lady Maxwell's, where we joined in prayer; and I unburdened my mind to her, and was refreshed. O what a comfort is a faithful friend in distress—how often have I seen the goodness of the Lord in strengthening and supporting me by her means! When I came home I got power to speak freely upon the most important truths of the gospel at table, and felt nothing of the false shame that used to assault me on such occasions. This evening I am very dull, and have been cold and dry in prayer; but I am not well in body, which may be the cause. I will therefore lay me down in peace, and quietly trust in the Lord Jesus, who is my wisdom, righteousness, sanctification and redemption. He knows my heart, that I would do his will; that my desire is to know him, to love him, and to serve him with my whole soul.

Monday, January 28.—This evening I felt somewhat like a slight stroke of the palsy in my tongue and side. Blessed be God, the fear of death, and what is worse, a useless life, is in a great measure taken away, and I can submit to the will of God without murmuring. When I got to my room, I fell down before him, acknowledging myself to be his creature in every sense, and besought him to do with my soul and body whatever was most for his glory. Blessed God, I thank thee for preserving me hitherto from the evils my sins have deserved! If thou shalt see good to prolong my life and the use of my faculties, let them be employed more faithfully in thy service than they ever yet have been. Let my whole soul, body, and spirit, be devoted to thee in time and eternity.

Tuesday, January 29.—The Lord has been pleased to add another day to my life, and has enabled me to arise betimes this morning, to dedicate myself afresh to his service; after which I went out to visit the sick, and have spent the day in endeavours to be useful to the souls of others. I have found the good effects of the warning I got last night; it has left a serious impression upon my mind of the certainty of an approaching eternity. I see more of the importance of securing an interest in Christ, and of living every moment to his glory. Lord, enable me to walk before thee with an upright heart all the days of my life!

Wednesday, January 30.—This morning I was waked by a loud clap of thunder, which caused me to arise and fall upon my knees before God, to be in readiness in case he should call me away. I had little comfort in prayer, being sorely tempted with wandering thoughts; but after breakfast I got a clear sight of the beauty of holiness in heart and life, and hungered and thirsted after perfect conformity to God. I besought him to make me wholly his in soul, body, and spirit. I went out to see Lady Maxwell, and had much comfort in talking with her, and in prayer with her, and felt a union of heart with her that I experience with few. I have had some opportunities of speaking for God to-day; but have cause to blush for my silence this evening in a company of gay people. Lord, give me power to be faithful to thee at all times!

Thursday, January 31.—This morning I wrote down some heads of examination for every evening; but, alas! upon reviewing them at night, what cause have I to be ashamed! I cannot with a safe conscience answer them. I have at best done nothing this day; and as an idle unprofitable servant, must beg for mercy through the blood of Jesus. I have endeavoured to speak to God; but my lips were sealed. O Lord, how unfit am I for thy kingdom! O grant unto me more faith, more life, more love, and cover me with thy robe of righteousness, that I may stand complete in thee in the sight of a pure and holy God.

Saturday, February 2.—This morning I felt great longings after Christ; my soul sought him, and eagerly thirsted for his salvation. I was convinced of sin, and saw more than usual of my vile heart; but the latter part of the day I have been idle, and done nothing to purpose. O when shall I live wholly to God!

Lady Glenorchy to Lady Maxwell.

" *February* 5. 1771.

" My dear Madam,—I hope you are well. I would have called on you this day, had it not been so damp, as I am far from being well, and wish to keep from getting more cold, for fear of not getting to the Canongate Church on Sunday; and this would be a great disappointment to me, for my soul hungers and thirsts for this ordinance; and the Lord's words come often to my mind, " With desire I have desired to eat this passover with you, before I suffer." I think it is possibly the last opportunity I may have. O that the Lord would make it a sealing time to his own children; and if it was his will to take me to himself, I think I could willingly at this time leave the world. No word yet of Mr De Courcy, nor any farther intelligence of Veritas. Lord Glenorchy suspects he has also written to Mr De C——, to frighten him from coming to the family; and this is not improbable. I have many uneasy thoughts about this same Veritas; but I will endeavour to wait on the Lord,—very animating indeed are the promises to him that overcometh. Alas! I am overcome of every thing—I sink under a load of uneasy thoughts. I am ignorant, blind, and helpless; sick in mind and body. All that I know is, that I ought not to trouble you with my distresses—you have your own portion to bear. I will, if the Lord enables me, endeavour for the future to speak no more of myself, except to God. If you can, remember me in your prayers. I am, in all situations and in all frames, my dear Madam, your obliged and affectionate,

W. G."

Thursday, February 7.—I rejoice in the view of the approaching ordinance, and went to church this day in hopes of a blessing; but all I heard seemed to make against me. When the minister spoke of an over-zeal, I thought the word was pointed at me. When he spoke to sleepers and carnal secure sinners, I felt as if I were the person meant. I resolved to keep this day by fasting, but my body was so feeble that I could not do it. My ideas are so broken and dissipated, that I can neither pray, read, or meditate with attention. O Lord, thou knowest all my thoughts and my ways—nothing is hid from thee. Give me that faith, love, and strength, which thou seest I stand in need of, and quicken my soul. Grant me the victory over all that opposeth my union with thee. Thy love is all I desire;—take from me whatever standeth in the way, and make me what thou wouldst have me to be, for thine own name's sake.

Friday, February 8.—This morning I heard an excellent sermon from Mr Walker, upon these words, "Wait upon God continually;" but my soul was dead, and it did not come with power to me. I had not the understanding heart.

Sunday, February 10.—This morning I got up early to call upon the Lord, and to seek his blessing this day at the sacrament. My spirits were composed, and my heart trusted in the Lord. I did not feel much joy while at the table, but was enabled to act faith on the righteousness of Christ, and commit my soul to him; and at coming away I felt much peace, joy, and delight in the Lord. I longed to praise him, and saw something of his unspeakable love in dying for sinners; and though I had not the full assurance of faith, nor any particular testimony from the Lord of his acceptance of me, yet I had a firm persuasion of my calling, and that he would perfect the work he had begun in me. I saw myself far from the mark, but at the same time that I had begun the race; and I looked to Jesus to draw me on, and give me strength to finish my course with joy. I had much delight in singing his praises. Upon the whole, this has been the most comfortable communion I have had since the twentieth of May last. Blessed be the Lord, for refreshing my weary soul in this wilderness! O that I may never forget his mercies, but may go on from strength to strength, till I appear before him in Zion! I have been assaulted to-day by suggestions of different kinds, particularly by doubting whether the peace I enjoyed was not a false peace; but I got rid of them by looking to the Lord, and begging of him to keep me from temptation. I cannot think my peace is false. *First*, because I now have lower thoughts of myself than I had before: I see that I am not worthy the name of a Christian. *Secondly*, I have a desire to pray, and resolve to spend more time in that delightful exercise than formerly. *Thirdly*, I feel more desire to confess Christ before men. *Fourthly*, I am more watchful over my heart, and more upon my guard, knowing how easily I am led away. *Fifthly*, I see my strength lieth only in Christ, and that it is by cleaving to him, and looking to him continually, that I can only hope for safety. *Sixthly*, That my peace proceedeth from seeing more of the love of God, in the sacrifice of his Son, than usual, and my heart in consequence thereof being drawn out to more confidence in him.

Monday, February 11.—This morning my soul was in a very dead frame, but I found some life in talking with a Christian. I went to church, and heard without feeling the word. Came home convinced of sin,—went to prayer, and got some comfort in pouring out my heart to God. I felt strengthened, and was enabled to confess Christ at table, and to speak boldly for him.

Tuesday, February 12.—I passed most of this day in great uneasiness from the fear of man. Mr De C. was expected, and I did not know how he would be received. I sought the Lord by groans that could not be uttered. Wonderfully has he helped me, and stengthened me in my soul. All things have turned out favourably. O, to have ever a single eye in all things to his glory!

Lady Glenorchy to Lady Maxwell.

"My dear Madam,—Mr De Courcy arrived here this evening, and I have had a great deal of private conversation with him. He is quite the person Mr Wesley represented him, of a sweet disposition, and wishes only to preach Christ to poor sinners, wherever he finds an open door. I have not as yet got an answer from Mr H., but I have, by a letter received from another quarter, some reason to think it very possible that cruel letter came from a different person,—I would gladly hope so. Beg of the Lord to direct us how to proceed with respect to St Mary's Chapel. We are poor blind creatures,—much need we have of wisdom from above; but the Lord is gracious, he surely will not forsake those who put their trust in him. I will endeavour to call upon you, and bring Mr De C. with me, to-morrow morning.—Yours affectionately. W. G."

"*Tuesday*, 10 *o'clock*."

Wednesday, February 13.—Mr De Courcy began to-day to expound in the family,—the word seemed accompanied with power. I have been all day in great darkness. Satan seems to have set all his forces in array against me. But in the name of the Lord I trust, he will be put to flight.

CHAPTER X.

Lady Glenorchy gives up all connexion with Mr Wesley's preachers—Letters from Mr Wesley to Lady Maxwell on this subject—Lady Glenorchy's separation from the Methodists affects Lady Maxwell, but does not interrupt their mutual friendship—Extracts from Diary from February 14. to March 4. 1771—Letter from Lady Glenorchy to Lady Maxwell—Diary continued from April 6. to May 26. 1771—Letter from Lady Glenorchy to Lady Maxwell—Diary continued—Lady Glenorchy goes to Taymouth—Extracts from Diary from July 7. to September 15. 1771—Lord and Lady Glenorchy leave Taymouth, and arrive at Barnton—Lord Glenorchy's sickness and death—Extracts from Diary from September 21. to November 24. 1771—Lord Glenorchy's funeral—Will—Generous act of Lord Breadalbane—Lady Glenorchy has a severe attack of fever—Extracts from Diary from February 12. to March 15. 1772.

For some weeks Mr De Courcy officiated in conjunction with Mr Wesley's preachers with great acceptance. Being, however, a decided Calvinist, the strain of his discourses must have been very different from theirs; so much so, indeed, does this appear to have been the case, that even Mr Wesley found himself called upon to disapprove of the open and pointed manner in which one of his preachers had impugned some Calvinistical points. This incongruity of doctrines was, as might have been expected, very unpleasant, and in fact injurious to Lady Glenorchy, and determined her to give up entirely all connexion with Mr Wesley's preachers. The sagacity of Mr Wesley had foreseen this, and in two letters, not written perhaps in the very best temper, he endeavoured to prepare the mind of Lady Maxwell for the event.

The Rev. Mr John Wesley to Lady Maxwell.

" *London, January* 24. 1771.

" My dear Lady,—Although Mr M'Nab is quite clear as to justification by faith, and is in general a sound and good preacher, yet I fear he is not clear of blame in this. He is too warm and impatient of contradiction, otherwise he must be lost to all common sense, to preach against final perseverance in Scotland. From the first hour that I entered the kingdom, it was a sacred rule with me, never to preach on any controverted point—at least not in a controversial way. Any one may see, that this is only to put a sword into our enemies' hands. It is the direct way to increase all their prejudices, and to make all our labours fruitless. You will shortly have a trial of another kind. Mr De Courcy purposes to set out for Edinburgh in a few days. He was from a child a member of one of our societies in the south of Ireland. There he received remission of sins, and was for some time groaning for full redemption. But when he came to Dublin, the Philistines were upon him, and soon prevailed over him. Quickly he was convinced, that 'there is no perfection,' and that 'all things depend on absolute unchangeable decrees.' At first he was exceeding warm upon these heads: now he is far more calm. His natural temper, I think, is good: he is open, friendly, and generous. He has also a good understanding, and is not unacquainted with learning, though not deeply versed therein. He has no disagreeable person, a pleasing address, and is a lively as well as a sensible preacher. Now, when you add to this, that he is quite new, and very young, you may judge how he will be admired and caressed! 'Surely such a preacher as this never was in Edinburgh before! Mr Whitefield himself was not to compare with him! What an angel of a man!' Now, how will a raw inexperienced youth be able to encounter this? If there be not the greatest of miracles to preserve him, will it not turn his brain? And may he not then do far more hurt than either Mr W—— or Mr T—— did? Will he not soon prevent your friend from 'going on to perfection,' or thinking of any such thing? Nay, may he not shake you also? He would; but that the God whom you serve is able to deliver you. At present, indeed, he is in an exceeding loving spirit. But will that continue long? There will be danger on the one hand if it does; there will be danger on the other if it does not. It does not appear that any great change has been wrought in our neighbours by Mr Wh——'s death. He had fixed the prejudice so deep, that even he himself was not able to remove it; yet our congregations have increased exceedingly, and the work of God increases on every side. I am glad you use more exercise. It is good both for body and soul. As soon as Mr De Courcy is come, I shall be glad to hear how the prospect opens. You will then need a larger share of the wisdom from above; and I trust you will write with all openness to, my dear Lady, your ever affectionate servant,

"JOHN WESLEY."

The Rev. Mr John Wesley to Lady Maxwell.

"*February* 26. 1771.

"My dear Lady,—I cannot but think the chief reason of the little good done by our preachers at Edinburgh, is the opposition which has been made by the ministers of Edinburgh, as well as by the false brethren from England. These steeled the hearts of the people against all the good impressions which might otherwise have been made, so that the same preachers by whom God has constantly wrought, not only in various parts of England, but likewise in the northern parts of Scotland, were in Edinburgh only not useless. They felt a damp upon their own spirits; they had not their usual liberty of speech; and the word they spoke seemed to rebound upon them, and not to sink into the hearts of the hearers. At my first coming I usually find something of this myself; but the second or third time of preaching, it is gone; and I feel, greater is He that is with us, than all the powers of earth and hell.

"If any one could show you, by plain Scripture and reason, a more excellent way than that you have received, you certainly would do well to receive it; and, I trust, I should do the same. But I think it will not be easy for any one to show us, either that Christ did not die for all, or that he is not willing as well as able to cleanse from all sin, even in the present world. If your steady adherence to these great truths be termed bigotry, yet you have no need to be ashamed. You are reproached for Christ's sake, and the Spirit of glory and of Christ shall rest upon you. Perhaps our Lord may use you to soften some of the harsh spirits, and to preserve Lady G——, or Mr De Courcy from being hurt by them. I hope to hear from you, (on whom I can depend), a frequent account of what is done near you. After you have suffered a while, may God stablish, strengthen, settle you. I am, my dear Lady, your very affectionate servant,

"JOHN WESLEY."

Lady Glenorchy, being fully aware how deeply the step she was about to take would affect Lady Maxwell, it was not till after many struggles and prayers, and then only by degrees, that she communicated to her Ladyship her intentions.

Lady Maxwell, as might be expected, was deeply affected by the communication, and it required some little time to recover from the surprise and pain which it occasioned her. Lady Glenorchy, by the prudent and cautious manner in which she finally made the separation, wisely and kindly prepared the way for this recovery. And it does infinite credit to the characters and memory of both, that what between ordinary persons would most probably have made an everlasting breach of friendship, did not divide them for an hour, and that during the whole of Lady Glenorchy's life, there never, on any occasion, appeared even the shadow of a variance between them. The extracts from the Diary and the letters which are now to follow, among other interesting occurrences in her Christian experience, give an account of this very trying event.

Thursday, February 14.—My temptations and unbelief are still strong. My soul is in great distress. How grievous is my ingratitude to the Lord, who, in answer to prayer, has sent Mr De C——; and yet, instead of rejoicing, I am discouraged and distressed more than usual.

Friday, February 15.—This day I have often prostrated myself at a throne of grace, yet feel nothing but darkness and wretchedness in myself, and no clear views of God. This evening Mr De C—— began preaching at my chapel; his prayers and sermon were good: towards the end my heart began to thaw a little. I endeavoured to humble myself before the Lord, and say, Thy will be done.

Saturday, February 16.—The Lord has given me more hope to-day concerning Mr De C——. This evening Lord G—— went with me to the chapel, and heard Mr T——.

Sunday, February 17.—This morning I went to church, and was much refreshed with the sermon. Afterwards heard Mr De C—— at my chapel, where many were deeply affected—some wept bitterly. My own heart was very full, particularly in the last prayer. The Lord was with us of a truth. In the evening had preaching in the great drawing-room to about forty people.

Thursday, February 21.—Mr De C—— preached again yesterday to a crowded auditory, some of whom seemed melted under the word. This day his exhortation in the family came with power to my soul. I was convinced of sin, particularly of hypocrisy. I see my need of Jesus. O what a sight have I got of my own heart this day!

Friday, February 22.—This day I am confined by pain and sickness. The Lord has shown me that I had need of it, and enabled me to say, Lord, what thou wilt, how thou wilt, and when thou wilt! I see his loving kindness in sending the rod; O that it may be abundantly sanctified!

Sunday, February 24.—I heard Mr Walker in the morning, but felt no life in my soul, and saw all around me as if they were dry bones. I was in anguish of spirit during the morning service, from a sense of our great deadness,—our distance from God,—our ingratitude to him,—and our want of spiritual life. In the evening I was refreshed by a lively discourse from Mr De C—— on these words, "One faith." Gracious God! work in my inmost soul that one faith which I have heard described to-night, and unite me so effectually to thee, that neither the world, the flesh, nor the devil, may ever be able to separate me from thee.

Monday, February 25.—This morning I found access in prayer, and was enabled to come to the Lord Jesus, and to put myself into his hands, and commit all my ways to him. I have found more peace to-day than usual. I begged of the Lord to open some door of more extensive usefulness to Mr De C——, and this afternoon I received an invitation for him to preach in the Castle. I have had another remarkable answer in prayer this day also in a temporal affair. O that my hard heart were melted into love and gratitude for all the repeated mercies of the Lord! This is thy work, O Lord. Give me, I beseech thee, a grateful heart, and open my mouth that I may show forth thy praise.

Thursday, March 14.—It hath pleased the Lord for a fortnight past to lay me aside, and to try me in soul and body in various ways. On the day in which I met with the accident that now confines me, I was much oppressed in spirit, and wished that the Lord would take me out of the world. But he has shown me since, that he can deliver me from some of my trials in a different way. I can perceive his love in the present dispensation,—thereby bringing my will into submission to his, showing me the pride, impatience, self-will, and vanity of my heart, and bringing off from dependance on the creature, and the outward means of grace, in order that I may receive every blessing when and how he sees meet to bestow it. I have seen more than ever my own helplessness, and have been led to seek for the righteousness freely imputed to us through faith. My former views of this doctrine of imputed righteousness have been restored, and my peace revives in proportion to my views of this blessed truth. O that the Lord would now establish and settle me in the true faith, and not suffer men or devils to shake my confidence in Jesus, as the Lord our righteousness!

About this time Lady Glenorchy wrote the following letter to Lady Maxwell:—

Lady Glenorchy to Lady Maxwell.

"My dear Madam,—It gave me great concern to hear of your illness. I really grow uneasy at your many colds and headachs, and fear you do not take that care of your health which it is the duty of all to do. I am persuaded also that your mind is uneasy, and that this affects your body; and if it did not appear like prying into other people's affairs, I would ask you what distresses you, knowing how often I have felt relief from unbosoming myself to you. But not being naturally inquisitive, and seeing your great reserve with me in what concerns yourself, I have never ventured to inquire into the nature of your trials, although I feel much for you, and would willingly help to bear your burdens. So very different is my temper in this respect to yours, that I cannot be easy till I open my heart to you on a subject upon which we now misunderstand each other. You think I am prejudiced against the Methodists. Against some of them I own I am, although my sentiments do not deserve the name of prejudice, being the result of matters of fact; and I wish much to see you, to shew you the cause of what I now say. You are as much concerned, my dear Madam, as I am in what relates to the glory of God, and the advancement of his kingdom upon earth; you will, I am certain, therefore, agree with me in sentiment, if you are as free of prejudice as I am at this moment. All I beg of you is to examine coolly what I shall shew you, and then tell me what you think I should do; and in order to this, I must beg, if you are able, that you will come and see me some day at four o'clock, as that is the only time I can be sure of seeing you alone; and if you will appoint the day, I will forbid any body to disturb us. Send me word how soon. And believe me yours affectionately,

"W. G."

April 6.—Severe and various have been my trials since the fourteenth of March; but one has been predominant. I have struggled with it in vain, and groaned all the day in the bitterness of my soul. I have been harassed by company, and got little leisure for prayer and meditation, but on Sundays. This day the Lord has been shewing me my backslidings. When confessing them before him this morning, Peter's fall came to my mind. I prayed that the Lord would look upon me, that I might be made sensible of my sin, and mourn for it. I continued wrestling with many cries and tears till he gave me access to him, and enabled me to make a full surrender of myself to him. I besought him to take from me (if necessary) health, fortune, friends, name, reputation, every comfort under the sun, even life itself, so that I might enjoy the consolation of knowing that he loved me, and never would forsake me. After this I went to the chapel; but how was my heart overwhelmed when Mr De C—— took for his text, "And the Lord turned and looked upon Peter." The whole sermon seemed to be a message from the Lord to my soul. O that the impression thereof may never be effaced! May I this day return to him who is willing to heal my backslidings, and to love me, even *me*, freely. Blessed Jesus, turn thou me, cause thy gracious face to shine upon me, so shall I be saved!

Sunday, April 13.—Blessed be the Lord for all his mercies! He has heard my cry, and revived his work in my soul. My heart and affections have been drawn out towards him throughout this last week, particularly for three days past. For some days I was in great trouble of mind, and set apart some time for seeking the Lord. It was then he removed my distress, and gave me liberty to pour out my soul in prayer. O that I may now go on striving against sin, looking unto Jesus to bring me off more than conqueror! I feel my weakness, and the need I have of supplies of grace moment by moment. Lord, help thy poor weak creature! Unto thee I commit my soul; preserve it from the rage of thine enemies, and clothe it with thy righteousness, then shall I never be ashamed.

Sunday, April 20.—The Lord has been pleased to refresh my soul by his word through the last week and this day. I hope he is establishing me more in the truth; shewing me every day more and more of the deep depravity of my heart, and of the fulness there is in Christ to supply my every need.

Saturday, April 26.—Every day I see more of the love of God, and of my own unworthiness. He enables me to pour out my heart before him, to plead his promises, and to cast my soul on the Lord Jesus for righteousness and strength. Yet still I have not clear views of him. The veil is still on my heart, and the scales on my eyes. I have not that testimony of his love to my soul which I ardently long for. O Jesus, wherefore dost thou hide thy face from me? O think upon me, and refresh my poor languishing spirit!

Sunday, May 5.—For some days past I have enjoyed much peace, and a sweet hope of attaining establishment in the faith. I begin to see my interest in Christ from the light I receive in reading and hearing his word. I see there is no condemnation to them that are in Christ Jesus; and from Scripture marks I can perceive that I have received him as my Saviour. This morning I was much comforted in reading Shepherd's Sound Believer. He answers an objection that has long kept me from comfort. I now see that it is not presumption to believe, but the bounden duty of every one who hears the gospel. The Lord hath given us two commandments in the new dispensation; which are, to believe in the Lord Jesus Christ for eternal life, and to love the brethren. These are equally binding upon all who hear them; and none ever thought it presumption to obey the latter. Ashamed of my past unbelief, I now ventured to obey this sweet command; and my soul was filled with peace and joy in believing. I could not refrain from crying out for some time together, Jesus is mine, and I am his! I saw that nothing but unbelief could prevent my happiness. My joy was exceeding great. I felt that I did believe. Lord, increase my faith; and suffer not the enemy to rob me of thy peace!

Wednesday, May 15.—I received this day accounts of the death of a very dear friend. Felt much reluctance to submit to the will of God, and could perceive two natures struggling within me: One saying, Wherefore didst thou do it? The other, The Lord does all things well.

Saturday, May 18.—This morning I have discovered many evils in my heart, particularly a legal spirit resting in the performance of duties, &c. A dream I had in the night was of use in discovering something of this, and causing me to examine myself more strictly. O blessed Jesus, bring me more and more out of self, and off from all dependance on any thing I have done, or can do! I would disclaim all, and beseech thee to pardon the sins of my holiest duties. O let thy glorious self be ever my object in view! to be found in thee, lost in thee, and nothing in myself!

Sunday, May 26.—This has been a comfortable Sabbath. I have had a sight of my backslidings, and felt a desire to return to the Lord. My soul thirsted for God. I have had access in prayer, and been enabled to see his work on my soul, and made to hope in his word.

At this time Lady Glenorchy wrote to Lady Maxwell the following letter:—

Lady Glenorchy to Lady Maxwell.

" *Wednesday Evening.*

" My dear Madam,—Your letter gives me real pleasure, as it affords me some hopes, that you will not wholly withdraw from me that friendship which I hitherto have, and do still esteem a singular blessing. The taking any step which endangered my losing it, was the greatest act of self-denial to me; and I do not think any thing less than the clear conviction I have for some time had of the propriety of it, could have supported me under the struggles I felt between the desire of your approbation, and what I thought duty to the cause in which I am engaged. I am sorry if I have offended you by saying, 'We boasted too much of a Catholic spirit.' I know that I have found fault with others for being too narrow-minded, whom I now see acted from more knowledge of the religious world than I had; and I am not ashamed to acknowledge, that I have in many things acted too hastily, and judged rashly. I hope the Lord will preserve me from this for the future. By what I have done, I would not have it supposed that I do not think the Methodists the people of God—Far be this from me; I only think they do not all preach pure doctrine, and therefore I would not have all of them to preach in my chapel, else I should frustrate my intention in opening it. Though I desire to have it open to every sect and denomination, yet there is but one doctrine I would have taught there,—and it is this and this alone which obliges me to do what I have done. If I have erred, I pray God forgive me, and I trust he will, as it is, I hope, more from ignorance of his will, than a rebellious spirit. I have now to beg once more, my dear Madam, that you will continue me some share of your friendship and prayers. This last you are bound to do as a Christian, if you think me out of the way of truth. I feel that I am very ignorant, weak, and helpless; and it is my desire that the will of God may be done in me and by me at all times. Help me then, by your prayers, to obtain more strength, and knowledge of the Lord Jesus; and I also beg, that you will write to me as often as you can, and say whatever you think may tend to stir me up to more diligence in the work of the Lord, or keep me from that spiritual slumber to which my heart is very prone. I shall not have time to call on you before I set out for Taymouth. I pray that the Lord may bless you with every spiritual blessing, and return a hundred-fold all the prayers and good offices you have bestowed on your most obliged and affectionate friend and servant, W. G."

Wednesday, May 29.—The Lord has shewn me many evils in my heart this evening; and, blessed be his name, he has imbittered sin unto me, by causing my backslidings to reprove me. He has made the creature as thorns in my flesh, and shewn me the folly of overvaluing it. O that I may learn wisdom, and no longer hew out unto myself broken cisterns, but cleave unto the Lord only, who is my best friend, my only real comforter! O that I may from this moment give up my whole heart to him, and seek no other portion! I am distressed and oppressed on every side. All seems against me, but I will still trust in the Lord. O that I knew his will, that I could hear his voice saying, This is the way, walk ye in it. Lord, thou only knowest my troubles; they are various and complicated, and greatly increased by a sinful heart. But what is this great mountain before thee? Speak the word, and it shall become a plain. What is this tempestuous ocean, that threatens to swallow me up? Say unto it, Be still, and there shall be a calm. O blessed Jesus, speak thou unto my perplexed afflicted soul, and say, Peace, be still. O bring my will into perfect submission to thine. My perverse nature shrinks back from the cross, even though I know that thou hast commanded me to take it up. But if thou wilt give me patience and strength, then, Lord, I will bear it after thee with joy. O heal the diseases of my soul, pour balm into the wounds which sin hath made; then shall I run with alacrity and joy the way of thy commandments!

Taymouth, June 28.—Before I left Edinburgh, I dismissed Mr Wesley's preachers from my chapel, as, from some writings of Mr Wesley which fell into my hands, and from the sentiments of some of his preachers of late officiating there, I found they held doctrines that appear to be erroneous. *First*, They deny the doctrines of imputed righteousness, election, and the saints' perseverance, which I think are clearly revealed in Scripture. *Secondly*, I found that none of our gospel ministers would preach in the chapel, if they continued to have the use of the pulpit; so that, by receiving them, I should exclude those who were sound in the faith, and thereby frustrate the end I had in view in opening the chapel, which was to have all who preached pure evangelical doctrine to preach there, of any sect or denomination whatsoever. *Thirdly*, I found by experience that my own soul had been hurt, and kept from establishment in the faith, by hearing some of the preachers, and I judged that others might be hurt by them also.

The consequence of this step has been, that all the Methodists have bitterly cried out against Mr De C. whom they suppose to have been the cause of my conduct, and my friend ——— has almost given up connexion with me. The Lord, I trust, will shew her their errors. Upon considering what I have done, I feel satisfied with it, and the manner in which I did it; which was by shutting up the chapel upon my leaving town. I bless God for not permitting me to join their party when they urged it.

Since my arrival here, my soul has been at times in very deep distress; but last Thursday these words repeatedly came to my mind, "Though he were a son, yet learnt he obedience by the things that he suffered." Upon considering the import of them, the snare was broken. I saw that I might be a child of God notwithstanding my present temptation,—my mind was set at liberty, and my heart encouraged to go on trusting in the Lord. I have since that time felt power given me over my corruptions, and have been enabled to speak for the Lord, and to him, before others;—he again draws out my affections towards him. O that I may never more depart from him.

Tuesday, July 2.—This morning the Lord permitted me to draw near unto him in prayer, and to wrestle for a blessing. He made me willing to give up all for Christ. I besought him to take from me every thing, however pleasing, that kept me from being wholly his; and if I was unwilling to part with it, to tear it forcibly from my heart, whatever pain it might cost me, if so I might obtain the assurance of his everlasting love to my soul. This day I wrote out a description of saving knowledge from Brooks, and prayed over it, which I found of use. The Lord has, in some measure, I trust, caused this divine light to shine into my soul, by which I see the sins of the heart, and the all-sufficiency of Jesus to heal and save sinners. I hunger and thirst for more of this divine knowledge. The desire of my heart is, O that I might know him, and the power of his resurrection!—Ignorance and want of love to Christ are my greatest grief, and occasion many doubts and fears respecting my state, lest I should still be unregenerate, deceiving myself and others—Lord, thou knowest!

Lady Glenorchy, as the reader would perceive from her Diary, went to Taymouth this year in June, and remained there till near the end of September. Nothing very remarkable took place during this period in her external circumstances; but it was the last time she was to preside there in her own right. With respect to the state of her mind, although she still complained much of fears, and was dissatisfied with herself, yet she admits that she was more established in the truth, and enjoyed more comfort, and sometimes rose to a happy assurance of the soundness of her state before God, and her acceptance with him, which appears by her Diary from the 7th of July to the 15th of September.

Sunday, July 7.—Glory be to God for the mercies of last week. He has opened up unto me a living way to the throne of his grace, and frequently enabled me to pour out my heart before him. He has shewn me my past errors and backslidings, and also that he has wounded and he will heal me. This morning I had much freedom of access to him, and gave myself wholly up unto him as a living sacrifice, committing all my ways and making known all my wants to him; laying hold of Jesus as my Saviour, in his threefold offices; resolving in his strength to follow him at all events; giving up all unreservedly for his name's sake. I took the angels, and all the host of heaven, and all creation, to witness that I belonged to Jesus, and accepted of him as he is offered in the word, and desired no other portion in time and eternity; and I now confirm with my pen what I then did most solemnly affirm with my tongue: And do thou, O most blessed and merciful Lord God, ratify it in heaven, and remember me thy poor, helpless, sinful creature, when thou comest to judge the world! Let me then have cause to bless this day in which thou didst make me willing by thy power to devote myself wholly to thee. I now desire hereby to protest against Satan and all his works, to renounce the devil, the world, and the flesh, not in my own strength, but trusting that by faith in thee I shall come off more than conqueror. I do humbly beseech thee to keep me from their snares, and suffer not sin to gain dominion over me. Grant me the whole armour of God, that I may fight the good fight of faith, and finish my course with joy. May I live to thine honour here, and be translated to thy glory hereafter, through the alone merits of Jesus! This is all I ask.—If thou seest fit to take from me all earthly comforts, grant me but the assurance of thy love and the graces of thy Spirit, and I am content, as witness my hand, this 7th day of July 1771. W. G.

Monday, July 8.—Yesterday was a day much to be remembered by my soul. During the whole course of it my heart was drawn out almost continually in prayer. This day I have not felt so much comfort in my soul as yesterday; but still I feel deeply convinced of future and eternal things, and have a relish for spiritual duties. My soul is more dead to the applause of the world, and I long for greater degrees of holiness and conformity to the image of Christ. I am sensible that our peace and comfort will be in proportion as we walk closely with God, reading his word, and watching unto prayer.

Thursday, July 11.—The Lord has been pleased to bless the reading of Dr Owen's treatise on Spiritual Mindedness, to my soul; and shewn me from it how far short I yet am from the temper and frame of mind to which every Christian ought to aspire. My soul has been stirred up to vehement longings for more of the image of Christ, for greater deadness to the world, and I have been more watchful over my thoughts, and more importunate at a throne of grace for faith and love, as the root of holiness of heart and life. Yet, alas! I am not earnest enough for these things; and I am still distressed by vain wandering thoughts in prayer; and when I would meditate, I seem to lose the very power of thinking.

Saturday, July 13.—This morning I waked with Psalm cv. 4. on my mind: "Seek the Lord, and his strength; seek his face ever more."—It was sweet to my soul. I arose to seek the Lord by prayer, and found great liberty and comfort in wrestling with him, with many cries and tears, for a blessing. I was made sensible of my own utter inability to think a good thought, or do any thing towards my own salvation; I therefore cast my soul upon the Lord, and laid hold on his covenant of grace, claiming his promises to helpless, weak, and impotent sinners. My mouth was filled with arguments from Scripture. I urged, that as he was manifested for the purpose of destroying the works of the devil, and to set the captives free, and as I was a bond slave to sin, and unable to release myself, I therefore would cast my soul upon his mercy, and claim his promise not only to grant me future redemption, but a present freedom from the guilt and power of sin, particularly from the sin of unbelief and the vanity of my heart. Since that time, I have been assaulted by temptations concerning the truth of the Scriptures; but I saw from whence they came, and looked to Jesus, and the tempter withdrew. O Lord, pardon mine iniquities, and wash me in the blood of the Lamb!

Sunday, July 21.—All last week I have had liberty and comfort in private duties. Yesterday, while reading Guthrie's Trial of a Saving Interest in Christ, I was led to see, that a real work of grace was begun in my soul, and could not but acknowledge the great love of God to me the chief of sinners. At the same time, I perceived there must be some hidden cause for the slow progress I make in sanctification; and I think the Spirit of God has convinced me, that it is my conformity too much to the world in my conversation.

Tuesday, July 23.—About two in the morning I awoke, repeating the 63d psalm; I could not help singing it aloud.

> Lord, thee my God, I'll early seek:
> My soul doth thirst for thee;
> My flesh longs in a dry parch'd land,
> Wherein no waters be, &c. &c.

I found much peace and sweetness upon my mind all the morning, and got access to God in prayer; towards evening I fell into a dead frame. Lord, quicken me by thy Spirit.

Wednesday, July 24.—This morning, after spending two hours in reading and prayer, I took up E. Cole on Election; and, on reading the marks of the elect, the Lord was pleased to witness to my heart his electing love to me. I was overwhelmed with joy, and fell down upon my face before him, crying out with many tears, "What shall I render unto thee, O my God? How shall I glorify thee? Why me, why me, O my God?" All day I have felt such peace, love, and sweetness in my soul, as cannot be described. Towards night this frame abated; but I did not let go my confidence. I was tempted; but the Lord kept me. I felt, however, the evil of not continuing more watchful unto prayer.

Sunday, July 28.—The Lord is still pleased to give me some measure of faith, and peace of conscience, through a sense of his everlasting love in Christ; although at times I am sorely tempted to unbelief, and to many other sins. My corruptions are as strong as ever. I groan daily, being burdened with an evil heart; and yet I also rejoice in the Lord as my righteousness and strength, and in the hope set before me in the gospel. This day I have had some access to God in prayer. The sermon was sweet to my soul, and I was enabled to meditate upon it, and pray it over. O to be devoted, soul, body, and spirit, to that God who has redeemed and bought me with his precious blood!

Thursday, August 1.—For some days I have been ill in body, and sorely tempted in my soul. Whenever I get upon my knees, the enemy suggests unbelieving, unprofitable thoughts and wishes, and a thousand vanities. My soul has been in anguish all the day, and full of evil tempers. It being a fast-day, I went to church, and heard a sermon on godly sorrow. I thought I had never felt it as then described. I wished to experience it, that I might mourn before the Lord for the abominations of my heart. But all within me is dead, and hard as the nether millstone. O Lord Jesus, deliver me from this body of sin and death!

Saturday, August 3.—Yesterday, the Lord gave me some comfort in prayer, and employed me through the day in his service, which I found very sweet. But to-day I have again had a sore struggle with my heart. In all things I feel myself to be a miserable helpless sinner. In my flesh dwelleth no good thing; my heart is desperately wicked. I sin while praying, reading, hearing, speaking, and singing, in every action of my life, and if God should enter into judgment with me for my best performances, I should inevitably perish; for I have sinned against light and abundant mercy: it is amazing that I have not been cut off long ere now. But this is the cause—Jesus came to seek and to save that which is lost. I am indeed lost and undone in myself; but, O Lord, I would come to thee this night, as a poor, blind, ignorant, helpless, wretched creature, and cast myself upon thy mercy, pleading thy promise, that those who come unto thee, thou wilt in nowise cast out. I come to thee to receive out of thy fulness the supply of all my wants. Grant me a living operative faith in thy blood and righteousness, and all its fruits; deliver me from an unbelieving heart, and save me from my cruel foes, the devil, the world, and the flesh. Grant me, O God, a new heart, a contrite spirit, a devout mind, a conscience sprinkled with the blood of Jesus. I entreat thee to lift up upon me the light of thy reconciled countenance, and when I approach thy table to-morrow, seal me to the day of redemption. Grant me some foretaste of that union and love to Jesus, which I hope to enjoy with him to all eternity. Amen! and Amen!

Sunday, August 4.—This morning I offered up my first thoughts to the Lord, and begged his presence in the duties of the day. When I was dressed, I prostrated myself before him, and renewed my covenant with him, confessing my sins, and solemnly declaring, in the presence of heaven and earth, that I took Jesus to be my Lord and Saviour, my Prophet, Priest, and King. I accepted of him as he is offered in the gospel, as my wisdom, righteousness, sanctification, and redemption. I renounced all other Lords, and committed my soul to him, for time and eternity. During all this transaction, my soul was remarkably dead, and continued so till I came to sit down at the Lord's table: at that time the 24th Psalm was sung, and I felt my heart as it were open to receive the King of Glory; it seemed to go forth to meet him; and I received the symbols of his blessed body as broken for me, and his precious blood as shed for the remission of my sins. I was enabled to act faith sincerely, although weakly, on him as my righteousness; and during the sermon afterwards, my heart was melted and refreshed. I saw many snares and dangers on every side, and a great warfare before me; but I felt strong in the Lord, and, in the power of his might, able to encounter all my foes. In the evening I was tempted to doubt of my state, on account of the deadness of my heart; but the Lord once more comforted me, by shewing me some evidences of my interest in Christ, under the discourse in the family, by which I was much comforted.

Monday, August 5.—This day I have had a sore trial of faith and submission to the will of God, in being threatened with the loss of a dear friend. My wicked heart has rebelled—my spirit almost overwhelmed; yet, after a severe conflict, the Lord has given me, in some measure, resignation to his will.

Thursday, August 21.—I have been much distressed for more than a week past in my soul, with doubts and fears; my spirit has been overwhelmed within me. O Lord, arise for my help, and deliver me from the snares of the enemy. Arise, help, and deliver me, O Jesus, for thine own name's sake, for I am thy servant!

Sunday, August 24.—To-day my soul has been refreshed in hearing the word. I was enabled afterwards to turn it into prayer, and my heart was drawn out in love to Jesus, and much comforted.

Sunday, August 31.—Last week I was much distressed with a crowd of worldly company,—my heart quite oppressed, and I had not freedom of access to God, to pour out my complaint to him. But, blessed be his name, I yesterday got liberty to draw near to him in prayer, and also courage to confess him before men. I felt willing to become vile in their eyes, so that I were approved in the sight of God, and found in Christ.

[Aged 30.]—*September* 2.—This being the day in which the Lord was graciously pleased to bring me into the world, I desire, with all the powers of my soul, to bless his holy name for my being, preservation, and all the numberless mercies bestowed upon me. How wonderful has his long-suffering patience been towards me! Notwithstanding my repeated provocations and backslidings, sins against light, careless performance of duties, an ungrateful, dead, cold heart, he yet spares me. Alas! Lord, wert thou to enter into judgment with me this day, I should undoubtedly perish! But blessed be thy name, thou hast no pleasure in the death of sinners, but in order to deliver them from going down to the pit, thou hast provided a ransom, even Jesus thy well beloved Son, who has finished salvation for miserable transgressors; and this salvation thou hast called me to partake of, and now I do most solemnly accept of thy grace freely offered in the gospel. I desire to receive Jesus as my Prophet, Priest, and King. I look for salvation only through his blood and righteousness. This is the foundation of my hope; I desire no other; neither seek I any other portion than thy love in Christ. As thou hast created me for thy glory, magnify, I beseech thee, the riches of thy grace in saving me from the guilt, power, and dominion of sin, that I may praise thy name with a pure heart and holy lips in the land of the living! Sanctify my soul by thy Spirit, and renew my will and affections, that I may hate sin, and flee from every appearance of evil, and may love whatsoever thou lovest. Thus being conformed to thy image, in thought, word, and deed, as far as this imperfect state will admit of, I may live to thy glory while I continue in this world; and in order that I may be carried cheerfully through the troubles and trials that every-where surround me, O grant me the full assurance of faith, even the testimony of thy Spirit in my heart, witnessing my adoption, and giving me an earnest of that inheritance of love, peace, and joy, which I look for in the world to come; so shall I experience that promise, "In me ye shall have peace." Thou hast caused me to hope that thou wilt perfect that which concerneth me. O fulfil now that good word unto thy servant; complete thy work, O Lord; work faith with power in my heart, that I may rejoice with joy unspeakable and full of glory! O come, blessed Jesus, and abide in my heart! cast out thine enemies, subdue all that rise up against thee, and reign thou in me, and over me, from this time forth, for ever more. Amen! So come, Lord Jesus, come quickly.

Upon a review of my experience this last year, I perceive that the Lord is gradually carrying on his work upon my soul. For eight months past I have had a sore fight of temptations and afflictions; oft in the depths, and my confidence almost shaken; but blessed be God, I have not been left to despair, nor to doubt of the willingness and ability of Jesus to save me. At my lowest moments I could say, "Though he slay me, yet will I trust in him." If I perish it shall be at his feet. Since I came to this place I have frequently tasted of the loving-kindness of the Lord, and have been more established in the doctrines of the gospel. I have also been more humbled before him for many things in my life, the evil of which I did not see before, and particularly for spiritual pride. I have been grievously assaulted by one temptation in particular, which often brings great darkness on my mind, because it is of such a nature as appears to me inconsistent with grace, and whenever it assaults me, I begin to doubt whether I am a child of God. I believe this has been a device of Satan to rob me of peace, and to mar my usefulness. I begin now to know more of the nature of his devices: whenever I get any peace or comfort in my soul, he either suggests that it is all a delusion, or strives to draw me into a careless walk and conversation, which grieves the Spirit and brings guilt on my conscience; and then he comes in again, and tells me to try now if I am a child of God. Thus he brings me into distress of soul, and then, by a false

Barnton, September 21.—Blessed be God for bringing me safe to this place, where I have long wished to be, having dedicated this house and all in it (so far as lies in my power) to the Lord. The gospel has been preached here to the poor, the word received gladly, and I trust the Lord intends great things to this people. I feel much thankfulness in my heart to the Lord for all things. O to praise him for evermore!

Sunday, September 22.—We had a large congregation this evening in the hall. The word came with power to many. O how gracious is the Lord! I resolve to set apart a day for prayer for this people.

Sunday, September 29.—This morning we had a very large congregation in the hall. The people seemed melted under the word. My own soul refreshed.

Sunday, October 6.—This morning Lord G—— was suddenly seized with a fit. I was quite stupified with fear, and could not pray. The Lord has in mercy spared him. O that this warning may be sanctified!

Sunday, October 13.—All last week my soul was in a dull frame, though, blessed be God, at times I have been enabled to cast my care upon the Lord, and listen to his voice in the dark dispensations of his providence. This day the word has been refreshing to my soul; and I can say, as far as I know my heart, I have sincerely given it up to the Lord, and desire him as my only portion, and am willing that the Lord should do with me whatever is most for his glory.

Monday, October 14.—This day it was impressed upon my mind to call my maid-servants together in absence of the chaplain, and pray with them. I felt very unwilling and very unfit for it, and had a sore struggle for an hour before the Lord, before I could submit to it. At length I obtained a little faith in him for help, and set about it. In the evening my heart was very heavy at the thoughts of meeting the servants again. But the Lord graciously relieved me by sending a minister in the way, who took this office from me.

I have heard to-day of some of the poor children at my school being under serious impressions, also of some attempts made to awaken others having been blessed to them. O what shall I render to the Lord for all his benefits! Surely my heart is harder than a rock, that it does not overflow with love and gratitude. O Jesus, soften this obdurate heart! fill my soul so abundantly with thy love that I may be constrained to live every moment of my life to thee! increase my faith; draw me, and I will run after thee!

Sunday, October 27.—During the last week, my soul and body have been afflicted,—the former with guilt upon my conscience. I am in great darkness, unable to pray or think. The Lord is just and merciful in punishing me for my great carelessness. I will bear his indignation, because I have sinned against him. O Lord, I would confess my sin,—enable me to pour out my complaints before thee. Mine iniquities have taken hold of me, and are as a heavy burden, so that I cannot look up; but if thou speak the word they shall be blotted out, and my soul shall once more live and rejoice in thee! Lord, pity and pardon me for thine own name's sake, and restore unto me the joy of thy salvation!

Sunday, November 3.—My soul continues in darkness, under the power of temptation; but this evening a gleam of hope darted in upon me from these words, "We have not a High Priest who cannot be touched with a feeling of our infirmities, but was in all points tempted as we are; and he knows how to deliver out of temptation," &c.

Wednesday, November 6.—I went in to town to the Chapel—found the word sweet to my soul,—felt humbled under a sense of sin. Lord G. was not well this morning; I was sorry to leave him.

Thursday, November 7.—Fast-day in Edinburgh. I went to church; but my spirits were much depressed with a sense of sin, my distance from God, and Lord G.'s illness.

Sunday, November 24.—I desire this evening, in the presence of the Lord, to recount some of his dealings towards me, in a way of judgment as well as mercy. May I learn wisdom from experience, and turn with my whole heart to that God who hath smitten, and hath also supported me while his rod lay heavy upon me. On Saturday the ninth, Lord G.'s illness increased; I went to town to seek a nurse for him, and to ask the prayers of the church then assembled, intending to return after the sacrament next day, leaving Dr R—— with him. Hearing next day that he was worse, I returned home before the ordinance; found him very ill, and sent for more assistance. On Monday I sent for several ministers, who came and continued in prayer and exhortation all next day. At eight o'clock on Tuesday night, as Mr De Courcy was concluding a very importunate prayer in his behalf, he died.—He had frequently that day expressed a sense of the evil of sin, and his inability to believe on Jesus; he said he had no hope but in the merits of Christ; he wished to believe, and attempted to pray;—seemed pleased with the prayers of others, desired them to continue to do so:—towards evening he grew delirious. This was a very great distress to me; I had always entertained a hope that my prayers for him would be heard, and that he would "have made a good confession" at the last. When the final stroke was given, I sunk under it, and fell motionless upon the floor. My heart rebelled against God, I inwardly said, "It is hard." At that instant the Lord said unto my soul, "Be still, and know that I am God." These words were accompanied with such power, that from that instant an unspeakable calm took place in my mind. Every murmuring thought subsided. I laid my hand on my mouth, and held my peace. Upon leaving the room, these words were impressed on my heart, "Thy Maker is thy husband; the Lord of Hosts is his name." The light which accompanied them gave new life to my soul. I saw the Lord as it were calling me to the high dignity of being espoused to himself by an everlasting covenant. My soul exulted in the prospect of being united to this glorious head, of being guided and led by his Spirit, and made a partaker of all the blessings he had purchased for his spouse, the church. The word of God was very refreshing to my soul all that night and next day. Many texts of Scripture came seasonably to my remembrance—when tempted to murmur, "Who art thou that repliest against God, or sayest What dost thou?"—When I felt sorrow for my husband, "The Lord liveth; and blessed be my rock."—If the snares and dangers of my new situation presented themselves, and I felt afraid of falling into them, "I will instruct thee and teach thee the way thou shouldst go; I will guide thee with mine eye." Thus did the Lord comfort, support, and refresh my soul during the first days of my widowhood; but the enemy was soon after permitted to assault me. A Christian friend was made the instrument of plunging me into deep distress, and for some days I felt an agony of mind not to be expressed, till one morning I was relieved by reading Boston's Crook in the Lot; my comforts were restored, and I once more tasted the goodness of the Lord. O that my soul may ever keep in remembrance his marvellous loving kindness in this day of my calamity! Blessed, for ever blessed be the Lord, who hath loaded me with his benefits. What shall I render unto him? I have nothing but what he hath already given unto me. I can only bring to him, what in truth are his own, my soul, body, and spirit; my fortune, health, name, comforts, time, and life, to be disposed of as seemeth best in his sight.—O my God, let my life be spent upon earth to thy glory. Let every thought of my heart be brought into the obedience of Jesus. Preserve me by thy almighty power through faith unto eternal salvation; and deliver me from every thing that stands in opposition to thy perfect and blessed will. Do with me in this world whatever may tend to thy glory, and the salvation of my soul. Grant that I may honour thee in my death, and afterwards be admitted to the eternal enjoyment of thee in glory. My whole desire is before thee; hear and answer me, for Jesus' sake. Amen. W. G.

The remains of Lord Glenorchy were conveyed to Finlarig, at the head of Loch Tay, the burying-place of his ancestors; and his widow, with a jointure of a thousand pounds a-year, took up her residence with Lord Breadalbane at the Abbey of Holyrood-house. On opening Lord Glenorchy's repositories, a disposition, as it is called in Scots law, was found, dated the 16th of April in this year, which was just six months and twenty-four days before his death. By this deed he gave Lady Glenorchy his whole real or landed estate of the baronies of Barnton and King's Cramond, and other lands, with the patronage of the parish of Cramond, and all things belonging to him, in full right to her and to her heirs for ever. In a second deed of the same date, he assigns to her by will, for the favour and affection, as he expresses it, that he bore to her, all his plate, furniture, linen, pictures, prints, books, and every other thing over which he had a disposing power, making her his sole executrix and legatee; and that of all which belonged to him in each of the houses of Taymouth, Barnton, and the Abbey of Holyrood-house, and which must have amounted to a considerable sum, under the following and no other provision.

First, Reserving a power to renounce this deed any time during his life. *Secondly*, Under the burden of his debts, funeral charges, and legacies, if he should leave any, at any future period. *Thirdly*, "With full power to the said Willielma, Viscountess Glenorchy," to use the words of the testator, "upon my decease, to convert the whole of my said estate, means, and effects, hereby conveyed, into money, and to employ or bestow the whole, or such part thereof as she shall see cause, for encouraging the preaching of the gospel, and promoting the knowledge of the Protestant religion, erecting schools, and civilizing the inhabitants in Breadalbane, Glenorchy, and Nether Lorn, and other parts of the Highlands of Scotland, in such a way and manner as she shall judge proper and expedient. And in case of her death before the whole funds to be destined by her shall be so employed in pious purposes, the remainder thereof shall be employed at the sight of, and by the direction of Charles, Earl of Elgin and Kincardine, and David, Earl of Leven, or the survivor of them; with power also to them, or the survivor of them, to assume, nominate, and appoint one or more trustees in their place, who shall have the same power with themselves in laying out and bestowing the same aforesaid, failing my wife by decease before the whole be so employed." Of the existence of these settlements Lady Glenorchy was completely ignorant, until they were, after Lord Glenorchy's death, produced. These deeds must have been very gratifying to Lady Glenorchy, not merely as they put her in possession of a large independent fortune, but because they were the most decisive proofs to the world, that notwithstanding his vexing behaviour towards her, she was the object of his esteem and confidence, and that her conduct met with his approbation. Barnton, as has been seen, had been very recently purchased, and a part of the price still remained unpaid; but Lord Breadalbane, having previously at his own charge completed the payment in a most handsome and generous manner, put her in the full and free possession of it.* She now, at the age of thirty, was her own mis-

* The reader cannot fail to be struck with the affection and confidence which Lord Glenorchy displayed towards Lady Glenorchy in this matter. With all his peculiarities, he was not wanting in real attachment to her; and a man with far less discernment than he possessed, could not be insensible to her talents and her worth. Actuated by these feelings, he took the most natural and effectual manner of exhibiting them, by leaving her all the wealth and all the comforts which lay in his power. By his conduct upon this occasion, he not only discovered the strength of his affection for her, and the high veneration in which she was held by him, but also indirectly showed, that he was not insensible to the value.

tress, without any restraint, and with an independent fortune of between two and three thousand pounds a-year. In these circumstances, deprived of the protection which the very name of a husband brings along with it, she was doubtless exposed to increasing trials and difficulties, which, however, she bore with firmness and resolution. Although her mind was much distressed on these accounts, she seems at times to have experienced peculiar peace and joy in believing, and wonderful supports and encouragements from her God and Saviour. Immediately upon the back of one of these delightful experiences, she was visited with a severe attack of fever, which confined her for several weeks, and interrupted her Diary. But what were her feelings, and views, and conduct at this period, only a few months after her widowhood, will be best seen by the following extracts.

Edinburgh, February 12.—For some time past I have omitted writing the Lord's dealings with my soul, which I find by repeated experience to be a loss to me. Many are the mercies I ought to have noticed. Many the sins and backslidings I ought to have lamented and

and importance of those schemes of usefulness, and of those plans for promoting the interests of religion, which he well knew constantly lay so near her heart. And beyond a doubt, this evidence of his confidence and regard must have made a deep and lasting impression on Lady Glenorchy's mind, while it at once showed her how high she stood in his estimation, and put it in her power to accomplish those schemes of benevolence and piety, the accomplishment of which gave, in her mind, to honour and affluence their highest charms.

Although she was entirely ignorant of the nature of Lord Glenorchy's will previous to his death, yet it is hardly possible to imagine that Lord Breadalbane was not acquainted with it, nay, it is very probable that it was done with his knowledge and approbation. From this circumstance, connected with his generous and noble conduct in paying up the arrears of Barnton, it may be fairly inferred, that Lady Glenorchy also stood very high in his estimation and regard.

down contented in false peace. O Lord, wherefore is it thus with me? Thou only knowest; search me and try me. Is there an Achan in the camp? let him be brought forth this day and slain before thee. Whatever pain it may give, yet spare it not, O my God! I am thy servant, let not mine enemies triumph over me. O rescue me from the powers of darkness; make haste to help me,—make no long tarrying, O my God! In the multitude of thy tender mercies, for Jesus' sake, blot out my transgressions, and pardon my sins, for they are great; and seal thy pardon to my soul, that a sense thereof may produce godly sorrow, and repentance not to be repented of. O revive and quicken my soul by the renewing influences of thy Holy Spirit, for thine own name's sake. Hast thou not brought me out from among the heathen, and given me a name among thy people, and by thine own almighty power preserved me hitherto, not for my sake, but because so it seemed good in thy sight? Do not then, O God, give me up into the hands of mine enemies, lest thine own glorious name be blasphemed; but rather manifest thy power and love, in turning me again from mine iniquities; and glorify thy grace in my salvation, that all who see me may say, "Let the Lord be magnified, that taketh pleasure in the prosperity of his servants." Hear this prayer, I beseech thee, O my Father, for Jesus' sake. Amen!

Upon recollection, I think the present comfortless frame of mind may proceed from one of the following causes:—The hurry of company and business I have been engaged in for half a year past, which, together with bad health, deprived me of many hours I used formerly to spend in devotion, and also of public opportunities of waiting upon God; or, it may be, the change in my outward circumstances; or my inward deadness and poverty may be the answer to my prayers. I have often solemnly begged of the Lord to guide me in the right way, though it might be most contrary to my inclination, and grievous to flesh and blood. Now, perhaps the Lord is in this way calling me to see more of my own vileness, and the unprofitableness of self-dependance and resting upon duties performed, or gifts in myself or others, and leading me to rely wholly on the finished salvation of Jesus;—he is perhaps calling me to follow him in the night, as well as by day, in order to try my faith; and by denying me the comforts of religion, and sensible enjoyment of him in ordinances, is proving whether I follow for the loaves and fishes, or for himself only. Whichever of these be the cause, I would now, in dependance on divine grace assisting me, resolve to redeem as much time as possible for private prayer—to go early to bed, that I may be able to rise early,—to be holy and circumspect in my conversation in company, as a probable means of keeping away unprofitable visitors. To look continually to Jesus, and consider him in the days of his flesh, pouring contempt on the pride of this life. As a means of curing high thoughts (it is by faith we overcome the world), to think of God manifest in the flesh, despised and rejected of men, exposed to hunger, to watching and fasting, and had no place where to lay his head, and at last crucified betwixt two thieves. Shall this be believed, and the world courted and admired? Forbid it, Lord. Let the servant be contented if he be as the Master. Upon the whole, I would exhort my soul still to hope in God, for he is my God, and I shall yet praise him as the health of my countenance.

This day I heard two rousing sermons from Mr Russel and Dr Erskine, and found myself convinced of sin and alarmed with my state, whilst hearing them;

in my soul. My faith is now stronger. I feel power to trust him, and resign myself up unto him wholly without any known reserve. I desire, O my gracious God, with my whole soul to bless thee for the mercies thou hast bestowed on me, of the least of which I am utterly unworthy! I acknowledge my sins deserved thine utmost wrath; and it is because thou art God, and not man, that I am not consumed. What shall I render unto thee for all thy benefits? Alas! I have nothing to bring but sin and misery in return for love and mercy. Lord, I prostrate my soul before thee, acknowledging my unworthiness, disclaiming all right and title to any favour from thee. Yet, imboldened by the precious promises made in thy word to the chief of sinners, I would now plead the fulfilment of them to me; and, as such, lay claim to the glorious salvation freely offered in the gospel to sinners. I would stretch forth the hand of faith to lay hold on that life which is offered to all who will come to Jesus. Lord, I believe, help mine unbelief, and seal me thine for ever! Amen.

Sunday, September 6.—Last week I have been in a cold and lifeless state of soul; sometimes inclined to impatience and unbelief. All this day I was unable to pray or think on spiritual things; but this evening I have been permitted to pour out my complaints before the Lord. I see pride as the cause of my doubts and fears. The humble soul looks away from self; it sees the promise made to Christ, and through him to the chief of sinners, and is desirous that he may be glorified by their salvation. The sinner, therefore, may come boldly for pardon and eternal life, and all the precious gifts which God is glorified in bestowing for Christ's sake.

September 12.—This day I have endeavoured, in the midst of darkness and unbelief, to close with Christ in all his offices, and to receive him into my heart; giving up myself wholly to him, and resting wholly upon him for salvation. Therefore I now, in his presence, subscribe myself to be the Lord's, as witness my hand.

W. G.

When Lady Glenorchy acquired wealth and opportunity, her first thoughts, like those of David, were to prepare a place for the Lord, a habitation for the mighty God of Jacob; and with this view she formed the design of erecting a chapel, which she intended should be in communion with the Established Church of Scotland; and for this purpose she employed her friends in Edinburgh to find a proper situation for it. Various places were pointed out; but at length she wrote from Taymouth to one employed in this business, stating her own sentiments on the subject in the following words: "I think the Orphan-park is the most desirable place; and should be so in the eye of Christians, who consider not the house, but the people, as the church. I begin to be easy about this affair, being persuaded the Lord's will concerning it shall be done." Soon afterwards the ground was purchased, and tradesmen were engaged; and on the 11th of August she writes thus: "Let no time be lost in laying the foundation. The Lord prosper the work, and send us wisdom from above to carry it on and finish it, for his own praise and glory! I have time for no more than to beg the prayers of all the faithful, that the Lord may not only build the walls of this house, but fill it with his presence; and gather into it a real church, an assembly of the faithful, to the praise of the glory of his grace!" Neither the views of the people in general at gentleness of manners, and was ever after this a counsellor of Lady Glenorchy's, and to her opinion she uniformly paid much deference.

In her Diary of November 26. and December 19. Lady Glenorchy takes notice of the circumstance of the foundation of her chapel being laid, and of some other events, with much thankfulness.

Barnton, November 26.—Since I came to this place, I have been much employed in outward things, in which the Lord has prospered me, notwithstanding much opposition. The church of Cramond is happily settled: the chapel in town is advancing. On Sunday the 3d, I went to the Lord's table in a very dead frame; felt a want of spiritual taste and relish for the great truths I heard: I was very miserable till I came to approach the table, when part of the 22d Psalm was sung: I then saw that I had fellowship with Christ in his sufferings, particularly in the hiding of God's face. This melted my heart; and I felt content to suffer, if so be that in any way I might be made conformable to Christ. Soon after this I met with a very severe trial from a quarter I least expected it; but the Lord supported, and carried me through beyond expectation; he enabled me to kiss the rod, and to acknowledge that he is not only just but merciful.

December 19.—For some weeks past I have had much anguish of mind from the above cause. I have been reproached, threatened, aspersed, and cruelly used, by one whom I had treated but too well; and whom, from an excess of compassion and friendship, I had continued to use with kindness and civility, even when I ought in prudence to have withdrawn all intercourse. The returns I have met with are a warning that I hope the Lord will enable me to observe: May he give me the sanctified use of this sharp trial; in the meanwhile, however, I am much hurt by it. My time and thoughts have been too much engaged with it, and my soul has suffered loss of spiritual life and strength. O Lord, undertake for me; I am oppressed and afflicted. Revive and quicken me; speak the word, and these dry bones shall live: For thy name's sake hear me!

The Diary of Lady Glenorchy was written in her closet under the immediate eye of God, before whom, in the simplicity and integrity of her heart, she unveiled all her thoughts and feelings, as well as her actions and their motives. She hence was ever led to say with the prophet, to "God belonged goodness and mercy, but to her, shame and confusion of face." Her very great humility deserves peculiar attention. She indulged herself in nothing; she devoted her rank —her fortune—her time—her widely extended influence, and all her fine talents, unreservedly to the service of God. Upon examining herself before God, she declared that she was not conscious of keeping any thing back from him which she could command; and it was her burden, nay, and it may be truly said, it was her constant and only burden, that she could not completely subdue every thought and every feeling to the obedience of Christ. Whilst she was thus certainly rich in grace and in good works, she poured forth incessant tears and groans in secret, considering herself, after having done all, to be but an unprofitable servant. These exercises of her mind are amply and fully expressed in the following part of her Diary.

1773. *January* 1.—I have resolved this day to observe, more strictly than ever, the state of my soul towards God, and to call myself to account every night for the manner in which I have spent the day. O that by any means it would please the Lord to revive his work in my soul, and stir me up to more diligence in making my calling and election sure! It is with shame and confusion of face that I look back on the year past; how trifling, how careless have I been! This day has been mostly spent in company and in spiritual conversation, yet my thoughts wander,—my mind is vain,—I feel insensible to every thing that is good,—I have done nothing for my Master to-day. I am ashamed to draw near unto him. O Lord, breathe on these dry bones that they may live! O revive and quicken my soul according to thy word!

Sunday, January 3.—Last night and this morning, under conviction of the deplorable state my soul is in, through distance from God, I have wept before him, and made my supplications for grace and strength to go forward in his ways. I heard Mr Walker on Psalm xxx. and Ezek. ix. 4. and was in some degree comforted, but saw that I never had mourned as I ought for my sins, nor the sins of others. My heart is not right with God; I have been tempted all day with worldly thoughts. Mr Balfour spoke this evening from the parable of the fig-tree. I was convinced that I was unprofitable, and that it is of the Lord's mercies I am not cut down as a cumberer of the ground,—yet still I am not enough concerned at this.

Monday, January 4.—Last night I got liberty to pour out my heart before the Lord, and got a view of his holiness and purity;—my soul longed for conformity to his image, and I sought it with some importunity. This helped to clear up to me my interest in his covenant, seeing that I truly desired the blessings of it, and sought the things he had promised. I was enabled to believe that I should receive them. This morning my mind was in a sweet composed frame, and through the day opportunities have been given me of speaking for the Lord. He gave me courage and utterance that astonished myself. Satan has tempted me since to be lifted up with this change. This shows how needful it is to watch and pray without ceasing, and never more than after enlargement in duty, or manifestations of the love of God.

Thursday, January 7.—I have endeavoured to speak to some persons this day about their souls, but had little liberty in so doing. I found most life when in the company of a Christian friend, but grew dead again when alone. This, I fear, is a symptom of hypocrisy.

Friday, January 8.—I had no liberty this morning in prayer for myself, but found enlargement for the Lord's work; and particularly for the parish to which I belong, and their new pastor.

Saturday, January 9.—I was led last night in prayer to see something of the amazing love manifested in the sufferings of Christ, and of our astonishing ingratitude in our forgetting it. I bewailed my own sin and that of others in this respect, and found much comfort in drawing near to God. This morning I have found liberty in prayer for more of the image of God, and conformity to his will. I desired nothing but him, and wished to be nothing in myself, that Christ might be all in all.

But how soon did this frame vanish! About mid-day I was seized with an old temptation, and have ever since been disturbed with it, and praying and fighting against it, yet without success. In different forms it again and again assaults me. O that the Lord would rebuke the enemy! then he would have no power over me. Lord, do thou speak the word, and it shall be done. Thou hast formerly delivered me from this; thy hand is not shortened, thy power is the same: deliver me, I beseech thee, from the hand of the enemy, and the glory shall be thine for ever. Amen!

Sunday, January 17.—For two days past I have been in general in a dull uncomfortable frame, though at times I have had some degrees of comfort. This morning I had great hopes I should find this a good day to my soul, but in this I was partly disappointed. I heard three good sermons, but cannot perceive that I have profited by them. After all, I remain in a dead lifeless case.

Monday, January 18.—Last night I had liberty to pour out my soul before God, and to plead his promises, and seek with earnestness the full assurance of faith. My soul was greatly refreshed, my hope strengthened; and, blessed be his name, I this day feel more power to believe, and more inclination and relish for spiritual things. Yet, alas! my wicked heart is still prone to start aside like a broken bow, and leads me away before I am aware on the mountains of vanity.

Tuesday, January 19.—This morning I asked counsel of God concerning visiting unconverted people, and read 1 Tim. chap. v. in order to see if I could find any directions there on this head. I found on examination, that my intention in keeping up this sort of intercourse with them was not to please myself, but to endeavour to draw them out from the world, and to prevent them saying that religion shut me up altogether from their society, and made me neglect social duties. As I did not see my way clear to give it up, after prayer I went out to return some visits, and endeavoured to introduce profitable conversation; but I am sensible I did not speak as I ought.

January 20.—Last night it pleased God to visit this place by an awful storm. A house was blown down, and several persons buried in its ruins. How does this call for thankfulness from us that escaped? and O that it may serve as a warning to repentance, lest we also perish! My heart has in some measure been affected by this dispensation, but I have not improved it as I ought in speaking to others.

Sunday, January 24.—This morning I was detained from public worship by bodily indisposition; but the Lord has made my room a little sanctuary to my soul. I found comfort in reading the Scriptures, and prayer, and this in greater measure than I generally receive in public ordinances.

Wednesday, February 3.—I was very ill last night. I found much sweetness and peace of mind in committing my soul, and all my concerns, into the Lord's hands, that my life and all might be disposed of as was most for his glory. This day I feel power to trust the Lord, that all shall be well with me whatever the event may be; I can say, thy will be done in me and by me: Let me glorify thee, and be found in thee, and it sufficeth!

Sunday, February 7.—Last night as I was pouring out my heart before the Lord in prayer, for a blessing upon the ordinances this day, the case of a young gentleman was deeply impressed upon my mind, who was ill of a fever. I had no acquaintance with him; I only knew that he was reckoned a serious young man. I was led to cry importunately to the Lord for his recovery. This morning I was informed that last night the fever took the turn, and it is thought he will recover. From this may I not infer, that the Lord sometimes lays the cases of his children on the hearts of his people, that they may ask the blessings he intends to bestow.

Sunday, February 14.—This morning these words came forcibly upon my mind: "If the Lord be God, serve him; but if Baal, then serve him." I was alarmed at this, and immediately sat down examining my heart, to see if I was halting between two opinions; but was not able to discover the least desire in my heart towards any service but that of the living God. Perhaps this scripture may have been suggested by the enemy, to perplex my mind on this morning of a communion Sabbath, as he is generally busy at such times, and I have been variously tempted this day, but in some measure got the victory by casting my soul upon Jesus, and resolvedly chusing him as my Lord and Master. I endeavoured to lay claim to him as such in defiance of Satan, and took all to witness that I this day gave up my soul to him, to be saved by him in his own way and time. At church I felt some exercises of faith on the sacrifice I saw represented before me as a sweet smelling savour unto God, and felt these words comfortable, "Be not afraid." The minister who preached said many things very opposite to my views of the gospel of peace. I felt my heart more inclined to fretfulness, than compassion for him, and I got into a careless spirit. At length Mr Walker rose to serve a table, and spoke to my heart. How glorious did the gospel appear, after what had gone before. Like the sun breaking out after a cold, dark, frosty day, so did it enlighten, thaw, and warm my frozen heart, and melted me into tears of love and contrition. This frame continued some time, till another minister succeeded, who spoke in a manner which much distressed me. O for the meek and compassionate mind that was in Christ, who wept over those who resisted his love and rejected his gospel.

About this time the Rev. James Stuart, minister of Killin, at the head of Loch Tay, represented to Lady Glenorchy the great need which the district of Strathfillan in his parish, had of additional means of propagating religious instruction.*

* "Strathfillan, originally a distinct parish, was united to Killin about the time of the Reformation from Popery, and together with Ardeanaig became one charge with it. It consists of Strathfillan properly so called, and Glenfalloch; the first of these, viz. Strathfillan, is a flat or bottom, of six miles in length, four of which miles are situated by the east, and two by the west of the chapel or place of worship in that part of this country. Glenfalloch strikes out towards the south from that flat or bottom, and is five computed miles in length; the most distant farm town thereof is fifteen computed miles from the parish church of Killin, and seven from the place of worship in Strathfillan. There are in these two places, Glenfalloch and Strathfillan, about two hundred and fifty examinable persons, exclusive of the workmen at Coninsh and Clifton mines, who, with their followers, are rarely below a hundred and fifty persons, and sometimes they amount to the double of that number. Few of the common people in Strathfillan and Glenfalloch, who are past thirty years of age, can either read or write; nor can they hear sermon

on my soul, his will done in me and by me, and the comfort of knowing assuredly that I am now savingly united to him, and that nothing shall ever be able to pluck me out of his hand.

I spread these wants before the Lord this morning, and solemnly gave up myself to him, accepted of Jesus as my only Saviour, and besought the Lord to fulfil my requests in his own time. I found after this much peace in my soul, and was enabled to perceive the work of God there, and to rejoice in his goodness. I went to church in expectation of farther manifestations; but when there I fell into a cold careless frame, and heard little of the sermon; and was unaffected by the amazing scene of love displayed before my eyes in the broken body and shed blood of Jesus. I went to the table in a stupid frame; was confused and distressed with several outward things, that drew off my attention. I did, however, endeavour to receive the elements as pledges of the dying love of Jesus, as the seal of the new and everlasting covenant; and viewed it as the one great sacrifice offered up once for all for the sins of many.

Glory be to God for any thing I have this day seen of his love, or of my own interest in the great salvation purchased with the precious blood of a crucified Saviour! When I look back upon my sins, and inward upon my ungrateful heart, how astonishing is this love that still follows me with mercy, and bears with my repeated backslidings, still saying, as in Jer. iii. 1. " Return again to me, saith the Lord. O who is a God like unto our God, that pardoneth iniquity, and passeth by the transgressions of his people? yea, he multiplies pardons." O that from this time forward he would take possession of my heart, and manifest his power in me, by subduing my iniquities, and bringing into captivity every thought to the obedience of Christ. Lord, speak the word, and it shall be done. O transform me by the renewing of my mind, and let me henceforth live to thy honour while here, and at length behold thy glory in thy kingdom! Amen and Amen!

CHAPTER XII.

A melancholy event occurs in the course of building Lady Glenorchy's Chapel in Edinburgh—Lady Glenorchy much affected thereby—Extract from Diary, and correspondence between Lady Glenorchy and Mr Walker on the subject of the accident—Lady Glenorchy anxious to keep her heart right with God—Extracts from Diary from November 27. to December 31. 1778—Difficulty of drawing the line with respect to Christians mingling with the world—Two admirable letters of Mr Walker's on conformity to the world.

Lady Glenorchy was by no means given to superstition; but a very melancholy event took place at this time, which would have made a perplexing as well as distressing impression on any ordinary mind. On Wednesday the 18th of August, by a most unpardonable neglect of the workmen, the scaffolding in her chapel, which was building, gave way, and the architect and his foremen were precipitated from its lofty roof to the floor, and killed on the spot. To this terrible accident her Ladyship indirectly alludes in her annual recollections on her birth-day. This incident gave occasion to an interesting correspondence between her and Mr Walker, which will be found in the following pages. In the close of which, with great address, he intimates his fears that she exceeded in her liberality, and might encroach on her capital; in which, however, he was completely mistaken, as she always took care that her expenses should be below her income.

[Aged 32.] *September* 2.—This being the anniversary of the day of my birth into this evil world, I would endeavour, according to custom, to record the present state of my soul, and recount the mercies of the Lord through the past year. But, alas! how painful is the task! Innumerable are the mercies received; inexpressible the ingratitude and folly of my backsliding heart, which seems to be hardened by prosperity. In the month of October last, the Lord allowed me to cause the foundation of a house to be laid, intended for the honour of his great name, in Edinburgh. Soon after which, he permitted a sore and grievous trial to come upon me, of a nature that tended to humble me in my own eyes, and bring down my proud heart to the dust. Thus was I kept from being puffed up, or elated with the work carrying on. This year also he has honoured me as the instrument of preparing a habitation for a minister at Strathfillan, where the people are destitute of the means of grace. A plan is also laid for sending missionaries through the Highlands, and several others of a like nature are in forwardness. What shall I render to the Lord for all his benefits? What can I say? I am vile, exceeding vile. My life has been a course of backsliding for a great while past. I have not followed on to know the Lord. I have gone too much into worldly company, in the hope of gaining them. I am led away with every gust of temptation, into behaviour unbecoming the gospel. I am not sufficiently serious, nor holy in my conversation. The world has got in upon me. The cares of this life, and many outward things, distract and divert my thoughts from the Lord. Sometimes I am permitted to cry for help, and God hears and answers my prayers, and for a short season I get power over my corruption: at such times I am happy, but too soon I yield again unto temptation, and all my peace is gone. In this fluctuating state I have been for many months struggling with unbelief, darkness, and sin, especially with the vanities of the world, which once had the possession of my heart, and would afresh regain their former throne. I feel the workings of pride and self-conceit more strongly than ever. I cannot conceive any thing more infinitely vile than my heart in every respect. I can perceive no mark of grace in me, but that of a spirit within striving against this self, accusing it to God, and seeking for strength to overcome it. Surely this must be the new nature warring against the old. I will therefore take comfort, and hope for a final victory over my spiritual foes; and while I wonder and stand amazed at the long-suffering patience that has spared me for many years in this sinful state, and still follows me with mercy, may I now offer up my soul, body, and spirit, a living sacrifice to God, and devote the remaining hours and days of my life to his glory: and I would now in thy presence, O gracious Jehovah! with all the solemnity and sincerity of which I am capable, embrace the offer of grace and salvation in Christ Jesus. I do renounce all claim to life eternal in any way but through thy free and glorious grace, manifested, by the appointment of thy beloved Son, to be a propitiation for sin, through the shedding of whose blood I look for the remission of all my sins. I desire to be washed, justified, and sanctified in the name of the Lord Jesus, and by thy Spirit. I acknowledge that my life is forfeited to thy justice. I now seek it back as thy free gift in the way thou hast appointed. I confess that since I knew the way of salvation, I have sinned against both mercy and light; and if thou shouldest enter into judgment with me, I could not stand in thy sight. I can, therefore, have no hope, but in the blood which cleanseth from all sin, and in him who ever liveth to plead the cause of his people. Hear, O God, that blood which speaketh better things than the blood of Abel; that crieth for pardon for a hell-deserving sinner! And, O my God, restore unto me the joys of thy salvation; wash me from all the filthiness of the flesh and spirit, and stamp thine holy image upon my heart; work in me both to will and to do of thy good pleasure; deliver me, for thine own great name's sake, from the snares and temptations of the devil, the world, and the flesh. Let thy power be manifested in preserving my soul in the midst of an evil world, from the contagion of sin, by faith unto eternal salvation.

O let this prayer be now heard and answered, as far as it may be agreeable to thy holy will, through the merits and intercession of the Lord Jesus Christ, who is my only hope; to whom, with thee, O eternal Father, and the Holy Ghost, be ascribed everlasting glory, honour, and praise, now and evermore. Amen.

W. G.

The Rev. Robert Walker to Lady Glenorchy.

"Madam,—It is with no small reluctance that I write to your Ladyship on so dark a subject as the melancholy event of Wednesday last. But a sense of duty constrains me to express as I can, how much I feel both with you and for you; and, at the same time, to remind you, of what you certainly know and believe, that he who hath done this, "giveth no account of his matters;" so that it must be equally fruitless and presumptuous to say to him, "what doeth thou?" or, "why dost thou thus?"

"One thing I must beg of your Ladyship, which is, to beware of drawing, from your connexion with, and peculiar interest in the building, any conclusions that may have the remotest tendency either to weaken your hands, or to discourage your heart. What hath happened speaks no other language to you than it doth to me, and to as many as the report of it shall reach. It is only a repetition of the alarm, that hath so loudly and so frequently been published of late, "Behold, I come as a thief in the night;" and, surely, the place where it was last published, whatever it may add, can take nothing away from its solemnity and weight.

"If it hath pleased the Lord to prevent every other preacher, by becoming the first who makes his own voice to be heard in your chapel; if it has pleased him to write in the very centre of it, and all the way down from the roof to the pavement of it, the interesting, but much neglected words I have quoted, and although the pen was dipped in blood, how erroneous would it be to pervert into a token of anger, or mark of disapprobation, what may lawfully be interpreted, and ought certainly to be improved, as an awakening but salutary preface to those good tidings of great joy, with which I trust that fabric shall resound, while one stone of it remains upon another. You will, no doubt, on this occasion, receive letters from other friends, who are better qualified to suggest what is proper than I am.

My wife sympathizes with you most sincerely, and offers most respectful compliments to your Ladyship, in which I beg leave to join her. I have the honour to be, with the highest esteem, your Ladyship's most obedient humble servant. ROBERT WALKER."

"*Edinburgh, August* 21. 1773."

Lady Glenorchy to the Rev. Robert Walker.

"Reverend Sir,—The kind and seasonable letter which I received from you some days ago, is a fresh proof of the friendly sympathy you have often shewn to me when in distress, and demands my grateful acknowledgments. You seem to have entered so much into my feelings upon this awful and dark dispensation, and make use of arguments so suitable to the particular situation of my mind, that one would think you had the gift of discerning the thoughts of the heart. I must acknowledge, that before I received your letter my heart was much disposed to murmur, because I could not see the meaning of this unexpected trial, and I apprehended that the enemies of the work would consider it as a judgment. I also feared, that the unholy, unthankful temper of the unworthy author of the work, had drawn down the divine wrath upon those connected with her. But these, and many more unbelieving thoughts, gave place to sentiments more becoming a dependent creature, upon reading your letter, which points out to me the way of improving this dismal event, and also reminds me of the presumption of seeking from the Almighty an account of his ways to the children of men. I am much obliged to Mrs Walker for her kind sympathy. Lady Jane Home joins in compliments to her and you; we both desire to be remembered to and by our dear Thursday's friends. We are in a starving condition here as to spiritual things; but I hope by the air and exercise I now have in such perfection, to get health to enjoy the outward privileges I hope to be a partaker of at Barnton. I am, Reverend Sir, with much esteem, your obliged humble servant. W. Glenorchy."

"*Taymouth, August* 28."

The Rev. Robert Walker to Lady Glenorchy.

"Madam,—I had the pleasure to receive, by Monday's post, your favourable acceptance of the poor attempt I made to express my sympathy with your Ladyship the week before last; and shall always reckon myself sufficiently rewarded, when any thing that God is pleased to suggest to my mind, contributes in the least to the tranquillity and comfort of yours. I am glad that you agree with me in the view I took of that awful dispensation, with regard to its general aspect and tendency. We have now, I think, got our feet upon firm ground, from which we may venture with greater safety to look around this doing of the Lord, which, like all his other doings, the better it is understood, the more wonderful will it be in our eyes. For my own part, I acknowledge that the more I consider it, the greater reason I find, not only to acquiesce in the event itself, but likewise to be reconciled to every circumstance with which it was accompanied. The selection of the sufferers, to whom the insufficiency of the scaffolding proved most fatal, hath no doubt a dark appearance. The builder and his foreman were indeed the capital persons upon whom the conducting and perfecting the work seemed chiefly to depend, so that any other two might have been wanted better than they; but, besides that the Maker of men can never want instruments, if any other two had suffered, would not their death have, with some colour of justice, been charged by many to the account of these very capital persons, as it was upon their supposed attention and skill that all the under workmen were naturally led, nay, in a great measure obliged, to trust for their security? In my opinion, the dispensation would have been more perplexing if this circumstance had been reversed. Humanity inclines us to wish that all had been preserved; but if some were to suffer, it is impossible to select any other two in whose case it might have been said, with such obvious propriety, that "righteousness was laid to the line and judgment to the plummet;" while, at the same time, their venturing their own lives upon the scaffold, sufficiently acquits them from that blame with which they would have been loaded, had others suffered and they remained safe.

"But it may be asked, for unbelief is very acute and obstinate in putting questions, was it not unlucky—for this too is the blundering style of unbelief,—was it not unlucky that such a fatal accident should have happened in building a house for the worship of God? Thou blind perverse querist, would it have been less unlucky either for the sufferers or their employer, had the house been intended for the service of the devil?

"But where hath God promised to confer strength upon weak and ill-chosen materials, merely because they are employed in rearing a fabric connected with his worship? Hath he done more in the present instance, than permitted a cause to produce its natural effect? And is not this event evidently calculated to teach us a general and most important lesson, which is, that in doing the Lord's work, no such protection or interposition is to be looked for, as will give the smallest encouragement to any degree of carelessness and inadvertency with respect to the means or manner of conducting it?

"Men are deservedly praised for discovering attention and prudence in the common affairs of life; and yet success in these is equally dependant upon God, as in those infinitely greater things which pertain to his own immediate service. Why then should the one be carried on in a more careless and slovenly manner than the other? We have no warrant that I know, to expect success in prosecuting the noblest end, if we neglect the means that are the most proper for attaining it. God is certainly most honoured when his servants conduct themselves with wisdom, and walk in the midst of the paths of judgment.

"Let me allude to the erecting the tabernacle in the wilderness. It was an easy matter with God to have reared it up at once, without the intervention of any means or instruments. Or he might have appointed Moses to collect the various materials, and then with a word of power, as in the first creation, commanded them to range themselves in due order; the goats' hair to become curtains; the scattered threads to become hangings of blue, and purple, and scarlet, and fine twined linen; and the unformed masses of metal and timber to rise up in the shape and dimensions of a complete tabernacle, furnished with altars, and basins, and candlesticks, according to the pattern shewed in the mount. Thus might God have revealed his arm, and secured to himself the entire and undivided honour of his workmanship: But it pleased him to do a greater thing; instead of displaying his power over passive matter, he rather chose to glorify himself in the high character of the Father of spirits, by manifesting his sovereignty over the active mind: For thus he spoke to Moses,—'See, I have called by name, Bezaleel the son of Uri, the son of Hur, of the tribe of Judah, and I have filled him with the Spirit of God, in wisdom, and in understanding, and in knowledge, and in all manner of workmanship.'

"Doth not more of God appear in his 'instructing the husbandman to discretion, and in teaching him to open and to break the clods of his ground, to make plain the face thereof, and then to cast in the appointed seeds in their place,' than if he caused the earth to yield its fruits spontaneously?

"It is an approved part of the good man's character, that whilst 'he sheweth favour and lendeth, he at the same time guides his affairs with discretion.' The metre version of Psalm xli. 1. doth certainly express the true meaning of the text—

> 'Blessed is he that *wisely* doth
> The poor man's case consider;'

for there may be excess even in works of mercy themselves, which, by disabling the giver, may defeat his kind and charitable intentions; and God hath no where promised to replace that wealth which a too profuse liberality may expend.

"But softly, Mr Scribe, are you not here introducing a side-wind that points a little towards my quarter?

"I declare, Madam, that I did not intend to give it any personal direction whatever; but now when I mark its course, I dare not positively affirm that it blows altogether clear of your Ladyship.

"I have often told you, Sir, my opinion of the world, that it is only to be valued as a means of glorifying God by those labours of love which are subservient to the present and eternal interests of others. And for my own part, nothing would give me greater pleasure than that the end of my estate and of my life should bear the same date.

"But your Ladyship doth not know how many years you have to live.

"I neither expect nor wish to live long.

"Just as long as God hath ordained; and if your means of usefulness be exhausted before life concludes, the remainder can be fruitful of nothing but sympathy and good wishes, which will neither feed the hungry, nor clothe the naked. Besides, it will be found upon a just calculation, that a proper application of your annual revenue, even for such a moderate term of years as your own desire to depart and to be with Christ might be reconciled to, would, upon the whole, be productive of greater and more extensive good, than the immediate distribution of all that you possess at present will amount to; with this advantage too, that your light will shine to the last with undiminished brightness, and, year after year, afford unto others repeated opportunities of seeing and tasting the fruits of divine grace, which may constrain them to glorify your heavenly Father.

"These, my Lady, to the best of my recollection, were once the outlines of an evening's conversation at Barnton. Little did I imagine when I began this letter, that I should be twisted about in the course of it to give a lecture on economy; but the pulpit door flew open so suddenly that I could not help stepping in, although I might, and ought to have foreseen, that I should not be able to get out again without running foul of my text, by loading your finances with the superfluous tax of a double postage for one letter.

"I frankly acknowledge, that nothing would give me greater pain than to see the smallest diminution of the state which belongs to you, even as to its outward gloss and lustre. It is an apostolical decree, 1 Cor. vii. 20. "That every one abide in the same calling wherein he was called." Now it was as a lady of rank and opulence that you were called into the vineyard of God; and you there occupy a place to which you are so well adapted, that were you to leave it but a hair's breadth, you would create a vacancy to which you have no right of presentation; and although you had, yet even that would be of little avail, unless another power was added unto it, which it is impossible you ever can possess—I mean the power of creating a presentee, who shall in all points be equally qualified to supply it.

"After all, I can assure your Ladyship that my mind is perfectly at ease upon this head. The only species of changeableness I ever could discover in you, was the inability of retaining any error, either in opinion or practice, after you discovered it; and upon that, or rather upon him who inspires it, I can safely depend for your filling up all the parts of the character I quoted from the Psalms.

"I am really ashamed to turn over another page, but shall blot no more of it than is necessary in asking pardon for this immoderate waste of your time and patience; in offering my wife's most cordial respects to your Ladyship, and our united compliments to good Lady Jane; and in subscribing myself, with ever growing esteem, your much obliged and faithful humble servant, ROBERT WALKER."

"*September* 1. 1773."

Keep thy heart with all diligence, is a divine commandment; and obedience to it is enjoined by a very weighty consideration,—for out of the heart are the issues of life. Lady Glenorchy revered this commandment. To keep her heart right with God was her incessant effort; and no deviation of thought, no failure of affection, no impropriety of motive, were ever permitted by her to pass unnoticed, unrebuked, unlamented, or unchecked. No deeds of piety however extensive, no acts of benevolence however splendid, appeared to be any thing in her sight; her exclusive aim was to have her heart right with God. Her deeds of piety and her acts of benevolence were unquestionably many; and of no small magnitude; but of these she takes little or no notice in her Diary, whilst the state of her mind occupies not only every page but almost every line. Of her it may be truly said, that she walked before God in the land of the living. The following extracts, like those which precede, evince this.—

November 27.—For some days after the 11th of this month my soul enjoyed sweet peace, resting on the word of God, and I had relish in spiritual duties; but a hurry of business coming on, my mind was disturbed, my time for spiritual things shortened, and I once more unhappily got into a withered, sapless state. I was, however, revived in family prayer; the minister was led to plead my case (without knowing it) before the Lord in a remarkable manner.

This day I have been comforted in reading Haliburton's Life, who has, I perceive, been tried and tempted in many respects as I have been. O what cause have I to lament my distance from God, my ignorance of him, my careless spirit and carnality!

Monday, November 29.—This morning these words came upon my mind, "Wait on thy God continually." I was led to think of their meaning, and to beg the Lord would give me grace to obey the precept. I have had several pleasant views of this privilege through the day; and my mind, upon the whole, has been more spiritual. I have sought this evening from the Lord more disinterested views, and to be enabled to seek his glory as the end of all my actions. I had freedom in praying for the prosperity of his kingdom, and the revival of religion. I found comfort in prayer, and of talking of the love of Christ to sinners. In family worship I was sorely tempted, and saw much of the desperate wickedness of my heart.

Tuesday, November 30.—I got up early this morning, and, after contending for some time with wandering thoughts, I got liberty in prayer, and felt a solemnity of spirit all the forenoon; but company coming to dinner, I fell into a dead lifeless frame. I find I am sensibly hurt by the company of the people of the world, unless when I try to do them good. Lord, enable me to be faithful to their souls, and then I shall not suffer loss!

December 2.—The Lord is letting me feel what an evil and bitter thing it is to depart from him in heart. I am brought very low, entangled, and have no strength to resist the enemy. O Lord, do thou deliver me, for thine own name's sake; restore me the joy of thy salvation; lead my feet into the way of peace, and keep them in it, that I may not return to folly! Save me, O Lord, for I am thy servant!

Tuesday, December 7.—I set this day apart for examining my heart, and seeking the Lord. No access to God in prayer all the morning—was much discouraged, yet persevered in seeking. At length the Lord inclined his ear unto me,—he heard my cries, and enabled me to pour out my heart before him, and to renew the dedication of myself to him without reserve; to be led and guided by his Spirit, strengthened by his grace, and kept by his power. I have committed my soul once more into the hands of Jesus, who is able to keep it to the day of redemption;—when he who is my life shall appear, I shall appear with him in glory. I am no longer my own. I have no right to murmur at any of his dispensations; for I have put a blank into his hands. I only pray that I may live to his glory, and that his power and grace may be manifested, by preserving me from sin, and making me a witness for his truth in the world. I would not prescribe,—let him do in what way he will. All I desire is, to be made by grace a partaker of his heavenly calling, and an instrument of promoting his glory. Even so, Lord Jesus; so be it.

Edinburgh, December 31.—Since I came to this place about three weeks ago, the Lord has been graciously pleased to shew me more of the beauty of holiness than usual, and has drawn forth desires after conformity to his image; and although I have little inward peace, owing to the intrusion of vain thoughts, which haunt me night and day, especially in prayer, yet, upon the whole, I find my heart more detached from the world. I get more power to speak to others, and to do them good; but still the Lord keeps me at a distance. O that the Lord would breathe upon my soul, and revive me by his quickening Spirit!

Every person truly devoted to God, will sometimes find it a very difficult task to settle how far it is duty to mingle with the world, and how far it may be necessary to retire from it. Lady Glenorchy experienced this difficulty, and applied to Mr Walker, and urged him to give his opinion in writing, on that kind of conformity which is required from a Christian by Scripture and reason, and especially from one situated as she was. This he at first declined to do; but Lady Glenorchy continuing to press the subject, and sending him a few questions for his consideration, he roused himself, and produced the following letters.

ON CONFORMITY TO THE WORLD.

Letter the First.

"Madam,—I did not feign an excuse, but spoke the truth in my heart, when I told you that my abilities were not equal to the task you had enjoined me; and I suspect, that your Ladyship's opinion of them is by many degrees too favourable. I am indifferent though the world should err a little upon that side, as the mistake may procure greater attention to my public ministrations; but why should I strut in buskins before the children of the family with whom I shall soon meet again in that world of light, where every one shall appear in his real dimensions, without addition, and without diminution? I am none of those who possess a large sinking fund of knowledge and experience, from whence they can borrow materials at any time they chuse. It is true, I have read much, and thought more, so that for a tract of years my mind hath been conversant with a variety of subjects, important and interesting. But my vanity hath never yet been gratified with the sight of a full pantry, and the key standing in the door, to be turned about at pleasure; I have all along been fed with what may literally be called daily bread.

"Indeed, had I got my wish in early life, I should ere now have been a fool by choice; for I thought and studied hard, with an ardent desire, and some degree of expectation, of having it one day in my power to say, 'Soul, take thine ease,—thou hast goods laid up for many years;' and it mortified me not a little to find myself crossed in that matter. I could not be satisfied with present supply. My proud heart was always attempting to take possession of what belonged to an hour that might never arrive. Thus I lost the relish of breakfast, by looking forward to dinner; and when the dinner, the good things of which I had not foreseen, was provided, instead of being thankful for them, supper immediately employed my imagination, which, in its turn, was imbittered with the premature question, What shall I get for breakfast to-morrow? So that when I went to bed at night, it might have been written over my head in capital letters, Here lies the fool, who hath devoured his three meals without enjoying one of them. Was not this, my Lady, a sore travail? And yet I can assure you, that it lasted for years;. till after repeated experience of the care and faithfulness of the great Master of the family, who provides seed for the sower, and giveth to every one his portion in due season, I came at length to discover, that when unbelief, or pride, or vain curiosity, like the heavy load of wood upon Isaac's back, pressed me to put the question, Where is the lamb for a burnt-offering? it was then the business of faith to reply with Abraham, while the sacrificing knife was in one hand, and the fire in the other, 'My son, God will provide himself a lamb for a burnt-offering.' Blessed be his name, he hath done it hitherto, and I dare not be so arrogant as to doubt, that he will continue to do so to the end. Often have my few barley loaves, and small fishes, been multiplied in the distribution. Often have I looked with anxiety upon the dry, withered, and ill-connected notes, which my best labour could furnish out, and said distrustfully, Can these bones live? When, lo! at the time of need, sinews and flesh have come upon them, the skin covered them above, and breath came from the four winds, so that they lived and stood upright. To this method of dealing with me, I am now so thoroughly reconciled, that it gives me far greater pleasure to receive warm from the hand of my gracious Lord, the supplies that are suited to the present occasion, than to be able, by the mere force of study, or the mysterious engine of memory, to draw forth, when I chuse, those gathered stores which have long been freezing in the cold repositories of a speculating head, and, alas! a too unfeeling heart. Not that I am negligent in preparing as I can, for public service. This kind of presumption, though of a different complexion, is nearly allied to, and equally criminal with the bold presumption of distrust itself. I still read, and think, and write, as much as ever. But in digging the pools I now can wait with some measure of patience, and hope for the rain to fill them; and can bear to look at my own broken cistern, when I am permitted to lift mine eyes upward to the ever full and overflowing fountain of living waters.

"I am already at the fourth page of my paper, and the principal subject of my letter is yet to begin. What shall I say of this intruding, overgrown egotism? I am truly ashamed of it, and the more so, because, though it wears the form of acknowledged weakness, yet I am utterly at a loss to determine whether or not it hath been dictated by genuine humility; for it is impossible I can have the remotest intention to lessen myself in your esteem. But whatever motive presided in making the confession, I can assure your Ladyship, that the truth of it may be depended upon: may I not therefore hope that you will permit it to remain with you, as a standing apology for every seeming neglect of obedience to your orders; as I am conscious, that were it wholly in my power, the execution of what you desire should always prevent your request, and every good wish that riseth in your mind should conceive and bring forth at the same time. I do not mean to avail myself of it on the present occasion. The obliging manner in which you refused my declinature, and renewed your request, lays me under an irresistible obligation to make, at least, an attempt upon your difficult subject in one shape or other: only I must beg your indulgence for a delay, as I feel myself restrained from immediate execution, by a principle of delicacy, which I shall now freely and in confidence impart to you.

"Be pleased then to know, that I have the honour to be acquainted with one, who is working upon the same subject; not in the way of writing, but in painting and exhibiting a series of pictures, with such power of expression, that they will more effectually give an answer to your queries, than any thing that either Mr —— or I could offer to the public. The great outlines were drawn some years ago; surprisingly bold indeed, but so just in their direction, that I can hardly think any part of them will need to be erased; for the little irregularities, (or if you please to call them the excrescences), which were unavoidable in the first rapid strokes of a full pencil, are so happily placed, that, with a few delicate touches, they may be improved into such real ornaments as will add greatly to the beauty and value of the picture.

"The principal figure, in the first picture, is a lady in the bloom of youth, with the world under her feet. She is raised so much above it, that a space is left vacant between the surface of the globe and her dress, and, by its appearance, it should seem that she had not leisurely retired from the world, but separated from it at once by a vigorous effort, and that the spot from which she took her departure had been hedged about with a mixture of briars and thorns, and, moreover, covered with an adhesive substance; for several pieces of the selvage, which bear all the marks of being violently torn away, are still attached to that part of the surface of the earth which she left.

"In the next picture, a perspective view of the lady is given in a dress plain but becoming, though rather disproportioned to her rank. She is not only attended by a few decent looking domestics, but beset with a pressing crowd of seemingly destitute creatures, among whom she is distributing bank paper, in exchange for humble petitions, while at a little distance you can discern some buildings for public use, rising at her sole expense, which of themselves are carrying off more than the superfluities of a very opulent estate. This picture is not to be retouched: and indeed there can be no reason why it should; for as the light comes from behind, it promotes and heightens the effect of the principal figure. In the third picture, the lady appears in a fine attitude; her dress exactly suited to her person and station, with the happy mixture of simplicity and dignity which distinguisheth what in poetry is styled the true sublime. She is here attended by a greater number of domestics than perhaps may seem necessary for performing any services she personally needs; but all of them find employment sufficient to prevent the pernicious effects of idleness, and their looks express a grateful consciousness that they are hired, not so much to render services to their lady, whose wants are few, as to learn heavenly wisdom from her instructions and example.

Real objects of charity are to be seen in her retinue, who, instead of intruding into her presence, keep at a modest distance, and patiently wait her kind invitation to come, and receive the supply they need. From a quarter much illuminated, you behold a youthful band of both sexes, who, animated by her example, have likewise made their escape from the pollutions of the world, hastening to follow her with every mark of cordial esteem and love. Here too the buildings appear finished, and each of them put to its proper use; but in the interval betwixt them, and where the shades are deeper, you may discover some motley groups of dark figures, fantastically dressed, who, under an affected disdainful sneer, betray every symptom of wonder and envy, whilst their mixed countenances express that shame and self-reproach which they inwardly feel.

"Your Ladyship will observe, that this picture is not, and at present cannot be finished; but I have the pleasure to inform you, that of late it hath received very considerable improvements.

"Nothing (so far as I can perceive) can be added to the face. It is natural to suppose, that when the emblematical lady first separated from the world, the sight of its deformity, and the sudden, unexpected discovery of its hostile intentions, would imprint upon her countenance, as is delineated in the first picture, those traces of displeasure, which the apprehension of impending injury can hardly fail to produce. But these, in the other pictures, have been softened down into the most expressive features of humble gratitude, for begun deliverance for herself, and tender compassion for those blind deluded wanderers she hath left behind her in the waste and howling wilderness. And now you can see exhibited in the liveliest colours that peace of God which passeth all understanding, which is the parent of true magnanimity, and guards the heart equally against the fear, or love, of earthly things, by rendering it altogether independent of them, either for its present enjoyment or its future hopes.

"But something in the first picture still remains to be done, for filling up the interval I remarked between the feet and the globe. One who has no idea of being upheld by everlasting arms, might be apt to suspect the existence of artificial support, so ingeniously contrived as to elude the eye, upon which the lady hath the dexterity to rest. To prevent a blunder of this kind, I am persuaded the artist will judge it proper to bring the lady so far, at least, into contact with the surface of the globe, as to make it appear, that though she is not of the world, yet still she is connected with it, which is certainly the case.

"How this is to be executed, I really do not pretend to say. A few strokes of the pencil may possibly extend the fretted borders of her robe, and by lengthening out the broken threads, may unite them in the manner in which they ought to be united to the native land she loves, and may give them the form of those fringes, which of old distinguished and decorated the garments of the true Israel of God, serving at the same time as useful monitors, 'that when they looked upon them, they might remember all the commandments of the Lord their God to do them.'

"This, however, will require some time, and till the pictures be completed, of which I wish and hope to avail myself, (as their amendments have already corrected some of my ideas and enlarged others), I cannot think of beginning to write upon the subject. I confess, that I long to see the finishing hand put to them, and yet I dare not be urgent with my much respected friend, who is a female artist; for though I have never been restrained by a false complaisance from telling her my opinion with the strictest honesty, even when it differed from her own, yet I never presumed to offer any advice to her. Neither have I any cause to repent of my reserve in that matter; for I candidly acknowledge, that I am able to recollect more instances than one, wherein, had she been to listen to the only advice I could have given at the time, her performances would have wanted some of those masterly strokes of true genius and taste, which now mark the originality, and heighten the beauty and expression of the whole. But if your Ladyship be very desirous to have it speedily finished, I shall, by your order, present to her any request you shall please to indite; or it will be still more effectual if you address her in person, for were I to tell you her name, you would readily acknowledge, that you are oftener in her company, and have more to say with her than I or any other in the world.

"The bulk of this letter is beyond measure oppressive, but I hope you will bear it with greater patience when I add, that it will probably be the last of its kind. Farewell, my honoured Lady: May light and truth be your constant guides; may you never lose sight of the pillar of cloud by day and of fire by night; and may the good will of him who dwelt in the bush, guard you through life, and enrich you to eternity.

"Robert Walker."

"*Edinburgh, 20th November* 1773."

Letter the Second.

"'Tell me, I pray thee, wherein thy great strength lieth, and wherewith thou mightest be bound to afflict thee.'"

"When your Ladyship reads the question that Peter put to his Master, 'Lord, how oft shall my brother sin against me, and I forgive him? till seven times?' Doth it not readily occur to you, that the honest disciple had, in his own opinion, made as liberal an allowance, and laid as heavy a load upon human patience as it either could or ought to bear? And that he plainly seems to have thought, that the addition of another injury would render the burden quite insupportable? And I cannot help suspecting, that one of these conclusions, after receiving the seventh offence, would have strongly inclined him to seek out some decent way of procuring the eighth, that he might be at liberty to shake off the burden at once. In which case, it is more than probable that a principle of strict justice might have disposed him to lay as much vengeance upon the last provocation, as would recover, with legal interest, the arrear due to his forgiveness from the other seven which had escaped with impunity.

"I cannot deny that a similar suspicion is raised in my mind when the question is put to me, How far may the Christian be conformed to the world? I could therefore wish, that the person who proposeth it would imitate the blunt honesty of Peter, by subjoining his own opinion, and describe as he can the utmost limit to which, and no farther, the Christian may or ought to go; otherwise I shall be apt to conclude, that instead of desiring to be informed how soon he may stop, (which was the true meaning of Peter's question with respect to forgiveness), he rather wants to be told, that the boundaries are so undefined, or placed at such a distance, that he need give himself very little concern about the matter.

"I could likewise wish, that the querist would come fully into the light, by assuming some known denomination, whereby his character may be clearly distinguished. This he cannot decline with any colour of reason. The very terms of his own question express an acknowledgment, that a distinction doth exist between real Christians and those who are of the world; and his putting the question not only gives me a right to demand, but obligeth me to insist upon it, that he discover to which class or denomination he belongs. Because though my answer, upon either supposition, would, in substance, be the same, yet the form and manner of it must be varied according to the character of the person who requires it.

"In the mouth of one who styles himself of the world, the question (unless it be dictated by mere curiosity, which I may gratify or not as I find leisure or inclination) must be proposed with an intention to avail himself of my answer, by taxing the Christian to the utmost extent of his liberty, and demanding every kind and degree of compliance with the maxims and manners of the world, that can be squeezed within the boundaries of the farthest line which separates the doubtful from the forbidden ground.

"I do not say that in this case I would refuse to give an answer, even though the querist should avow the use he was to make of it; for I am thoroughly satisfied in my own mind, that the most enlarged and accurate description of the just measures of Christian liberty, instead of inviting his solicitation, would most effectually deter him from every attempt of that kind. But I should certainly be disposed, and judge myself entitled to ask a few preliminary questions, to which honour, as well as courtesy, should oblige him to reply without evasion or circuit.

"The term *world* is so general and vague, that till some descriptive epithet, such as learned, polite, gay, busy, and the like be prefixed to it, nobody can know what it means. Hence it comes to pass, that in current style there is an almost endless variety of worlds. Some of them, indeed, of so neutral a complexion, that the most rigid casuist hesitates to determine on which side of the discriminating line they ought to be placed; while the lurid aspect of others approacheth near to the blackness of darkness itself.

"How remote from either of those reputable places* dedicated to the improvement of music and graceful motion, where the noble and gentle youth of both sexes are introduced into the polite world, and gradually formed to appear in it with fashionable propriety—how remote, I say, from these, is that profane, opaque sequestered cell into which no ray of the sun hath access;† where (if report may be credited) blasphemy, gaming, and foul debauch, insult the first day of every returning week? and yet, betwixt these distant extremes, the whole intermediate space is crowded with apartments of different colours, forms, and dimensions, each of them contending for the pre-eminent, if not the exclusive title of *the world*. I should, therefore begin with asking him to which of these worlds he himself doth at present belong?

"I would next inquire, what security he can give, that the particular world to which he avows his own relation, and whereinto he no doubt means to invite the Christian, shall retain its present state, and make no alteration in its form and position, without asking and obtaining the consent of its new guest?

* The then Concert-Hall and Assembly-Room, Edinburgh.

† This alludes to a meeting or club of libertines from the higher classes of society, which, according to general report, was held at Edinburgh. The members met about mid-day, on a Saturday, and, having excluded the light of day, remained together in that state till Monday.

"This question proceeds upon a supposition, that the world he is connected with, is at least situated within the limits of what I formerly styled the doubtful ground; for, were it confessedly on the wrong side of the line, the conference would be at an end. Nay, it must be further supposed to have a complexion, if not absolutely neutral, yet, at most, nothing worse than ambiguous; and, moreover, to lie so near the verge of the unexceptionably lawful ground, that the Christian may readily pass over to it, if not altogether unobserved, yet without incurring the suspicion of a formed design to proceed any further in that direction.

"It would surely be unhandsome, (to say nothing worse of it), to allure one with flattering promises of additional pleasure, and more agreeable companions, into a place where he expects to find rest, if, soon after his arrival, he may be told by the very person who brought him there, that the company is just about to decamp, so that he must either go along with them, or be left alone. Nay, if when he hath reluctantly attended them to the next stage, he may in a few weeks or days have the intimation renewed to him of another removal to a place still more distant, where, for any thing he knows, a third summons may await him, which may be repeated again and again, till he be carried as far from the place of his first outset, as the Prodigal went by choice from his father's house.

"This is no chimerical supposition: the thing hath often happened; it is common. Even while I am writing, many awful examples occur to my remembrance, of persons, in different stations and seasons of life, who, by steps in appearance short at the beginning, but too rapidly progressive, have soon gone such lengths in conformity to the world, that had any pretended to foretell it at the time when the downward motion commenced, they would have shuddered with abhorrence at the prediction, and been ready to reply in the language of Hazael to the prophet Elisha, "Am I a dog, that I should do this thing?"

"Now, it is evident, that no man of ordinary understanding would consent to such loose capricious terms of conformity, were they fairly set before him, as in common honesty they ought to be. So that the meaning of my second question is abundantly plain, and the aim so just and honourable, that I should not need to make any apology for putting it, and demanding a clear and direct answer.

"But the third and last question I would ask is of a higher importance than either of the former two. I should certainly press him to tell, without disguise or reserve, from what motive he is so solicitous to gain the Christian over to a conformity to the world in any kind or degree whatever.

"It cannot be, that his character as a Christian may acquire dignity and lustre from his connexion with the world, and shine forth to public view with more attractive grace. This pretence would be confuted by the very title he hath assumed. For how is it to be supposed, that a man of the world should exert himself to advance the honour of a character, to which his own stands in the most direct and hostile opposition?

"Neither can his motives be, that the addition or mixture of worldly pleasure may heighten the relish of those which are peculiar to the Christian; for, with respect to pleasure, the man of the world would certainly chuse to be at least on an equal footing with the Christian; and, therefore, if once he admit that there is any real enjoyment in religion, when he presseth his own sweet cup on the Christian, he should at the same time ask permission to pledge him in his, that the whole compound quantity of pleasure may be as equally divided betwixt them as possible: so that, according to the genuine influence of this motive, just as far as the Christian cometh into the world, so far should the man of the world go out of it, and sally forth into the Christian ground. But as this promiscuous intercourse and reciprocal participation of pleasure, would annihilate at one stroke the distinction we have all along supposed between the Christian and the world, and upon which, indeed, the question at issue is entirely founded; and as the man of the world appears firmly determined to keep within his own ground, it is plain, that we must look somewhere else for the true motive of his zeal and activity.

"But why should I affect to be in suspense upon this head? It is certain, and the querist will not presume to deny it, that he hath and can have no other aim, than either to strip the Christian by little and little of every badge of distinction, and to gain him entirely over to his own party; or, at least, that he may disarm him of the power to hurt his favourite interest, by clothing him with such motley apparel as will render him an object of contempt and ridicule, and either cover, or, if possible, totally extinguish, that penetrating light and overpowering splendour of pure and undefiled religion, whereby the despicable meanness and hateful deformity of the maxims and manners of a corrupt world, are most clearly detected and most severely reproved.

"'Pray, Sir, what have I to do with your querist? You know well, that the inquiry was proposed by one who does not profess to be of the world. Why then have you introduced a person with whom I neither have nor desire to have, any connexion, and wasted so much of your paper upon him, that you have not left yourself room to fulfill the promise you made to me?' I suppose you are going to add, ' And, now that I have brought my preliminary questions to this conclusion, it would be superfluous to proceed any farther in the subject, as it could serve no good purpose to give such a querist an account of——'

" Your Ladyship may stop. I confess you have got the start of me, and hit upon almost the very words I was just about to write. But I hope you do not suspect me of a serious intention to fight off, as it is called, by a feigned rencounter with a combatant from whom I can with such ease disengage myself at pleasure? I assure you, that I have no design to elude, by any artifice whatsoever, the performance of my promise to consider the subject you recommend to me, with all the attention and accuracy of which I am possessed. It is my fixed purpose to lay before you as full a description as I can, of what appears to me to be the just measure of Christian conduct in relation to a present world.

" But as you have laid me under no restrictions, either as to time or manner of execution, I think myself at liberty to chuse my own road, and even to digress from it occasionally to any moderate distance, when an object which is inviting happens to attract my attention.

" I frankly acknowledge, that I was under no necessity of laying hold upon the gentleman who hath offended you, but might have let him pass on quietly, without seeming to take notice of him. And yet, however strange it may seem, such persons are apt enough, of their own account, to thrust themselves into the company of serious Christians; and which is equally surprising, though they affect no concealment, but appear without disguise, yet their solicitations not only obtain a patient hearing, but too often make an impression upon, and even prevail with some, who bear that honourable appellation.

"I am truly at a loss to determine which of the two is most astonishing: whether the confidence of an avowed enemy in presuming to offer counsel, or the simplicity of those who are capable of hesitating for one moment about the reception that is due to it.

"I can look back upon a time, and it is not very remote, when they that were styled of the world pleaded for nothing higher than a toleration to follow their own way. Instead of pressing the Christian to be conformed to them, and reviling him for an opposite course, they only begged the favour of him to turn his eyes some other way, that he might not be offended by looking at their conduct. They seemed contented that others should frequent places of worship, and be as devout as they pleased, provided only they themselves might be indulged to resort freely to other places that were better suited to their inclinations and taste.

"Whence the amazing revolution we now behold hath proceeded, deserves to be seriously inquired into; and I have little doubt, that the result of such an inquiry would afford just matter of shame and sorrowful regret to many yet living, who still retain the name of Christian, and would complain loudly of injury, if you should apply to them the opposite denomination.

"But I have detained you too long, and shall only add, that I have the honour to be, &c. &c.

"Robert Walker."

CHAPTER XIII.

Lady Glenorchy complains of want of spiritual comfort—Inquiry into the cause of this—Extracts from Diary, from January 5. to April 3. 1774—Note of Lady Glenorchy to Lady Maxwell—Situation of Lady Glenorchy's chapel in Edinburgh—Correspondence between Lady Glenorchy and the Presbytery respecting her chapel—Chapel opened for public worship—Extract from Diary—Lady Glenorchy goes to Taymouth—Finds much delight in the retirement she there enjoys—Extracts from Diary, from July 18. to September 11. 1774—Lady Glenorchy returns to Edinburgh—Is exposed to new trials—Extracts from Diary—Lady Glenorchy goes to England—Remarkable occurrence in Pinner's Hall—Visits her friends at Hawkstone—Extracts from Diary, from March 14. to August 13. 1775—Lady Glenorchy goes to Taymouth—Extracts from Diary, from August 17. 1775.

Lady Glenorchy almost always complains in her Diary of the want of religious comfort. This is a very common case among Christians; and by many it is frequently ascribed to a want of integrity, to negligence in the use of the means of grace, to the indulgence of known sin, to undue conformity to the world, and to a heart but partially devoted to God. None of these things, however, with truth could be charged against Lady Glenorchy. Her integrity was evinced in all her thoughts, and words, and deeds; she was most diligent in the use of all the means of grace, both public and private; she was, in an uncommon degree, separated from the world, and her heart was unreservedly devoted to God; yet she enjoyed comparatively little peace of mind and religious comfort. It may not be improper, therefore, to inquire, What was the cause of this? It was attributed by her to wandering and vain thoughts, to cold affections, to guilt on the conscience, to sensible distance from God, and to the want of liberty in prayer. But these are rather to be considered as the effects than as the causes; for if the mind has peace and comfort, these things have no place,—it is only when they are absent that they exist. The truth is, as the Scriptures teach, salvation is of the Lord, and the peace and joy which flow from it are also from the Lord, (for every good gift and every perfect gift is from above, and cometh down from the Father of lights; and as we are saved by grace through faith, and that not of ourselves, it being the gift of God), so we receive the peace, and joy, and comfort of salvation in the same manner, that is, by grace, through faith given us of God. This enables the believer to apply the doctrines and promises of the Scripture respecting the saving virtues of the blood of atonement and reconciliation to his own mind and conscience, and hence arises his peace, and joy, and comfort. The moment he ceases so to apply the blood of atonement, his peace, and joy, and comfort, wanting their only support, will fail, and like Samson, when deprived of his hair, he will become, in these respects, like other men. No integrity, no diligence, no separation from the world, no devotedness to God, can be of any avail in these circumstances. Lady Glenorchy was indeed occasionally enabled to apply these doctrines to her conscience, and at these seasons she did enjoy a certain degree of peace and comfort; but not applying them with that habitual perseverance which she ought, and which is emphatically styled in Scripture, living by faith, she, as might be expected, notwithstanding her eminent attainments in religion in other respects, became not unfrequently very comfortless and distressed.

These remarks will receive illustration from what is next to be exhibited from her Diary.

January 5.—I had great comfort in reading Owen on Communion with God, and felt my heart drawn out towards him, in love and gratitude for his numberless mercies towards me, but especially for his love manifested in Jesus. All night and next day I experienced great joy and peace in believing.

January 6.—I had more than usual comfort in hearing Mr Walker preach from 1 Thess. v. 16, 17, 18. "Rejoice evermore. Pray without ceasing. In every thing give thanks: for this is the will of God in Christ Jesus concerning you." The Lord enabled me to hear and retain the things spoken, and the word was refreshing to my soul. I saw it to be my privilege in every thing to give thanks: this sweet frame lasted during Friday and Saturday. Perhaps I was lifted up and thought my mountain stood so strong, I should never be moved, for on Sabbath the 9th, as I was dressing for church, and full of the hope of being refreshed there, a sudden temptation came across my mind; at first I repelled the thought, but at church it returned with more violence; a seeming accident made it more plausible—it took possession of my mind, and I could not attend to any thing I heard. Haste, Lord, to my help, for thy own name's sake.

Sunday, January 16.—This evening I got uncommon liberty and comfort while speaking to some of my servants about their souls. My temptation ceased while I was thus employed.

Monday, January 17.—I called on a Christian friend to whom I communicated my case and asked counsel. This seems to have broken the snare. I am now relieved from the temptation.

Sunday, January 30.—All last week my time has been consumed in fruitless attempts to conquer vain thoughts. I have had much time alone, which I endeavoured to spend in meditation, reading, and prayer. One evening I attempted to write something for the benefit of a backslider, which brought my own backslidings to remembrance, and filled me with apprehensions about my state. In the night I lay some hours awake, and got a sight of the holiness and purity of God, and of my own unholy life. I saw myself as an unclean thing in his sight, utterly unfit to partake of the pure and holy life to which I aspired in the world to come:—towards morning these words, "Deny thyself, take up your cross and follow me," came forcibly upon my mind; I saw that I had not obeyed this command. I got up and besought the Lord for power and strength to obey him, and obtained liberty to plead for mercy to pardon, and grace to help in time of need. I was desirous to hear what the Lord would say to me from the pulpit. The Psalm first given out was the lxxxv. 8.

I'll hear what God the Lord will speak :
To his folk he'll speak peace,
And to his saints ; but let them not
Return to foolishness.

The sermon, Ezek. xxxvi. 31. "Then shall ye remember your own evil ways, and your doings that were not good, and shall loathe yourselves in your own sight for your iniquities and for your abominations." Both were suited to my case. The afternoon's sermon also came home to my heart. I found it good to be there.

This evening my frame has been dull; I attempted to instruct a child and pray with her, but to little purpose. I have cause to bewail my negligence in my family; in all things I come short. God be merciful to me a sinner!

Monday, January 31.—This day Lady Maxwell and I agreed to set apart an hour or two every Friday forenoon, to pray for a revival of religion in our souls, and in the souls of the Lord's people, and that he would pour out the influences of the Holy Spirit on the church in general; and that we should ask others to join in doing the same.

Tuesday, February 8.—This morning I got freedom to put up my requests, particularly for the fruits of saving faith, love, joy, and peace. Afterwards in reading Owen on the Evidences of Saving Faith, the Lord was pleased to shine upon his work in my soul, and give me the inward testimony of his Spirit bearing witness with my spirit that I had saving faith, and thereby filled me with wonder, love, and joy. It was an abasing humbling view I got of his mercy to my soul in particular, which filled me with shame at my past unbelief, and was accompanied with a sense of unworthiness, and at the same time an ardent desire to live wholly to the glory of God,—to have my heart weaned from all created things, and altogether fixed on Christ as my alone portion and hope. By this I know it was the Spirit of God. What comes from him leads to him, exalts the Redeemer, and abases the creature. O for a grateful heart! O to retain for ever a sense of his amazing love! Lord, help me to praise. Glorify thyself in me, for I am thine. Glory be to thy name for ever!

March 5.—For some time past I have had many ups and downs; sometimes rejoicing in hope, at other times cast down through the prevalence of sloth, and carelessness, and a carnal spirit, which leads me to waste precious time, and opportunities of seeking intercourse with God. For some time past I have been much engaged with some who lately appear to be under serious impressions; my desire to help them forward has been inordinate; they are become a temptation to me; I have forgotten that it is the Lord's work, not mine.

On Wednesday last I went to see a dying person, who was awakened only a fortnight ago. She said, "When I lay down on this bed I was a polluted miserable sinner, but now I hope I am pardoned and redeemed. I cannot find words to express the joy I feel in the view of the glory I believe I am about to enjoy."

She longed to depart and to be with Christ, but said she waited patiently God's time. She seemed to enjoy a full assurance of hope, and a clear view of the glory of Christ in the redemption of sinners. She was afraid of returning again to the world, and longed to depart. She was twenty-one years of age.

Sunday, March 20.—I have this day been at the Lord's table. My heart was dead and wandering, yet I was enabled to believe on him as the bread of life, and to receive the elements with calm composure of spirit, in the full persuasion that his body was broken for me, and his blood shed for the remission of my sins.

Friday, March 25.—I was much distressed all this morning with confusion of thought, and inattention in hearing the word.

The Lord's dealings with me are mysterious. Sometimes he seems to withhold support from me in duty, either by laying sickness on my body, or withdrawing the influences of his Spirit when I would perform them. I am permitted to help others, while my own soul is left a barren desert, as if I was only an instrument to be thrown aside when the work is done. I have many misgivings of mind about my state, yet no power to wrestle with God for a better one; like a door on its hinges, I move, yet get no farther on. Sometimes I fear he has taken his Spirit from me as a punishment for not improving the grace bestowed. I am tempted and harassed by vain thoughts, and can get little comfort from the promises, nor from any creature; the only thing which yields me any consolation is, to see the work of grace going on in others. They are increasing, whilst I am decreasing; but if the Lord be glorified thereby, I will rejoice, and do rejoice. Let him do with me what seemeth good in his sight.

Sunday, April 3.—For some days past I have been indisposed in body, but more so in mind. Yesterday these words came to my mind, Isaiah xli. 17. "When the poor and the needy seek water, and there is none, and their tongue faileth for thirst, I the Lord will hear them, I the God of Israel will not forsake them." I saw they were applicable to my case; but being in company, could not at that time retire for prayer. This day, being confined from public worship, I got an opportunity to pour out my complaint before the Lord with many cries and tears, and was enabled to commit my body, soul, and spirit, with all my burdens, to the Lord. I had no manifestation of his divine presence, or particular assurance of my prayer being heard; but I have a comfortable hope that it was the Lord who enabled me to pray, and that the needy shall not always be forgotten; the expectation of the poor shall not perish for ever. I have had some comfort in reading the first epistle of John: I can apply the marks given of the children of God, and think I do keep the two great commandments, of believing on the Lord Jesus Christ, and loving the brethren: at least, if I trust not on him for salvation, I know not on what I trust; and if I love not his disciples, I love no other creature. I desire to say with David, "Whom have I in heaven but thee, and there is none upon earth that I desire besides thee!"

On Thursday the 5th of May Lady Glenorchy writes thus in a note to her friend Lady Maxwell: "I hope you will remember to unite with me to-morrow in seeking the Lord's blessing and countenance on the house to be opened next Lord's day in his name, and do not forget one that stands much in need of your prayers for wisdom and direction, and other spiritual blessings. The strong are called upon to bear with the weak, to comfort the feeble-minded, and to strengthen them. You now have an opportunity of doing this for me, for I am weak, feeble-minded, distressed, perplexed, and tossed about with many fears, and not comforted."

Lady Glenorchy's chapel in Edinburgh is a plain but substantial stone building, commodiously fitted up to hold two thousand people, and when very crowded may hold more. Its situation is unfavourable with respect to access, being at the east end of the deep hollow which separates the Old Town from the New Town. It may be seen from the North Bridge, contiguous to the College Church and the Trinity and Orphan Hospitals.

When the building was nearly completed, as Lady Glenorchy had intended that her chapel should be in full communion with the Established Church, she wrote to the Presbytery of Edinburgh in the following terms:—

To the Rev. the Moderator of the Presbytery of Edinburgh.

"Rev. Sir,—It is a general complaint, that the churches of this city that belong to the Establishment are not proportionate to the number of its inhabitants. Many who are willing to pay rent for seats, cannot obtain them; and no space is left open for the poor but the remoter areas, where few of those who find room to stand, can get within hearing of an ordinary voice. I have thought it my duty, to employ part of that substance with which God has been pleased to intrust me, in building a chapel within the Orphan-house park, in which a considerable number of our communion, who at present are altogether unprovided, may enjoy the comfort and benefit of the same ordinances that are dispensed in their parish churches; and where I hope to have the pleasure of accommodating some hundreds of poor people, who have long been shut out from one of the best, and to some of them, the only means of being instructed in the principles of our holy religion. The chapel will soon be ready to receive a congregation, and it is my intention to have it supplied with a minister of approved character and abilities, who shall give security for his soundness in the faith, and his loyalty to government. It will give me pleasure to be informed that the Presbytery approve of my general design, and that it will be agreeable to them that I ask occasional supply from such ministers and probationers as I am acquainted with, till a congregation be formed and supplied with a stated minister. And I beg you will do me the favour to present this letter, with my respectful compliments, to the Rev. Presbytery of Edinburgh, at their first meeting. I am, Rev. Sir, your most humble servant,

"W. GLENORCHY."

To this letter she received the following reply from the Presbytery clerk, Mr James Craig.

"The Presbytery unanimously approved of Lady Glenorchy's general design; and desired that she might be informed that her asking occasional supply from such ministers and probationers as her Ladyship is acquainted with, till a congregation is formed and supplied with a stated minister, will be agreeable to the Presbytery."

This place of worship was opened on Sabbath the 8th of May 1774. The morning service was conducted by the Rev. Dr John Erskine, at that time one of the ministers of the Old Grey Friars' Church, and colleague to the distinguished historian, Dr Robertson, then Principal of the University. He preached from the 8th chapter of the book of Proverbs, the 33d and 34th verses: "Hear instruction and be wise, and refuse it not. Blessed is the man that heareth me, watching daily at the posts of my doors." The service of the afternoon was conducted by the

Rev. Robert Walker.* He took his text from the 6th chapter of the Epistle to the Galatians, 15th verse, "For in Christ Jesus neither circumcision availeth any thing, nor uncircumcision, but a new creature." The few persons who survive, speak of this day with much satisfaction and delight. Fervent prayers for the usefulness of this institution were offered up to Almighty God, which we have every reason to hope and believe have already been heard and answered, and will be answered for ages and generations yet to come. Lady Glenorchy, in her Diary of the day, mentions the event with much modesty and great conciseness.

May 8. 1774.—This day, through the blessing of God, my chapel in Edinburgh was opened, by Dr Erskine and Mr Walker; each preached a very suitable discourse to crowded audiences. I went in the interval between sermons to St Cuthbert's Chapel of Ease, and partook of the Lord's Supper, and returned again to my own chapel in the afternoon. I had much freedom in devoting myself, and all that I am and have, unto God, and had sweet joy and peace in believing. I have felt all day much desire to praise the Lord, and to call on all within me to bless his holy name, who hath done for me great things. All his ways towards me have been mercy and truth. To him be ascribed glory, and praise, now and for ever more. Amen.

The external quiet and retirement of Taymouth, together with its beautiful and sublime scenery, and the pastoral and orderly habits of the people, were

* See page 94.

peculiarly congenial to the views and feelings of Lady Glenorchy, and contributed in no small degree to sooth her mind and promote her health. Hence she repeatedly expresses pleasure at her return to it. This place must have necessarily inspired useful recollections and associations. Here she once lived in worldly grandeur, and with high ambitious prospects, without God in the world; and, but for divine grace, she would have been left to perish in the midst of them all. Here God, however, had been pleased to visit her in mercy, and to call her to a saving knowledge of himself; and now she felt herself little more than a stranger and pilgrim in it, looking for a heavenly inheritance. Here, unattended, she traversed the fields, walked with God, recounted his kindnesses and his grace, and with faith unfeigned, offered up fervent prayers and praises. Here, in her wanderings, she often communicated sacred instruction to the poor, which, in many instances, issued in their experimental knowledge of God. Here she generously and seasonably distributed alms to the necessitous she met with by the way, and then returned to her closet to record in her Diary, in the sincere and unaffected lowliness of her heart, how unworthy, and how sinful, and how unprofitable she felt herself to be. But such are the wonderful effects of the grace of God.—This will be seen by reading the extract which follows.

Taymouth, *July* 18.—Once more the Lord has been pleased to bring me to this place, for which I desire to bless his holy name. It was here I first found the Lord to be my God, and the Saviour of sinners. It has been here I have generally experienced more of his loving-kindness, and found his favour better than life, and have had the clearest views of his glory in the face of Jesus Christ.

July 25.—Last week I enjoyed sweet fellowship with the Lord, and peace in believing; but my mind is still harassed with vain thoughts, through my unwatchfulness. O, what an evil is this! Unwatchfulness and sloth eateth like a canker, and, when the disease cometh to a height, it is incurable to human skill. Yesterday I got into a sad, stupid, careless frame, from which I was in some measure roused, by reading Mr H. Dorney, "On God as a Sanctuary." I felt my heart drawn out towards God, with inexpressible longings and earnest desires for sanctification, and was enabled to seek, with some degree of fervency, the blessing I stood in need of. I had power to believe the Lord will accomplish his promise of sanctifying me wholly, and redeeming me from all iniquity; and that he will present me faultless before the throne of his Father, being washed from all my sins in his own blood. Lord, increase my faith! perfect that which concerneth me, for thy mercy endureth for ever. Forsake not the work of thine own hands! O let my soul live before thee. Let Christ live in me; and work in me all the good pleasure of thy goodness, and the work of faith with power: bring every thought of my heart into thy obedience; restore my diseased soul to health, and give me the spiritual mind, which is life and peace. Cleanse me from all filthiness of the flesh and spirit; and glorify thy name in me, and by me. Even so, Lord Jesus; and thine be the glory for ever. Amen.

August 14.—I have been very miserable for a fortnight past, through the power of indwelling sin, and outward temptation. I have murmured at my situation, and forgotten that the fault lay in my rebellious heart. Yesterday, as I walked in the fields alone, and attempted to sing the Lord's praises with a heavy heart, he was pleased to bring conviction upon my mind, of my past carelessness in duty, remissness in seeking strength from him, and the danger I was then in of going back into the world. I felt strong desires of turning to him, and was enabled to give up myself anew to him without reserve, to be disposed of according to his will. When I came home, I sought him by prayer and supplication, and made all my wants known unto him, with thanksgiving. This morning I went to his table with a dark confused mind, and hard heart; yet I had faith to lay hold of Christ, as the propitiation for my sins, and to trust in his perfect sacrifice as the only atonement and hope of a perishing sinner. I have little light, and no joy; but a calm peace, and quiet acquiescence in the Lord's will and way of salvation: on this salvation I trust, and desire to wait for the accomplishment of his promises, believing he will deliver me from the remains of corruption, and grant me eternal life, according to his word. So be it, Lord Jesus!

August 28.—This morning I had much comfort in prayer, and great joy in believing the glad tidings of the gospel. I saw the sin of unbelief; I acknowledged my backslidings; and was enabled to believe the Lord will heal them. I felt the spirit of adoption crying Abba Father, and had liberty to approach him as an adopted child. O for stronger faith! O for perseverance in seeking it, and grace to live by it every moment!

[Aged 33.] *September* 2.—Upon this day of the year it pleased God to call me into being, and to give me a place among the works of his hands. He hath ever since followed me with mercies, preserved me from dangers, and restrained me from innumerable evils, to which my nature was prone. O that my heart were sensible of the amazing love displayed in all his dispensations towards me. Bless the Lord, O my soul, and be stirred up to praise and thankfulness; for he hath done for thee great things; he hath called thee out of darkness into his marvellous light; he hath taken away thy filthy garments, and clothed thee with the robe of his imputed righteousness; he hath sprinkled thee with the blood that cleanseth from all sin; he hath given thee an eternal inheritance among his saints in light; and hath promised, that he will not turn away from doing thee good, but will perfect that which concerneth thee; for his love is from everlasting to everlasting, and his mercy endureth for ever. Now, what return hast thou made for all this love? Thou hast abused his mercies; neglected his precepts; been careless, slothful, and negligent in seeking him by prayer. Thou hast bestowed upon the creature, and every trifle, that time and thought which were his due. Vain wandering thoughts have got possession of thy heart; and thou hast not striven against them with all thy might. Thy prayers against them have been so cold and lifeless, that they seemed to beg a denial. Thou hast yielded too much to the snares that have been laid for thee by the world, and well nigh slipped into the paths of error. Thou hast not kept thy heart with all diligence. Thy zeal hath cooled; thy faith is weak; thy corruptions strong; thou hast left thy first love; and the things that remain are ready to die. What shall be done in such a case? Is there no remedy? Yes, blessed be God, the blood of Jesus cleanseth from all sin: To this I would fly this day. Lord, wash thou me, and I shall be clean! O grant unto me strong and lively faith to purify my heart, and overcome the world. It is by this alone I can hope for victory; it is by this alone I can give glory to thee, or obey thy will. Faith is thy gift. Grant me faith to receive all thou art willing to bestow: enlarge the capacity of my soul; enlarge my desires; and let me be filled with all the fulness of God, to the praise of the glory of thy grace for ever more. Amen!

W. G.

Sunday, September 4.—All this day I have been opposing an evil heart of unbelief, and have received no good from any thing I have heard or read. O for Abraham's faith, who staggered not at the promises of God through unbelief. Lord, I would also believe thy bare word. In Christ, thou hast given me life. What though I feel it not in my soul, and shall soon lay this body in the dust; yet, believing in him, I shall live; nay, I have life, even eternal life, now in him; and when he, who is my life, shall appear, I shall also appear with him in glory. Lord, I believe! help my unbelief!

Sunday, September 11.—I was very dull and uncomfortable, till about eleven o'clock, when the Lord poured out upon me the spirit of grace and of supplication, and enabled me to confess sin, and plead his promises for myself, and the places of worship he has raised by my means. Also for the church in general, and for all my own friends and connexions.

I found much comfort in singing his praises abroad in the fields. We had no sermon in church; but blessed be God, it has not been a silent Sabbath to my soul.

In the month of November Lady Glenorchy was again in Edinburgh, exercised it would seem with some new and unexpected trials. Lead us not into temptation, but deliver us from evil, is a petition which our Lord has enjoined every one of his disciples, in every age, daily to offer, and which implies that every one of them in every age is daily exposed to temptation, and to suffer by it, and that it requires the interpositions of divine power and grace to preserve them from it. If any disciple of Christ might be supposed to be placed beyond the reach of temptation, one would think that a person so abstracted from the world, so cautious, so watchful, so tremblingly alive to the most distant appearances of evil as Lady Glenorchy was, must be that favoured disciple. She however was not exempted from the common lot of humanity, and although she was not permitted to fall by temptations, she was assailed by them. She however found that God did not suffer her to be tempted above that she was able to bear; but with the temptation also made a way to escape, with some account of which she closes her Diary for this year.

November 20.—For some weeks past my mind has been so much agitated, that I could not continue my Diary, being unable to judge of the real state of my soul. The Lord hath been pleased in the course of his providence, to appoint me a trial of a new nature. I have been tempted by the world in its most alluring form, to forsake the narrow path; and the bait was so artfully hid, and so much suited to my natural temper, that I have felt a very severe struggle to escape from it. What the Lord is to teach me by this I know not; but surely I may learn much of my own weakness from it.

December 11.—Since writing the above, the Lord has been pleased to send bodily affliction upon me, which has, I hope, in some measure been sanctified. During the first part of it, I was in a very sad and miserable frame, unable to pray or think a good thought. I seemed to be cast out from his presence; but at length he sent deliverance, he rebuked the tempter, and gave me liberty in pouring out my complaint before him, and has restored the light to my benighted soul, which shows me once more the vanity of all things here below, and the unspeakable privilege of being wholly devoted to God, in a life of self-denial and holiness. I feel my spiritual strength renewed, and have pleasure in hearing the word and in prayer. Last Friday I had a humbling view of the low state of religion in this country, and was enabled to plead for the people with many supplications and tears, and to pray for success to Mr Grove's ministry, who seems to be a faithful minister of the gospel. These things have been a burden upon my mind. I now feel power to believe in invisible things, and am deeply impressed with the thought of eternity, and that the Lord is at hand. The love of the world seems taken out of my heart. I am willing to leave it. I have a comfortable hope that the Lord indeed is my God, and that he has begun a good work in me, and will perfect that which concerneth me. I see much of his goodness in delivering me from the snare which was lately laid for my feet. O that he may continue to guide me by his counsel, and keep me from falling!

February 20. 1775.—For some months past my life has been chequered with hopes and fears concerning the state of my soul; but, upon the whole, I have had more comfort in hearing the word, and in talking of the things of God, than formerly.

March 1.—I arrived in London under great apprehensions of being left of God to dishonour him by going back into the world.

Lady Glenorchy's chapel had hitherto been supplied partly by the clergymen and probationers of the city and neighbourhood, and partly by two respectable dissenting ministers from England, Mr Edwards of Leeds, and Mr Grove of Wooburn, in Buckinghamshire. Dissenting ministers from England, at this time, were admitted freely to the pulpits of the Established churches, and even allowed to receive presentations to parishes, there being no law to the contrary. Lady Glenorchy had been confined all January by sickness; but early in February she went to England, among other objects, to seek supply for her chapel. There is a weekly meeting in London among the orthodox dissenters, which is held every Tuesday morning, called the Merchants' Lecture, because it was originally instituted and supported by that class of men, and has subsisted for a century. Six of the most distinguished ministers of the city and its environs, elected by the subscribers, are the lecturers, and preach alternately. On the 14th of March Lady Glenorchy attended this lecture. By one of those incidents that sometimes happen in human life, the writer of these memoirs, passing through London, was taken that morning by a friend to Pinner's Hall, the place where these lectures were then delivered. Mr Webb, pastor of a church in Fetter-lane, Holborn, was the lecturer for that day, and preached from the 18th verse of the first chapter of the Epistle to the Ephesians, "The eyes of your understanding being enlightened, that ye may know what is the hope of his calling, and what the riches of the glory of his inheritance in the saints." The house was very small, the congregation not numerous, the preacher advanced in life, and read every word of his sermon, with no grace in the delivery: in short, there was no external embellishment to give the discourse the least force; but there was a gravity, a sincerity, a pathos, an uncommonly rich display of evangelical experimental truth, accompanied with a holy unction that made every word irresistible to a mind disposed to receive the impressions of divine truth, the effect of which six-and-forty years has not effaced from the mind of the author of these pages; nor will any number of years be able to do so, whilst his faculty of memory remains. Lady Glenorchy was seeking a minister for her chapel: little did she think that there was at that time present a stripling, perhaps within her view, not then twenty years of age, who, in that moment, in sentiment and feeling, held close religious fellowship with her, and who, within five short years was to become the minister of her chapel, and after having laboured in it between forty and fifty years, was to take this manner of attempting to do justice to her memory and character. Little did this stripling think there was then in that small congregation, and among the citizens of London, a person of her rank and influence, to whom before the close of the next year, by what some men call accident, but by what he considers a very peculiar and gracious providence of Almighty God, he should be introduced; and on which introduction, by the blessing of Heaven, nearly all his future usefulness and comfort for a long life would depend: But thus it was, for so it seemed good in the eyes of the wise and beneficent disposer of all events.

Lady Glenorchy left London in May, having previously paid a visit in Bedfordshire, probably to her sister-in-law, the Marchioness of Grey; thence she went to her friend, Miss Hill, at Hawkstone, and afterwards to Buxton and other places. The incessant hurry and bustling necessarily occasioned by removing from place to place, was extremely irksome to one accustomed as she was to great regularity and order; and she returned about the beginning of August with very perturbed feelings. These, however, as in other similar instances, she turned to a good account, by using them to lead her to close examination of herself, and to flee with much earnestness to God for aid, as will be seen by the extracts from her Diary which will next appear.

March 14.—I was delivered from my fears by hearing a sermon at Pinner's Hall, from Mr Webb, on Ephesians i. 18. and from this time forward, for two months, I experienced peace and joy in believing.

May 15.—I went to pay a visit at W—— in Bedfordshire, where I staid two days; and there lost sight of my privileges, and got into darkness and distress of mind. Thence I went to Hawkstone and other places, still continuing in a sad dark frame of mind. At my return to Edinburgh I met with many trials, and my heart yielded but too much to the suggestions of the enemy. I endeavoured to pray, and the Lord poured out the spirit of supplication upon me. I then had a sight of the evil of backsliding in heart, and was enabled to pray for healing.

August 13.—This morning I arose early to call upon God, but found my heart cold and dead. I could neither pray, read, nor meditate in a profitable manner.

O Lord, search my heart, and try my inward parts; shew me what my real state is: I may deceive myself and others, but I cannot deceive thee. Graciously discover to me the deep deceits of my wicked heart, and sweep away every refuge of lies. Leave me no covering but that of the unspotted robe of a Redeemer's righteousness, under which do thou enable me to flee; for his sake I ask it who shed his precious blood to redeem such wretched sinners as I am from guilt and misery. O Lord, let me not enjoy one moment's peace till I find peace in thee. Imbitter every thing to my taste, until I taste that thou art gracious!

After this period Lady Glenorchy went to Taymouth somewhat later in the year than usual. In this earthly paradise she hoped to find quiet; and she did so, and something more than quiet. Immediately on her arrival there she determined to seek the Lord by a day of extraordinary private fasting and prayer. The account which she gives of her preparation for this, in which she enumerates her many wants, and of the manner in which she observed it, together with the effects which followed, is very edifying: her recollections and reflections on her birth-day are also truly affecting. She appears this summer to have enjoyed more peace and divine consolation than ever she did before; and on this account the Diary of this period will be read with peculiar pleasure.

Taymouth, August 17. 1775.—I arrived at this beloved place, which is peculiarly endeared to my soul, being the place of my spiritual birth, and frequently has since been a place of revival and refreshment to my spiritual life. I purpose setting apart to-morrow as a day of prayer, in order to seek the Lord. I have been considering the wants of my soul, that I may plead for a supply at the throne of grace. They are as follow:—

I want an abiding sense of the presence of God, a filial fear, a hatred of sin, love to holiness, more faith exercised in the promises of God, especially that in John xiii. 13, 14. "And whatsoever ye shall ask in my name, that will I do, that the Father may be glorified in the Son. If ye shall ask any thing in my name, I will do it."

I want to have sin subdued and mortified in me by the Spirit of God, and that the Holy Ghost may shed abroad his influences in my heart, to purify, enlighten, and sanctify me; to testify of Jesus, teach me what I know not, lead me into all truth, and refresh me with his consolations.

I want to have my backslidings healed, my soul restored to the vigorous exercise of grace, awakened from drowsiness and sloth, and that the things which remain and are ready to die, may be strengthened.

I want the Holy Spirit to witness with my spirit that I am born again, and that I am now a child of God.

I want the improper love of myself destroyed, that internal principle of selfishness which stains, mars, and spoils all I say and do.

I want my besetting sin mortified, which, the Lord knows, has harassed and distressed my soul for years past; and although now it prevails not, but rather seems dead, yet I fear will revive on the first temptation.

I want to know more of God, of his perfections, of his glory as it shines in the person of Jesus Christ our Lord, of his love to sinners in the work of redemption.

I want an experimental knowledge of the truths I have been taught. I would feel their influence on my heart and life, that it may appear unto all that I belong to Jesus Christ.

I want to be made willing that all should know this, that I may not be ashamed at any time, or any place, of my Christian profession.

I want more humility and lowliness of heart, and self-denied and constant obedience to all the commands of Christ.

I want the image of Christ stamped on my soul, and more love to him, and more conformity to him in all things.

I want wisdom to direct me how to behave towards my unconverted relations, seeing that all the ways I have hitherto tried have proved ineffectual in reconciling them to the truths of God.

I want gravity and dignity of behaviour at all times, becoming my profession, and the high calling of God. I would carry about with me the dying of the Lord Jesus.

I want also wisdom to direct me in temporal affairs, that I may act the part of a faithful steward of the things intrusted to my charge, so that I may neither by profusion nor narrowness bring a reproach upon religion.

I want more of the spirit of prayer, and power to meditate and delight in reading the word of God; a tender conscience to feel the first approach of sin; an evangelical repentance, that looks on him I have pierced, and that mourns because of sin, as the procuring cause of his sufferings; and which leads to flee from sin as from the face of a serpent.

I want more love to the brethren, for the Lord's sake, and a more single eye to his glory in all I do for them.

I want to have no will of my own in any thing, but ever to find the Lord's will precious to me, even when it crosses my will. I know he cannot err, therefore I would rejoice when I am disappointed, for when his will takes place my end is answered; for I desire only to advance his glory.

I want to know his will concerning the manner in which I ought to settle the chapel in Edinburgh, and that in Strathfillan, and the parish of Cramond.

I want to know my wants, and to have access at all times to spread them before a throne of grace, where I know they can be abundantly supplied out of the fulness of Christ.

August 25.—I arose early to spend an hour in confessing my sins unto the Lord. My soul was rather dead in the duty, yet, through grace, I attained to something of simplicity of heart,—a desire for sincerity, and consciousness of deficiency.

I afterwards spent some time in reading the Scriptures. The Lord was present with my spirit. I afterwards retired to a place unknown to others, where I sought the Lord, first for his church, and then for myself. He was graciously pleased to permit me to spread my wants before him. I felt enlarged in prayer, and got somewhat of a fervent spirit for two hours, and had some degree of comfort from the secret testimony of the Spirit, of the love of God to my soul. This was not in so great a measure as on former occasions of this sort; but I was made to perceive the Spirit of Christ was indeed making intercession for me, and I had confidence of being heard. I have since this time been rather in a dull frame; corruption still assails me; but the Lord will deliver me in his own time. I desire to praise him with my whole soul for all that is past, and to trust him for all that is to come.

August 26.—This morning I had sweet access to a throne of grace, and felt some meltings of heart in the view of my Redeemer's sufferings for sinners, and for myself in particular. I could say that I looked upon him whom I had pierced. I felt abhorrence at the part I had in crucifying the Lord of glory.

This day I made a disposition of my chapel and school in Edinburgh, and I believe I have done it under the direction of the Lord, in the way most likely to promote the end I have in view. To him be the praise!

Sunday 27.—Before going to church, I prayed the Lord to enable me to look beyond the instrument, and to receive his word in the love of it. The sermon was a good one, and my soul was refreshed by it.

Friday, September 1.—This day I endeavoured to keep as a day of prayer, for the revival of religion in our land. I found some degree of sorrow for the abounding iniquity of it, and liberty to plead with the Lord that our backslidings might be healed; and I also remembered all my Christian friends particularly by name before the Lord.

[Aged 34.] *September* 2.—It hath been my custom, ever since I knew the grace of God, to observe this day as a day of humiliation for my sins, and of thanksgiving for the mercies conferred upon me by God my Saviour, from my birth to the present hour. To see my own vileness, I must at the same time behold the infinite perfections of a Holy God. O that I had a clearer view of his glory and excellence, of his amazing love to the sinful sons of men! Then should I indeed be humbled under a sense of the ingratitude and insensibility of my cold wretched heart, which is so little moved by all his tender mercies and loving kindnesses to me, preserving me from evil, restraining me from outward sin, redeeming my soul from hell, and adopting me into his family. He has given me a goodly inheritance in this world, and in that which is to come an inheritance incorruptible, undefiled, and which fadeth not away. Surely none ever had such cause to extol free sovereign grace,—a brand plucked from the burning,—a backslider restored,—a poor worm raised up and employed by infinite grace as an instrument in the Lord's work! Was it for any foreseen good in me, any greater measure of love or faithfulness, that the Lord has thus distinguished me by his grace? O no! at this day my vile heart is still prone to depart from him by unbelief,—at times it is filled with all evil,—sin still warreth in me, and deceives me, so that I am frequently led captive by it, and made to cry out for the bitterness of my soul. Sometimes I am ashamed of my gracious God, and fall into conformity to the vain conversation of his enemies; and thus spend precious time in a most unprofitable manner. I sometimes restrain prayer, neglect meditation, and reading the scriptures. I am careless in reading, and inattentive in hearing, the word of God, and omit many known duties. Oh, my sins of omission are many and grievous; had the Lord dealt with me as I have sinned, I should now have been lost. But, glory to his name, his thoughts are not as our thoughts. How hath my heart, like that of Joseph's brethren, misinterpreted the Lord's dealings, and foreboded terror and destruction, while his thoughts have been of good, and not of evil. How hath he overruled my sins and follies for his own glory and my everlasting good. O how much have I learnt this year of my own weakness, ignorance, pride, worldliness, and desperate wickedness of heart! I hope I have also learned to trust it less, and to expect no safety or stability but in the ways of God, and from himself. As to outward things, I have been blessed by an increase of income, in proportion to what I have laid out in his cause. He hath hitherto helped me, and owned the work I have been engaged in to be his, by blessing his word to some souls.—For all these things I desire to praise him, and to ascribe unto the Father, Son, and Holy Spirit, one God, as is most due, all the glory, now and for ever more. W. G.

Sunday, September 3.—This whole day has been spent in inward conflict with the corruptions of my heart. The enemy within opposes me in every thing I do. When I would read, meditate, and pray, some vain thought is suddenly suggested, that leads me away, and causes me to lament in sorrow the deep depravity of my nature, and the carelessness and sloth of my past life.

Monday, September 4.—Last night, after writing down my exercise during the day, I took up my Bible, and read in Revelations, from the sixth chapter to the end; during which the Lord was pleased to give me such hope and comfort in the faith of the glory to be revealed, and of my own part in it, that I could hardly read for tears of joy. I had sweet peace through the evening,—the enemy seemed to have left me,—and this morning I awoke with these words: "He hath made him to be sin for us, who knew no sin, that we might be made the righteousness of God in him." I made haste to get upon my knees, and the Lord poured out upon me the spirit of grace and supplication with thanksgiving. I got much liberty of access to God, and made known my suit with boldness, and confidence of being heard; in particular, for the church of Christ, for my chapels, ministers, schools, my bosom friends Lady Maxwell and Lady Henrietta Hope, their parents and mine. I felt much love for them, and all the saints, as being one with them in Christ;—was astonished at the grace and mercy of the Lord, in calling such worms to partake of his glory, and particularly myself, the vilest of all. I got new light upon some Scriptures while praying over them, especially Heb. xii. 1—6. "Wherefore, seeing we also are compassed about with so great a cloud of witnesses, let us lay aside every weight, and the sin which doth so easily beset us, and let us run with patience the race that is set before us. For whom the Lord loveth he chasteneth, and scourgeth every son whom he receiveth;" and Phil. ii. 5. 11. "Let this mind be in you which was also in Christ Jesus." "And that every tongue should confess that Jesus Christ is Lord, to the glory of the Father." I got a sight of one great evil in my heart, namely, being unwilling to become of no reputation for Christ. I prayed earnestly to be made willing; and also for a spiritual mind, and to be delivered from vain thoughts. I asked power to persevere in the use of the means for attaining spirituality of mind, and that I might be kept from temptations which have hitherto overcome me, and now threaten me. Glory be to God for the mercies of this morning. I note this to the praise of his glorious rich free grace to the most unworthy of all his redeemed creatures.

Sunday, September 10.—This last week I have again been tried with vain company, and have cause to lament my numberless miscarriages and omissions. I yielded too much to their spirit, yet I have cause to bless the Lord for enabling me to confess him before them. I have had little life or comfort to-day in my soul, yet at bottom there is a hope I would not part with for a thousand worlds. There *is* a state of life and immortality beyond the grave.

Sunday, September 17.—During the course of last week I have had much occasion to lament the deep depravity of my mind, and the power of old habits; yet, notwithstanding my folly, the Lord has at times been very gracious to my soul, particularly one day when reading in the fields an old book, Christ in you the hope of Glory, by Brown, or Christ dwelling in the Believer by the Spirit. I was made to believe my union with him, and his actually dwelling in my heart by faith, in so clear and satisfactory a manner, that I was filled with joy and wonder unspeakable. My soul was transported with a view of invisible things,—it seemed too much for the body.

This morning, after trying to pray, being very dull and dead in it, I took up Vincent on the Coming of Christ to Judgment, and had not read far before my soul was filled with unspeakable joy and peace in believing. I was made to see my willingness to receive him, and consequently my interest in him. I was overwhelmed with a sense, or foretaste as it were, of the glory to be revealed, and astonished at the sovereign rich grace of God, that had written my worthless name in the book of life before the foundation of the world. I fell at his feet overcome with love, unable to speak, and could only adore in silence, uttering my feelings by sighs and tears.

At church the Psalms were refreshing to my soul. I could sing heartily to the Lord, my Strength and Redeemer. The text was, " Rejoice that your names are written in the book of life."—I did rejoice. The four last verses of the 97th Psalm, which were afterwards sung, were very pleasant to my soul:—

For thou, O Lord, art high above
 All things on earth that are;
Above all other gods thou art
 Exalted very far.

For all those that be righteous
 Sown is a joyful light;
And gladness sown is for all those
 That are in heart upright, &c. &c.

I saw much in that verse, Light is sown for the righteous, and gladness for the upright in heart. But this pleasant frame did not last long. Upon the whole, this has been a blessed day to my soul. Glory be to God!

Sunday, October 8.—The Lord has been very gracious to me during the course of last week and this day. This is a time of prosperity with me in soul and body. I enjoy health, riches, friends, comforts of various sorts; spiritual mercies, peace of conscience, freedom from many evils, and some measure of faith in the glorious things that await me when time shall be no more. The dangers I have now to fear are spiritual pride, high-mindedness, self-seeking, self-righteousness, impatience, sloth, carelessness, omission of known duties, and carnal security. Gracious Lord, deliver me from these, and every other sin and snare thou seest me in danger of,—undertake for me,—preserve me now in this day of wealth, lest I be full, wax fat, and kick against thee. Let thy grace and power be manifested in keeping my soul near to thyself, in a humble dependance on thee for all things. Sensible of my own nothingness and emptiness, may I come every moment to receive from thy fulness, wisdom, righteousness, and strength. Grant this, for thy holy name's sake. Amen!

CHAPTER XIV.

Lady Glenorchy returns to Edinburgh—Some circumstances with respect to her chapel there cause her much uneasiness—Extracts from Diary—Letter from Lady Glenorchy to the Presbytery of Edinburgh concerning Mr Grove—Answer from the Presbytery to her Ladyship—Mr Grove determines to return to England—Lady Glenorchy still further distressed with the circumstances of the chapel—Resolves to leave Scotland—Her friends' remonstrances against this resolution, particularly Lady Henrietta Hope—Lady Glenorchy determines to invite a minister to her chapel to whom the Presbytery could have no objections—Extracts from Diary, from January 14. to April 20. 1776—Lady Glenorchy makes choice of Mr Balfour as the minister of her chapel—Correspondence of Lady Glenorchy with the Presbytery of Edinburgh on the subject—Difference of opinion in the Presbytery on the measure—The matter brought by complaint before the Synod of Lothian and Tweeddale—Lady Glenorchy goes to Taymouth—Extracts from Diary, from July 11. to September 2. 1776.

Lady Glenorchy returned to Edinburgh in October, where circumstances soon occurred which gave her much and long vexation. Some of her religious friends had scruples with respect to their continuing members of the established church, and they separated from it, and became zealous and censorious sectarians of different denominations. These occurrences affected her very much. Mr Grove had preached in her chapel three months at the close of the last year, and after going back to England, he returned in October, bringing his family with him, and preached for as long a period at the end of this present year. He was very generally acceptable to the congregation, and desirous to settle amongst them; nor was Lady Glenorchy averse to it.

There were some, however, who were not satisfied with Mr Grove's sentiments with respect to church order, and they expressed their dissatisfaction in a way which made Lady Glenorchy very uneasy. However, to put an end to this, she applied by letter to the Presbytery of Edinburgh, informing them of her wishes to gratify the congregation of her chapel, by appointing Mr Grove to be their minister, and respectfully requesting their countenance therein; to which she received an answer, stating the terms on which they were disposed to acquiesce in Mr Grove's settlement.

Of these circumstances the reader will be further informed by an extract from her Diary, and copies of these letters.

Edinburgh, Sunday, October 22.—I came yesterday to this place; found my soul refreshed in conversing with some dear Christian friends. To-day the word of God, and the whole services of the church, have been comfortable. To him be the glory!

December 20.—On Wednesday the 14th of November I got a cold, which brought on a long confinement and bad state of health: I was at the same time much afflicted in my soul; had no comfort from the Scriptures or prayer.

On Sunday the 17th I begged the Lord to shew me what my real state was before him; my trouble increased; I began to murmur at my situation. The enemy for a season was permitted to plead the cause of his votaries, and drew a comparison between them and the church to the disadvantage of the latter: thus my mind was drawn aside into awful and dangerous depths. Upon this I ventured to pray that God would manifest himself and his work of redemption to my soul. In bitterness of spirit I arose from my knees, took up the Bible, and cried to the Lord to give me faith in his word, and an answer of peace from it. On reading, the snare by which I was held gave way, and my soul escaped as a bird. From meditating on the Scriptures, peace was restored to my soul, my doubts and distresses vanished away, and my relish for the word of God and access to the throne of grace have been restored. Glory be to God!

The letter to the Presbytery of Edinburgh which has been mentioned, is in the following terms:—

To the Moderator of the Presbytery of Edinburgh.

" *Edinburgh, December* 27. 1775.

" Rev. Sir,—I acquainted your reverend Presbytery, in a letter sent to them in March 1774, that the chapel which I had built, for the purposes mentioned in that letter, would soon be ready for the reception of a congregation; that I intended to have it supplied with a minister of approved character and abilities; and was persuaded it would be ageeeable to the Presbytery, that, in the mean time, I should ask occasional supply from such ministers and probationers as I was acquainted with.

" The Presbytery having been pleased to signify their approbation of my design, several ministers and probationers have cheerfully given their assistance; and I have no doubt they will continue it, which in future will only be necessary at particular times, as the chapel is now statedly supplied by the Rev. Thomas Grove, a minister of established character and abilities, who for several years has been pastor of a Protestant dissenting congregation in England, and as such gave the security required by law in that part of the kingdom for his loyalty to Government, and his adherence to those essential doctrines of the Reformation in which the established Confessions of both churches are happily agreed. He is well known to several ministers of this city and suburbs, with whom he has joined in ministerial communion; and to those who attend at the chapel, having preached to them during the space of three months last year, and as many this year; to whom his ministrations are so acceptable that they have expressed their earnest desire of his continuance among them as their pastor, which it is my intention to comply with, that, besides the preaching of the word, they may enjoy the comfort and benefit of the other ordinances of religion, which are dispensed to their brethren of the same communion in their parish churches. I beg you will do me the favour to communicate this letter to the Reverend Presbytery at their first meeting, with my respectful compliments, which will oblige, Rev. Sir, your most obedient and most humble servant,

"W. GLENORCHY."

To this letter Lady Glenorchy received the subjoined reply :—

To the Right Honourable Lady Glenorchy.

"Madam,—Your Ladyship's letter was laid before us; and although we continue to approve of your pious intentions in establishing the new congregation within our bounds, we cannot give countenance to any person's being admitted minister thereof, until we have satisfying evidence of his having been regularly licensed and ordained, of his loyalty to Government, and of his conformity to our standards. We have the honour to be your Ladyship's most obedient most humble servants. H. MONCRIEFF WELLWOOD, *Moderator*."

1776.—Mr Grove was a gentleman of some landed property, of good address and talents, and of pleasant manners. He was one of the six young men, who, in the year 1768, were expelled from the University of Oxford, for praying extempore in a private house; but was by his severe judges acknowledged to be the least exceptionable of them in every respect: and although with great humility and earnestness he petitioned for restoration, and the Vice-Chancellor admitted that his case was very hard, his application, notwithstanding, was refused. This harsh treatment made Mr Grove a decided dissenter in his own country, and gave him a distaste to national religious establishments in general; and as he found Lady Glenorchy determined not to separate her Chapel from the Church of Scotland, of which she was a member, and with which her oldest, ablest, and best friends were connected, he determined, but not without much reluctance, to return to England.

This event occasioned Lady Glenorchy considerable perplexity, and the suspicion and clamour and evil speaking to which it gave rise, hurt her so much, that she seriously meditated a plan of selling her estate, and leaving Scotland altogether. This resolution both alarmed and distressed her friends, who did not fail to remonstrate against her intention in very strong terms: among these was Lady Henrietta Hope, who wrote to her, on the 18th of January, in the following manner:—

"I did not receive your's, my dear Madam, till this morning; and then, I must own, I felt sensations which your ever welcome letters have not been used to excite. So little am I reconciled to the plan you have eventually formed, that the determined manner in which you write of it as if really to take place, was more than I could bear unmoved; and I know not how long the damp it threw on my spirits would have continued, had it not been brought to my remembrance, that *you* might *propose*, but that *God* would *dispose*, and surely overrule all things for his glory. To me it appears next to impossible, that by such an event this great end should be advanced; but, as your Ladyship seems at present to be absolutely fixed in your determination, I shall not trouble you more on the subject, till some better occasion offer to remonstrate more strongly."

The circumstances of Mr Grove's family would not admit of his immediate return to England. He therefore remained, and no objection being made to it, preached in the chapel till the end of February, when it again was supplied by the ministers and probationers of the city and neighbourhood.

When Mr Grove finally left Edinburgh, Lady Glenorchy consulted her friends with respect to the most eligible mode of conducting and settling her chapel. She herself was of opinion, that the best way to prevent all suspicions and jealousies with respect to her objects and designs, would be to invite a minister from the church, of whose ecclesiastical views no doubt could be entertained, either by the Presbytery or the public; and having fixed upon the mode of management, her mind became tranquil and easy as will appear from her Diary.

Sunday, January 14.—The Lord has seen meet to afford me some glimmerings of light on the path of duty. I have seen it right to give up my own plans and wishes concerning the settlement of the chapel, and simply to follow whatever seems most likely to promote faith, peace, and love, in the Church of Christ.

I have permitted Mr Grove to return to England, as he was not willing to sign the formula, and I did not find myself at liberty to separate from the Established Church. I now think of procuring a minister from among ourselves, for stated pastor, who will consent to the occasional visits of preachers from England. My mind is more composed since this was settled. I now wait for light whom to chuse, and how to proceed. But my soul is still at a distance from God. Strong temptations assault me in prayer; so that I cannot continue many minutes in it. My thoughts are unfixed; my body threatened with a painful and dangerous malady. I have no great fears of death: I seem more afraid to live to dishonour God. I almost look on an early death as a privilege; and should rejoice to think it near, were my soul as comfortable as in times past.

Sunday, January 28.—The Lord has been graciously pleased to loosen my bonds, and permitted me to pray with some degree of faith, to commit my way unto him, and to give up myself wholly to him for time and eternity. I found sweet composure of mind, and power to rest on his word this forenoon in secret. I was however disappointed in public worship, my mind wandered, and I got no benefit, and returned home ashamed and confounded at the deep and unutterable depravity of my nature, yet thankful for the ground

I have to hope for deliverance through the Lord Jesus Christ.

Sunday, February 10.—The Lord hath permitted me this day to sit down at his table, and partake of the symbols of his broken body and shed blood, with some degree of faith. Blessed be his name for creating in me a hunger and thirst for spiritual blessings, and for letting me feel my wants.

He has also restored, in a measure, my health, delivered me from the fear of an incurable and painful disease, and relieved my mind from many other heavy weights: he enables me to cast my care upon him, and to believe that he careth for me. The 103d Psalm was sweet to my soul this morning,—I could praise the Lord in the language of the Psalmist, believing that he had indeed forgiven mine iniquities, and pardoned my sin;—that as a father pitieth his child, so did he pity my helplessness and my infirmities.

This evening I have felt like the workings of true repentance and godly sorrow for backslidings, vain thoughts, short-comings, and backwardness to duty. My soul longeth after holiness and conformity to the image of Christ. I have, I think, from the bottom of my heart, asked the Holy Spirit to abide in me, and sit as a refiner's fire, to purify me from all my dross, to sanctify every power and faculty of my soul.

February 23.—Last Lord's day my soul was in a very dull frame in hearing, and at home I had little liberty in prayer till the evening, when the Lord was pleased to give me a praying spirit for increase of faith, and the work of sanctification in my soul.—Blessed be his name, he hath answered me, by giving me all this week a sensible increase and revival in my soul, more of the spirit of prayer, and more watchfulness over my heart and tongue. This morning I continued some hours in private exercises, and found in a measure his presence with me.

My heart this night is cold, and my affections languid; but my hope remains as an anchor, fixed within the veil, sure and steadfast. I will hope in Jesus, who (though my frame changeth) remaineth the same yesterday, to-day, and for ever. I have, for some days past, found great benefit in reading the Scriptures.

March 17.—Since writing the above, it pleased God to send a severe illness upon me, which has reduced my body very low, and I have seldom had any sensible life or joy in my soul. But, blessed be his name, my hope concerning the life to come has never failed; my sweetest moments have been those when death appeared near. This day I have had the privilege of sitting down at the Lord's table. My body was very weak, and I could not get to a lively frame of spirit; but I was enabled to receive the tokens of his unspeakable love with a thankful heart, and to bless the Father for giving the Son, the Son for giving himself up to the death for us, and the Holy Ghost for applying the benefits of his death, and opening my understanding to know the truth, without which I must for ever have remained in ignorance, and perished eternally. This evening I see my great need of fresh supplies of grace, and have got power to plead for more life, wisdom, knowledge, faith, love, holiness, strength, and power over sin, and a thankful spirit for mercies received.

April 20.—For a month past I have been much engaged in outward things, yet I have had sweet moments in the contemplation of the divine promises, and in laying hold of them by an appropriating faith. On Sunday the 7th, I enjoyed a lively sense of the love of God all the day, both in public and in private devotion. The week following my joy was interrupted by the business in which I was engaged, and a weak body, which clouded the mind; but my hope remained immoveable. On Saturday last I heard a sermon on brotherly love, from Mr S——, under which I was convinced that I had hitherto failed greatly in this duty, and determined, through grace, to observe more carefully the commands of Christ concerning it, particularly in 1 Corinthians, 13th chapter.

The first movement of Lady Glenorchy in the execution of her plan for her chapel, was to select a proper person to be proposed to the congregation and Presbytery, as the future minister. The clergyman on whom she fixed, was the Rev. Robert Balfour, minister of the parish of Lecropt, near Stirling, and afterwards, for nearly forty years, the justly admired and beloved pastor of the Outer High Church of Glasgow, whose memory will long be dear, very dear, indeed, to the hearts of all who knew him, for his piety—his integrity—his great talents—his kindness—his candour—his usefulness, and every grace, virtue, and action that bind close Christian to Christian, and man to man. No choice could be more judicious than this. He was a native of the city of Edinburgh, he had been educated at its schools and university, he was a licentiate of its Presbytery, and well known to the most of its members from his very childhood. The people were delighted with this choice; Mr Balfour cheerfully accepted of the offer, and no one dreamt of opposition from any quarter; but the great Lord of the vineyard had destined him for a much higher station, and a sphere of much greater usefulness.

Lady Glenorchy was not destitute of able advisers. In the church she numbered Dr Webster, Dr Dick, Dr Erskine, Mr Walker, &c. &c. and out of it, Mr Crosby, Advocate, one of the most distinguished men at the bar in his day. They appear to have informed her, that there were two sorts of chapels in connexion with the Established church, the one, chapels of Ease strictly so called, entirely dependant in their operations on the minister and session of the parish within whose bounds they are situated, and in which the ministers are in fact little, if any thing, more than assistants to them; the other, free chapels, accountable for their conduct only to their Presbyteries and the superior courts. Lady Glenorchy's chapel was of the latter class. As institutions of this kind were but few at this period, laws and regulations for them did not exist, and therefore Presbyteries admitted them on such terms as they judged expedient,—the proprietors and people generally struggling for as much liberty as they could possibly obtain, and the church courts gradually drawing tighter and tighter the cords of restraint. By a law enacted since this period, the rules by which every chapel that is erected is to be conducted are prescribed by the General Assembly, before it is admitted to the communion of the Church. This statement will enable the reader better to understand the nature of the contest into which Lady Glenorchy, much against her inclination, was brought with certain individuals in the church courts.

All things having been prepared for the inducting Mr Balfour, she, on the 15th of May, sent the following letter to the Presbytery :—

To the Moderator, &c.

" *Edinburgh*, 15*th May* 1776.

" Rev. Sir,—As the chapel I lately built in this city is private property, and not meant to be put upon the footing of the Establishment, I was informed, that what related to the settlement of a minister there, could not with propriety be brought before your Presbytery. But it appeared to me a piece of respect due to so venerable a body, to acquaint them of my intention not to settle any person but one of established character, loyal to Government, sound in the faith, and firmly resolved not to follow any divisive courses.

" This I did, some time before the chapel was opened, in a letter directed to the moderator. And in December last I acquainted them, in another letter, that the Rev. Mr Grove, a dissenting minister in England, having for some time officiated in the chapel, I had occasion to be fully satisfied that he was, in all respects, a person to whom the above character justly belonged; and therefore had a view of calling him to be minister of the said chapel. To this letter I was favoured with the following answer :—' Your Ladyship's letter was laid before us, and though we continue to approve of your pious intentions in establishing the congregation within our bounds, we cannot give countenance to any person's being admitted minister thereof, until we have satisfying evidence of his having been regularly licensed and ordained, of his loyalty to Government, and of his conformity to our standards.'

"It gave me pleasure that the Presbytery approved of my general design, and were satisfied of the integrity of my intentions. They have, no doubt, a title to demand evidence of what they judge necessary, previous to their fixing a pastoral relation between a minister and any congregation within their bounds; and I am persuaded, if circumstances had permitted Mr Grove to remain in Scotland, he would have given such satisfaction, with respect to the above particulars, as would have removed all difficulty in the way of their granting that countenance to his ministrations, which I meant to have asked of them.

"This is now unnecessary, Mr Grove has returned to England, and I intend that the Rev. Mr Balfour, minister of Lecropt, one of your own licentiates, with whose ministerial abilities and good character you are well acquainted, shall be pastor of the foresaid congregation.

"As at his ordination he subscribed, and is still ready to subscribe, the standards of the Church of Scotland, my nomination of him cannot fail of being agreeable to your Presbytery, especially when I add, that such is his regard for them, and his resolution to hold communion with the ministers of the Establishment, that he declines taking any step toward the loosing of his pastoral relation from his parish, until he is assured that your Presbytery will countenance his admission to the chapel, by appointing one of their number to preach on the occasion. This you will please to signify to them at their first meeting, who, I doubt not, will comply with Mr Balfour's request. I am, with respect, Reverend Sir, your most humble servant.

"W. Glenorchy."

The Presbytery unanimously approved of Lady Glenorchy's choice of Mr Balfour, as being possessed of all the qualifications they had required; but he having intimated his desire to be introduced to the chapel, by one *appointed* by the Presbytery to preach on that occasion, this gave rise to a debate,—a few members being of opinion, that, in order to authorize such appointment, it was necessary that there should be a call from the congregation, and legal security for the stipend to the minister; and that the collections should be put under the administration of the managers of the Charity Workhouse. The majority of the Presbytery thought these requisitions improper and unnecessary, but, desirous to preserve that unanimity which had hitherto subsisted, they agreed, without a vote, to appoint a committee of their number to converse with Lady Glenorchy on these points; and as the minority differed amongst themselves as to the precise things they demanded, the Presbytery, instead of specifying particulars, gave a general instruction to their committee, and through their moderator wrote to her as follows:—

To the Right Honourable Lady Glenorchy.

" *Edinburgh*, 17*th May* 1776.

" Madam,—I this day laid your letter of the 15th current before the Presbytery, and have received their directions to assure your Ladyship, that the nomination of Mr Balfour to be minister of your chapel, is very agreeable to them; and that they will, upon proper application being made to them, appoint such a day for his admission to be minister of the chapel, as shall be convenient for your Ladyship; and have recommended it to Dr Webster, Dr Erskine, and Mr

Robert Walker, to converse with your Ladyship upon their ideas of a proper application. I have the honour to be, in the most respectful manner, Madam, your Ladyship's most obedient and very humble servant.

"H. MONCRIEFF WELLWOOD, *Moderator*."

Pursuant to the above recommendation, the committee gave Lady Glenorchy a full account of what had passed in the Presbytery; and, in consequence of this, she wrote the following letter to the moderator:—

To the Moderator, &c.

"*Edinburgh, May* 24. 1776.

"Rev. Sir,—On Saturday last I received your letter of the 17th current, informing me that the nomination of Mr Balfour, minister of Lecropt, to be the minister of my chapel, is very agreeable to the Presbytery; and that, upon proper application made to them, they will appoint a day for his settlement.

"What application is here pointed at, I have just learned from the reverend gentlemen to whom you refer for that purpose. This gives me an opportunity, which I cheerfully embrace, of explaining more fully the nature and design of my chapel, and shall take the liberty to express myself in words that cannot be mistaken.

"I have already acquainted the Presbytery, that the chapel is private property, and was never intended to be put upon the footing of the Establishment, nor connected with it as a chapel of ease to the city of Edinburgh, in such a manner as the chapels of ease lately erected in St Cuthberts and other parts of Scotland are connected with their respective parishes.

"Having built the chapel wholly at my own expense, for the accommodation of my family, and numbers of poor people who at present are deprived of the best, and to many of them the only means of being instructed in the principles of our holy religion, I think myself entitled to name the minister thereof, especially as no person is under any obligation to join with him in his ministrations, but such as shall voluntarily choose so to do. The Presbytery, however, may rest assured of my steady adherence to what I have often declared, that I will at no time nominate any person but one of established character, sound in the faith, loyal to Government, and firmly resolved not to follow divisive courses. They may also rest assured, that, in such nomination, due regard will be shewn to the sentiments of those who statedly attend during divine worship in the chapel.

"Pursuant to these resolutions, I made choice of Mr Balfour. With this choice the Presbytery have expressed their satisfaction; and as the great body of the hearers have declared their approbation in a manner stronger than words, (by taking seats in the chapel, which were all vacant at Whitsunday last, and which I would not suffer to be let anew till intimation was made that I had nominated Mr Balfour to perform divine service there), I had no doubt that, when his relation to the parish of Lecropt should be loosed, the Presbytery would, agreeably to his own desire, have appointed one of their number to introduce him to the chapel, by preaching on that occasion. In this desire of his I concurred, in order to satisfy the Presbytery that nothing was farther from my thoughts than to promote any interest in opposition to the Church of Scotland; and to convince them of my sincere wish, that the minister of the chapel, though not on the

Establishment, should hold communion with the ministers thereof, as brethren in Christ, and servants of the same Lord and Master, which was all I ever meant in my application to them.

"I have taken no notice of my agreement with Mr Balfour respecting his benefice, because this is a matter which properly belongs to us. His acceptance of the chapel is a proof that he is fully satisfied; and I flatter myself that the Presbytery are too well acquainted with my sentiments, to doubt of my taking care that he who serves at the altar shall live by the altar.

"I have only to add, with respect to the collections, that all who attend at the chapel know that trustees are appointed for the distribution of them; so that if they do not approve of that mode of administration, they may dispose of their alms in any way they choose. I owe it, however, in justice to myself, to inform the Presbytery, that the sums collected at the chapel are applied, agreeably to the intention of the contributors, for the support of poor and indigent persons, whereby the parochial funds are relieved in part of a burden that would otherwise fall upon them. Besides this, I have sent once and again part of these collections, small as they are, to the treasurer of the Charity Workhouse, for which his receipts lie before me.

"This letter has far exceeded the bounds which I first proposed; but, upon second thoughts, I judged it proper to give you and your brethren a full view of the facts which they seem desirous to know. I am, with due respect, Reverend Sir, your most humble servant. "W. GLENORCHY."

The majority of the Presbytery being fully satisfied with this letter, and with the report of their committee, it was moved, that in case Mr Balfour's relation to the parish of Lecropt should be loosed, the Presbytery, upon intimation thereof being made to them, should appoint Dr Webster, who had previously declared his willingness to obey the appointment, to introduce him to the chapel, by preaching upon the occasion. But the motion being opposed by some members, the question was put, Appoint or not? Which being determined in the affirmative, Mr Chiesly dissented, and craved liberty to complain to the Synod of Lothian and Tweeddale. To which Mr Robertson of Ratho adhered; Dr M'Knight dissented.

There was no dispute about continuing the chapel in communion with the Church, for in this all the members of Presbytery agreed; neither did the opponents object to any minister of the Presbytery preaching at Mr Balfour's introduction to the chapel, if he chose to do so, but only to a formal judicial appointment for that purpose. Hence it was expected, that after Mr Balfour's settlement in the chapel the complainants would fall from their complaint; and with this impression Lady Glenorchy left town, and went, at her accustomed time, to Taymouth. Here she experienced her usual spiritual exercises, often complaining of distress, and sometimes finding peace and joy; but always endeavouring to have a conscience void of offence towards God and man. The feelings of her mind, on her birth-day this year, are fully expressed, and most decidedly evince the simplicity and godly sincerity of her heart and life, and her entire devotedness to God, and subjection to his blessed will, as will be seen by the following portions of her Diary.

Taymouth, July 11. 1776.—Having formerly enjoyed much of the Lord's presence here, and felt relieved from the cares that often distract my mind when at Edinburgh, I came hither this year in hopes of finding a seasonable time of refreshing to my soul; but hitherto the Lord has seen fit to deny me the comforting influences of his Spirit, and for three days past I have been left to a state of deadness and dissipation of thought.

July 21.—I continued all last week in the above uncomfortable state of mind, groaning under a sense of my unprofitableness, yet unable to pray, meditate, or read with understanding. On Friday, my heart was a little softened with reading Mrs Rowe's Devout Exercises of the Heart; and on Saturday morning I got access in prayer, and liberty to spread my wants before the Lord. Yesterday I experienced a quiet waiting on God.

Sunday, July 28.—Last Friday I determined to seek the Lord by prayer, with fasting. In the forenoon I had some liberty in pouring out my complaint before him. I also got some comfort in meditation and reading the Scriptures; but company came to dinner, and I was taken up with them all the rest of the day. On Saturday forenoon I enjoyed some refreshing moments when thinking on Romans viii. 33. to the end.

I found some comfort this morning in reading and prayer; but, alas! I have much cause still to complain of a hard heart, want of the spirit of grace and supplication, and of wandering thoughts. O to be more spiritually minded! Yet this I perceive, my heart is more weaned from earthly objects, and the enjoyment of God in Christ is my chief desire, for which I would forego all that the world calls pleasure. This is surely the Lord's doing, and if he has begun the work he will perfect it; for faithful is he that has promised. I may therefore rejoice in hope of being delivered from sin, and rest assured that when Christ, who is my life, shall appear, I also shall appear with him in glory. Glory be to God! Halelujah!

Thursday, August 8.—The Lord was pleased last week to give me at times peace and joy in believing. I had more access to God in prayer, and ability to meditate, than for some time before. For several mornings past I have had a longing for more of the image of Christ, and an ardent desire to give up all for him. I am resolved to sell my estate as soon as I can, that I may have more to spend in promoting the interest of his Church: I see nothing worth living for but to do good to the souls or bodies of men. To feed the hungry, to clothe the naked, to comfort the distressed, to support the feeble, to instruct the ignorant, to relieve the destitute—brings heaven into the soul. Can I better employ my time, talents, or fortune, than in such offices of kindness to others? The Lord hath enjoined it—hath given an example of it,—and hath connected with the performance of such duties a peace which surpasseth all understanding.

The Lord has of late delivered my mind from anxious cares about the several works in which I am engaged, and has shewn me his overruling hand bringing to pass whatsoever he hath purposed. I have committed all to him, and spread all my desires before him concerning those things he knows I intend for his glory. I leave them there, and wait the issue with tolerable composure of spirit, desiring to praise him when he overturns as well as when he fulfils my plans.

Sunday, August 11.—Last Friday I spent alone, and found comfort in drawing near to God, and had a sense of his presence with me. Saturday I got liberty in prayer for the whole church militant. This day I have been at the Lord's table, but my spirit seemed sunk within me,—I had no sensible outgoings of heart towards the Lord, nor intercourse with him. I could barely keep hold of the word of promise, and receive the outward elements as a memorial of his love, and a testimony given to my senses that Jesus was crucified on Calvary for the sins of many; and that as surely as I did eat the bread and drink the wine, so surely were my sins atoned for, and washed away by his blood, and that he would come again the second time without sin unto salvation. I was employed at the table in calmly and coolly considering the grounds of my hope; but, alas! my heart was unaffected. I had no mourning for sin, no love in exercise,—my feelings were more suitable to a stoic than to a redeemed sinner. I have been still more dead since I left the church, absolutely incapable of thinking a good thought. I seem as if left to feel the utter depravity of my heart, and my absolute dependance upon God for all things.

[Aged 35.] *September* 2.—This day I may set up my Ebenezer, for hitherto the Lord hath helped me. When I look back upon the number of years I have lived in this world, what a scene do I see of sin and folly on my part,—of goodness and mercy from the Lord. How oft have I been rescued by his gracious interposition from evils brought upon me by my own folly, and from dangers I could neither foresee nor prevent. How hath he taught me by afflictions, pains, and trials of various sorts, yet still I have need to be taught the same lessons over and over again. Surely the greatness of my stupidity and obstinacy can only be equalled by the patience and long-suffering of my God. I would review the Lord's dealings with me since this day twelvemonth, and first call to mind my fears, perplexities, and distresses experienced about ten months ago, when a snare was laid for my feet to draw me into the world,—a bait was offered in a pleasing form, while at the same time the professors of religion were permitted to afflict me, and my corrupt nature seemed to say, why tarry any longer among those who misunderstand and grieve you? get into this resting-place, accept of the ease and comfort now offered you. Satan also, like a roaring lion, came upon me, crying, "Where is now thy God?" In that day, when my soul was oppressed beyond measure, did the Lord appear for my help,—he sent his word and healed me, he rebuked the enemy, and, by his gracious interpostion, caused my unbelieving heart, with Thomas, to cry out, My Lord, and my God!

How did he bring down my pride by pains and sickness, and cast me into a furnace for a season, to purify me from my dross. My body was afflicted, and my mind agonized with the bitter spirit of some, and the hypocrisy of others, the disappointment and frustration of all my plans, uncertainty about the path of duty, and darkness as to my own state. At length the Lord saw fit to mitigate my pains, restore my sight, which was in danger, and bring my mind into a submissive frame. He made me willing to be esteemed nothing before others, so that his will might take place, and his name be glorified. He gave me at times a desire to depart and be with Christ, and made me willing even to suffer a painful death, if by that means I might shew forth his love and power to a careless world.

I desire to call to remembrance his goodness when I was taken ill upon a journey, when he gave me songs in the night, and made my bed to feel as one of roses; saying to my soul, "Be not afraid." After my return home, he not only relieved me from my illness, but caused light to arise concerning some of my most perplexing affairs, and overruled them in so wonderful a manner, that the end was gained I had in view. How mysterious are the ways of Providence! and how gracious hath he been to me this morning, in drawing forth my affections towards himself, and quickening my soul, when in a most lethargic state, bringing his mercies to remembrance, giving a desire to be more than ever devoted to his service, and enabling me to seek, with some degree of sincerity and fervency, those blessings he hath promised to give, and is willing to bestow. I have been led in particular to ask a lively operative faith, working by love; the sanctifying influences of the Holy Ghost, to purify the heart and life, and to seal the soul to the day of salvation; and to be delivered from a heart-sin lately discovered, which I thought had been subdued. O bless the Lord, my soul, and forget not all his benefits: What shall I render for the same? I will, in the name and strength of Jesus, set out afresh in the good ways of the Lord, determined to count all things but dross and dung for the excellency of the knowledge of my Redeemer. I will seek to know nothing but Christ, and him crucified. I will put my trust in him in time and for eternity. I will confess him before men, and count the reproach of Christ greater riches than all the treasures of Egypt; in short, I will give up soul, body, and spirit, unto him as his lawful property, to be disposed of as shall be most for his glory; to go where he will, to be what he will, to do what he will. Here, then, O Lord Jesus, I do most sincerely give myself away to thee, and cast my soul upon thee, believing thou art able to keep that which I commit unto thee; and that, when thou shalt appear, I shall also appear with thee in glory. I will endeavour to be without carefulness, and wait with patient expectation for the grace that shall be brought unto me at thy second coming. Do thou confirm my faith, increase my love, and cause me to abound in hope; and thus may I bring forth much fruit unto thee, whereby thy name may be glorified. Hear this my earnest prayer, O my God, which I offer up in the all-prevailing name of Jesus. Let it be registered in heaven, and answered in thy time, to the joy of my heart; and thine shall be the praise for evermore. W. G.

CHAPTER XV.

Mr Balfour gives up his nomination to Lady Glenorchy's Chapel—Lady Glenorchy, thrown into renewed perplexity, actually leaves Scotland—Extracts from Diary—Letter from Lady Glenorchy to Mrs Walker—Decision of the Synod of Lothian and Tweeddale, respecting her Chapel in Edinburgh—Lady Glenorchy at Exeter—There the author first becomes acquainted with her—She visits Exmouth—Erects a Chapel there—Goes to Plymouth Dock—Extracts from Diary, from December 1. to December 15. 1776—Letter from Lady Glenorchy to Lady Maxwell—Goes to Dorsetshire—Visits the Isle of Wight—Crosses over to Southampton—Arrives in London—Extracts from Diary, from January 27. to February 19. 1777—Meeting of the General Assembly of the Church of Scotland—Sets apart a day of Prayer to God, to request, that he would overrule the Decision of the General Assembly—Favourable Sentence of the General Assembly—Lady Glenorchy returns to Scotland—Letter from Lady Glenorchy to the Rev. Mr Jones—Extracts from Diary.

In prosecution of the design of Mr Balfour's settlement in Lady Glenorchy's Chapel, he, at the first meeting of the Presbytery of Dumblane, in whose bounds the parish of Lecropt is situated, tendered his resignation of the charge of his parish into the hands of the Presbytery, when, contrary to all expectation, and to general practice, they refused to receive it. This new and serious difficulty, which would have required a long and vexatious contest in the Church Courts to remove, determined him to give up his nomination to Lady Glenorchy's chapel. This threw Lady Glenorchy back into her former state of perplexity and distress, and led her not merely to resolve, but actually to take measures for leaving Scotland. This appears from the following extract and letter :—

October.—After frequent prayer to God for direction, I was led to determine upon leaving my own country for a season, perhaps for ever. The bad state of my health, which seemed partly owing to the trials I have met with, together with the opinion of the physicians that I should live in a warmer climate, made me see it to be my duty to go to the South of England, which I preferred to that of France, on account of having the benefit of the ordinances of the gospel. I earnestly begged of the Lord, that if his presence went not with me, I might not leave home; and that, if I did go, he might make me a savour of Christ in every place. About the middle of October (1776) I set out with one man and one maid-servant, after selling off my cattle and horses, and leaving orders to sell my lands, when a purchaser should offer. I felt much heart satisfaction upon the road, from a sense of the eye of the Lord being upon me as a guide. To him I committed my way, desiring to settle wherever I might receive good, or be of use to his church. I had occasion to remark an answer to this prayer in several instances upon the road; being undesignedly led to stop at places where some things were attempted for the good of souls. From Hawkstone, my friend, Miss Hill, accompanied me, and we travelled on to Bath and Wells, where we first met with ————————, who promised to meet me at Exeter, and accompany us to any place we fixed on, and to act as my chaplain.

Lady Glenorchy to Mrs Bailie Walker.

"*Hawkstone*, 19*th October*."

"My dear Madam,—I wrote you a few hasty lines from Carlisle, which I hope you received: Since then, I have continued my journey under the protection of the same gracious God, who hath never left me, but preserved and comforted me in all places and times, in sickness and health, and brought me safe to this place, where I found my kind friends all well; their souls, I trust, prospering, as well as their material part; and their hearts as much inclined as ever to glorify God with their bodies and spirits, which are his. My friend and I are to set out from this place on Wednesday for Bath, where I purpose staying till after the 30th of October, which is a day I wish to observe with my family, in imploring the direction of God how to proceed in the affairs of the chapel; and also for his blessing upon every means used for the spread of the gospel in all places, in Scotland in particular, pleading, as in Psalm lxxxv. ver. 6.

> That in thee may thy people joy,
> Wilt thou not us revive?
> Shew us thy mercy, Lord, to us
> Do thy salvation give.

"I hope to meet you, and many others that day, at a throne of grace.

"We have not yet determined any thing farther than to go to Bath, and to pay a visit to Mrs Tudway at Wells, and there to consider where to go next. The Lord, I hope, will guide and lead us to the place where he would have us to be, and where he will employ us in his work, and refresh our souls with his presence. This is all I desire, if I know any thing of my own heart. To his care and infinite grace and love I commend you, my very dear friend, begging to be remembered by you, as an unworthy but needy sinner, and as such, a proper object of the Saviour's compassion; and in every situation with sincere affection yours,

"W. G."

At Wells, Lady Glenorchy and her friend, Miss Hill, paid a visit to Mrs Tudway, the Lady of Clemant Tudway, Esq. who was many sessions member of Parliament for that city. Here she received an account of the decision of the Synod of Lothian and Tweeddale with respect to her chapel. She had written a letter to Dr Webster, requesting him to inform the Presbytery, that she intended to give them no further trouble with respect to Mr Balfour's settlement in her chapel, as he had determined to remain at Lecropt. This intimation was received by the Presbytery without remark, and ordered to be inserted in their minutes. In these circumstances, the friends of the chapel concluded, that as the occasion of complaint to the Synod was thus taken away, the complaint itself would consequently be withdrawn, and under this impression some of them did not attend the meeting of Synod. The complainants, however, collected their friends on the occasion, all of whom together did not amount to nearly the number of the members of the Presbytery of Edinburgh, who were excluded from judging in the question, being parties. After much discussion, the Synod, without a vote, on the motion of Dr Carlyle, minister of the parish of Inveresk, pronounced a sentence reversing that of the Presbytery of Edinburgh, and discharging all the ministers and probationers within their bounds from officiating in the said chapel; and further discharging the ministers of this church to employ any minister of the said chapel to officiate for them; a sentence which was considered both extraordinary and extrajudicial.

Against this judgment, Dr Erskine, Mr Walker, and Mr Johnston, (minister of the parish of North Leith), protested and appealed to the ensuing General Assembly, and on the day following Dr Webster joined in this protest and appeal, which, at the next Presbytery, these ministers were appointed to support at the bar of the General Assembly.

On the last day of November, Lady Glenorchy and her fellow-traveller proceeded westward, literally as Abraham, not knowing whether they went, but like Abraham also, walking before God towards the inheritance which fadeth not away, and both receiving and scattering blessings as they went along. At Exeter, she met with Mr Holmes, a gentleman of a congenial spirit to her own. He had been, in his youth, a merchant trading to Lisbon, and early in life had acquired an ample fortune: he had now, however, retired from business, and was the kind and generous friend of every good man who happened to be brought within the sphere of his notice, and the munificent patron of every work of piety and charity. His house was made by him and his excellent lady, the welcome home of every approved minister of the gospel who passed through their city, where they found every thing which could delight a well informed and well disposed mind. For the space of two years and a half, the writer of these pages resided at Plymouth Dock, as assistant to an aged minister in that place; during which period, many weeks never elapsed without his visiting their hospitable roof. In the beginning of December, he accompanied a young gentleman of rank and fortune in the west of England, from Plymouth to Exeter, and on entering Mr Holmes' house, they were met by him, and informed that Lady Glenorchy and Miss Hill were expected in a few minutes to dine there. His companion had seen Lady Glenorchy before, but this was the writer's first introduction to her Ladyship. When she went away, she requested him to conduct the family worship at her lodgings that evening and the next morning, which he accordingly did. She then made many inquiries about Plymouth and its environs.

In ten days or a fortnight afterwards she came to Plymouth Dock, and during the six weeks she remained there, he officiated morning and evening in her family as domestic chaplain.

Exmouth is well known as a place to which invalids resort, on account of the warmth of the climate, and the salubrity of the air. Thither Lady Glenorchy went, and having a preacher with her who was distinguished for his popularity and zeal, a congregation was collected. She procured a house, and formed it into a chapel in this place, which has been eminently useful, and continues to be so to the present time.

How often does God bring good out of evil! Had it not been that Lady Glenorchy was forced from home by ill health and vexation, as we have seen, it is, according to human views, more than probable that the rude inhabitants of Exmouth might have been left without the gospel to this day, and many who in that place have slept in Jesus, might have died in their ignorance and their sins. The writer of this book, too, had possibly otherwise never crossed the Tweed, and most assuredly had never attained to the place of comfort, respectability, and usefulness which he has so long enjoyed. Lady Glenorchy's own account of this her pilgrimage to the west of England, and of the interesting circumstances which attended it, will be given from her Diary, and by an extract of a letter to Lady Maxwell.

December 1.—We spent one Lord's day at Taunton,—got acquainted with Mr Reader, who informed me of Mr Holmes' character at Exeter. Next day we arrived there, and went to Mr Holmes, who fully answered the character we had got of him. On the 3d of December we went to Exmouth, where we remained some days. Mr —— began preaching there in the long room on the 6th, and we continued three days there, my chaplain preaching in different places to crowded auditories, some of whom seemed impressed by the word. Here we met with much opposition from a neighbouring Justice, who sent a press-gang to the long room to disturb the congregation, and ordered the landlord to give no more admission to such preachers, on pain of taking away his license. This made me wish much to have a house licensed in the town, large enough to contain the people who were willing to hear. This desire increased in proportion as I saw the eagerness of the people to hear and receive the gospel. I mentioned it to Mr Holmes, but he seemed to think Exmouth so wicked a place, that it would be in vain to attempt any thing there. The thought, however, never left me, and some weeks afterwards I wrote to Mr Holmes, to look out for a house in the town which I might purchase, which accordingly he did, and found one, which I bought, and repaired and fitted up for a place of worship, and in which a congregation of some hundreds has been gathered, and is now (in 1783) in a very flourishing state.

From Exmouth we went to Teignmouth, but could not stay long, on account of the damps which prevail there in the winter.

December 15.—We had the privilege this day of joining with the church at Plymouth Dock in celebrating the Lord's supper. It was a good day to my soul, —truly a refreshing season. I could hear of no comfortable lodgings;—at length a good man offered to quit his house in order to accommodate us. This I accepted of, and sent immediately to hire a woman-servant. Providentially, one came that morning from the country to seek a place. My maid liked her appearance, and hired her.

It pleased the Lord to make this circumstance the means of bringing this woman to the knowledge, belief, and obedience of the gospel. And the day before I left Plymouth, being uneasy about parting with her, her father, whose house she had left in consequence of some family dispute, sent a message to her, requesting her to return home, his mind being changed at the critical moment, and the hand of the Lord was made visibly apparent in the whole affair. I cannot but note here another remarkable incident: A female servant belonging to the master of the house, had scoffed at my young woman's profession of religion. I therefore, when about to depart, sent for her, and set before her the evil of her conduct, and the danger to which it exposed her, and urged her to seek the Lord as she should answer for it on the day when we should meet before the judgment-seat of God.

The admonition was blessed, as I afterwards learnt, for from that time this poor girl gave good evidence of being a new creature. After having experienced deep convictions of sin, and being brought to the knowledge of the gospel, and the experience of its liberty, she became a member of a dissenting church to which the family in which she served belonged; and I lately was informed that, after having adorned her profession of religion for several years, she died in the Lord.

During my stay at Plymouth, I received some very remarkable answers of prayer.

Lady Glenorchy to Lady Maxwell.

" *Plymouth Dock, January* 6. 1777.

" My dear Madam,—I have often thought of you since I came to this place, wishing you could partake with me of the refreshing ordinances we enjoy here and at Plymouth. The word indeed is clothed with power, and it is good to be under the droppings of the sanctuary. Yesterday we had two heavenly discourses from Mr Kinsman, one from Jeremiah xxxi. 3. " The Lord hath appeared of old unto me, saying, yea, I have loved thee with an everlasting love: therefore with loving kindness have I drawn thee." The other from Isaiah xl. 1, 2. " Comfort ye, comfort ye my people, saith your God. Speak ye comfortably to Jerusalem, and cry unto her, that her warfare is accomplished, that her iniquity is pardoned; for she hath received of the Lord's hand double for all her sins." And one from Mr Jones, from Ecclesiastes ix. 10. " Whatsoever thy hand findeth to do, do it with thy might; for there is no work, nor device, nor knowledge, nor wisdom, in the grave, whither thou goest." I have got Mr Jones to come in twice a-day as chaplain, and he expounds the Scriptures morning and evening in the house.

"The Lord has been very gracious in leading us to this place, and making it, in the best sense, a place of rest and refreshment to our souls. Much cause have I to wonder and adore the kind Providence that hath directed my steps since I left home, and kept me in all places where I have been, restoring my bodily and spiritual health, and causing all grace to abound towards me. O for a heart to praise the name of our God and Saviour, who has loved us with an everlasting love, therefore with loving kindness hath he drawn us, and comforted us on every side!"

In the end of January Lady Glenorchy and Miss Hill went first to Dorsetshire, then to Hampshire, and the Isle of Wight, where they remained till the month of April, when they crossed over to Southampton, and in the beginning of May went to London; at which place Lady Glenorchy intended to wait the decision of the General Assembly with respect to her chapel, and by which she proposed to direct her future movements and conduct.

January 27.—I left Plymouth, and came to Dartmouth; in which place Mr Jones, who came with us, preached in a meeting-house belonging to a pious lady, Mrs Newcomon. The people were rude, and behaved ill.

At Totness I met with a good man from Scotland, of the name of Little, who requested me to send a preacher to the town, and he would give him board, and find a place for him in which to preach.

February 1.—We came to Honiton. Mr ——— preached the next day in the meeting-house there. That night we were burned out of the inn. We were greatly alarmed, but lost nothing, nor did we suffer in our health from being exposed to the open air in the middle of the night in the streets, although the weather was cold and damp. Next night we came to Dorchester, where Mr —— preached in Mr Edward's meeting-house.

February 7.—We arrived at Southampton, and by a providential mistake we went to an inn at which we did not intend to stop, and were very ill accommodated, and not civilly treated by the people of it; but the Lord overruled this for good, by touching the heart of the waiter with what he heard, and there is reason to believe he was savingly impressed with the truth and importance of religion. He almost immediately left the house, and was taken into the employment of a respectable gentleman.

Mr Kingsbury gave Mr —— the use of his meeting-house, where he preached frequently; also at Romsay, Titchfield, and various other places in the neighbourhood, and there is reason to believe several were savingly brought to God at that time by his ministry.

February 19.—We sailed for the Isle of Wight. Upon our first arrival we met with discouragements, and I began to think we had nothing to do there; but remembering the Lord's promise, that when two or three shall agree to ask any thing he will do it, I mentioned it to ——, and we agreed to ask the Lord to open a door for his gospel in the island, so that all the islanders might have an opportunity to hear it. That very day a meeting-house was offered to ——, where he preached statedly. Opportunity was also given him to preach the gospel in every part of the island, which he embraced.

Miss Hill and I then departed by Portsmouth to London.

When in London Lady Glenorchy set apart a day, according to her usual practice in matters of difficulty and importance, for solemn and extraordinary prayer to God, that he would overrule the deliberations of the General Assembly respecting the chapel, for his own glory. The preparation which she made for this exercise of devotion will be seen in the next extract from her Diary.

May 23d I set apart as a day of prayer for the following things:—

That the Lord would be pleased to overrule the counsels of the Assembly respecting my chapel, that they may give such a decision as may promote his glory, and the good of the church. That he would leave me no doubt how to act, but make my path plain, that my mind may be delivered from its perplexities concerning it; and that he would shew me whom he has chosen to be the pastor, and not permit me to anticipate, but to wait the issue of his will in this matter.

That the Lord would prosper his work at Strathfillan, and encourage the hearts of the little flock there.

That he would grant success to Mr W—— at Exmouth and elsewhere, and to other works of a like nature attempted in his name.

That I may be helped and assisted by the Spirit in family prayer, and not be left to a dry, formal, burdensome worship; but be enabled to do it to God's glory, and the comfort and edification of my own soul, and those of my servants.

That I may be directed concerning my future place of residence, and led to fix wherever I may be of most use in the work of God; and be kept from all selfish motives whatever in my choice.

That the Lord would search me and try me, and bring forth to light any hidden idols, any secret corruptions, any concealed enemy to him or his ways, that may be lurking in my heart, and deliver me from them, and the love and power of every sin.

That I may henceforth follow him fully, and give up all I have to him without reserve, and be wholly devoted to him all the days of my life, and made meet to enjoy him in glory through the endless ages of eternity. Amen and Amen!

On the 27th day of May the cause of Lady Glenorchy's chapel, which had excited no small interest in the church and in the public mind, was heard at the bar of the General Assembly.

There appeared as appellants, Mr David Johnston, minister of North Leith; Mr John Macfarlan, one of the ministers of the Canongate; Mr Robert Walker, senior minister of the High Church; Dr Webster, of the Tolbooth Church; Dr Macqueen, of the Old Church; and Dr Erskine, of the Old Greyfriars' Church,—ministers of Edinburgh. And as respondents, Mr Robertson, minister of Ratho; Mr Robertson, minister of Dalmeny; Mr Chiesly, minister of Corstorphine; Mr Grieve, minister of Dalkeith; Dr Carlyle, minister of Inveresk; Dr M'Cormick, minister of Prestonpans.

There being twelve persons at the bar, each of whom spoke, and some of them at great length, the whole first day, to a late hour, was consumed by the pleadings.

The argument of the appellants naturally divided itself into two parts. First, the informality of the complainers in bringing, and of the synod in taking up the complaint, when the ground of it was removed by Mr Balfour remaining at Lecropt. And, secondly, the synod's not only taking up the complaint, but extending their interference to things in no way brought before them; as censuring the Presbytery of Edinburgh for admitting the chapel into communion with the church, and pronouncing a sentence of separation against it.

The answer of the respondents was, that the complainers had a right to bring the complaint to the synod; and that the synod had a right to review the whole merits of the case, and decide accordingly.

On the next day the cause was again argued in the Court. The principal speakers on the side of the appellants were, Mr Hunter, one of the ministers of Dumfries; Mr Duff, minister of Tippermuir; Mr Taylor, one of the ministers of Paisley; Mr Campbell, minister of Renfrew; Mr Blenshall, minister of Dundee; Alexander Belshes, Esq. advocate; and the Lord Chief Baron Montgomery.

On the side of the respondents were, Professor George Hill of St Andrews, Professor John Hill of Edinburgh, Principal Campbell of Aberdeen, and Buchan Hepburn, Esq. advocate.

It was considered a remarkable circumstance at the time, that none of the noblemen, gentlemen, nor any of the law-officers of the Crown, who generally took a share in the debates of the Assembly in matters of importance, attended on this occasion, or if they were present, that they were silent, with the exception of the Lord Chief Baron.

In the course of the debate it became evident that there was a considerable majority in favour of the appellants: a division of the house, therefore, was not attempted; but a good deal of discussion took place with respect to the terms of the sentence. At length, at a late hour, on the motion of the Lord Chief Baron, they agreed to and pronounced the following sentence:—

"The Assembly, waving the consideration of the first part of the synod's sentence, disapproving of the Presbytery's appointing Dr Webster to introduce Mr Balfour to the chapel by preaching on that occasion, agreed, without a vote, to reverse, and hereby do reverse the second part of the synod's sentence prohibiting all the ministers and probationers within their bounds to officiate in the said chapel, and discharging the ministers of this church to employ any minister of the said chapel to officiate for them; and in case the matter shall again be brought before the Presbytery, the Assembly recommend it to them to take proper care, that the person to be admitted to the said chapel conform himself to the standards of the church."

The respondents in this cause, and those of the members of the Assembly who supported their views on it, are now no more; but they lived long enough to see, that their apprehensions of evil, arising from the admission of Lady Glenorchy's chapel into the communion of the church, were groundless; and also to shew that their hostility towards it was completely removed, by evincing, on every occasion that offered, their anxiety for the welfare both of the chapel and its minister.

On the third of June following, Lady Glenorchy had occasion to write to the author of these pages; and in her letter she very incidentally mentions the decision of the General Assembly, but in such a way as to make it plain, that she was under the impression that it was an event that, stranger as he was to the country and people, and placed as he was at the distance of six hundred miles from the scene of action, it could be of very little interest to him. The way of God, however, is in the sea, and his path in the great waters, and his footsteps are not known; two short years were not to pass away, before he was to become the person principally interested in this decision.

Lady Glenorchy's mind being now set at rest with respect to her chapel, she immediately prepared to return to Scotland, and arrived in Edinburgh in the month of June. The state of her mind on this occasion, will be seen by the following letter, and extracts from her Diary.

Lady Glenorchy to T. S. Jones.

Rev. Sir,—You know, by happy experience, the exquisite pleasure it gives one to be made in any degree instrumental in bringing souls to Christ; and therefore you can guess my feelings when I look back upon last winter, and view the Lord's hand leading me from place to place by a way unknown, making crooked things straight, and rough places plain, still granting the request with which I set out upon that journey—that I might, through grace, be a savour of Christ in every place. O, what cause have I to praise and adore rich, sovereign, free, unmerited grace, that has thus made use of a brand plucked from the burning, to kindle the flame of divine love in these poor souls! I am every day hearing of some good effects of ——'s preaching in the Island, and at Southampton. I hope there is a work begun in the former that will increase and flourish. The enclosed letter to ——, I commit to your care, as I don't know where to direct to him: It is informing him of the General Assembly's having reversed the decree of the Synod, and granting full communion to the minister of my chapel with the Church of Scotland;—this is what I did not expect from them. I am to set out, God willing, on Thursday, for Scotland; and having much business on hand, can only assure you of my best wishes for every spiritual blessing to your own soul, and success to your labours, and that I am, Rev. Sir, your sincere friend and well-wisher in Christ,

"W. GLENORCHY."

"If you have any good news to send me, or any thing you wish to communicate by letter, my address is now at Edinburgh."

June 11.—I arrived safe at Edinburgh; was much comforted on my way hither by a sermon from Mr R——, junior, at Northampton, on Psalm cxix. 117. "Hold thou me up, and I shall be safe; and I will have respect unto thy statutes continually;" and by hearing and conversing with Mr Edwards at Leeds. The Lord has preserved me in my outgoings and my coming in; he has been with me in the way, and guided me with his eye; he hath led me to places where I have either got refreshment to my own soul, or been the means of carrying the gospel to others; he hath never left me nor forsaken me; so I may here raise my Ebenezer, and adore the matchless love and grace of Jehovah to me a poor worthless worm, less than the least of all saints, yet the greatest debtor to free grace. All praise and glory be to my God, for ever and ever!

[Aged 36.] *Taymouth, September* 2.—When I take a survey of the last year of my life, I am filled with wonder and astonishment at the goodness of God my Saviour, and at the ingratitude and folly of my vile incorrigible self. My life, since this day twelvemonth, has been a series of gracious dispensations of Providence. The Lord hath manifested himself to me as the preserver of my life, the hearer of prayer, the deliverer from temptation, the Saviour from sin, the giver of every needful blessing, spiritual and temporal. Yet, notwithstanding this, my ungrateful heart is this day as prone to wander from him as ever, as averse to pray as if he had never answered my requests, as averse to read and meditate on his word as if I never had found comfort therein. I am led away by every trifle; and, though convinced in my judgment that God is an all-satisfying portion to the soul, an all-sufficient fountain of every desirable blessing, yet still I do not abide with him as such. Strange perverseness! Yet let this perverseness endear a Saviour to me. The Lord Jesus is able to heal my soul; he never rejected any who came to him in the days of his flesh. Have compassion then, O Lord, on my poor soul; say to me, thy sins are forgiven thee, go in peace; and O that power may accompany the word, that soul and body may be invigorated to run in the way of thy commandments. Lord, thou knowest it is the desire of my heart this night to be wholly devoted to thee, to glorify thee with soul, body, and spirit, which are thine. I wish to live for this end. Do with me, for me, and in me, thy whole will; and let me serve thee here, and dwell with thee for ever. Amen. W. G.

CHAPTER XVI.

Lady Glenorchy looks out for a Minister for her Chapel in Edinburgh—Makes choice of the Rev. Mr Sheriff—Mr Sheriff falls into bad health—Obtains an assistant—Forms the congregation into church order—His health gradually declines—Extracts from Diary from November 2. to December 30. 1777—Lord's Supper dispensed for the first time in the Chapel—Death of Mr Sheriff—Extracts from Diary, from February 2. to June 14. 1778.

After the decision of the General Assembly, the chapel was, for four months, chiefly supplied by the ministers and probationers of the city and neighbourhood, while her Ladyship was actively endeavouring to find a fit person who might be settled in it as pastor. At length she heard of Mr Francis Sheriff, who, she thought, would in every respect suit the situation. He had been educated at the University of Edinburgh, licensed and ordained by the Presbytery of Haddington, and was now a chaplain in one of the Scots regiments in Holland,—a situation which he could resign when he pleased without the intervention of any church court. He was twenty-seven years of age, accomplished, of good appearance, and had fine abilities; and was possessed of all the simplicity, integrity, and ardour of one recently brought to the knowledge and experience of the gospel. He had friends in Edinburgh, and through these Lady Glenorchy invited him to come over and preach in her chapel, and reside in her house, with the understanding, that if, on due acquaintance with each other, all parties concerned were satisfied, he should be settled as their minister. About this time he began to be unwell, and was advised by the medical men of Holland to return to his native land, as the best remedy they could prescribe. The union of these two things led him to consider it to be his duty to accept of the invitation.

Accordingly, he left Holland in the middle of September, arrived in Edinburgh in the end of that month, and on the first Lord's day afternoon of October, he preached in the chapel. He also officiated in it two whole days of the same month. The conducting of the worship of a whole day in so large a house was too much for his strength: he therefore did not attempt it again. Lady Glenorchy, aware that it was not probable that he would ever be able for the entire duty of the situation, engaged one to assist him who had repeatedly preached in the chapel, and was very acceptable to the congregation.

Her Ladyship, understanding that Mr Sheriff was universally approven of by the stated hearers in the chapel, and that it would be most agreeable to them that he should become their pastor, gave him, on the 14th of November, a letter directed to her trustees for the management of the affairs of this institution, informing them that she had appointed him minister of it; and the next Lord's day intimation to this effect was made from the pulpit. As the question agitated in the Church Courts concerning the chapel had arisen out of the mode of settling an already ordained minister in it, and as there then was not any known determinate rule by which to regulate the matter, Lady Glenorchy dreaded the experiment of again applying to the Presbytery. Mr Sheriff nevertheless considered it to be his duty to go to the first meeting of Presbytery, to inform them that he had received and accepted of Lady Glenorchy's appointment to be minister of her chapel, and to offer to sign the formula and standards of the church, in terms of the sentence of the General Assembly. He did so, but was received very coolly by some of his old acquaintances; and in consequence of murmurs of threatened opposition reaching his ear, he thought it prudent to retire without making the attempt.

Immediately, however, upon his appointment, he began, with the aid of his assistant, to form the congregation into church order. The state of his health did not permit hin to visit the members of it in their houses, but he invited, from the pulpit, those indigent persons who were admitted to free seats, to meet him on appointed days, and he conversed with each of them separately. This duty employed him to the middle of the following February.

On the forenoon of the 14th of December, Mr Sheriff again conducted the worship of his people in public. Lady Henrietta Hope happening to be in town, heard him on this occasion, and in her Diary has given this account of it: "Mr Sheriff sung the 100th Psalm, and preached from Psalm xxxvii. 4. 'Delight thyself also in the Lord, and he shall give thee the desires of thine heart.' And truly his words were trying and quickening, and, blessed be God for the riches of free grace, though humbling, yet also comfortable; for, alas! although far short of the degrees in which they ought to be, yet surely he named the chief desires of my heart. I was wondrously encouraged by this sermon, and my spirits raised, and I think I received it of the Lord. I was grieved for Mr Sheriff; it is the first time I have heard him, and there is reason to fear it will be the last. I am grieved for my friend,—I am grieved for the congregation, who seem in him to have a faithful pastor. But what the Lord gives, may he not take away? and if he gave him, cannot he give another? O for firm faith and absolute trust in his power and goodness!"

The fears of this excellent lady were too well founded; for although Mr Sheriff did again appear in the pulpit after that, twice to make intimations, and once at the administration of the Lord's supper, to fence the tables, and give the closing exhortation, of which we shall shortly take notice, he never preached again.

As Lady Glenorchy had been somewhat elevated at the prospect of seeing her chapel, at the first arrival of Mr Sheriff, likely to be desirably settled, she was now proportionally distressed when these prospects were thus overcast. This, with other things, seems to have even more than ordinarily disturbed the course of her Christian comfort, as appears from her Diary during this time.

Edinburgh, November 2.—This day and some preceding ones it hath pleased God to give me convictions of having backslidden from him in heart and life. A ray of divine light from time to time has darted into my mind, and shewn me various heart sins and corruptions that have, like noxious weeds, overrun my soul, so that the seeds of grace are almost choked up, and cannot shoot forth. Some degrees of conformity to the world in dress and behaviour have rendered my company too agreeable to the people of the world, and this has caused my being oftener with them than formerly. I was led into this from what I took to be a desire of doing them good; but I find they have robbed me of precious time and peace of conscience. My soul has also been hurt by unfaithfulness to acquaintances and relations, who are going on in the broad road, unmindful of their eternal concerns, yet I have not warned them of their danger. I have suffered worldly prudence and fear to keep possession of my heart, and unbelief has gained ground, and inability to speak properly to them increased. My zeal has cooled.—These things have produced distance from God, carelessness, slothfulness of spirit, forgetfulness of God's omnipresence, neglect of frequent prayer, wasting of precious time, want of self-examination, meditation, searching the word with diligence, and, in short, every symptom of a heart estranged from God; and what is worse, I was insensible to the evil of this state, till within these few days, that the Lord, in his abundant mercy, has sent a choice servant of his, Mr Sheriff, into my house, who hath been the instrument of shewing me from whence I have fallen, and by his own life and conversation, as well as preaching, called upon me to strengthen the things that are ready to die, convincing me, that for some time past I have been as one long dead. What shall I render to the Lord for his mercy? O to be thankful! to be now enabled through grace to set out afresh,—to redouble my speed from the city of destruction, towards the heavenly city,—to redeem the time, and to pray that the Lord may restore the years that have been devoured by the locust, the caterpillar, and the canker-worm,—and that he may yet be glorified in his servant, by shewing forth his power in subduing every base lust, and bringing down every high thought and imagination of my heart, to the obedience of Christ. He has this night permitted me to rest my soul upon Christ with some measure of confidence, and also to commit my way and concerns to him. Confirm my faith in thy blessed word, O my God. Strengthen, stablish, and settle my base wandering heart. Rule in me, reign over me, and guide my feet into the way of peace;—conduct me by thy counsel here, and afterwards receive me to thy glory, for thy own great name's sake. Amen and amen!

November 3.—This morning I felt great deadness and wandering in prayer; had no nearness to God till the afternoon, when I went to seek his presence and blessing upon the meeting we were to have in the evening. At six o'clock some Christian friends met to pray, and deliberate on the proper method of proceeding to dispense ordinances in the chapel. Mr Sheriff began by prayer. I felt that the Lord was indeed with us, and attended to the voice of our petition. The intended rules of my chapel were read, and all seemed pleased and of one mind concerning them. Difficulties were removed, the light shone clearly, and discovered to us the way we should take; the desire of all was, that God might be glorified in the conversion of sinners, and the edification of saints: The meeting was closed before nine with a prayer by Mr Bonar.* We afterwards supped together, and eat our bread with gladness and singleness of heart. I found a sweet peace and acquiescence in the Lord's will all this evening, and desire to praise him for bringing matters thus far. We appointed Monday next for another meeting upon the same subject.

November 4.—I found some liberty this morning in prayer, and had a view of the perfections of God as they are revealed in the word, and particularly of his na-

* The late Alexander Bonar, Esq. of Ratho, the first named trustee for her chapel; and who, from its establishment, had been her confidential adviser in all its concerns,—a man, whose memory will be ever dear for every Christian grace, and every benevolent and generous action.

ture under the title of love; got freedom to ask power over besetting sins, and to commit my concerns into his hands. This evening I was led to write faithfully to an old friend. I had some pleasing converse with Mr Sheriff, and find that I get more insight into the corruptions of my heart daily. O that this may lead me more to Christ, the fountain that cleanseth from all sin!

November 8.—After some hours of distress, I at length had liberty to pray to God, and to plead for his own name's sake that he would make me what I appear to be to others; that he would give me what he knows I want,—a powerful application of the blood of Christ to my heart and conscience; and that I may be led into the highway of holiness, and kept from conformity to this present evil world. I feel some degree of persuasion that I made this prayer in the sincerity of my heart, and that I really desire nothing so much as to glorify God upon earth, and to enjoy him for ever. I therefore conclude I am not a hypocrite; but, alas! much hypocrisy dwelleth in me, for which I ought to be deeply humbled, and led to strive with all diligence for more singleness of heart in duties.

November 9.—This morning I awaked with these words, "Can a woman forget her sucking child," &c. This text did not come with much force at first; but it afterwards grew sweet and comfortable to my soul when meditating on it, and gave me encouragement to hope for a blessing at his table. I went to church, and was very dead all the time of the sermon, and had no power to think of any thing till the 43d Psalm was sung, when my heart began to melt, and I got some hope that I should yet praise the Lord. Mr Walker afterwards, addressing the communicants, described my case so exactly that I thought somebody had told him of it. My bonds were now loosed; I got power to believe on Christ as now ready to receive me, and bear my burdens for me; and as able and willing to save me from all my infirmities, to heal my backslidings, and to carry me through future trials. I got up with joy and went to the table, where I had liberty in pouring out my requests to the master of the feast, who drew, as it were, near, and said, What is thy petition? I saw myself as less than the least of all his mercies, yet permitted to sit among his children. I then gave myself away to him for ever.

November 10.—This morning I heard Mr Bonar,* and in the afternoon Mr Sheriff, but was not much affected by the discourses, although excellent. In the evening I had a meeting of the trustees of my chapel: I found the Lord near to us in singing and prayer. I was much hurried all this day: I received much spiritual food, but had no time for digesting it.

November 11.—This morning I had a sweet time in prayer and reading; felt a melting of soul, and found the Lord near; had a sort of foreboding that trouble was at hand; but I was enabled to give up all to Jesus. At twelve o'clock I was seized with a violent cough; and I continued ill all day: Mr Sheriff also very ill.

* The late Rev. Archibald Bonar, who, through life, was much esteemed for his very amiable temper, his talents, his eminent piety, and his usefulness. He was a younger brother of Mr Bonar of Ratho, and was presented by Lady Glenorchy to the parish of Cramond, a few months before her death.

November 12.—I was very distressed in body all night, and all this day; unfit for spiritual duties. Mr Sheriff very ill; the doctor afraid of a consumption. This is a dark providence: I am trying to get my will brought into subjection; find it hard indeed. Lord, help in this!

November 14.—Mr Sheriff better; myself also better, yet still in a hard dead frame. This night there was a meeting of the trustees of the chapel: I sent a letter by Mr Sheriff to them, appointing him to be the minister of it. The meeting was very unanimous, and every thing carried on in order and in love. Glory be to God who has heard my prayer for this!

December 30.—I have risen early, and endeavoured to seek strength and power from God. I have daily sought him with tears and groans, but he frequently shutteth out my prayer, and, as it were, leaveth me in the bitterness of my own soul. My state is such, that I cannot examine nor humble myself before him, from weakness and want of recollection. My whole mental powers are in disorder and confusion. I am amazed and confounded: I am afraid of what may be coming upon me. I seem left of the Spirit, and as dead to spiritual things as if I had never known them. When I look on the year past, I see nothing but mercy and love multiplied from God, but little beside ingratitude, carelessness, and wanderings, on my part. What can I think of these things? Lord, thou knowest, and thou alone can'st pardon and deliver me!

Since writing the above, I have had some liberty in prayer, and have been enabled to plead for deliverance from my sins, under a sense of belonging to God. I therefore can claim his promise, that sin shall not have dominion over me, not being under the law, but under grace.

1778.—Mr Sheriff having begun to form a congregation from the holders of free seats, intimated from the pulpit, on the 15th of February, his desire, that all the other seat-holders, who intended to become members of the congregation, would give him an opportunity of conversing with them; and that if his time would not suit them, that they would converse with his assistant. There was in the terms and manner of this intimation, something so solemn and so affectionate, arising in part, perhaps, from his evidently dying appearance, that it was very generally and cheerfully complied with. A fortnight after this, he intimated his intention of administering the Lord's supper, at the same time that it was to be celebrated in the other churches of the city,—the 15th of March. On this, as on the occasion of his intimation to the free seat-holders, he took the opportunity of avowing his attachment to the doctrine and discipline of the Established Church of Scotland, and of his determination to conform his ministry to its rules.

On the fast day preceding the administration of the Lord's supper, the morning service was conducted by the late Mr Dickson, then minister of Liberton, near Biggar, afterwards of the New North Church, Edinburgh, and the afternoon service by the assistant of the chapel. On the Saturday the late Mr Innes of Gifford officiated; and as Mr Sheriff was unable for the duty, the late Mr Randall of Stirling conducted both the morning service of the Lord's day, before the communion, and also the evening service after it. Mr Sheriff, as has been already mentioned, only fenced the tables, and gave the closing exhortation. This was the last public duty which he performed. The former minister elect, Mr Balfour, led the devotion of Monday, which he continued to do for forty years afterwards. Soon after this, all hopes of the recovery of Mr Sheriff were abandoned. Every thing, however, that could be thought of, was done to stop the rapid progress of his disease; but all was in vain, and nothing remained but to make his last days as comfortable as possible. For this purpose, his noble patroness removed him to Barnton; sent for his mother to attend him; and not only assisted her in performing the mother's part, but did that which his mother could not do for him; she helped him to elevate his mind from earth to heaven—to Christ—to God—and to the hope of being for ever with the Lord. His last days and hours were those of a man of God, full of faith and peace. His whole spirit and conduct were highly edifying, and such as became his character as a Christian, and his office as a minister of the gospel. After lingering to the 13th of June he expired, and was buried in the Barnton vault, under the church of Cramond.

The history of his ministry in the chapel is very brief: He formed the seat-holders into a congregational body; he preached to them seven times; thrice, on the occasion of making intimations, he gave a few admonitory words; once, he dispensed to them the sacramental bread of life; and afterwards, by all its blessings and obligations, he exhorted them to be faithful unto death. For six months, he was a bright example to them of the work of faith, and the labour of love, and the patience of hope in our Lord Jesus Christ, in the sight of God our Father; and then his warfare was accomplished, and he received his reward. A short account of him, and the circumstances of his illness and death, were drawn up by Lady Glenorchy, and printed and circulated among her friends: it has since been reprinted, and published. The exercises of mind, and the spiritual experience of Lady Glenorchy, from the beginning of this year, till Mr Sheriff's death, will be seen by the extracts from her Diary, which follow.—

Monday, February 2.—I was in a very dead frame all last month. The Lord has seen fit to send an alarming complaint of body; but it has not had any other effect on my mind than to stupify and confuse me. This day I began to entertain hopes that the Lord will appear in my behalf, and save me out of the hands of my spiritual enemies, that would destroy my soul. Lord, hear the cry of my necessities, and send deliverance from above! Thou alone knowest my case, and thou alone canst help and save me. Manifest thyself as a God of power, by rescuing my soul from the mighty; deliver the lawful captive. Save now, I beseech thee, for I am thy servant,—thine own purchased and redeemed servant. Let none pluck me out of thy hands, for thy great name's sake!

February 6.—Glory be to God, the hearer of prayer, who hath graciously listened to the voice of my supplication! All day yesterday I felt the drawings of his love upon my soul, and a strong desire to return to him. I got some access to God in prayer both alone and with a friend, and found it good to my soul. At night I had liberty to seek blessings for others; and this morning I waked with these words on my mind, "God is love." I felt their power, and found liberty to go to him under this endearing character. I perceive the Lord is at work with my soul, mortifying my corruptions, and bringing me forth from the fearful pit and the miry clay, into which my soul has been plunged for some time past. He also has raised in my heart a strong desire to seek him at his table, which I did not experience till yesterday. I conclude, from this and other things that he is about to restore my soul. Let me not in this be deceived; but revive thy work, renew my strength, increase my faith, animate my hope, shed abroad thy love in my heart, give me victory over my heart sins, and power to run in the way of thy commandments, for the sake of Jesus, thy beloved Son, and glory be thine for ever! Amen.

February 13.—This morning I set apart for seeking the Lord by fasting and prayer. I endeavoured to begin the work of the day by confessing my sins, but my heart was very dead. At length the Lord was pleased to permit me to pour out my petitions before him. I then found liberty to give myself to the Lord without reserve; to beseech him to cleanse my heart from every evil felt or feared; to plead the promise, Ezek. xxxvi. 26. " A new heart also will I give you, and a new spirit will I put within you; and I will take away the stony heart out of your flesh, and I will give you an heart of flesh;" and to seek direction for Mr Sheriff in his work, to remember the nation, the church, the afflicted, the giddy and profane; enemies, friends, and, in particular, all those who have desired my prayers. I sought to know the reasons of past deadness and backslidings, and they appear to be the following: Neglect of redeeming time in the evening; forsaking the Lord, and neglecting his word; not persevering in meditation and self-examination; not observing opportunities given through the day for prayer, and when in company not using ejaculatory prayer; not improving opportunities for social prayer; not searching the Scriptures with diligence daily; slothfulness in the performance of relative duties, especially in my family; unwatchfulness over my temper, desires, words, thoughts; suffering the heart to be engaged with trifles, vanity, &c.

I desire this day, in the strength of Jesus my Saviour, to set out afresh in the good ways of the Lord; to make conscience of redeeming time every evening for solemn prayer and reading God's word before going to bed; also for self-examination of the manner in which the day has been spent. I intend through grace, when in health, to rise early, to have at least two hours before family worship for prayer, reading, and meditation; to keep a sense of God's presence upon my spirit through the day; to come again before him at twelve o'clock; to redeem some time for private prayer before tea, and also before supper. These things, with the blessing of God, I look upon as the best means of keeping my soul in life, and preserving me from falling again into my past miserable state. I therefore beseech thee, O Lord, (who now seest my heart, and knowest that I desire to love and serve thee), that thou wilt give me grace to follow the above plan, as far as it is for thy glory, and my soul's advantage! Keep me from resting in duties performed; preserve me from despising the means of growing in faith and love. Let thy grace be sufficient for me in all things, and at all times, and thy name glorified through me, and by me, now and for evermore! Amen.

Saturday, February 14.—I rose between six and seven; spent some time in prayer; was dead, and troubled with wandering thoughts; read, and tried to meditate on the Scripture, but felt little life in my soul.

After breakfast spent two hours in writing, reading, and prayer; found much comfort in the latter at twelve o'clock, and had a comfortable sense of my calling and election through rich sovereign mercy; saw that the Lord had chosen me as a vessel of mercy, and my heart was overwhelmed with a sense of it. I felt the drawings of divine love upon my soul, and afterwards light and comfort in conversation with Mr Sheriff; found some little time for prayer before tea. Afterwards went out to get some spiritual conversation with Mrs ——; on coming home found people waiting for me on business, and got no time for prayer before supper, but have this night had some liberty of access to a throne of grace. Glory be to God for all his mercies!

Sunday, February 15.—This morning I waked in a spiritual frame, desirous of spending the day to the Lord; experienced some liberty in prayer, and comfort in reading the Scriptures; found a desire for the increase of the Redeemer's kingdom, and sought for his presence to all his people. Went out in hopes of finding it a good day to my soul, but was disappointed. I have not had such freedom from outward distractions as I could wish, and the word preached did not come with power. One thing I must, however, remark, that the Lord answered prayer in behalf of Mr Sheriff, who was enabled to go to the chapel. He made an intimation, and give an exhortation to the people, and was assisted wonderfully beyond expectation; every word he spoke came with power. I saw him more fitted than ever for the charge of the chapel, yet feared I should be called to give him up; and my mind was agitated with different sentiments of grief, joy, fear, and hope.

Thursday, February 19.—I got some liberty this morning in seeking deliverance from my heart evils. After breakfast found access to God, and some comfort in prayer; was better through the day than for some time past. Heard a good sermon from Mr Walker on Isaiah xvii. 14. "And behold at eveningtide trouble; and before the morning he is not. This is the portion of them that spoil us, and the lot of them that rob us." Lost ground at night; could not pray in the spirit at going to bed.

Saturday, February 21.—This morning I wrote letters and received visits; had no time for private prayer before dinner. Company with me till supper time: no private duties performed to any purpose this day, and little good (if any) done in company. Some comfort in family prayer this evening, but my heart is still very dead. May the Lord revive and quicken, and cause me to hear his voice to-morrow in the word preached, so that I may yet live before him!

Wednesday, February 25.—This morning I spent some time in prayer,—found liberty to give up all to God. I saw that my present trial is needful to wean my heart from too great an attachment to creature comforts, also to subdue my will respecting the manner of helping forward the Lord's work. I think also that Satan sometimes accuses me of sin, in order to weaken my hands and prevent the discharge of present duty. I found liberty to commit my soul, and the Lord's work, into his own hands, with some measure of faith in his power and willingness to perfect what concerneth them, and to make all issue in his own glory and my good. My heart was much enlarged in seeking spiritual blessings for Mr Sheriff, insomuch that I thought I would willingly suffer any spiritual deprivation myself, so that he might obtain joy and peace in believing, and strength for his work; or, if obliged to give it up, that he might have patience and submission. After breakfast I went to see a poor woman on her death-bed. She bore a noble testimony to the faithfulness and love of God. She said all the promises she had ever been brought to believe had been accomplished to her,—the last was "even to hoary hairs I will carry you," and that he was now fulfilling it to her. She said, no believer need fear to pass through this wilderness, or to enter the stream of Jordan; that she had been like the Israelites, who saw the wonders of the Lord, had tasted of the manna, and had sung his praise, and then, like them, soon forgot his works, and sinned again and again by unbelief; yet God had again and again forgiven her sin, and had for seven years past not suffered her to doubt her interest in his promise. She now believed she was on the threshold of glory, just about to enter her Father's house, and her joy at the prospect was great. Last night she thought she heard the sound of his chariot wheels, but was disappointed; but she hoped he would not be long in coming. She feared she sinned in being too desirous to die and unwilling to live. She still felt the workings of sin leading her thoughts away from Christ to the trifling things of the world, and she longed to be free of that clay tabernacle that imprisoned her soul. I asked her of what nature she thought the happiness was to which she was going? She answered, It consists of seeing Christ as he is, in being changed into his image, perfected in holiness, attaining new discoveries of the wisdom, power, love, and grace of God, and freedom from all sin: But this body, said she, is a bar in the way of comprehending that happiness, for flesh and blood cannot enter the kingdom of heaven;—she wished to say more, but strength failed her. Mr Bonar then prayed at her desire, and I left her.—May my last end be like hers!

This scene left a sweet savour of divine things on my mind all day, and I had an opportunity of speaking of it at night to some of no religion, who, I hope, may be the better for it.

Sunday, March 1.—For two days past I have been in a dull frame. This day, by the good hand of the Lord upon us, the ordinance of the Supper was intimated for this day fortnight, in the chapel. Mr Walker lectured in the forenoon, and preached in the afternoon upon the nature of the ordinance,—an excellent discourse. I see great cause of thankfulness, yet feel surprisingly dull in my soul. For some days I have not been quite well, which may partly be the reason of this deadness; for sure I have much cause to rejoice, since the Lord seems about to bless us, and give me the desire of my heart for many months and years past, and to overrule all the counsels of those I have intrusted with the chapel, so as to make them act agreeably to all my wishes and prayers, and that without my appearing in it myself. The spirit of love seems shed abroad in their hearts, so that they are all as one soul; no party spirit, no by-ends, no boasting, but much prayer, and diligence in the use of means, seems at present to be their happy attainment. Not unto us, O Lord, not unto us, but unto thy thrice holy name be the praise and glory, now, and for evermore!

Sunday, March 8.—During the course of last week, about two hundred persons have been admitted as church members, who have to all appearance experienced a work of grace upon their souls: this is cause of much thankfulness; but my soul is kept in heaviness through manifold temptations. I know not whether I shall venture to join with them in that blessed ordinance, being altogether unworthy of the crumbs that fall from the children's table. O for more faith, and love to Christ! O for power to walk up to light! O for a victorious faith to overcome the enemies of my soul, by laying hold on the arm of Omnipotence, and so put to flight the army of the aliens. This day has been a lost Sabbath,—no comfort in hearing, no communion with God, no breathings of the Spirit; my mind in a state of woeful confusion, unable to do any thing to purpose. O that the Lord would come over the mountains of my sins and provocations, and surprise me with his goodness; then should I loathe and abhor myself for my sins and iniquities, and be ashamed, and never open my mouth more.

Saturday, 14.—All this week I have continued distressed with temptations and wandering thoughts,—no comfort in prayer, nor in hearing the word. On Thursday Mr Dickson and the assistant preached. Yesterday we had a meeting for the distribution of tokens; nearly four hundred communicants were admitted. This morning I set apart to examine into my state, and I feel incapable to pursue any thought almost for a minute together. In general, I fear I have committed much sin by approaches to the Lord's table without due preparation. I also see, that my heart sins have partly been the cause of my past darkness. I have not been circumspect in all my ways. I have not denied myself, and taken up my cross. I am unholy in many respects, and have grieved the Holy Spirit. I have endeavoured to confess my sins. O that the Lord would give me true repentance, and effectually turn me again, for his own name's sake, and now enable me to partake of this ordinance with a suitable frame and disposition of heart.

Sunday, March 15.—This morning I got up early, and obtained some liberty in seeking for the Lord's presence this day in his ordinances. I found much desire for a blessing to his people, even although I should be left in a dry and comfortless frame. During Mr Randall's sermon, I saw something of the glory of God in the way of redemption, and felt some small measure of his love shed abroad in my heart, and a sense of his presence. As Mr Sheriff fenced the tables, I felt a melting of heart and a spirit of prayer accompany the word. When I went to the table, my mind was in a thoughtful frame. I exercised some degree of faith in Jesus as the atoning sacrifice for sin, and I felt power to believe that his body was broken for me, and his blood shed for me. My heart said, is it possible that thou shouldest die for me, Lord? Yes, for me, even the chief of sinners! I felt assured that the ordinance was the pledge for sitting down at the table above, and drinking of the wine in my Father's kingdom. My thoughts were somewhat confused, yet I had a relish for divine things all the day, and this afternoon I was much refreshed by Mr Randall's sermon, and in the last psalm. I was enabled to act faith on the promise, and to rejoice in hope. I came home rejoicing, and have had my hope increased by hearing that this has been a remarkable day to the souls of many. Glory be to God in the highest, for peace on earth, and good will to the sons of men! Blessed be God for his unspeakable gift! O, that all would praise him, for his wonderful goodness to the children of men! Bless the Lord, O my soul, and forget not all his benefits! Let heaven and earth praise him! Let every thing that hath breath praise the Lord! Amen, so be it! W. G.

March 22.—This has been a silent Sabbath to me; detained at home by a cold and headach, I was unable to fix my thoughts upon any subject till seven at night. I attempted in vain to pray or read,—all was fruitless till then, when the Lord enabled me to pour out my heart before him for myself and for my sick friend, whose case calls for much sympathy. I felt much liberty in looking for the coming of Christ, and my heart seemed weaned from the world and all in it. I desire only to live while I can do any thing to advance the kingdom of Christ. This night I may look back with shame and confusion of face upon the week past, in which I can see nothing but misimproved sickness and distraction of thought, neglect of prayer and serious discourse, and all this after receiving much comfort and many exhortations to the contrary, during the late ordinance. O! the amazing depth of sin that is in my nature, drawing me away continually into the abuse of mercies, and the neglect of commanded duties. Surely it can only be equalled by the depth of love that devised a way in which God can be just and justify the ungodly: and blessed be his name, this not only equals, but surpasseth the other, for where sin abounded grace has much more abounded. Here then is my hope. To this grace I would flee for help in time of need. May I now be enabled, in the strength and by the grace of Christ Jesus, to set out afresh, and run with renewed vigour in the highway of holiness, continually looking unto Jesus as the author and finisher of faith.

This evening, upon coming down to prayer, I found Mr Sheriff uncommonly serious. He told me, that since I had gone up stairs, the Lord had been very gracious to him, and poured much joy and consolation into his soul. He had got a view of his illness that he had not had before, and believed that his end was near. We had much profitable conversation on this subject, and I felt resigned to the will of God. My spirit was wonderfully composed and solemnized.

Sunday, March 29.—This last week Mr Sheriff has been much worse:—his animal frame fast dissolving, and his spirits flat; but he has shewn no fears of death, nor desire to live. He seems to have a great dislike to company, and has something upon his mind which he seems desirous to disclose, but cannot accomplish it. My own soul has been very dead in prayer this last week, and my thoughts so much taken up about Mr Sheriff, that I have neglected many other concerns. This day I received no benefit from two sermons I heard: To-night my spirits are quite sunk.—My case is complicated. None but the Lord himself knows my various distresses, and none but he can help or support me. On him will I depend, on him will I put my trust. He is my hope, my refuge, my aid, in every time of need. My Lord and my God, none ever trusted in thee and was ashamed: thy mercy endureth for ever,—forsake not the work of thy own hands; for thy name's sake help and deliver me from every unbelieving fear.

Barnton, Sunday, April 5.—This last week I have been much taken up in the same way as in the former;

—Mr Sheriff continuing worse,—his doctors flattering him with the hopes of recovery, when they and every one that sees him knows that his end approaches fast. I am uncertain as to duty; for fear of hurting him if I tell him what I think, and I fear sinning against his and my own soul if I deceive him as to his dangerous state. To-day he told me that he now entertained hopes of recovery, and had got power for some days to pray for it. This threw me into such agitation, that I was forced to leave the room; yet I cannot prevail upon myself to tell him the real state of his case, my own mind is so greatly agitated.

June 7.—For two months past I have been employed in attending the dying bed of Mr Sheriff, who this day lies at the point of death. He has borne a noble testimony to the power of faith in supporting and quieting the mind under bodily distress, and the certain approach of death. For six weeks past the Lord has given me much heartfelt submission to his will in this trial. He has shewn me wherefore it was sent,—convinced me of the expediency and necessity of it, to subdue my will in those things I judged not only lawful, but in which I thought I might be zealous. He has brought me to give up the chapel wholly to himself, being the Head, Governor, and Lawgiver of his church; and last night and this day he enabled me to surrender up myself and all my plans wholly to him, without any known reserve. I got power to ask much for the chapel for ages to come,—that it might be a lamp and a witness for the doctrines and discipline of the true church in future generations. A place where true vital experimental religion might be taught, and where souls might daily be born again, and savingly united to Christ. I had some degree of faith for this, and that a proper pastor would be provided for it by the Lord in his time, and I sought patience to wait upon him for the answer of this prayer. And now, O my gracious Saviour, as I have devoted myself, and all that I am and have unto thee this day upon my knees, and with my heart and tongue, I would now in thy presence confirm it with my hand, and with all the sincerity of heart with which I am capable, solemnly giving up and committing to thee my soul, body, and spirit, my life, reputation, goods, friends, relations, health, and outward comforts—my understanding, will, and affections; in short, all that I am and have, to be disposed of as shall be most for the glory of thy name, and the eternal good of my soul. Guide and conduct me through life,—be with me to support and comfort me in death,—and receive me at last into thy kingdom and glory, to be ever with thee throughout eternity. And the whole glory and praise shall be ascribed unto the Father, Son, and Holy Ghost, one God, for ever and ever. Amen. W. GLENORCHY.

Barnton, June 7. 1778.

The closeness of Lady Glenorchy's attention to Mr Sheriff in his illness, and the edification she derived from it, will be seen from the following note which she at this time wrote to her friend Miss Hill.

Lady Glenorchy to Miss Hill.

"My dear friend will pardon my sending her a very few lines, when I tell her that my worthy pastor lies in the next room at the point of death. He has been growing weaker every day since he came here, and now is confined to bed, every hour expecting the joyful summons from his dear Lord to enter into eternal glory. His mother and I attend him constantly, and as she has not yet attained a taste for spiritual conversation, (though I hope she is in a fair way of doing so), he has nobody but myself to whom he can open his mind on spiritual things. This makes me incline to be with him constantly, as also to hear the many precious things that drop from his lips from time to time. I never saw any person enjoy so much uninterrupted peace of mind, or so strong a faith as he does. The particulars I shall send you after his decease, when I get time to write out at length the notes I am taking from day to day."

Saturday, June 13.—Yesterday, at nine o'clock, it pleased God to take to himself my very dear friend and pastor, Mr Sheriff. He was enabled on Thursday to speak from ten in the morning till near ten at night, almost without intermission, to the praise of glorious grace. He gave me many exhortations, and said, Submit, it is the Lord's doing; we shall live together with him for ever: he has saved me; he will save you, my dear friend. His last words were—All is well. The Lord most wonderfully supported me during the last two days and nights of his life, enabling me to attend him during that time, without weariness. I felt uncommon power to believe and acquiesce in the Lord's will. He is now with his God. O that his dying words may make a suitable impression on my heart; may I never forget the awful but instructive scene; may I listen to the voice of God through him, and persevere in his work to the end. May I give up all for Christ, and bear all his dispensations with patience. May I see my friend in glory, and be for ever with the Lord. Amen and Amen.

Sabbath, June 14.—This day I was enabled to attend public worship, after which I visited the place where Mr Sheriff was to be laid. These words came with much force to my remembrance, His flesh shall rest in hope—sown in weakness,—raised in power!—Afterwards I was present at the * chesting, and I was supported wonderfully through the whole ceremony; and at the evening sermon in the Barnton chapel I was enabled to believe that all was well.

* The last melancholy services due to the dead, are not in Scotland left to undertakers and their attendants.—The body is washed and swathed, and laid out by the sick nurse, or servants of the household. When it is to be put into the coffin, the relations, and most intimate friends, to whom affection and respect are intended to be shewn, are invited to attend as witnesses. The performance of this duty is done by the nearest relations, with great solemnity, and profound silence. This office being performed, if a clergyman is present, which is often the case, he closes the solemnity by appropriate prayer, and this is called the chesting.

When the company invited to the funeral are collected, immediately before carrying out the corpse to the grave, a clergyman also offers a suitable prayer; and this is the only religious funeral service used in Scotland, excepting by those of the Episcopal church.

CHAPTER XVII.

Lady Glenorchy directs her attention to supply the vacancy occasioned by Mr Sheriff's death—The offer of the chapel is made to the Rev. Mr Hodgson—Extracts from Diary—Lady Glenorchy goes to Taymouth—Extracts from Diary, from July 13. to September 13. 1778—Lady Glenorchy returns from Taymouth, and comes to Edinburgh—Mr Hodgson declines accepting the chapel—Lady Glenorchy again thrown into perplexity—Mr Dickie sent to London to offer the chapel to the Rev. Mr Clayton—Extracts from Diary, from October 28. to December 27. 1778—Letter from Lady Glenorchy to Mr Jones, requesting him to aid her in inducing Mr Clayton to accept of the chapel—Mr Clayton declines—Letter from Lady Glenorchy to Mr Jones, inviting him to supply the chapel for a few months, which he complies with—Offer of becoming the minister of the chapel made to him, which he accepts—His ordination in London—Returns to Edinburgh, and enters on his ministerial duties—Extracts from Diary, from January 3. to May 30. 1779.

When Mr Sheriff's remains were removed to their long home, and his mother, and other friends who had attended him in his last days, had departed, Lady Glenorchy left Barnton, and went to Edinburgh. From the comfortless state in which her mind is usually seen, it might be thought that this event would have much increased it; but it should be remembered, that it was not temporal afflictions altogether that occasioned her distresses; for these she could bear with a fortitude rarely shewn by her sex; her distress was occasioned chiefly by spiritual mortifications, on account of imperfection in the sight of God, and these may be said to be the only source of her mental pain: hence, on this occasion, her attention being turned aside for a little from the old subject of her complaints, she appeared not merely composed and resigned, but rejoicing in tribulation. On her return to Edinburgh, her first employment was to supply the vacancy which had occurred in her chapel. She called together for this purpose, those friends who most interested themselves in her concerns. After prayer for divine direction, she advised with them what was best to be done. Their unanimous opinion was, that Mr Joseph Hodgson, minister of Carmunnock, ought to be invited to accept of the office of pastor. They sent, therefore, a deputation to converse with him. He received them kindly; but requested time to make up his mind with regard to their proposal. Her mode of expressing her views on these events, will be seen by the subsequent extract from her Diary.

Edinburgh, Saturday, June 27.—Since I came to town, I have experienced much of the loving-kindness of the Lord, in comforting and supporting me, and carrying me above the present affliction, to seek for comfort in himself. My heart is depressed, yet my spirit rejoices in God my Saviour; and he, as it were, says, Am I not better to you than ten pastors? Yes, Lord, thou art my portion; my chief good; my only desire. O that I may never, never seek any other good but thee!

"Take thou my heart, and let it be
For ever closed to all but thee."

Truly my soul has experienced something of the peace that passeth understanding, even when outward things appear most gloomy. I feel a secret power enabling me to rest in the will of God, and believe, that all is working together for my good, the good of his church, and the glory of his name. O for ever blessed be the Lord my God, now and evermore!

Sunday, June 28.—Yesterday was a day of mercy from the Lord; begun in distress of body, but afterwards strengthened, and carried on in much peace and comfort of mind, particularly in the evening, when I had a meeting of some Christian friends for prayer, to seek the mind of the Lord concerning the steps which ought to be taken for obtaining another pastor. After prayer, and singing the 147th Psalm, I asked them what occurred to them as the most scriptural and proper method of proceeding. I mentioned some ministers, particularly Mr Hodgson, as one I supposed would be agreeable to the congregation: they all were of opinion that he would be the most acceptable of any that could be procured. It was then agreed that two of the number should go to him, and lay our plan before him; this, after another meeting for prayer with a view to him in particular, was done. There was a spirit of love and unanimity appeared so remarkable in our conversation, that surely the Lord himself was with us. We concluded with a very lively and fervent prayer by Mr Scott Moncrieff, and then sung part of the 102d Psalm, and parted. My heart was lifted up in thankfulness to the Lord for giving me such helpers in his work; their hearts appeared to be full of love to the Lord, and their eye single to his glory. This morning I have had some comfort and pleasure in hearing Mr Bonar lecture on the ascension, and preach from Psalm lxxii. 20. "The prayers of David the son of Jesse are ended." I have since been able to pour out my heart in prayer, and to commit the providing a minister to the chapel wholly to the Lord, with a degree of confidence in his answering my request; also for myself, that he will perfect that which concerneth me, and grant me eternal life through Jesus Christ our Lord.

As nothing more could be done in this business till Mr Hodgson's determination was known, Lady Glenorchy went, as usual at this season of the year, to Taymouth. Nothing remarkable occurred during her residence in the Highlands. The chapel was supplied by the assistant, while she and the people were waiting Mr Hodgson's decision.

In August she experienced another unexpected stroke, in the death of the master of her school in Edinburgh; a man of high respectability, and greatly beloved. Her mind at this time was much more comfortable than usual. The following reflections on her past experience and conduct, and on the events of the preceding year, are uncommonly interesting.—

Taymouth, Monday, July 13.—I came to this place last Saturday. I was rather in a dead frame on the road, and since I came here: but I feel strong desires after the Lord; my mind goes out towards him; I want to be wholly dead to the world, and alive to him. The Lord, I trust, will keep me from the snares which surround me, else I know I shall fall. I hope the Lord, who is my strength, will manifest his power in preserving me from this present evil world. O grant this, blessed Jesus, for thine own holy name's sake!

Friday, July 17.—This morning I set apart some time for seeking the Lord by self-examination, meditation, and prayer. I have been convinced of much practical atheism in my heart, particularly want of right apprehensions of the majesty of God, want of reverence in my approaches to him, and want of intercourse with him in my thoughts; so that my heart prefers every trifle to thinking on him, who is the source of all perfection. Perpetual wanderings of heart and affection shew the natural tendency and bent of my depraved nature. I have got a clearer view than ever of the necessity of divine power being exerted to reconcile my heart to God, and cause my thoughts to flow in a right channel; and that he that begins this work must also carry it on and finish it. I have seen much self-seeking mixed with all my past plans for promoting the cause of religion. I have often limited the Lord to work in the particular way that I marked out. I trust in some measure he has now enabled me to say, Not my will, but thine be done. I have discovered a great proneness in my heart to lean more on the instruments employed in his work, than on the hand which holds the instrument; and thus have often been left to feel the bitterness and evil of trusting to the creature, and departing in heart from the living God. I have again been convinced of my sinful negligence and slothfulness in not seeking the Lord more constantly by prayer and meditation; in letting my heart grow estranged from him, thus grieving the Spirit, and causing him to depart and leave me to my own desires; not improving spiritual blessings when received as earnests of still greater things, and thus following on to know more and more of the Lord. I am persuaded that all true happiness consists in the knowledge of him. If we know him, we must love him; if we love, we shall obey him; if we love and obey him, he will come unto us, and manifest himself unto us as he doth not unto the world; nay, the

Father and the Son will come and make their abode with us, and in that day we shall know that Christ is in the Father, and we in him, and he in us. O the inconceivable, unfathomable love of God, to admit such vile polluted worms as we are to this close and intimate union with himself! But can this union subsist when the love of sin remains in the creature? Surely not. It is the new nature, the new born soul, that consents to the law of God as holy, just, and good; that abhors evil, and groans under it, and a vile body of sin and death, which is thus made a partaker of a divine nature. This new nature comes from God, is imparted by him, and therefore must be united to him, and will continue to be so to all eternity.

I this day desire, in the strength of the Lord Jesus Christ, to renounce all selfish views and aims in his work; to seek no great things for myself; but that his glory may be promoted upon earth, his kingdom come, his will be done; and that this may be my only end in every action of my life. I would earnestly implore the aid of the Holy Spirit to mortify and crucify this self in me, that Christ may be established on the throne of my heart, and reign the only sovereign there. I earnestly beg the grace of perseverance in known duty, whatever trouble it may cost. I beseech thee, O Lord, to make me willing rather to suffer any thing than sin against thee. O for a more quick sense of the exceeding sinfulness of sin, for a tender conscience, a more constant breathing and panting after holiness in heart and life. O for power to resist temptation, and to flee from the beginnings and appearances of evil. O to see enmity against a God of love written upon the smallest deviation from the path of duty! My soul longs for more clear impressions of thy image, O God, to be stamped upon it; and that it may begin here to taste those divine and exquisite pleasures which flow from thy right hand for evermore: it already feels that happiness consists in a holy nature, and believes that perfect holiness will bring the perfection of happiness. O when shall I live wholly to thee, my chief good, my only portion, my all in all! When shall the thoughts of my heart be brought into subjection to thee, my only Lord? When shall sin be destroyed, my soul delivered from its bondage, and brought into the glorious liberty of the children of God? When shall I behold thy glorious and gracious face, and join with the redeemed in songs of praise to him who has loved us, and washed us from our sins in his own blood? Lord, whenever it shall be for thy glory and the good of my soul, I believe thou wilt grant me these petitions. Even so come, Lord Jesus, and do as thou hast said! Amen and Amen.

Sunday, July 19.—Yesterday and to-day my soul has been in a very dull frame, particularly to-day. In public worship it was bodily service only that I performed;—I returned ashamed and confounded. In private I have been very dead; unable to reap any other benefit from reading than a conviction that I never have worshipped God aright; that he might justly bid me depart from him for ever for the sins of my best duties. I have endeavoured to confess before him my great wretchedness, and to implore a new heart and a right spirit; but even when engaged in this, and making supplications with cries and tears, my perverse heart started aside, and led me away to the mountains of vanity ere ever I was aware. I see I cannot of myself command one good thought, although my soul were at stake; I therefore renounce all dependance upon myself for every part of my salvation

If I am saved, God must have all the glory through Jesus Christ, now and for evermore.

Sunday, July 26.—I still find my heart cold and dead, and sometimes averse to prayer, and oftener to meditation. This morning I had some small degree of liberty in asking spiritual blessings, yet I have not found my soul more alive through the day: On the contrary, I feel more dead than ever; wandering thoughts distress me continually; I get no benefit from what I read or hear; I have the faith of the presence of God without feeling its power; I believe God sees every thought in my heart, yet I cannot keep out one vain, trifling, impertinent thought which offers to come into it; and even when praying against them, I am most harassed by them. Well may I cry out with Paul, O wretched creature that I am, who shall deliver me from the body of this death! O that I could with equal faith say, Thanks be to God through Jesus Christ! and that with the mind I myself serve the law of God.

August 8.—Last Thursday was the day set apart in this parish for humiliation and prayer. I kept my room in the morning, and had some comfort in prayer and meditation till I went to church; but then all vanished, and I became as dead and comfortless as ever.

This day I have in vain attempted to examine myself, and meditate upon the word. I have many fears about approaching the Lord's table to-morrow in this frame of mind. As this ordinance, however, is a means of growth in grace, (and I never had more need than now of spiritual food), I dare not stay away, lest by neglecting the means I grow worse, and the things die which are now ready to perish. O Lord, thou knowest my case! Thou art able to heal the diseases of my soul, and can'st give me a lively faith. Grant now, I beseech thee, whatever thou seest I stand in need of, to prepare my soul for drawing near to thee in thy ordinance; undertake for me, for I put my trust in thee.

Monday, August 10.—Yesterday morning I was enabled to examine myself, and found that I had reason to conclude, upon scripture grounds, that I had truly believed upon the Lord Jesus Christ for salvation, and that I was now willing to depart this life to be with him, were he to call for me. I therefore thought I might approach his table to remember his death, and shew it forth till he come. I found power given me during the whole day, to attend to the things spoken, with more composure of mind than for many days past. I was also enabled to exercise faith on the perfect sacrifice of Christ, as having for ever perfected them who were sanctified; and, upon the whole, I had a better day than I expected. Glory be to God! This was a sort of preparation for the afflictive news I received, upon coming home in the afternoon, of the death of John Robertson, the teacher of my school in Edinburgh, whose uncommon abilities for his office rendered him very useful to me. The rod is once more lifted up. O that I may lay it to heart, to search and try wherefore the Lord is thus sending wave upon wave!

August 23.—For some days past I have felt my heart more drawn out after spiritual things than it was in the beginning of the week; and this day I found comfort in prayer, and in reading the word. Having no sermon at church, I endeavoured to spend the whole morning in those exercises in which I believed most Christians were then engaged, and I had sweet fellowship with them in spirit; and even with the church triumphant, as employed in thanksgiving for redeeming love. I have this day got a little more insight into the deceitfulness of the heart, and saw the impurity of the best actions of my life. I have been led to cry for pardon for the defects of my holy duties, and particularly for my rash zeal in the first years of my religious profession; whereby I did in many things hurt the cause I wished to promote, and this from pride and self-conceit; not being enough sensible of my dependance on God for all things, and of my nothingness before him. I think I did this day truly renounce all hope in myself, and rest on Christ as my only Saviour. Lord, thou knowest. O! do thou search me and try me, and see if there is any wicked way in me, and cleanse me from secret faults. What I know not, teach me; and lead me in the way everlasting, for thine own name's sake. Amen!

Sunday, August 30.—Last week I had a visit from Mr and Mrs Balfour, which was refreshing. He preached twice this day; and in the evening we had some spiritual conversation, which was like water to the thirsty.

[Aged 37.] *Wednesday, September* 2.—This day I would, as usual, look back upon the last year of my life, and endeavour to record the mercies I have received from the Lord; of the least of which I confess myself utterly unworthy. How difficult the task! Every day is marked with his long-suffering kindness, and my ingratitude. This has been a year of awful dispensations; of dark and mysterious providences.

The Lord's ways have been in the deep; how little of them can we discover! Yet this we know, that he hath done all things well. He is of unerring wisdom: great is his faithfulness. I therefore believe, that all his ways towards me have been dictated by mercy and truth, and shall be productive of fruits to his praise and glory; and what I know not now I shall know hereafter.

I desire to bless the Lord, as the hearer of prayer, in providing a pastor for the chapel, such as was every way suited to begin the work intended, of gathering a people into church order and discipline. The peculiar circumstances attending him were remarkable: Eminently called of God, and fitted by various means for the situation, and thereby enabled to begin and set a-going the work, which to any other person would have seemed impracticable, ability was given him for bringing it such a length as to render it easy in future. The ordinances dispensed agreeable to the scripture plan; a number of lively Christians formed into a society for managers and helpers in the work; peace preserved, without infringing on holiness, or strictness of discipline; all things done by prayer; love and unanimity in councils; the Lord visibly directing to wise and prudent measures; an assistant provided every way agreeable and proper;—and when all this was done, the pastor was advanced from the church militant to the church triumphant, and had an abundant entrance given him into the kingdom of his dear Lord. I ought also to bless the Lord for permitting me to be a witness to his holy life, and triumphant death, and for making me any way instrumental in alleviating the evils of disease and sufferings, and assisting his servant in his last moments, both in temporal and spiritual matters. This was an honour

I asked and obtained by prayer, for which I desire to be thankful. O that I may suitably improve the precious blessing. What support and consolation did not the Lord afford me under this trial, beyond all expectation remarkably overruling all matters concerning him, according to repeated and united prayers! So that, while my heart was ready to break with grief, I was constrained to say, All is well. I would not have it otherwise. The Lord is wise, and just, and merciful, and faithful in afflicting me. He manifests his love in every stroke. He stayeth his rough wind in the day of his east wind. I desire to bless God for convincing me that there is enough in himself to satisfy the soul; that he can by his presence, and the sensible communications of his love, make up for the loss of every other thing; and that he has given me a desire to seek no other portion in time but himself, which I take to be an evidence that I shall dwell with him throughout eternity. He has also convinced me of past misconduct in many respects of self-seeking, and impatience under the cross; of discontent with my lot, and wandering without a warrant from the place allotted me by Providence; and he is now giving me a willingness to give up all schemes of comfort in life, so that God may be glorified in me, and his cause promoted by my instrumentality. This summer, he has convinced me more than ever, from experience, of the deep depravity of my nature, and the absolute necessity there is of depending upon God for every right thought, word, and deed; of the danger I am in of falling again and again into those very errors and evils I now renounce and abhor, if left one moment to myself. I now see more of the worthlessness and unprofitableness of the creature in its best estate, and of the continual necessity of abiding in Christ by faith, in order to have peace with God. When I look to myself, I see nothing but death; when to Christ, I behold life and immortality, and rejoice in the hope of being freed from this state of sin and corruption: and I have cause to bless God for interposing in my behalf this summer, in preventing evil which I had great reason to fear, and was led to pray against; also for preventing me from murmuring, when he took away the worthy master of my school by a sudden stroke, and giving me faith that this also was to work for good, although I knew not how; and, soon after, he unexpectedly provided me with another. I have much cause to record to the praise of free grace, that the Lord has lately given me much composure of spirit concerning the calling of another minister for the chapel in Edinburgh; enabling me to trust in him, that one shall be appointed according to his own heart; making me satisfied, that his will in all things shall take place, even although it should be in demolishing of the whole work, or in my not being permitted to see its prosperity: this I feel to be a new temper of mind, wrought in me by repeated trials, afflictions, and disappointments. Glory be to his name. What shall I now render to the Lord for all his benefits. It is of thine own only, O Lord, that I have to offer. I am thine, in every sense of the word; thine by creation, redemption, repeated self-dedication. I can now only renew this day what I have often done; and I now afresh solemnly do, as in thy presence, devote my whole soul, body, and spirit, to thy service, beseeching thee to rule over and reign in me. Dispose of me in whatever way is most for thy glory; guide me by thy counsel whilst I am here; leave me not one moment to myself. Let me live under an abiding sense of thy presence, and of thy love in Christ Jesus; and when I can no longer serve thee here, receive me into the heavenly kingdom, to dwell with thee for evermore: and thine shall be the praise and glory, through Christ. Amen! W. G.

Sunday, September 6.—I have still cause to lament the very dead and unprofitable state of my mind; harassed by wandering thoughts, and little comfort in reading or prayer. Having this day no service in the church, I endeavoured to examine into the cause of my deadness; but I have got little light concerning it. I had some enlargement in the afternoon in prayer for spiritual blessings: I can say, my soul truly panteth after God; the knowledge and enjoyment of him was my chief desire. Blessed be his name for the day of small things. I trust I shall yet see greater, and have much cause to praise him.

Sunday, September 13.—I was enabled this evening to give a faithful warning to a young lady, which, I trust, will be blessed to her.

At the usual season Lady Glenorchy returned from Taymouth, and without spending any time at Barnton, as she used to do, came directly to Edinburgh, anxious to accomplish without delay the settlement of a minister in her chapel. Mr Hodgson not having as yet given an answer to the offer made him in July, she invited him to a conference in Edinburgh. He complied with this, and had repeated conversations both with her and the managers of her chapel. They agreed in all points excepting in the manner of admitting persons to church privileges, on which Mr Hodgson held some peculiar opinions, from which he could not deviate, and to which neither Lady Glenorchy nor her friends could accede. With mutual regret they were therefore obliged to terminate the negociation. Lady Glenorchy was thus again placed in a state of anxiety and perplexity how to proceed.

The usual sacramental fast-day of the city was at hand, and she and the congregation agreed to keep it, and in doing so to have particularly at heart their present circumstances, and to implore the great Head of the church to provide them with a pastor that might repair the loss they had experienced. As no eligible person appeared in Scotland, she turned her eyes towards England. She had heard of Mr Clayton, who had lately been settled in a presbyterian meeting in London, whose character and talents were highly respectable. She thought it probable that he might be induced to come to Edinburgh, and sent therefore Mr Dickie, one of the managers of the chapel, to hear him, and, if he thought he would answer the situation, to invite him to visit Edinburgh with a view to his settlement there. These things appear from the following extracts.

Wednesday, October 28.—In the afternoon there was a meeting of the managers for solemn prayer, to request direction in the choice of a minister. They were unanimously of opinion that they must give up Mr Hodgson. I was led to commit the matter wholly to the Lord, and enabled in some measure to believe he would provide.

Friday evening, October 30.—Another meeting for prayer, and a proposal agreed to of using next Thursday as a congregational fast with respect to the circumstances of the chapel, as it was the fast-day before the celebration of the Lord's supper in the city.

November 5.—This day being set apart for fasting and prayer in the chapel, Mr Martin of Monymeal and Mr Bonar preached; the former on Psalm li. 3. "For I acknowledge my transgressions, and my sin is ever before me;" the latter on Revelations i. 17. "And when I saw him I fell at his feet as dead; and he laid his right hand upon me, saying unto me, Fear not; I am the first and the last." The interval betwixt the worship in the forenoon and the afternoon was spent by the managers in prayer. My own soul has been very dead all day,—no liberty in prayer,—my sins are as a heavy burden,—I am weighed down, and have no power to raise myself up, or to lay hold by faith on the remedy. I feel my heart full of vain wandering thoughts, sensible of the state I am in, yet not enough distressed on that account. I have no power to plead in prayer for a minister, nor for myself, although I see the need of both. O that the Lord would have compassion upon me, and melt this frozen heart with a sense of his love. This I know would effectually remove the darkness and ignorance of mind which I now groan under. O that he would enable me to look upon him whom I have pierced by my sins, and mourn as one mourneth for her first-born. My heart is hard as the nether mill-stone.

This night Mr Dickie has written to London to inquire about a minister for the chapel:—may the Lord overrule and direct in this matter. To thee I commit it, O thou great Head of the church! Send whom thou wilt send,—let thy will be done, thy glory advanced, our souls quickened and built up in the faith, for thy great name's sake. Amen.

Saturday, November 7.—I have been this day endeavouring to examine myself, and I plainly perceive that

I have suffered much from not giving more diligence in redeeming time, and in suppressing vain unprofitable thoughts. I have no strength to perform any duty, yet I dare not for this reason absent myself from the Lord's table to-morrow, because the more weak and the more sickly my soul is, the more need I have of spiritual medicine and nourishment. Viewing the ordinance in this light, I will venture forward, as the poorest and most needy of all the flock. Perhaps the Chief Shepherd may cast an eye of pity upon me, and lead me into his green pastures, beside the still waters of comfort. Perhaps it may be a day of revival to my soul.

Sunday, November 8.—This morning my temptations were strong, and my faith weak. I went out in much darkness of mind. When I entered the church they were singing the two last verses of the 43d Psalm:

Why art thou then cast down, my soul?
What should discourage thee?
And why with vexing thoughts art thou
Disquieted in me?

Still trust in God; for him to praise
Good cause I yet shall have:
He of my countenance is the health,
My God that doth me save.

This gave me some comfort, and Mr Plenderleath's first prayer seemed very suitable to the state of my mind, and his sermon was refreshing. I found that I desired to see Jesus, and, blessed be God, when I went to the table I got some degree of light and liberty, and was made to see my own vileness and unworthiness, and something of the love of Christ in dying for such a sinner. I was enabled to give up myself wholly to him, for time and eternity, and to put all my concerns into his hands. I found a readiness to do or to suffer whatever he saw meet for me. I also got a sight of the vanity of the creature, and felt a desire to have my all in God. My burden was taken off, so that the rest of the day I have felt comfort in joining in songs of praise to him who has turned my night into day, and delivered me out of the hands of my cruel foes. I felt joy and triumph in singing a part of the 23d Psalm.

Monday.—I was delivered from an imminent danger this day, for which I desire to praise and magnify the Lord, who has been my help and protector in the time of need.

Sunday, November 29.—This morning I was led to expect some comfort from the word preached, having asked it in prayer; and accordingly I did find more comfort than usual in hearing. Mr Bonar preached, and seemed directed to speak to my particular case; and while I heard I was refreshed by it. But this evening I cannot recollect it. I only think it has left an indistinct impression on my mind, by which I have been led to pray more earnestly to God, that performeth all things for me, with firmer faith than is common to me of being heard. I have put myself, and the affairs of the chapel, into the Lord's hands, and besought deliverance in any way he thinks fit.

Sunday, December 6.—Last week I have been much taken up with company, both at home and abroad; but found more liberty in prayer, and composure of spirit, than usual at such times; particularly on Friday morning I had near access to God, and besought him to help me through the day.

Tuesday, December 8.—It was determined that Mr Dickie should go to London to invite Mr Clayton to come to the chapel.

Sunday, December 27.—This day I have had little benefit at church; my mind was exceedingly dead this afternoon. Since I came home I have had a sight of my heart sins, and of the evil of my past life, and have been able to mourn before the Lord on that account, and to lay hold on Christ as he is freely offered in the gospel. Surely this proceeds from a work of grace begun in my soul; and if begun, it shall be perfected. Why then art thou cast down, O my soul? and why art thou disquieted within me? Trust in God, for thou shalt yet praise him; for he is the strength of thy heart, the light of thy countenance, and thy God.

1779.—In the close of the month of November, Mr Clayton was ordained pastor of the church and congregation of the Weigh-house, East-Cheap. The author, at Mr Clayton's request, was present at that solemnity, and remained in London some weeks afterwards. While there he received a letter from her Ladyship, requesting his attention to the son of a noble friend of hers, who lay ill at Plymouth Dock. Being unable to comply with her request, he immediately wrote her Ladyship to that effect; and in course received the following answer, under cover to Mr Dickie, begging that he would aid him in his negociation with Mr Clayton.

Lady Glenorchy to the Rev. T. S. Jones.

" Rev. Sir,—I received your letter last night, and could not help esteeming it a kind providence to me, your being in London at this particular time, as you now may be very assisting to me in an affair that I have much at heart, and is as follows:—

"From what you formerly wrote to me of Mr Clayton, and from the character I have heard of him lately from others, I am led to form a very favourable opinion of him. And hearing lately that he was ordained minister of a Presbyterian meeting in London, (a circumstance absolutely necessary to qualify a person for usefulness here), I have sent a gentleman from this place to hear him, and if he thinks his manner of preaching the gospel suitable to our congregation, he has powers from me to invite him to the pastoral care of it. But Mr Clayton being perfectly a stranger to me, and the people of this country may possibly be startled at such a proposal, and without due inquiry or consideration may reject it, I shall therefore be exceedingly obliged to you, if you will do what you can to remove any prejudices he may have formed against it. You know pretty nearly my views and plans, though you cannot let him into the extent of the sphere of usefulness he will have here, without having seen it. But of this you may assure him, that if he comes, and is acceptable to the people, (which I do not in the least doubt will be the case), he will have an opportunity of preaching the gospel to more souls in one year, than he can have in London in twenty, unless he goes to Tottenham-Court Chapel or the Tabernacle,—because, besides his own stated congregation of two thousand persons, the whole town will endeavour to hear him, and I have a chapel in the neighbourhood which he may supply whenever his time permits.

"Mr Clayton being already qualified for this, by his ordination to the Weigh-house congregation, is a circumstance that appears so providential, that I cannot help thinking it points him out clearly as the person destined for us. The event will shew whether I am right or not. If he should be of a different opinion, I hope you will be so kind as assist, by your advice, Mr Dickie, (who will probably give you this letter), in search of some other ordained minister, who may suit us. I shall make no apology for giving you this trouble, as I am fully persuaded you wish well to Zion, and will be glad to forward the work of God in this, as well as your native land. Mr Dickie is one of the managers of my chapel, and can inform you that the work of God still goes on among us: the Spirit of the Lord remaineth, though not in that measure we desire.

"That he may be continually at your right hand, to give you the support and assistance you stand in need of, is, Reverend Sir, the hearty desire of your well-wisher in the Lord. W. GLENORCHY."

Mr Clayton, after a very short deliberation, declined the offer. This occasioned a second letter from Lady Glenorchy, in which she pressingly invited the author to visit Scotland immediately, to supply her chapel for a few weeks, and to which he assented. The letter was in the terms subjoined.

Lady Glenorchy to the Rev. T. S. Jones.

"Reverend Sir,—I received your letter, and one from Mr Dickie, this evening, from which I perceive that my expectations from your friendly zeal have been fully answered. I feel more obliged to you than I have at present time to express. Mr Clayton's three first objections may be easily answered. The last four have more weight; and I feel so much the want of a lively gospel preacher here, that I know not how to urge him to leave a congregation destitute, who are attached to him. Yet the much greater sphere of usefulness here, might render such a request lawful.

I would very willingly set out immediately for London, to try what influence I could have, were it not from present indisposition, and also that Lord B—— has been complaining for some days; so that I cannot leave this place immediately, nor can I fix any time for so doing. Meanwhile, it would give me very great satisfaction if you could accompany Mr Dickie, and pay us a visit of a few weeks here; as much longer or shorter as you please: but I should like to see you, and consult with you upon what can be done in this important affair. You can then see the congregation and the country, and could give Mr Clayton a more distinct idea of every thing concerning them; and we should have the benefit of your labours for a few Sabbaths, which would be very refreshing to myself, and, I believe I may say, to the whole congregation. If you do this, I shall write your apology to Mr Kinsman, and take the blame upon myself. You used to express a desire of seeing Scotland: you now have a good opportunity of doing so; an agreeable companion on the road; when you arrive you shall have a room in my house, and two thousand people to preach to, as often as you please. I think this will be a more useful expedition than that into Gloucestershire; and I hope you will consent to it: and may the Lord send you to us in the fulness of the blessing of the gospel of Christ.

I have only time to beg you would remember me to Mr Clayton, and tell him I enter into all his feelings upon the subject in question, and am sorry his way does not appear more clear. I hope the God whom we serve will not permit us to err, but will overrule this important matter in the way that shall be most for his glory. In haste, I must subscribe myself, your obliged friend. W. G."

When the author consented to visit Scotland, he had not the least expectation that the result would be his remaining there. After however having preached a few Sabbaths, at the request of the managers and congregation, Lady Glenorchy made him an offer, to which she added her personal request, that he would become the minister of her chapel. In the middle of March he returned to London, where he soon after received a written invitation, in the form of a call, from her Ladyship, the managers, and the whole congregation. He had previously been known to, and had repeatedly preached for some of the members of the Scots Presbytery in London. On application being made to them, they received him on trial, and on the 9th day of June ordained him to the office of the holy ministry, before a crowded congregation, in a Scots Presbyterian chapel, Peter-street, Soho. Lady Glenorchy, being at that time in London, was present, and in a few days afterwards went to Buxton, and thence to Edinburgh, to attend his admission to be the minister of her chapel.

On July the 25th, Mr Walker, of the High Church, preached in the chapel, and introduced him to the congregation as their minister and pastor. Thus, after seven years' contest and anxiety, Lady Glenorchy's vexations with respect to this institution terminated. And here it may be proper to remark, that whatever usefulness, whatever respectability, whatever comfort have attended the institution, much may be ascribed to the many fervent prayers with which Lady Glenorchy, and those upright and pious persons with whom she associated, accompanied their exertions in carrying it forward. They are now in glory; they rest from their labours, and their works do follow them.

What were Lady Glenorchy's thoughts and exercises during this period will be seen by the following extracts from her Diary.—

January 3.—Last week, my mind has been almost wholly taken up with the affairs of the chapel. Thursday morning I set apart for prayer; but felt little light or liberty to plead with God; I could only groan out my complaints before him, and confess my unworthiness of being heard, and his justice, if all my plans were brought to nothing. I was oppressed and overwhelmed in spirit, and was led to believe that the Lord was doing all things well, although not according to my designs and wishes. On Friday, a letter from Mr Dickie gave me grounds of hope, if not of Mr Clayton, of another equally suitable. This rebuked me for past fears, and misgivings of mind concerning it.

This morning I was confined to the house, and had a very profitable time in pouring out my heart before God, and in confessing my sin, which I saw was done away by the blood of Jesus. Unbelief, I see, is the root of all sin; and faith is the grace which can procure all I need. I sought it with fervour, and endeavoured to exercise it. In the afternoon and evening I have had some comfortable moments.

Thursday, January 14.—This day Mr Jones arrived; and on Sunday the 17th he preached twice in the chapel. On Tuesday he preached again. On Sabbath the 24th he preached twice. On Monday some persons came to beg I would desire him to remain, and that I would take steps to procure his settlement as their pastor. On Tuesday the 26th, he preached again to their great satisfaction. All this time my health has been very bad.

Thursday, March 18.—Since writing the above, my disorder has increased, and the Lord has seen meet to lay me on a bed of affliction. The night before I was confined to bed, (being the 29th of January), I was enabled to cast my cares upon the Lord, beseeching him to relieve me from anxiety of mind, and to order all concerning myself and chapel as seemed good in his sight. This prayer has been wonderfully answered; for, during the course of a six weeks' fever, I was never permitted to have an anxious thought, either about myself or others; and, during that time, the Lord was pleased to carry on his work in the chapel, by inclining the people's hearts so much to Mr Jones, that an invitation and a call is now given him, and I trust he will return to us in the fulness of the blessing of the gospel of Christ.

Sunday, April 18.—For the last fortnight my health has continued improving. Last Sabbath I went out to public worship, and also this day, but my soul was not profited. I have been very dead and comfortless in my mind for many weeks past, till last night, that I felt a growing desire after spiritual blessings; and this day have had some liberty of access in prayer, and comfort in pouring out my heart to God, under a sense of his being my God. I found the workings of faith on my heart, leading me to cast my burden upon him, and to trust him with my lot.

London, Sunday, May 30.—The Lord has been pleased to bring me to this place a fortnight ago, in health and safety. I have cause to bless him for many mercies; in particular, for strength and spirits to go through the business and fatigue that I have had since I came here; for rendering my journey prosperous, with respect to Mr Jones's ordination; and giving me the near prospect of accomplishing it to my wishes.

CHAPTER XVIII.

Lady Glenorchy goes to Taymouth—Extracts from Diary, from August 8. to September 19. 1779—Lady Glenorchy returns to Edinburgh—Extracts from Diary, from October 3. 1779, to April 23. 1780—Lady Henrietta Hope accompanies Lady Glenorchy to England—Lady Glenorchy returns to Scotland, and goes to Taymouth to attend her father-in-law—Extracts from Diary, from May 17. to August 13. 1780—Mr Jones lays the evidence of his ordination before the Presbytery of Edinburgh—Subscribes the Confession of Faith, and Formula—All misunderstanding between Lady Glenorchy and the Presbytery happily terminated—The Rev. Thomas Fleming settled at Kenmore—Lady Glenorchy much satisfied with this event—Extracts from Diary, from September 2. to September 10. 1780—Lady Glenorchy returns from Taymouth—Sets out for Bath—Extracts from Diary, October 22. to December 31. 1780—Lady Henrietta Hope takes up her residence with Lady Glenorchy—Extracts from Diary, from January 1. to April 30. 1781—Lady Glenorchy purchases and supports a chapel in Carlisle—Lady Glenorchy goes to Taymouth for the last time—Extracts from Diary, from July 22. to September 2. 1781.

IMMEDIATELY after the writer's admission to his pastoral charge, Lady Glenorchy set out for Taymouth; and by the following extracts from her Diary at this period it will appear, that her religious experience was on the whole similar to what it had formerly been.

Taymouth, Sunday, August 8.—This day I have joined in celebrating the dying love of Jesus. I hope I was enabled to exercise faith on him as the propitiation and sacrifice for sin, and to plead his broken body and shed blood as sufficient to atone for my sins, and as the procuring cause of every blessing, spiritual and temporal. I endeavoured to give myself up to Jesus as his lawful property, purchased by his blood; and begged of him to dispose of me as seemed good in his sight. I besought him to keep me back from doing any thing dishonourable to his name, and I trust he will hear and answer me in due time. Some parts of the 119th Psalm was very comfortable to me to-day. I felt with the Psalmist an earnest desire to be taught the will and commandments of God;—every verse seemed applicable to me. I believe it is in faithfulness that the Lord has afflicted me, and I have a comfortable hope that my soul shall live, and taste of his loving kindness in heaven, and enjoy his favour, which is better than life. Let him lift upon me the light of his countenance, and I am content to face a frowning world. Only shew me thy will, and give me power and grace to obey it: I ask no more, O ever blessed God!

[Aged 38.] *Taymouth, September* 2.—How dark and mysterious are thy ways, O Lord, to the children of men! yet we are bound to believe that all thy ways are mercy and truth to such as fear thee. The last year of my life has been deeply marked with judgment and mercy. I have in myself a witness that God is almighty in preserving my life, notwithstanding the diseases of body which I have gone through. I do not yet see the meaning of my trials, but I believe I shall yet praise God for them, and be made to acknowledge, that in faithfulness, and loving kindness, and in tender mercy, he has afflicted me. My only comfort is in committing my way to the Lord, and trusting in him, that he will do with me whatever is for his glory and my good. I find that my will is subdued, and my desire is, that his whole will may take place.

This year the Lord has graciously vouchsafed me another minister to the chapel, who has been brought to us in so providential a manner, that I can have no doubt of his being an answer to those prayers put up in faith for this blessing, especially as those we at first cast our eyes upon were prevented from coming by the most uncommon interpositions of Providence. It is satisfactory to reflect, that Mr Jones's call and ordination was carried on in the most scriptural and acceptable manner, and with much ease, the hearts of men being wonderfully turned to it, that the Lord's hand appeared conspicuous in the whole, agreeable to the petitions every day offered up in my house, that the Lord's hand might appear in it.

I have also had the comfort this year to hear of good being done at Exmouth, and a prospect of that work being established on a permanent footing. Many are the particular mercies I have received from the Lord as an individual; preservation from dangers, recovery from pain and sickness, protection and direction in journeyings, and frequently pleasing and refreshing moments in the ordinances, when by faith I could realize the invisible world, and lay hold on the promise of life eternal in Christ. I have also had comfort in seeing my own past miscarriages, and in viewing the hand of God chastening me in infinite wisdom and mercy, in the way most likely to cure the predominant diseases of my soul; thus convincing me, that it is the rod of a Father that is laid upon me, and that I am not a bastard, but a lawful child, an heir of glory. O, joyful transporting thought! who would not suffer, nay, desire to suffer chastisement, when it is to bring us nearer to God, and render the soul meet to behold and enjoy him. O my God, I desire with my whole heart to submit to thy fatherly correction, and to receive it as a proof of thy tender care for my eternal welfare. I ask not deliverance till the end of it is obtained, and every high thought and imagination of my vile heart brought into subjection to Christ. I beseech thee not to leave me to my own devices, or to follow the desires of my carnal heart, but lead me into thy holy will, whatever pain it may give me;—let my own corrupt will and affections be crucified,—let Christ live in me, that the life I lead henceforward may be a life of faith on him, receiving from him continual supplies of life, so that it may be no longer I that live, but Christ that liveth in me. If I have erred, convince me of it, that I may humble myself before thee, and seek pardon; and do thou overrule my errors for the glory of thy name, and the good of thy people. Dispose of me, and all that is called mine, in the way which seemeth good in thy sight. I would no longer seek honour from the world, but desire that honour which cometh from thee only. O, let me never be ashamed of my hope;—thou art my refuge, my strength, my high tower, my only hope. In thee I desire to put my trust. On thee I depend for deliverance out of my present perplexities and troubles. Surely thou wilt never let me be ashamed.

Sunday, September 5.—We had no public worship this day in church, but the Lord has abundantly made up the loss to me, by permitting me to draw near to him in private prayer, and giving me some sensible communications of life to my soul; giving me the joyful hope of eternal life in Christ Jesus, and causing me to believe the things that are freely given me of

God. I also read the Bible with delight, and had some small measure of light thrown on some passages of it, which afforded me delightful meditations. In this way I passed four comfortable hours. Glory be to God for this profitable exercise. O that a sweet savour of divine things may continue through the week, that every day of it may be a Sabbath to my soul, by my resting in the work of Christ. O for an increase of faith, for more love, for greater degrees of spiritual life and light, that I may go on from strength to strength, till I appear before my God in Zion!

September 19.—I was last week mostly in a dull frame, two mornings excepted, when I found some comfort in prayer, and was enabled to cast my care upon the Lord. This day I have been much harassed by vain worldly thoughts. I have striven against them, and prayed for deliverance from them, but have gained little ground; so that I must number this among my lost Sabbaths, for I do not know of any thing obtained to-day, unless it be a more feeling sense of my total inability to do any thing good of myself.

The state of Lady Glenorchy's mind at this period to the end of the year, although on some occasions depressed, yet often rose into high religious enjoyment. Nothing could satisfy her unless all her thoughts, and words, and actions, were conformed to the will of Christ. This, as well as the principal employments in which she was engaged, will appear by the next extracts from her Diary.

Edinburgh, *Sunday*, *October* 3.—Through mercy the Lord has brought me again to this place, and permitted me to join this day in the great congregation;

but, alas! how cold and insensible is my heart to all his mercies. O to be thankful! O for more seriousness in the things of God, that I may walk continually as in his presence, as seeing him who is invisible! I do experience some measure of faith in approaching him as a reconciled God.

Barnton, October 10.—Once more the Lord has permitted me to come to this place. The day I came I was seized with a cold and fever, which confined me to my room for two days. My mind was dark and gloomy in the evening, but I felt through the night some stirrings in my soul towards God. Some portions of Scripture were brought to my remembrance, but in the morning this frame was gone, and I was harassed by foolish idle thoughts. After combating them some time, the Lord was pleased to lead my thoughts towards the state of my mind, and enabled me to lay it before him. I felt the Spirit of God bringing my sins and follies to remembrance, shewing me my backslidings, and pointing out wherein I had erred and grieved him, and brought darkness and distress upon myself. I saw the wisdom and goodness of God in bringing that sort of distress upon me which was most likely to cure my soul, and wean me effectually from created good. I thought I could perceive the cure in a measure begun; I felt willing it should be completed in any way the Lord saw fit. After some time spent in confession of sins, of which I hope I was deeply convinced, I was led to view Jesus as the propitiation for them. I saw his death as a sufficient atonement for all of them; and that when he was nailed to the cross, the curse of the law was removed, and my transgressions blotted out; and when he arose from the dead, my acquittal was declared; and when he ascended on high, it was to give me assurance that I also should be received into glory, where he now is making intercession for transgressors, and appearing in the presence of God for us. I found that the belief of this, so far from tending to slacken my diligence in duty, was the strongest and most powerful motive to holiness; for in the view of being redeemed by his blood, I felt a holy indignation against sin, and could say with Paul, "Shall we sin because grace abounds? God forbid." I had this testimony in myself of belonging to him, that I hated all known sin, and particularly that which separated my soul from him, and may be called my besetting sin. This evening the Lord has been pleased to fill my soul with joy unspeakable, manifesting his name to me as the Lord God merciful and gracious, and giving me a glorious hope of life and immortality beyond the grave. Death seemed a joyful prospect, the invisible world was realized, and this world and its vanities disappeared. The Lord seemed to draw nigh to my soul, and permitted me to present my petitions. I felt that I was utterly unworthy of the least of his mercies, and that he would have compassion upon me because he would have compassion. His love appeared wonderful, and his grace infinite. I was enabled to commit all my concerns fully into his hands, and to put my trust in his name, and to believe that I should never be ashamed of my hope. This frame has continued less or more for ten hours past, my eyes often pouring out tears of joy when I think of the love of God manifested through Christ to me, a vile worm, the least of my father's house. O what a debtor am I to free sovereign grace! I desire to record it to his glory, who delighteth in shewing mercy to the evil and the unthankful. Satan has thrown fiery darts at me through the day to shake my faith: but thanks be to Jesus, in whose name I bid him defiance! My vile heart also started aside while I was deeply engaged in prayer, and led me more than once after lying vanities; but I saw this to be the effect of my fallen nature, and made use of it to humble myself before the Lord, and to rejoice the more in his salvation. Upon the whole, this has been a sweet day to my soul. Thanks be to him, who on this day triumphed over sin, death, and hell, and purchased deliverance for all who believe in him! Hallelujah! Glory to God in the highest!

Sunday, October 17.—Every day through the week past I have cause to bless the Lord for spiritual blessings. I have less or more had a sense of his presence, some liberty in prayer, and found peace and joy in believing. I have been indisposed in body, and deeply engaged in family affairs; yet during the intervals of business I have felt much sweetness within, through a sense of the pardoning mercy of God, and the hope of eternal life.

Saturday, October 23.—Last night I was much indisposed in body, I almost got no sleep; yet I was free from pain, and had much sweet meditation upon the goodness and faithfulness of my God. I saw it was my privilege to leave it to him, when, and where, and how he was to take me to himself; and also that I ought to trust him with what was to befall me during my abode here.

Sunday, October 24.—This morning I got liberty to seek a blessing for all the churches of Christ, and in particular for our own congregation, where I was once more permitted to attend. Mr Jones and the assistant had excellent discourses; I trust they were as fruitful as they were faithful. I was enabled through grace, which I obtained by prayer, to speak a few words to my family assembled, and to read an awakening sermon to them before evening prayer. I found much comfort in this exercise, and saw it clearly as a sin I ought to repent of, that I had not of late been diligent in instructing my family; and I feel resolved, through grace enabling me, to be more faithful to their souls in time coming. This day my own soul has not been so lively as I could wish, although I feel a sweet peace and composure of spirit in the belief of the truth. This night I have been frequently tempted by pride. Lord, preserve me from this hateful sin, for thy name's sake!

Wednesday, October 27.—Yesterday, going into town in the coach, my heart was suddenly filled with joy at the thoughts of death, and complete deliverance from all sin, and being for ever with the Lord. In the evening, upon reading a serious book, the love of God was again so manifested to my soul, that I could not see to read any longer for tears of joy. This morning I have had delightful access to God in prayer, and my heart drawn out to praise the Lord for his goodness to the children of men.

I have had so much more comfort of late in my soul than usual, that I sometimes think it is a preparation for suffering. At other times I think death is near; for my views of it have been so pleasant, and it appeared so desirable, that this looked like a forerunner of it. Perhaps these thoughts are a temptation. Whatever is in it I am sure of this, that the Lord doth all things well, and sends either peace or any other blessing in the best way. I desire to have no will of my own concerning life or death. All I ask is to live to God's glory here, and to enjoy him for ever when time shall be no more, through Jesus Christ our Lord!

Edinburgh, Thursday, November 4.—I came to this place on Monday, in order to enjoy the privilege of waiting upon God in public ordinances; but it has pleased him to lay the rod upon me, and keep me at home. I apprehend fresh trials coming upon me; and I am willing that they should, provided God may be glorified by me in the furnace; but flesh and blood shrink back at the prospect of sufferings.

Sunday, November 7.—I was permitted to attend public ordinances yesterday, and to-day in the forenoon. The Lord has vouchsafed his presence in the assembly of his people; my soul desires to magnify him, but my frame is not so lively as I could wish, from great bodily infirmity.

Sunday, November 21.—This day I have benefited but little from what I heard at church, although very excellent. I this night have had liberty to spread my case before the Lord, and to believe that he will save and deliver me out of all my distresses. I see trouble on every side, and many trials before me; yet he that has hitherto helped me in many past trials, can still support and carry me through those which are to come; and I believe he will at last bring me to his heavenly kingdom, where all tears shall be wiped from my eyes. I look to him for light upon my path, and wait for his salvation. Surely, O Lord, thou wilt hear and help me in thine own time, for thou never yet didst forsake the soul that trusted in thee! Wait thou, my soul, with patience upon thy God; for he that shall come will come, and will not tarry!

Sunday, November 28.—This day I have been very cold and dead under a lively ministry, and this evening unable to do any thing to purpose: wandering thoughts are the canker-worm and moth that eat out the spirit of my duties, and mar every thing I do. Oh that the Lord would spiritualize my heart and affections more and more, and set them apart for himself!

Sunday, December 12.—Last week I was confined to my room by sickness. I endeavoured to take the opportunity of settling my affairs. I have been enabled to do much in this way with a degree of composure of spirit and peace of mind. This day I was confined from public worship, but I have found it good to draw near to God. I found my will swallowed up in his; and discovered that the prevailing desire of my heart is, that he may be glorified in me either by life or death, or in any way that seemeth good unto him. I have had unusual liberty in prayer for guidance and direction in what lies before me. I have put myself and all my concerns once more into God's hands, to be disposed of as he sees fit, praying only that I may be kept from sin, which is surely much more to be dreaded than affliction.

Friday, December 31.—Help, Lord, for the godly man ceaseth, and the faithful fail from among the children of men! I this morning received the painful tidings of the death of Mr James Young, one of the managers of my chapel.

1780. *Sunday, January 2.*—Another year is gone,—a new one begun. Oh to be seriously affected by the shortness and value of time! Now is my salvation nearer than when I first believed by many years; yet, alas! how little progress do I make in attaining the temper and language of the country whither I am bound. Instead of growing more spiritual, more self-denied, and dead to the things of time, I fear I grow more slothful and carnal. O Lord, do thou strengthen the things that are ready to die! Grant that I may now set out afresh in the Christian course, and run with redoubled speed in the way to Zion; redeeming the time that is past, and which cannot be recalled. Renew my strength, and give power to my fainting soul. I ask it for Jesus' sake, and the glory shall be thine for ever!

Sunday, January 9.—Blessed be God for giving me some desire through the last week to deny myself, and to seek his face! I cannot say I attained to more than desires, but even this is matter of thankfulness. My eyes are towards the Lord for counsel, and for power to do his will. Surely he will not suffer a soul that hangs on him to perish, neither will he suffer the footsteps to slide of any who commit their ways to him. He has promised to keep the feet of his saints, therefore I will believe. Lord, help my unbelief, strengthen my faith, confirm my hope, for thy name's glory!

February 3.—This day being set apart for a general fast, and being detained by sickness from public worship, I endeavoured to seek the Lord in private. I began by writing down all that I felt I stood in need of at this time. I found I was spiritually poor, sadly deficient in every grace, a backslider, careless, unable for any thing good. After making a catalogue of my wants, and of my cause of thanksgiving, I looked into the Bible, and read Psalm 69th; and was struck with the 32d and 33d verses, "Your heart shall live that seek God; for the Lord heareth the poor, and despiseth not his prisoners." This enabled me to go with confidence to a throne of grace, where with much liberty I poured out all my desires before God, putting myself and all my interests into his hand with assurance of being heard; and I believe that he will order all things well that concerneth me. I endeavoured also to remember all my friends, and their different circumstances, together with the church and the land.

Sunday, February 20.—It pleased the Lord to send a severe illness upon me in the night of Thursday the 3d, which for some days deprived me of ability to continue in spiritual exercises, being oppressed with sickness; but although unable for present duty, it was a great comfort to me during my illness, which appeared a dangerous one, to think that I had so fully and freely given myself into the Lord's hands on the day in which I was seized with it. I therefore was enabled to believe that it would be for his glory and my good whether the issue was life or death. Since my recovery I have felt desires of soul for more of the image of God. The Lord knows that I desire to be spiritually minded. O that he would arise and make bare his arm, and get himself the victory over these enemies of my heart, and set up his throne there for ever! This day I have again been permitted to enter into the congregation of the chapel, and felt some comfort in hearing a discourse from Mr Jones. I thought I could lay hold on some of the marks given of those who loved the saints.

Sunday, March 1.—The Lord has been pleased during the course of last week to continue serious impressions upon my soul of the necessity of holiness, and of self-denial, and of watchfulness over my heart, in order to obtain and promote it. At times I have had much comfort from a conviction of my acceptance in the beloved, and had clear and evident marks of my adoption, and begun sanctification. I feel persuaded that the Lord will perfect what concerns me. O that this were the abiding frame of my heart!

March 26.—I wound and I heal, I kill and I make alive, saith the Lord. This has been fulfilled in my experience for three weeks past. The Lord has been pleased to shew me the mouth of the pit from which there is no return, and to snatch me from it by his own omnipotent arm. Much cause have I to sing of mercy and judgment, yet my heart is so dead this day that I feel I cannot command a good thought. The Lord knows I desire to serve him with my whole heart and soul. He knoweth my frame, he is of infinite compassion; I will therefore hope in him, and quietly wait for his salvation.

Sunday, April 23.—For the last fortnight both my health and spirits have been very bad. On this last Sabbath I had much enjoyment in hearing Dr Erskine preach. My heart witnessed that I sought the Lord, which was the subject of his discourse,—I therefore concluded that I should yet praise him. The savour of his sermon continued some days, and gave me a strong desire to attend at Leith upon the sacramental solemnity. On Thursday I went there, having unexpected health and strength. On Friday I was taken ill, but had much comfort in the morning by a clear view of my own interest in Christ, and my thorough acquiescence in the Lord's will respecting all that should befall me. Yesterday my health was bad, but

I had composure of mind all the day. Last night I was enabled to pour out my heart before God, and to lay hold of his covenant, and to set my seal to every article in it, and to take God to be my God, and to offer myself entirely to him for ever. I felt joy unspeakable in believing that he doth care for me, and will bring me to his everlasting kingdom.

On the 10th of May, Lady Glenorchy wrote to her friend Miss Hill, informing her, that Lord Hopetoun had given his daughter Lady Henrietta permission to accompany her to England, without restricting them either to time, or the places which they might visit, and that she intended to be at Hawkstone in her way home. Accordingly, on the 17th of May these two friends left Edinburgh for London. On the 27th they reached that city, where Lady Glenorchy was taken alarmingly ill, and the most eminent physician of the day being called in, he pronounced her complaint to be a gout in the head and stomach. From this she never afterwards was completely free. By the 28th of June she was so far recovered as to be able to leave town, and set out for Exmouth. There she found the chapel which she had formerly fitted up, and in the welfare of which she was much interested, in a very prosperous condition. After paying a visit to her friends, Mr and Mrs Holmes, at their country residence near Exeter, she returned by Bath to Hawkstone about the middle of July, and on the 20th of that month arrived at Buxton. A place of worship in that neighbourhood being unoccupied, she, during her stay, procured a minister to preach in it every Lord's day. On the 18th of August she left Buxton for Taymouth, to attend her father-in-law, as usual, where she arrived at the end of the month. Some account of these movements, and of the state of her mind at this period, will be seen by what is contained in her Diary, from the middle of May to the middle of August.

May 17.—Set out for London,—arrived there the 27th, not in good health,—continued growing worse every day till the 20th of June, when my situation appeared alarming, and Dr Fothergill was called. He pronounced my complaint to be gout in the head and stomach.

On Wednesday the 28th of June I left London, and came to this place (Bridport) the 1st of July;—my mind composed, and health rather better. God's path is in the deep, and his footsteps are not known. O for a more lively faith in his promises, and more knowledge of his perfections! This would bring peace to the soul in the midst of trouble.

Buxton, Sunday, July 23.—Through mercy I arrived at this place last Thursday in tolerable health and composure of mind. I had some comfort in meditating on Psalm xxxii. ver. 8. and 9.

> I will instruct thee, and thee teach
> The way that thou shalt go;
> And with mine eye upon thee set,
> I will direction show, &c. &c.

I saw that Christ was bringing my soul into that quiet and tractable state which is there required, that is, to be easily led into the will of God, guided by his eye (or providence), ready to forego our own plans and ways when called to it. I see something of this temper wrought in myself;—glory be to God! I feel willing to do and to suffer whatever he has appointed for me. Only let me know clearly thy will, and give me power to obey, O my God, and command what thou wilt,—I can do all through Christ strengthening me. This is a silent Sabbath to me,—my heart very dead. O revive my soul, blessed Saviour! say unto me, Live, live in the knowledge, love, and enjoyment of all thy privileges as a redeemed and sanctified soul; and this shall suffice, till mortality is swallowed up of life. Speak the word, O blessed Jesus! breathe upon me, and say, "Receive ye the Holy Ghost," and my soul shall be revived and strengthened, and enabled to glorify thee. Come down as the rain on the mown grass, as showers that water the earth. Be it unto me according to thy word.

Sunday, August 13.—Since I came here the Lord has been pleased to give me once more another warning of the frailty and uncertainty of this life, by sending a fever, and other complaints, on my body; but, blessed be his name, he has also sent his servants to be comforters to my soul; Mr Edwards, who preached in the meeting here, and spoke to the family in private, for one week, and then Mr Scott, whose conversation and preaching have ever been a reviving cordial to my soul:—O that I may profit thereby. In some measure, I trust, I have been stirred up to more earnest desires of God; but, alas! how cold and faint are they still. How far short do I yet come of that spiritual mind and close walk with God that I long for. O when shall I live a life of faith on the Son of God? I see my privileges, but still labour under a dead, lukewarm, careless spirit. I have been a grievous backslider in heart;—quicken me, for thy mercies' sake, by the influences of thy Spirit, that my soul may live and praise thee for ever.

The writer of these pages had now resided in Edinburgh as minister of Lady Glenorchy's chapel for twelve months. He had formed habits of intimate friendship with a considerable number of the members of Presbytery, and was known to all of them. The hostility of those who had formed prejudices against the chapel had subsided, and a general understanding took place, that if he appeared in the Presbytery, and there produced the evidence of his ordination, and of having qualified to government, and also signed the formula, he would be received without opposition. He did therefore attend the Presbytery, and laid before them a certificate of his ordination, as will be seen from the following minute of Presbytery.

"At Edinburgh, the 28th day of July, 1780 years. Which day the Presbytery of Edinburgh being met and constituted,

"Dr Webster represented to the Presbytery, That the Rev. Mr Jones, who has been employed for some time to officiate in the chapel built by the Right Hon. Lady Glenorchy, had acquainted him, that he had been ordained a minister by a class of Presbyterian ministers in London, who are in full communion with the Church of Scotland, of which an attestation by the Rev. Dr Hunter, late of South Leith, and Dr Trotter, late of Ceres, was produced and read to the Presbytery. Dr Webster further represented, That Mr Jones earnestly desired, in order to give full satisfaction to the Reverend Presbytery of his firm adherence to the discipline, as well as to the doctrines, of the Established Church, that he might be permitted to subscribe the Confession of Faith, and Formula, in their presence. The Doctor therefore moved, That Mr Jones should be called upon for that purpose, in consequence of his own request. Which motion being agreed upon by the Presbytery, Mr Jones was called, and having compeared, he subscribed the Confession of Faith and Formula enjoined by the Assembly 1711, and expressed, in proper terms, that though he did not enjoy the emoluments of the Establishment, it would always give him the highest satisfaction to be in communion with the ministers and members of this church."—Extracted from the records of the Presbytery of Edinburgh by

THOMAS MACKNIGHT, *Clerk.*

Thus ended all misunderstandings between Lady Glenorchy, the Presbytery of Edinburgh, and the other Church Courts, respecting her chapel,—a desirable event, of which she afterwards spoke with much satisfaction.

Few persons equalled Lady Glenorchy in diligently embracing opportunities of doing good. But far from taking the least credit to herself on that account, she viewed them as gifts from Heaven, which called for gratitude to God. Among the many instances she mentions in her Diary, we may take notice of the settlement of a clergyman of talents and usefulness at Kenmore, the parish church of Taymouth, the Rev. Mr Thomas Fleming,* of whose ministrations she speaks with great approbation, which will appear by what is contained in the following extracts.

[Aged 39.] *Taymouth, September* 2.—Again I am arrived at this place after another year, in weakness of body, and depression of mind. How marvellous are

* Dr Fleming, the present minister of Lady Yester's Church, Edinburgh.

thy ways, O Lord, to me! Thy judgments are a great deep.

This last year has been marked by mercy, as well as by judgments. I have cause to remark the great goodness of the Lord, in giving me at times much comfort in prayer, a lively faith in my own interest in his love, and a strong desire to do his will. I have also cause to praise him for letting me see the grace bestowed on the people at Exmouth, and in making me instrumental in bringing the gospel to Buxton and other places, and in being the means of relieving some of his distressed members. O that I were suitably affected by his goodness, and could now not merely devote, but actively employ my whole heart and life in his service. Lord, I would be wholly thine without reserve,—take possession of my whole soul, and keep me through faith unto eternal life. Into thy hands I commit my body, soul, and spirit, for time and eternity.

September 10.—This morning I had some liberty in seeking the presence of the Lord, and his Spirit, to help me to sanctify this holy day. I heard an excellent sermon on regeneration from Mr Fleming. My heart was filled with gratitude to the Lord as the hearer of prayer, in bringing such a minister to this place. At my return home I went to thank God for the same, and to pray for a blessing on the word; and my soul was led out in holy desires and fervent prayer for that renewed nature of which I had heard. I felt a strong hungering and thirsting for righteousness, and a desire for the second coming of Christ to redeem me from all sin, and destroy the works of the devil. Blessed be God, I have this day felt the influences of the

Spirit leading my thoughts to spiritual things, and restoring a relish for them to my soul! O Lord, vouchsafe the continuance of these desires; cleanse the thoughts of my heart; give perseverance in known duty; and fulfil in me all the good pleasure of thy will, that thy name may be glorified in thy servant, and my soul eternally blessed in thy enjoyment! I ask it for Christ's sake. Amen.

On the 14th of October Lady Glenorchy returned to Barnton from Taymouth, where she passed a few weeks. In November she attended the celebration of the Lord's supper with much comfort. On the 23d of that month she set out for Bath, where, on account of her health, she intended to winter. After having made several visits on the road, she arrived there the 9th of December. The Rev. Mr Tupin, whose ministry she had purposed to attend, not being at Bath, she joined in worship in Lady Huntingdon's chapel, and received much edification. A more particular account of these things may be gathered from the following extracts from her Diary.—

Barnton, October 22.—I came to this place on the 14th instant. When I think of the comfort I enjoyed in this place twelve months ago, I cannot but inquire how it comes to pass that I now feel so differently? The Lord's hand is not shortened, nor his ear heavy; he is still the same. Why then am I so cold and lifeless, having no enjoyment in any thing? Is there any sin which lies unrepented of in my heart? Do I allow any known evil to cleave to me? Lord, thou knowest; search and try my heart, and see if there be any evil way in me, and lead me in the way everlasting!

Sunday, October 29.—All this last week I have been confined by a severe cold to my room. This has been a silent Sabbath; little ability for religious duty, and much indisposed both in body and mind. The Lord enable me to be thankful that it is not worse with me; that I am not now beyond the possibility of hope, but still in the land of the living; the door of mercy open; and the Lord Jesus, the same to-day as yesterday, still willing to save to the uttermost every soul that comes to God through him. To him I look, and would flee from the depth of my misery unto the depth of his love, and cast my soul at his feet, to be washed, justified, and sanctified by his Spirit. Even so let it be, Lord Jesus!

Sunday, November 12.—Last Thursday was our fast-day, and the Lord was pleased to convince me of the need I had of true repentance for the sins of my heart and life, particularly the former. He enabled me in the evening to confess them, and to plead for pardon in the prevailing name of Jesus. On Friday something perplexed and distressed me, and I was much afraid that the enemy would gain an advantage over me; but this morning the Lord was pleased to deliver me from my perplexing thoughts, and enabled me to attend to Mr Jones's excellent discourse on John xvi. 20. "Verily, verily, I say unto you, that ye shall weep and lament, but the world shall rejoice; and ye shall be sorrowful, but your sorrow shall be turned into joy;" and to believe for myself that my sorrow indeed should be turned into joy. At the table I was assisted to exercise faith on a present Saviour as the sacrifice for my sins, and to receive the pledges of his dying love as a sure token of the pardon of sin, and of obtaining eternal life through him. I particularly offered three petitions; first, that the love of God may be the motive, and his glory the end of all my actions; secondly, that he would give me the spirit of prayer constantly; and, thirdly, that he would make me a spiritual worshipper. I asked similar blessings for my dear friend Lady Henrietta Hope, who was this day unwillingly absent from our solemnity. If I am conscious of any thing, I must conclude that my chief desire is to live to God.

November 23.—Set out for Bath; came to Penrith the third day. Mr Jones, who so far accompanied me, preached in the evening, and twice the next day, being the Lord's day.

Bath, December 29.—On arriving here I was much disappointed at finding the dissenting meeting-house shut up, as there was no other place of worship that I could attend with satisfaction but Lady Huntingdon's chapel, and I was not clear about uniting with them in the Lord's supper. I went there on Christmas day, with the disposition to come away at the beginning of the communion service. When the clergyman, however, gave the invitation to all who were sincerely and devoutly disposed to come and partake of the ordinance, I asked myself, If I durst refuse? Here was a company of devout worshippers assembled to shew forth the Lord's death; the Lord's presence, according to his promise, was to be expected. Why, being invited, should I decline to join them? Was I more holy than they? By no means; perhaps the most unworthy there. Was it the form? This was not a sufficient reason to neglect the Lord's command, and especially as I had no opportunity of obeying it elsewhere; and, moreover, the Lord looks upon the heart, and not the attitude of the body. I thought myself a believer; I was desired as such to unite. The question was, Durst I refuse? I found I could not. I therefore staid and partook of the ordinance with more than usual comfort. My heart was dissolved with love and joy in believing the great and glorious things held forth: it was broken under a sense of sin, and the grace of a pardoning God. My affections were drawn forth in an unusual manner at the table, insomuch that it was with difficulty I refrained from crying aloud. My faith was strengthened; I was enabled to receive a whole Christ to save me from the guilt and power of sin, and to sanctify and glorify my soul. I came home rejoicing, and my heart more enlarged towards his people of all denominations; and confirmed in the opinion, that a catholic spirit is acceptable to God.

December 31.—Much cause have I to bless God for the mercies of the year which is past. Frequently have I found deliverance from bodily and mental afflictions. In a particular manner, I have to praise him for bringing me to this place this winter, where I have leisure to examine into the state of my soul, and opportunities of conversing and joining in worship with some lively Christians. O to be suitably impressed with a sense of the goodness of God in once more putting into my heart an earnest desire to be wholly devoted to him, and thus restoring in some measure that light I at first had of the vanity of all created good, and the desireableness of giving up every thing to Christ! May I now be enabled to live up to that light!

1781. Lady Glenorchy's Diary this year, and especially that part of it which refers to the time prior to her going to Taymouth in July, is remarkably brief.

One short entry made in January, another in March, and a third in April, form the whole. This was occasioned partly by the state of her health, and partly by her frequent and long journeys, from which she seemed in general to get much relief. In February she removed from Bath to London, in March from London to Bristol, and in June she went to Buxton.

During this period an event took place which added much to the comfort of her after life. On the death of John Earl of Hopetoun in the beginning of this year, his numerous family, as is usual on such occasions, were dispersed. His eldest daughter, Lady Henrietta, soon after went to London, to which place Lady Glenorchy, who was then at Bath, hastened to meet her. In June she by appointment met her at Buxton; and from this time Lady Henrietta constantly took up her abode with Lady Glenorchy, and commonly accompanied her wherever she went. They were of one heart and of one mind in all things, and united in promoting every work of faith and labour of love. To Lady Glenorchy she was a most valuable acquisition. With a happy temper and high accomplishments, she was distinguished for sagacity and prudence,—talents which she inherited from her father. Perhaps the sympathies of these two friends were excited and strengthened by their extremely delicate state of health.

Bath, Monday, January 1.—This morning my heart went out after God in holy desires for his salvation—a present salvation from the dominion and power of all sin. I asked power to resist sin, although it were to blood, so that I might be saved from its tyranny. I went to church, and joined in celebrating the Lord's supper, and experienced comfort from the exhortation, especially from what Mr Penticross said upon the sanctification of the heart. I was conscious, that I desired to put off the body of sin, and longed to be holy as God is holy. I went in the evening and heard Mr Taylor, from Psalm cvi. ver. 4. "Remember me, O Lord, with the favour that thou bearest unto thy people: O visit me with thy salvation!" It was a profitable discourse. May the Lord enable me to follow the exhortations given in it.

Bristol, March 27.—I arrived yesterday at this place, in a very poor state of health, temporally and spiritually. My mind is much discomposed by various occurrences which have of late perplexed me. Some desire, however, still remains to glorify and enjoy God. Blessed be his name, although I change, he doth not. I trust he will revive his work in my soul, and bless me in this place. Lord, to thee I look for healing. There is nothing too hard for thee. O help and deliver me from every thing that is contrary to thy holy will, although dear as a right hand or eye. Hear me for myself, and hear me for my friend. Save us, O Lord, from the hands of our enemies.

April 30.—This day I was seized with a violent and dangerous illness, which has kept me six weeks longer in this place than I intended. This has been blessed as a means of delivering my soul from spiritual disease, and quickening my views of invisible and eternal things. Glory be to God for this dispensation, evidently sent in love.

A circumstance must be here mentioned, which farther illustrates Lady Glenorchy's uniform anxiety to embrace every opportunity of doing good which presented itself in the course of providence:—

The state of religion in Carlisle at this time was like that of the Church of Sardis, in the days of St John—it had greatly decayed, and the remains of it were ready to die. Among other proofs of this, an old Presbyterian meeting-house, which in former days had flourished, was now deserted, and shut up. Lady Glenorchy, passing through this place in her way home from Buxton, observed the fact, and, in compassion to the people, purchased this Ichabod, and exerted herself to restore its glory. She procured a minister for it, and aided the congregation, whom he collected, in providing a salary for him. After her Ladyship's death, Lady Maxwell, her executrix, continued to assist in this good work as long as the funds intrusted to her management would permit, and finally settled the institution in the hands of trustees for the purposes for which Lady Glenorchy intended it. The house has since been enlarged, and continues to this day, (forty years from its establishment), to flourish, and its minister to be useful.

About the middle of July, Lady Glenorchy, with her friend, Lady Henrietta Hope, spent a few days at Barnton, in her way to Taymouth, where she arrived about the end of the month.

Since April, her Ladyship had, as we have seen, travelled much, and met with occurrences which deeply interested her. The feelings to which these gave rise will appear in the following extracts:—

Taymouth, July 22.—From Bristol I went to Buxton, where I met my dear friends, Lady Henrietta Hope, and Mr and Mrs Scott. Staid ten days, and came by the west road to Edinburgh. The Lord, in his gracious providence, called on me to purchase a meeting-house in Carlisle, where the gospel, I trust, will be preached. I staid four days at Barnton, and then came to this place in a very poor state; my health seems daily declining, and my soul is dull and inactive. This morning I had some comfortable meditations on the free grace of the gospel, as offered to all, and consequently to me; and my soul seemed to rest on the word of promise. This was after a great conflict and much anguish of spirit, from a recollection of past sins, and some doubt concerning the pardon of them. I have, upon the whole, felt more spiritual life this day than for some time past; and I hope the Lord is about to revive his work before I go hence and be no more seen.

Sunday, July 29.—All last week I was in a very poor state of health and low frame of spirits. This day we had no public worship; but the Lord has graciously made up the want to my soul, by giving me liberty of access to his throne, and enabling me to pour out my wants before him with some degree of faith. May the Lord uphold my faith, and keep me waiting in hope till he is pleased to perform his word unto me! The xvth chapter of 1st Corinthians has been peculiarly sweet to me this morning, by the reading of it with application to myself. I have felt my faith increased.

Sunday, August 12.—This day I have been permitted to wait upon the Lord, in the ordinance of the Supper. At the table, I made some feeble efforts to exercise faith on the sacrifice once offered up for the sins of many, and received the sacred symbols as a sure pledge of the thing signified. The whole day my thoughts have been dull and confused; yet, through all, I can look to Jesus as my Saviour, the same yesterday, to-day, and for ever. My safety depends not on my frames, but on that finished work I have this day been commemorating. On this I rest my hope, and from his peace-speaking blood I look for pardon and eternal life; nay, I believe I have obtained them already: and though my life is now hid, yet when he who is my life shall appear, I shall then appear with him in glory. Lord, confirm this hope more and more! Increase my faith, love, and joy, and glorify thy grace in the complete salvation of my soul!

[Aged 40.] *Taymouth, September 2.*—This day I have, as usual, endeavoured to review my past life, and, in particular, the last year of it, in order to humble my soul before God for sin, and render thanks unto him for his creating and preserving grace. But O what a heart-rending sight has he given me of the unspeakable vileness and ingratitude of every period of my life! This day, I have endeavoured to call upon the Lord for deliverance by his almighty power; and have besought him to renew a right spirit within me, that I may set out afresh in his ways. My health has been very bad for many months past, and my spirits weak. Great and manifold, however, have been the mercies of the Lord during all my distress, giving me support, and carrying me through beyond all expectation, raising me up Christian friends in a distant land, when sick, and given over for death, to pray for me, and comfort me. In the hour of the greatest need, he hath given me a dear and faithful bosom friend, who is to me as mine own soul; and who is a kind and faithful companion to be with me at all times, and to dwell in my house. He has enlarged my sphere of usefulness in his church, by opening new doors for the spread of the gospel; and still continues to me the heart and ability to help forward his cause. Innumerable are the mercies I receive; unspeakable is my ingratitude. O Lord, have mercy upon me; forgive my sin; restore thy image in my soul; prepare me for the society of the saints above, and the enjoyment of thyself in glory.

I now commit and commend my soul, body, and spirit unto thee; glorify the riches of thy grace in my salvation.

Lady Glenorchy having remained at Taymouth, as usual, during the summer, left it early in October, never more to return; for, before the next season, the venerable proprietor was gathered with his fathers and his children, and laid with them in the long resting-place of Finlarig, the lonely repository of the remains of his ancestors for many generations.

CHAPTER XIX.

The Lord's Supper is begun to be administered in Lady Glenorchy's chapel every second month—Lord Breadalbane's death—Extracts from Diary, from January 1. to March 3. 1782—Lady Glenorchy's health rapidly declines—Two Letters of Lady Glenorchy's—Extracts from Diary—Lady Glenorchy's health somewhat revived—Her Ladyship goes to Moffat with Lady Henrietta Hope—Letter from Lady Glenorchy to Mrs Bailie Walker—Lady Glenorchy and Lady Henrietta Hope return to Barnton—In order to extend her sphere of usefulness, Lady Glenorchy purposes to sell Barnton—Extracts from Diary, from January 1. to June 3. 1783—Almost all the remaining part of Lady Glenorchy's Diary lost—In 1784, Lady Glenorchy accompanies Lady Henrietta Hope to Moffat—Proceeds to Carlisle—Reaches Matlock—From a singular occurrence in Providence, is led to purchase a chapel there—Returns to Edinburgh—Is again in bad health—Leaves Barnton, and never returns—Purposes to reside in future at Matlock—Concluding extract from her Diary—She sells Barnton—Death of Lady Henrietta Hope—Letters from Lady Glenorchy to Lady Mary Fitzgerald—Letter to Mr Innes—Letter to Lady Maxwell—Lady Glenorchy settles a plan for Hope Chapel—In her way to Scotland, purchases ground for a chapel at Workington—Returns to Edinburgh—Her health declines—Completes the sale of Barnton—Her last illness—Death—Character—Funeral—Will—Conclusion.

[1782.] THE Lord's supper was at this time in Scotland rarely celebrated more than once a-year, excepting in cities and great towns, where it was generally celebrated twice during that period.

On those occasions, it was the practice to have public worship on other days besides the Sabbath. One whole day was set apart for humiliation and prayer, generally a Thursday. On the afternoon of Saturday there was an exercise of preparation; on the forenoon of Monday there was another of thanksgiving; and on the Sabbath two long sermons were usually preached, besides the other acts of devotion, which were considerably extended. This practice began in the hateful days of persecution under the Stuarts, when numerous congregations, collected from every district and corner of the land, were constrained to encamp, and hold their solemn assemblies in the fastnesses of the mountains. As these meetings could only be held in the middle of summer, the people, when they came together, devoted the whole time to religious purposes, and could not therefore employ it more reasonably or usefully, than in their fasts, and preparations, and thanksgivings. But this practice, like many other ancient customs, has extended to times which do not require it, and in which, to say the least, has the inconveniency attending it, of preventing the more frequent celebration of the ordinance.

Lady Glenorchy, and the congregation worshipping in her chapel, were aware of this, and venturing to face the prejudices which ran very strong against any innovation, they, on the second Sabbath of the month of January this year, began to celebrate it with public worship only on the Thursday and Saturday evenings preceding, and which they have continued to do, much to their comfort and edification, without intermission, every alternate month for these forty years, excepting in May and November, when they observe the fast, preparation, and thanksgiving days, with the other churches of the city. This practice is now adopted by some parish churches in the Establishment, by many chapels of ease, and by a great proportion of the Presbyterian seceding congregations, so that it is no longer considered as a novelty or peculiarity.

In the end of January Lady Glenorchy was called upon to perform the last sad offices to her valuable friend and much revered and beloved parent Lord Breadalbane, who died at an advanced age, on the 26th of the month, in his apartment at the Royal Palace of Holyrood-house.

Lady Glenorchy could not be indifferent to his spiritual state, and she omitted nothing, through a long course of years, that she could with propriety do to direct his attention to the things which belonged to his peace; and there is reason to hope her attempts were not altogether in vain. The writer of these pages has been informed by the late Mr Lea, who for many years was his household steward, and always about his person, both by night and by day, and whose veracity, integrity, and piety, were well known, that for years before his death, and much more so at the time of its approach, his Lordship was frequently employed in reading his Bible, and in fervent prayer; and that he repeatedly told him his only hope for a happy eternity was founded on the mercies of God, and the merits of Christ Jesus his Saviour.

The state of Lady Glenorchy's mind at this period, and for some months after, may be gathered from the following extracts from her Diary.

Barnton, January 1. 1782.—Blessed be God for the mercies of the past year, and a happy commencement of a new one, begun indeed with pain and weakness, but with strong desires for spiritual blessings, and grace to glorify him more than I ever yet have done. The Lord was pleased to give me a minister this morning to speak to my family in a suitable manner, and we began this day with exhortation and prayer. I was afterwards enabled to speak to three of my family with earnestness about their souls, and felt comfort therein. O to be thankful for undeserved mercies!—my soul is too full for utterance. I cannot express what I see in the wisdom, goodness, and compassion of the grace of God to me, a poor sinner. Surely none ever had such cause to praise, yet no one has been ever so remiss in this duty as I have. Open my lips, O Lord, and let the dumb speak.

January 13.—This day the ordinance of the Lord's supper is to be dispensed in my chapel, Edinburgh, for the first time without being accompanied with the usual days of devotion, and at a different time from the churches of the city. I am detained from being a partaker of it by ill health, but I have endeavoured to have fellowship in spirit, exercising faith on the body and blood of Christ. I felt my heart drawn forth in desires for the whole body of Christ, that as our head is holy, we also might be holy through his grace imparted to us, that he may be glorified. My soul has been led to seek more sensible fellowship with the Father and the Son, through the Spirit, and to know my union with Christ by his Spirit.

Sunday, January 20.—I am still detained from public worship, but the Lord has made it up to me by giving me liberty in prayer, and comfort in reading the Scriptures.

This last week I have been called to a trial in seeing my very aged parent, Lord Breadalbane, deprived of his mental faculties, and laid to all appearance on his dying bed: but with God nothing is impossible; he may yet be restored to bear testimony to the truth, if it seems good unto the Lord. May his will be done, and his name glorified, in all things.

Sunday, January 27.—Yesterday it pleased God to take Lord Breadalbane suddenly away, ten minutes after Dr Cullen had pronounced him much better, and that he probably would be up in his chair in a few days. I have cause to remark many kind providences in this event with regard to myself, that I was so much recovered as to be able to go to town on Thursday to attend him, and had the comfort to see him pleased and happy in having me about him. This day I feel more sensibly the loss than yesterday, yet I dare not murmur, —to the Lord belongeth the disposal of all events,—to his sovereignty I desire to bow, and to rest assured that he doth all things well. What am I that I should reply against God? Be still, my soul, and harbour not a thought inconsistent with total submission to God! The Lord he is God: Let his blessed will be done!

Thursday, February 7. *General Fast.*—This day I arose early, and attempted to humble myself for my sins, and those of the land,—but with what coldness! I read Henry on Isaiah the lviiith, and other similar passages of Scripture. I prayed for holiness, and for a revival of vital religion in the churches of Christ in general,—for the out-pouring of the Spirit as in former years,—for quickening grace to ministers, and for furnishing them with every necessary gift,—for the congregations and schools in which I am particularly interested,—for friends,—for relations,—for my parish and its minister,—my tenants and servants,—the afflicted,—the sick,—the wounded,—the dying,—the destitute,—the unconverted,—for prisoners,—and for those who have begun to seek God,—for the king and for all in authority.

I gave thanks for private mercies, and for public blessings. I felt some measure of faith. I went to public worship, but was cold and lifeless in hearing, and returned in the same frame:—much cause have I to be humbled this day, under a full sense of my total worthlessness, and utter insufficiency to think a good thought.

March 3.—This day the Lord has given an answer to prayer, in sending me a chaplain, Mr J. Campbell,* who has preached in the chapel here this afternoon to a large congregation of attentive hearers. May he send down the plentiful influences of the Spirit, to make the word effectual! We have also heard an excellent discourse at church from our parish minister Mr Walker,† who improves from day to day;—blessed be the Lord for this mercy also. O how manifold are his loving kindnesses to the unworthy race of men, and to my sinful self in particular! Much I have seen to-day of my past backslidings, and present hardness of heart. I have a desire for the salvation of others, yet do not embrace the opportunities which offer to do them good. I am grieved for the low state of religion in my soul. Lord, help; revive and quicken me, for thine own name's sake!

In the end of May Lady Glenorchy and Lady Henrietta Hope went to Buxton, and at the close of July they returned to Barnton. Lady Glenorchy's health now rapidly declined. Of this she complained as the cause of what, it would seem, was thought inattention to her friends, and pleads it as her excuse, as will be seen from the following extracts from her letters, and her meditation on her birth-day, which closes her Diary for this year. To one lady she writes thus:—

* Dr Campbell, now (1822) one of the ministers of the Tolbooth Church, Edinburgh.

† Nephew of Mr Walker of the High Church.

"*Barnton, May* 27.

"My dear Madam,—The reproof you no doubt meant to give me in your two last notes, was so gently and kindly expressed, that I am at some loss how to understand them; and therefore I must beg you would in plain terms tell me in what I have offended you, and why you have of late adopted the style of distant formality in your addresses to me. I am sensible, that for some time past I have had very little intercourse with my friends in Edinburgh. But as I believed the cause of this was understood by them, it did not to me appear necessary to make an apology for it. The long and dangerous illness I had last summer has reduced both my mind and body to that feeble state, that a small exertion of either is apt to throw me into a fever, under the experience of which I am now labouring. I neither am able to make visits, or to receive many, without feeling very severe effects from them. I must therefore consider myself as called in providence to a state of retirement and patient submission to the will of God in those things in which I formerly took pleasure. I desire to wait his time for a removal of the bars which in a measure seclude me from the comforts of the society of my Christian friends; but I shall think it hard, if that which ought to make me the object of their sympathy and prayers, should become a means of estranging their hearts from me, or of incurring their resentment. I am conscious that my heart is the same towards them that ever it was.—I wish them happiness and prosperity here, and look forward with joy to the period when these feeble bodies and sickly minds will be no hinderance to our communion; and it would now be a great satisfaction to me to obtain an interest in their prayers, for a sanctified use of the repeated strokes of my Heavenly Father's rod, that I may no longer be a stubborn or rebellious child, but yield up my whole self to him in meek submission, that his will may be done in me, and that his name may be glorified in every dispensation of it towards me. I am, dear Madam, yours affectionately. W. G."

To another lady she writes in these terms:—

" *Barnton, August* 23. 1782.

" Madam,—With regard to the state of my health, I can truly say it is worse than ever, having lately been brought to the brink of the grave by the gout in my head: I have not enjoyed a day free from pain for many months, yet I mean not to complain. The Lord has wise ends in afflicting his people; he has chosen them in the furnace, and has promised to bring them forth in due time. I would not exchange my present suffering state for uninterrupted ease, and every thing this world calls good and great, if in so doing I should lose my title to the precious promises made to an afflicted believer. Forgive me, Madam, for taking this opportunity of bearing my feeble testimony to the power of religion. I am desirous, while any strength remains, to recommend to others the good and gracious Master I have endeavoured to serve, who does not, like the world, cast off his servants in the time of their distress, but generally makes the time of their extremity a season to display his compassion towards them, by giving them the peace which surpasseth all understanding, and a hope full of immortality. That you and yours may experience this blessing in all its fulness, is the sincere prayer of, Madam, your most obedient humble servant, W. G."

[Aged 41.] *Barnton, September 2.*—Another year is past of this short uncertain life. Examine, O my soul, thy state; see what thou hast gained, what progress thou hast made in thy Christian course! It has been a time of trial; the rod has not been spared; and, blessed be God, it has not been sent in vain! This last year seems to have been a season wherein the Lord has called upon me to cease from earthly comforts, and to seek for happiness in himself alone. My soul would obey the call; I see the grace and goodness of this; I am sensible of the propriety of compliance with it, and my heart longs for its attainment. O to love God above all, to love him in all, and all for his sake! Nothing less can satisfy me. He is my only resting-place; how painful are the consequences of any separation from him; what solid peace may be obtained by continuing in him as an all-sufficient portion! This seems to have been the language of all the dispensations of Heaven towards me. I begin to attend to his voice; and the answer of my heart is, Whom have I in heaven but thee, and there is none upon earth I desire besides thee! O that this may become more and more the confirmed and abiding frame of my heart. With regard to outward things, I have little to record, having lived mostly in retirement, being laid aside by sickness, and have only had the privilege of privately assisting others to act for the Lord. Perhaps this has been a more safe state than one more conspicuous in the eyes of the world. Blessed be his name if in any way he grants me the privilege of helping forward the interest of Zion! My health is now so precarious that it is very possible this may be the last birth-day I shall have to record upon earth; therefore I here set down, to the praise and glory of God, that goodness and mercy have followed me all the days of my life; the Lord has fulfilled his promise of being a father to the fatherless; he has made himself known to me as such in every sense of the word, and has given me power to believe that he never will leave me nor forsake me; but that he will guide me by his counsel while here, and afterwards receive me to his glory, so that I shall dwell in his house for ever. In this glorious hope I desire to rejoice now, and to ascribe unto the Father, Son, and Holy Ghost, one Jehovah, the glory and praise, world without end! Amen and Amen. W. G.

[1783.] In the course of the spring of this year the health of Lady Glenorchy somewhat revived, and her spiritual comfort was much improved. Lady Henrietta Hope had been accustomed to visit Moffat for the benefit of goat whey; she accordingly went thither in June with her sister Lady Jane, afterwards Lady Melville. Lady Glenorchy soon after followed, and remained with them till the end of August. In this place, as indeed wherever she went, Lady Glenorchy followed out that plan of doing good to the souls of her fellow-creatures which always lay so near her heart. Of this she thus wrote to her friend Mrs Bailie Walker:

Lady Glenorchy to Mrs Bailie Walker.

" *Moffat, August* 9. 1783.

" My dear Madam,—The Lord has been pleased to visit me by sickness once more, after having attained to a measure of health I had not known for several years past. May I not say with Job, Shall I receive good from the hand of the Lord, and not evil also? He gave me health for a season, and now he has taken it away; blessed be his name, for he doth all things well. Yes, I am fully persuaded that this very illness is one of the all things that are working together for my good, and my heart freely acquiesces in the dispensation.

"This is a sad benighted place, but there is a remnant in it that fear God. I have found out about eight humble folk, who, though in poverty, are yet rich in faith. One has lain nine years in her bed, rejoicing in the goodness of God. When I was able I had much comfort in visiting her and some others. They have private prayer meetings, and many good books among them: They speak favourably of the minister who is coming among them, and say that he preaches the gospel; so I hope their situation is on the mending hand. Believe me to be yours affectionately. W. G."

In the beginning of the month of September Lady Glenorchy and her friend Lady Henrietta Hope returned to Barnton, where they remained during the following autumn and winter. The liberal mind, says the Prophet, deviseth liberal things. Much had Lady Glenorchy done, and much had she expended, in promoting the cause of benevolence and the interests of piety; yet after all she was not satisfied; she thought she had never done enough while there was a possibility of doing any thing more. Little or nothing indeed did she expend on herself more than was absolutely necessary, yet she contracted even that little in order that she might be able to do more good. Her economy became great, but it was the economy of piety and benevolence, as will be seen from the extracts from her Diary.

[1783.] *January* 1.—The Lord has been pleased, (most unexpectedly by me), to lengthen out my life to see the beginning of a new year. He has not only preserved me, but restored me to health and strength, and crowns me with every blessing my heart can wish of a temporal nature. I also enjoy the means of grace in abundance; but, alas! how unworthy do I feel myself to be of such favours; how ungrateful, careless, negligent, and forgetful of my best friend and benefactor. I stand astonished at the goodness of God, and at my own total unworthiness. O that I had a heart and tongue to praise him, and power to shew forth to others the grace of God by a holy and useful walk and conversation! May I this year increase in faith, love, and power in my soul, that God may be glorified in me and by me. Let my soul live, O Lord, and it shall praise thee! Amen and Amen.

January 26.—The Lord seems to be changing his dispensations towards me: for some time past my health has been wonderfully good, which has enabled me to rise early; and for some days past I have had more liberty in prayer, and more comfort in secret duties than usual, particularly in the morning; and sometimes in the night when I awake, I have been constrained to praise him for his mercies.

I have had several instances of his answering my prayers for spiritual blessings, and find my mind led out to trust and look for yet greater blessings than any I have hitherto experienced. I want to be more habitually spiritually minded, and to live under a constant sense of his presence; to act as in his sight, with a single eye to his glory. My soul longs for the mind which was in Christ. O Lord, grant me all thou art willing to bestow on a creature here, and then take me to thyself to behold thy glory without a veil.

May 11.—For some months past I have at times experienced peace and joy in believing, at other times great deadness of soul; but on the whole I have cause to bless God for keeping me from many evils to which I formerly have been exposed, and giving me in some measure a composed spirit, and an habitual desire for heavenly blessings. This day I have found it good to wait on God in his ordinances; the word came with power to my soul; I have been both reproved and instructed: Reproved for not being sufficiently zealous in promoting the salvation of others, and for not being more diligent in known duties. How deficient have I been in faith and love! O that the Lord would now vouchsafe me an increase of these radical graces, without which nothing can be done to good purpose! Write, Lord, on the tablet of my heart the instructions I have this day heard; let them never be effaced!

May 29.—For some time past I have had convictions of my defectiveness in zeal and activity in the Lord's work, and I fear being found among those who dwell at ease in Zion. I feel strong desires to break off more than I have ever yet done from the world; to forsake every thing which mars my progress in the divine life. I have felt desires to leave this place, and give up every unnecessary expense; and follow the Lord whithersoever he may lead me, where I may be of most use to his church. This desire is strengthened by finding myself of little use here; yet hitherto Providence has not pointed out where I should go. I desire to wait on the Lord to know his will. Here I am, Lord, do with me whatever seemeth good in thy sight! Amen and Amen.

June 8.—My convictions grow stronger daily of the call I am under to live more to God, and less to the world than I have done. My spirit is weighed down under a sense of the shortness of time, and of having already wasted many precious years in carelessness; and of the folly of spending it in idleness or vanity, while I possess the great privilege of improving it in works of piety and mercy. I long ardently to set out afresh for God; to run in the way of his commandments; to employ every talent committed to me in promoting his glory. A field of usefulness has been opened to my mind within these few days. I must become more vile in the eyes of the world if I follow the suggestion of my conscience. May the Lord enable me to forsake all if called to it! He knows at this moment that the secret desire of my heart is to have no will but his; to have no end but his glory; to seek no enjoyment in any created thing separate from him. Let Christ be all and in all to my soul! Amen and Amen.

That Lady Glenorchy continued her Diary to nearly the end of her life, the writer has not the least doubt; for a leaf corresponding in size and paper to the third volume of the Diary which belongs to the year 1785, the contents of which will be given in their proper place, has been found among a mass of other loose papers, and bears evident marks of having belonged to a book which seems to have formed a fourth volume of her Diary. The writer is possessed of a copy of the minutes of a sederunt, as it is called in Scottish law, of the agents or attornies employed in Lady Glenorchy's affairs soon after her funeral, from which it appears that an iron chest, containing, as they express it, "parcels and manuscripts," had been sent by them to Lady Maxwell as her executrix.

These they probably considered as of no use, and mentioned this as their opinion to Lady Maxwell, as she seems never to have looked into them. That this conjecture is well founded may be presumed from the circumstance, that she uniformly expressed an aversion to meddle with any thing which had been connected with Lady Glenorchy's person. Both the writer and the late Rev. Dr Hunter repeatedly, not only at that time, but at the distance of years afterwards, asked her Ladyship if there were any documents, &c. remaining from which some account of the life of Lady Glenorchy might be drawn up; to which she uniformly replied, that there were none. The Honourable Miss Napier, Lady Maxwell's executrix, however, after the lapse of twenty-four years, opened the chest, found the Diary, examined the letters and papers, and gave some of them away to friends. When confined to her room in her last illness, and chiefly to her bed, she permitted them to take away and read the Diary and other papers; and as several of them resided at a considerable distance from Edinburgh, it is probable that the loose parts of the Diary were thus lost. This conjecture is strengthened by the circumstance, that some of Miss Napier's papers were (by a person unauthorised) destroyed at the time of her death, from the fear of their falling into the hands of persons who might publish them.

Some little account of the remaining part of Lady Glenorchy's life will now be given, from what the writer himself personally knew, and from letters and other documents in his possession.

[1784.] Her Ladyship spent the winter of 1783 and the beginning of 1784 at Barnton, and remained there till June; when her friend Lady Henrietta Hope went to Moffat, where she lived with her until the middle of August. Leaving Lady Henrietta at Moffat, she proceeded to Carlisle; from which place she wrote to the author, expressing her high satisfaction with the character and conduct of the Rev. Mr Muschet, then the minister of the chapel which she had bought in that city, and how much she was gratified by the promising appearances of good being done there. Passing on from Carlisle, probably in her way to Buxton, she reached Matlock on a Saturday: There her carriage broke down, which obliged her to remain over the Sabbath. On making inquiries, as she usually did wherever she went, concerning the state of religion in this village, and finding it very low, she was induced to make proposals for purchasing a small but neat house, originally built for the residence of the managing partner of a cotton-mill; and which had a chapel adjoining, capable of containing three hundred persons. This purchase she finally accomplished. The chapel remains, and much good has been and still continues to be done by the preaching of the gospel in this place: So wonderful are the ways of Providence, and so trifling are the circumstances which, by the blessing of Almighty God, often lead to useful and important consequences.

In October she visited her friend Miss Hill at Hawkstone in her way home, and in November arrived in Edinburgh; where, for the better accommodation of her friend Lady Henrietta Hope, she took for the winter the house of Lord Leven in Nicolson's-square.

[1785.] In the months of January and February Lady Glenorchy was so ill that her life was despaired of. She however revived, and spent some time in the beginning of summer at Barnton, and about the end of June left it, never to return. Even had she lived she probably would not have resided there, as she thought it led her to expend money which she might better employ in doing good elsewhere; and she seems therefore to have intended to make Matlock her summer residence in future. The purchase of the house and chapel having been concluded in the beginning of this year, she accordingly left Scotland, and took up her residence there till September. On the second of that month she wrote her usual recollections on the single small octavo leaf of paper to which we have already alluded, and which was the last of these grateful and devout memorials which she annually wrote; for before the returning day of the next year she was removed to that better world, for which she had been so long preparing, and to which she was now rapidly advancing. Although it is by very much the shortest of these meditations, yet, being the last, it will no doubt be read with peculiar interest. It is as follows:—

[1785. Aged 44.] *Matlock, September 2.*—I endeavoured this morning to call to remembrance the mercies of the Lord to a poor unworthy creature ever since I had existence among the work of his hands, and to humble myself before him for the base returns I have made to his goodness. Alas! how little have I experienced of either a humble or a grateful spirit. I found a deep conviction of having backslidden in heart and life from his ways, and I hope I had a sincere desire to return to him with my whole heart. I was enabled to plead the 14th chapter of Hosea for this purpose, and had some faint hope that the Lord would revive his work in my soul, and renew my spiritual strength, before he takes me hence.

This last year has been marked with a wonderful interposition of divine power in my behalf, when brought to the gates of death by pain of body and distress of soul, and given over both by physicians and friends: The Lord, in answer to prayer, revived me again, and put a new song into my mouth, even praise to his blessed name. He has also given me a delightful habitation in this place, and the prospect of some souls being brought to the knowledge of the gospel, which is preached under my roof.

My every attempt to sell Barnton has proved hitherto unsuccessful. The Lord knows my design is to glorify him with my substance, as well as with every power and faculty he has bestowed upon me. I will still wait upon him for this thing.

I desire once more, on this day of my birth, to dedicate the remaining days and years of my life to that gracious God and Saviour, who has given me both life for this world and for that which is to come. Fulfil in me, O Lord, the good pleasure of thy goodness, and the work of faith with power. Let my soul live, and it shall praise thee. Let it be sanctified and accepted through the peace-speaking blood and the purifying Spirit of the Lord Jesus, and made meet to enjoy him for ever and ever. W. G.

In this extract, her earnest desire to dispose of Barnton, and her deep regret at not succeeding, are peculiarly striking. At the end of this year, however, it was purchased by William Ramsay, Esq. then an eminent banker in Edinburgh, to whom she sold it for twenty-eight thousand pounds. The reflection here necessarily forces itself upon our notice, How different are the views and wishes even of Christians at different periods! The reader will recollect how anxious she was to obtain this place, and how often she made it the subject of her request before the Lord, and how thankful she was when it was accomplished; but now she is equally solicitous to dispose of it. Opposite as these things may appear to be, there is no inconstancy, no fickleness whatever discovered;—the principle was one and the same on both occasions. She desired to buy it to enable her to extend the sphere of her usefulness, and with the same object in view she desired to sell it. Times and circumstances had changed, and she wisely endeavoured to accommodate herself to them; but in motive, heart, and conduct, she remained the same.

Leaving Scotland, Lady Glenorchy and her friend went to Matlock, and remained there till September. At the end of this month, or the beginning of the next, she removed to Bristol hot-wells for the sake of Lady Henrietta's health, as well as for her own. Here Lady Henrietta grew rapidly worse, became dropsical, and suffered much during the months of November and December.

On Saturday morning, January the 1st, 1786, this excellent lady was released from her sufferings, and entered into the joy of her Lord. Some idea of her situation in her last moments may be gathered from the following letters, written at this time by Lady Glenorchy to Lady Mary Fitzgerald.

Lady Glenorchy to Lady Mary Fitzgerald.

" *Bristol Hot-wells.*

" Mr Ford will inform your Ladyship that things here remain much in the same state as when I last wrote. Lady Henrietta Hope is much increased in size, but Mr Ford does not seem to apprehend her to be near her end. I have therefore almost given up thoughts of going to Bath this winter, and shall not give your Ladyship any more trouble about lodgings. I find the situation here in some respects adapted to my taste, and were I more at liberty to go out, it might, by the blessing of the Lord, be very profitable, as there is a variety of good gospel preachers of different denominations in Bristol, and some excellent Christians, from whom I might receive spiritual benefit. My dear Miss Morgan is also a strong and powerful attraction to me. I find her conversation a means of drawing me nearer to our blessed Lord, whose presence alone can satisfy the believing soul. Lady Henrietta Hope's situation too, is such, that I am necessarily much in her room, and it is very uncertain in what state she may be in a few days hence. I am, Madam, your affectionate and obliged humble servant,

"W. G."

"*Albemarle Row, November* 22. 1785.

"My dear Madam,—I am exceedingly obliged to your Ladyship for the favour of your letter by Mr Ford, for which I ought to have returned my grateful acknowledgments sooner; but the painful situation in which I at present am, will, I know, plead my excuse with you for this, as well as for sending only these few lines, to say that my dear friend grows worse every hour. Her precious life draws near a close in this world, but I am persuaded there is a life begun in her soul that can never end. This is at this moment the only consolation I have in the event of losing one who has been to me for years as my own soul. If it shall please God that I live to perform the last offices to this inestimable friend, I wish to go to Bath, and shall gladly accept of your Ladyship's kind offer of seeking a suitable lodging for me, which I hope will be somewhere near your own; and whenever there is a prospect of my leaving this place, I shall take the liberty of letting you know when I shall want it, and the kind I wish it to be. In the mean while, permit me to add my best wishes for every blessing your soul desires in this life and that which is to come, and that I am, with sincere esteem, your affectionate and obliged humble servant, W. G."

" *Sunday, January* 1. 1786.

" My dear Madam,—It has pleased our blessed Lord to release his dear handmaid, Lady Henrietta, this morning, from a body of sin and death, and to call her soul to enter upon an eternal Sabbath, where I trust she will enjoy him in the church triumphant for evermore. It has not pleased him to grant me my request respecting a more explicit declaration of her steadfast faith and lively hope in the hour of death. This I wished for others,—not on her own account. Some wise and gracious end, no doubt, is to be answered by denying me this comfort. I have had such repeated instances of the goodness of the Lord to his poor unworthy creature, that I cannot but believe there is a blessing in every dispensation, although for the present it may be grievous. That every spiritual and heavenly blessing may be your portion, is the prayer, my dear Madam, of your affectionate and obliged humble servant, W. G."

Lady Henrietta, it seems, had united with Lady Glenorchy in the design of building a chapel near

Bristol hot-wells at their mutual expense, and for this purpose she left Lady Glenorchy two thousand five hundred pounds. Lady Henrietta's death was a severe stroke to Lady Glenorchy, which, however, she bore with Christian resignation and fortitude. The separation was but short. Two letters, one written to the author, and the other to Lady Maxwell, shall now be given, which will shew the state of Lady Glenorchy's mind upon this melancholy occasion, and the manner in which she continued to pursue her plans of doing good, without ceasing.

Letter to the Rev. T. S. Jones.

" *Bristol, January* 16. 1786.

" Rev. Sir,—I am much obliged to you for your kind and seasonable letter, in which you point out to me the best and only grounds of consolation under a bereavement such as mine is. The great pain I have felt, and do still feel, is, I acknowledge, altogether selfish, and it is my endeavour to forget, as much as I can, my own particular loss, and to turn my thoughts towards my friend's unspeakable gain. It was no small mercy to me, that, from the length of her illness, my mind was in some measure prepared for the event, whilst her great sufferings made me more willing than I otherwise should have been to see her released. How wise and gracious is our God, even in the most bitter dispensations. I am now about to remove from this place, to spend some weeks at Bath. I hear Mr and Mrs Holmes are to be there next month, and I have some thoughts of returning with them to Devonshire. I am, Rev. Sir, with much esteem, your friend and servant,

" W. G."

Letter to Lady Maxwell.

"*Bath, February* 28. 1786.

"I have received, my dear Madam, both your kind letters: The first found me at Bristol labouring under a severe cold; but which, through mercy, is now gone. Since I came to this place my time has been much employed with attending on places of worship, and visiting my friends, some of whom came from a distance to see me, and I thought myself obliged to be much with them. I find this place much more agreeable than it used to be, from the society I have met. Those I converse with are desirous of pressing forward themselves to heaven, and of helping others. There is a new meeting-house here, and an able gospel preacher in it, which is a great addition to our privileges. We are to have the Lord's supper there next Lord's day. You will suppose from this, that my spiritual life grows and flourishes. Alas! this is by no means the case: amidst all this variety of improvement, I carry about a cold heart, a confused mind, and a deep sense of want. I feel, however, strong desires, both for faith and love. My soul at times is ready to break with longing for a more intimate acquaintance with and conformity to Christ: yet it seems to be his will, that I should bear the cross, and to be made more acquainted with the depth of the fall in my own experience. This is a painful state; but perhaps a safe one for me. New opportunities seem to offer from different quarters of spreading the knowledge of the gospel, and a blessing seems to accompany it, especially at Matlock, where a young man, educated at my academy, is remarkably useful. I cannot get away from this till the chapel at Bristol is begun. I have procured a plan for a neat place of worship, plain, but elegant, and which will be a suitable monument for my dear friend, Lady Henrietta, and which I mean to call Hope Chapel. The estimate is L.2200. It is to be finished this summer, and will be opened next spring. I purpose to go about the 20th of March, if health permits, to Devonshire, to open a new place of worship there, and to visit my first attempt in that county at Exmouth, where there is now a stated congregation. After this, I must return to Bristol, and then pay a short visit to my mother in London, in my way to Matlock. I wish to be there by the 1st of May, to stay that month; and if during that time you come to England, it would give me much pleasure to see you. I have made an appointment with Mr Grove to go to Edinburgh, by Workington and Carlisle, in June; and he is to preach, and aid me in settling matters at these places. It would be very comfortable if you would join our party; but, at all events, I hope you will come to Matlock, as that cannot be far distant from any road you take. May the Lord overrule and direct all your movements to his own glory, and the advancement of his kingdom, both in our hearts and the world. To his grace I commend you, my dearest Madam, who, though very unworthy, am your very affectionate friend, W. G."

Lady Glenorchy followed out the designs she had formed, and which are mentioned in the preceding letters. She settled on a plan for Hope Chapel, entered into a contract with workmen to execute it, and saw its commencement. Soon after this she, accompanied by her intimate friend Miss Morgan of Bristol, went to Devonshire, and there accomplished her generous and pious purposes of promoting the interests of religion. After which she returned to Bristol and Bath.

In the beginning of May she went to London. On the 16th of that month she wrote from Derby, in her way to Matlock, to Lady Mary Fitzgerald. Her stay at Matlock was short. In her way to Scotland in June she seems to have visited Workington in Cumberland, purchased ground there for the erection of a chapel, and saw the work commenced. On the 19th of June she came to Carlisle. On her arrival at Edinburgh her friends observed with regret a most unfavourable alteration in her appearance. Her time at first was a good deal occupied with the completing the sale of Barnton. This was the last business in which she was engaged; and which had she not accomplished, as she seems to have made no destination of her landed property, all her plans of benevolence and piety, excepting the chapels of Edinburgh and Matlock, would have perished with her; but this being effected, her work it seems was finished, and it only remained that she should die in the Lord, rest from her labours, and receive the heavenly reward.

On Friday evening, the 14th of July, the writer, intending on the Monday following to leave home for some weeks, waited on her Ladyship to pay his respects, and take his leave of her. He found her sitting in her dressing-room, easy and cheerful during the hour or more that he spent with her. They talked of many important things, and her conversation was not only seasoned with grace, but had that vivacity and innocent pleasantry which often made it so fascinating. When the writer, fearing he had fatigued her by the length of the interview, gave indication of his being about to depart, she said to him with a tone and manner that could not be mistaken, If you are to be away so long, I shall not see you again. Unwilling to receive this sentiment in the absolute sense in which it was given, he replied, What! is your Ladyship about to leave us so soon? Resuming the gaiety of her tone, she said, I am thinking of going south. What! said he, to the south of France? Why, replied her Ladyship, perhaps I may. The physicians say I ought not to winter in Britain. I have written to the Holmeses to ask them if they will go with me; and if they consent, it may be I shall be on my way there before you return. She kindly gave him her hand, and bid him farewell. These were the last words he heard from her lips.

Soon after he left her, Mr Alexander Pitcairn, a gentleman who had for a considerable time gratuitously taken charge of her schools and other charitable institutions, called upon her; and she talked with him easily and with spirit on business for upwards of half an hour. He left her about eight o'clock in the evening. She afterwards took an emetick, the operation of which continued much longer than was desirable,—a circumstance that was not uncommon with her. Her aunt Miss Hairstanes, who was with her, sent to Mr Alexander Wood, her usual medical attendant, at ten o'clock at night, informing him of her state, and asking him if she might give her Ladyship a few drops of laudanum, which used to remove the irritation, and which with that gentleman's approbation was done. The sickness, however, continued all night. On Saturday morning Mr Wood saw her, and said it would leave her in the course of the day. She lay still, and although she spoke but little, she seemed remarkably composed. Some time in the forenoon, the curtain of her bed being drawn, Miss Hairstanes approaching as softly as possible, for fear of disturbing her if asleep, heard her say, Well, if this be dying, it is the pleasantest thing imaginable!—It may here by the way be remarked, that although her spiritual experience was so habitually painful, among all the causes she assigns of her uneasiness, she never once complains of the fear of death, or a dread of entering into eternity. It was the want of a more satisfactory conformity of heart to the divine image and will, which was alone the source of her distresses.

Having fallen asleep on Saturday night, she did not awake at the usual time on the Sabbath, but continued to sleep softly. Her medical man saw her in this sleep about ten in the morning, and said she would awake well. This not being the case, about noon, Miss Hairstanes becoming alarmed, sent for Dr Hope, who being a relation of Lady Henrietta Hope, was accustomed as a friend, as well as professionally, to visit her. Being told the circumstances of the case, he gave the same opinion with Mr Wood. He returned in an hour; and suspecting that it might proceed from gout or some other disease, desired that more assistance might be called in. Dr Cullen, her ordinary physician, was accordingly sent for; but he could give no decided opinion on the case. At ten o'clock the writer received a note from Lady Glenorchy's servant, stating that he feared his Lady was at the point of death. This was the first notice he had got of her situation. He instantly hastened to her Ladyship's residence, which was in Lady Sutherland's house, George's-square; and being admitted to her bed-side, found her reclining on her right side, the posture in which she had fallen asleep the night before, breathing it is true, but so imperceptibly as to require close attention to discover it. In this state she passed the night, and about half past eleven on Monday forenoon, the 17th of July, she expired.

Thus lived and died Willielma, Viscountess Glenorchy, a character distinguished by every qualification that could adorn exalted rank, and endear her to all who knew her. Her person was to the last agreeable, and in her youth must have been handsome. Her manners were polite, elegant, and dignified. She naturally was endowed with talents far above mediocrity; and these were highly cultivated and improved, and brought to bear with full effect on her whole conduct in life. But when she became a recipient of the grace of God, they were rendered by her peculiarly subservient to the interests of religion, not merely personally, but in promoting it in her fellow-creatures. Her imagination was lively, and her spirits constitutionally gay, on which perhaps she laid too severe restraints; and she had a vein of ready wit and pleasantry, which gave a delightful air of ease and frankness to her conversation. Her piety was unaffected and deep; her views of divine truth clear and distinct; and her attachment to the peculiar doctrines of the gospel decided, firm, and not to be shaken. No one could possibly possess a more delicate sensibility and tenderness of conscience, or feel stronger the obligations of moral and religious duty. Obedience, in her mind, was the only satisfactory test of Christian discipleship. Although she acutely suffered under the many trials and afflictions which were appointed her, yet she seems carefully to have endeavoured to suppress her feelings on those occasions, lest indulging her griefs and talking of her distresses might be construed into any thing like the most distant murmurings against divine Providence; and from a conviction that all events were ordered by unerring wisdom and infinite goodness for the best, and that as regrets were unavailing, so they might in many cases prove sinful. Of the truth of these remarks we have a striking example in her behaviour on the death of her friend Lady Henrietta Hope. Her attachment to her was unbounded, and had been confirmed by years of the closest and most endearing intercourse; but when the unalterable event by the will of God took place, she thought, that although she felt the loss to be the most severe and the most irreparable that could be inflicted, yet both good sense and piety forbade her to discover useless sorrow, and she conformed her conduct to their dictates. Her anxious desire to be the instrument of doing good in the world, led her to devote the whole of her life in contriving plans of beneficence, and her whole fortune in executing them; and the institutions which remain to this day shew that her views of usefulness had been by her extended beyond her abode upon earth. But what perhaps forms the most striking feature in her character, is the proof she has given of the efficacy of true religion to resist the mighty snares and temptations of high rank, great fortune, and powerful worldly influence and friends; no one of these, nor all of them combined, although employed with all their subtlety and all their powers, ever shook her fidelity to God and religion. And it is a proof to those in high life what may be done for the cause of Christ, if there be integrity, in the midst of the most unfavourable circumstances, for such for one-half of her religious life were those of Lady Glenorchy. How superior her character to the mass of our wealthy and titled population! While they were gratifying their unhallowed passions, and passing away their precious time in splendid vanity, she devoted herself to usefulness, and considered it to be her highest happiness to be the instrument of doing good to the world.

To say that she was faultless is to say that she was more than mortal; but all who knew her will unite in testifying, that there has seldom lived a person in whom individually so many excellent traits of character were so richly combined.

Undoubtedly there were persons who might equal, or even excel Lady Glenorchy, in some particular graces and virtues, but as an entire character, she did not leave behind her one who might be compared with her. Her talents, and her opportunities for employing them, arising from her high rank and fortune, were things over which she had no controul, and for which no praise can be due to her, for they were the immediate gifts of Heaven, and were certainly great; but her diligence and fidelity in the use of those things over which she had controul, were equally great and uncommon; and in this she is peculiarly an object worthy of praise, and admiration, and imitation.

Her Ladyship had expressed a wish to be buried in her chapel in Edinburgh. The persons who took the charge of her funeral accordingly ordered a vault or catacomb to be prepared to receive the body. On taking up the flooring, the ground was found to be solid rock. With considerable difficulty an excavation was made, just sufficient to contain the coffin. The head of it lies directly under the middle of the communion table. A stone, with a brass plate inserted in the centre, on which is deeply engraved her name, age, and time of death, and hermetically sealed, closes the opening of it. On Monday the 24th, fourteen days after her death, the body was deposited in this place. The present Earl of Breadalbane, who came from London for the purpose, attended as chief mourner.

Her silent obsequies* took place in the midst of a great multitude of weeping spectators, who crowded the chapel on this occasion. This heavenly grain was sown in weakness, but it shall be raised in power. It was sown in dishonour, but shall be raised in glory.

On the Lord's day after Lady Glenorchy's interment, two funeral sermons were preached in her chapel in Edinburgh, that in the morning by the minister of the place, from Luke xii. 42.—48. "And the Lord said, who then is that faithful and wise steward, whom his Lord shall make ruler over his household, to give them their portion of meat in due season? Blessed is that servant whom his Lord, when he cometh, shall find so doing; of a truth, I say unto you, that he will make him ruler over all that he hath: but if that servant say in his heart, my Lord delayeth his coming, and shall begin to beat the men-servants and maidens, and to eat and drink, and to be drunken, the Lord of that servant will come in a day when he looketh not for him, and at an hour when he is not aware, and cut him in sunder, and will appoint him his portion with the unbelievers. And that servant which knew his Lord's will, and prepared not himself, neither did according to his will, shall be beaten with many stripes; but he that knew not, and did commit things worthy of stripes, shall be beaten with few stripes; for unto whomsoever much is given, of him shall be much required; and to whom men have committed much, of him they will ask the more." That in the afternoon was preached by the then Professor of Divinity in the University, the Rev. Dr Andrew Hunter, from Psalms xii. 1. "Help, Lord, for the godly man ceaseth; for the faithful fail from among the children of men."

* See note, page 420.

Lady Glenorchy, ever mindful of the uncertainty of life, had for many years kept her will in readiness. The frequent changes which took place in her circumstances, however, required her repeatedly to alter it. On the 17th of February 1785, immediately on finishing the purchase of Matlock, she, by a separate deed, gave the house there, with its furniture, and the chapel, to the Rev. Jonathan Scott, and after him, to his wife, without limitation or restriction.

On the 26th of January this year (1786), she executed a trust-deed of her chapel and school-house in Edinburgh, to five gentlemen: Alexander Bonar, Banker; Andrew Hamilton, Deputy Comptroller of Excise; James Ogilvy, Deputy Receiver-General of the Customs; John Pitcairn, and Alexander Pitcairn, merchants; with full power to nominate their successors.

Lady Glenorchy left more than L. 30,000 in money. A will was found, regularly drawn, and executed at Bristol, dated the 6th day of December 1785, in which she made Lady Maxwell her executrix and residuary legatee, burdened with L. 5000 to the Society in Scotland for Propagating Christian Knowlege; the interest to be employed in supporting schools, and for other religious purposes, on the estates of Sutherland and Breadalbane, provided the noble proprietors gave due encouragement; or otherwise, to be employed for the general objects of the Society. L. 5000 to the Rev. Jonathan Scott, for the educating of young men for the ministry, and other religious purposes. To her mother, her aunt, and others, large legacies and annuities, besides a number of smaller ones, amounting to the half or more of her fortune.

Lady Glenorchy evidently intended to have made a new will. Memoranda and other papers found in her cabinet after her death, prove distinctly that she had been preparing for it. In fact, the scroll of it, together with the stamp paper on which it was to have been written, were found, and she had actually appointed her attorney and his clerks to attend her for the execution of it the evening of the day on which she died.

This occasioned her executrix considerable trouble and expense, as some of the memoranda clashed one part with another, and yet by the gentlemen of the law were considered to have codicillary powers. Lady Maxwell, however, by much patience and labour, adjusted the whole to the satisfaction of all parties.

Lady Glenorchy had left a sealed letter addressed to Lady Maxwell to be delivered after her death, requiring her to finish Hope chapel at Bristol-wells, and to aid those of Carlisle, Workington, and her other chapels and institutions, which she did, and not long before her death had completely exhausted all the funds Lady Glenorchy left.

Lady Alva survived her daughter more than twenty, and Miss Hairstanes died only three or four years, ago.

A neat marble slab has been placed at a considerable height, directly above the pulpit in her chapel in Edinburgh, on which is the following inscription:—

IN MEMORY
OF
THAT MOST EXCELLENT LADY,
WILLIELMA MAXWELL,
VISCOUNTESS GLENORCHY.
Few characters in the religious world were better known,
or more universally and justly respected.
Her many amiable personal qualities, and superior
understanding, improved by education,
genuine religion, reading, and experience,
greatly endeared her to her numerous acquaintances,
her family, and select friends.
And
this house, with several other places of worship in
Scotland and England, founded by her,
together with the large sums she bequeathed
to the Societies for Promoting Christian Knowledge,
will be a lasting monument how much
she had at heart the glory
of the Redeemer,
and the best
interests of mankind.
She died July 13. 1786, aged 43.
Her remains are deposited in the centre of this chapel.
This monument was erected as a tribute of respect,
by her executrix,
LADY MAXWELL.

Lady Glenorchy's friends, after her death, expressed a wish to have her picture engraved; but although there was one in Lady Sutherland's house in George's-square, painted in Italy, in which she is represented as playing on a lute, it bore no resemblance to the original. There is another in the hall of the Society for Propagating Christian Knowledge: this was painted by *Martin*, at the particular request of the Directors;

but as he had no personal knowledge of her Ladyship, and therefore drew from imagination, and the description of her person which he obtained from others, he did not, as indeed it was impossible he could, succeed. On this account, the wish of her friends could not be gratified.—It matters not: her likeness can never be effaced from the memory of those who knew her; and those who knew her not, may discover the features of her mind, and the dispositions of her heart, in the lasting productions of her beneficence and piety, as long as they shall endure; for,

The righteous shall be in everlasting remembrance.

FINIS.

Printed by Walker & Greig,
Edinburgh.

Lightning Source UK Ltd.
Milton Keynes UK
UKHW020338281218
334537UK00009B/660/P